PROBLEMATICS
of
MILITARY POWER

CASS SERIES: MILITARY HISTORY AND POLICY
Series Editors: John Gooch and Brian Holden Reid
ISSN: 1465-8488

This series will publish studies on historical and contemporary aspects of land power, spanning the period from the eighteenth century to the present day, and will include national, international and comparative studies. From time to time, the series will publish edited collections of essays and 'classics'.

PROBLEMATICS

of

MILITARY POWER

Government, Discipline and the Subject of Violence

MICHAEL S. DRAKE

School of Economic and Social Studies, University of East Anglia

With a Foreword by Paul Hirst

FRANK CASS
LONDON • PORTLAND, OR

First published in 2002 in Great Britain by
FRANK CASS PUBLISHERS
Crown House, 47 Chase Side, Southgate
London N14 5BP

and in the United States of America by
FRANK CASS PUBLISHERS
c/o ISBS, 5824 N.E. Hassalo Street
Portland, Oregon, 97213-3644

Website: www.frankcass.com

British Library Cataloguing in Publication Data

Drake, Michael S.
  Problematics of military power: government, discipline and the
  subject of violence
  1. Violence – Social aspects 2. Violence – Political aspects 3. Military
  history I. Title 303.6

ISBN 0-7146-5202-4 (cloth)

Library of Congress Cataloging-in-Publication Data

A catalog record for this book is available
from the Library of Congress

Drake, Michael S., 1958 –
  Problematics of military power: government, discipline, and the
  subject of violence/Michael S. Drake; with a foreword by Paul Hirst.
    p. cm.
  Includes bibliographical references and index.
  ISBN 0–7146–5202–4 (cloth)
  1. Sociology, Military. 2. Civil–military relations. 3. War and society.
  4. Violence–Social aspects. I. Title.
  U221.5 .D73 2001
  302–dc21

                                                          2001032310

Typeset in Sabon 10½ on 12pt by FiSH Books
Printed in Great Britain by
Bookcraft (Bath) Ltd, Midsomer Norton, Somerset

PROBLEMATICS

of

MILITARY POWER

Government, Discipline and the Subject of Violence

MICHAEL S. DRAKE

School of Economic and Social Studies, University of East Anglia

With a Foreword by Paul Hirst

FRANK CASS
LONDON • PORTLAND, OR

First published in 2002 in Great Britain by
FRANK CASS PUBLISHERS
Crown House, 47 Chase Side, Southgate
London N14 5BP

and in the United States of America by
FRANK CASS PUBLISHERS
c/o ISBS, 5824 N.E. Hassalo Street
Portland, Oregon, 97213-3644

Website: www.frankcass.com

Copyright © 2001 Michael S. Drake

British Library Cataloguing in Publication Data

Drake, Michael S.
  Problematics of military power: government, discipline and the
  subject of violence
  1. Violence – Social aspects 2. Violence – Political aspects 3. Military
  history I. Title 303.6

ISBN 0-7146-5202-4 (cloth)

Library of Congress Cataloging-in-Publication Data

A catalog record for this book is available
from the Library of Congress

Drake, Michael S., 1958 –
  Problematics of military power: government, discipline, and the
  subject of violence/Michael S. Drake; with a foreword by Paul Hirst.
  p. cm.
  Includes bibliographical references and index.
  ISBN 0-7146-5202-4 (cloth)
  1. Sociology, Military. 2. Civil–military relations. 3. War and society.
  4. Violence–Social aspects. I. Title.
  U221.5 .D73 2001
  302–dc21

2001032310

Typeset in Sabon 10½ on 12pt by FiSH Books
Printed in Great Britain by
Bookcraft (Bath) Ltd, Midsomer Norton, Somerset

Contents

Acknowledgements

The author wishes to thank Alan Scott for his persistent encouragement throughout; Paul Bellaby for reading an earlier version; Paul Hirst for his Foreword; Howard Caygill for his generous comments; Tarak Barkawi for reading, and recommending, the manuscript to Frank Cass; Andrew Humphrys for his original editorial interest; and Georgina Clark-Mazo for seeing the publication process through.

Foreword

This is one of the most original books on the sociology of power in recent years. It starts with a criticism of the new historical sociology of power, the chief exponent of which is Michael Mann. Mann and others argue that there are a variety of sources of social power, and organized violence is one. As a counter to the excessive emphasis in sociology on either the economy or culture, this argument has some force. The problem is that it presupposes the capacity to utilize violence.

This is where Michael Drake begins. How is the capacity for organized violence created and exercised over time? How are men persuaded to be ready to fight and die? Drake shows how organized violence can only exist on the basis of definite social and discursive conditions, thus greatly weakening the role of the means of violence as an independent variable. He does this by the detailed analysis of the historical literature of four periods: the Roman Republic and Empire, the decentralized violence of the feudal era, the late Medieval centralizing monarchies, and the formation of the modern state in the Early Modern period. Unlike most sociologists, he has taken the trouble to master the substance of military history in its considerable complexity. Drake also realizes that the political and social domains in which violence is exercised are not constants. Power is neither given nor just instrumental. It is also prefigured and defined in its discourse. Thus, along with close attention to military history, there is a parallel reading of key political texts. These define the role of armed power within governing institutions and the wider society. Special attention is given to those texts that operate across the boundaries of politics, legitimation, and the role of the armed man, for example, Julius Caesar, Vegetius, Machiavelli, and Justus Lipsius.

This is a demanding work because of its scope, its complexity, and its recognition of the need to go into military detail. It more than repays reading, however, and not just by political scientists or sociologists, but by all those interested in the transformations of military power. Traditionally, social scientists have found it hard to integrate war within the core of their conceptual schemes. They have behaved as if societies were normally peaceful, even if such peace rested on domination. The new historical sociology of power tried to some extent to rectify this defect. This work goes further, showing how the various forms of the military have been conditioned by, but have also shaped and defined, social relations. Thus it would be impossible to understand Roman citizenship in the Republic without reference to military obligation. It would be equally difficult to understand the concept of 'civilian' in England, and thus civil society, without reference to the Mutiny Act of 1688. This book will set the terms of discussion of the role of military force in social power for some time to come.

Paul Hirst

Introduction

This study has taken inspiration from a project outlined by Michel Foucault in 1976:

> One theme I would like to study over the next few years is that of the army as a matrix of organisation and knowledge; one would need to study the history of the fortress, the 'campaign', the 'movement', the colony, the territory.[1]

Foucault envisages this research project as a mobilization of his work up to that time, a way of enrolling the work on 'formations of discourse and the genealogy of knowledge' in relation to the problem of power, linking the 'micro-physics' of power in *Discipline and Punish* (first published in 1975) to a 'geopolitics'. Foucault never took up this project, but the theme of 'military power' has been taken up by historical sociology in its attempt to escape the economist legacy of historical materialism, shifting the object of its grand-narratives from capitalism to modernity, and the criteria of historical characterization from relations of production to relations of domination. This provides the starting point for the most prominent strands of grand-theory historical sociology as represented by Anthony Giddens, Michael Mann and Charles Tilly.

Theory, method and historical sociology: critiques and premises

However, these approaches either associate organized violence with 'the state', or else with some functional substitute, as in the conception of a military feudal system that fulfilled the ruler-function of protection and fiscal extraction in a socio-historical context where it could not be achieved centrally. The sociological function of domination as social integration is thus built into the terms of conceptualization through an *a priori* concept of 'society' itself, but once again displaces the thesis

1

that society is based on domination ultimately secured by violence, since the forces of coercion are possessed by those who have power and therefore fulfil integrating functions. These formulations of grand-theoretical historical sociology also reintroduce the accumulation model of social processes from Marxist theory.

The work of Tilly offers the greatest space to acknowledge the role of force as immediate domination, unrelated to any essential functional role, but the same conclusion is arrived at in his work as the outcome of a reason inherent in historical development, operating through processes of evolutionary competition wherein the form of the state proves the most efficient accumulator of capital and the means of coercion, eliminating rival forms of political organization. The development of forces of coercion is modelled on the same conception as that applied to capital formation, simply providing a parallel and complementary dimension of historical development. With Giddens, modernity is contrasted to other modes of domination by the appearance of 'containers', which 'generate power', but the power to create containers, to circumscribe a domain of activities so that they may be subjected to surveillance and regulation, is explained largely by reference to the resources of the state. The power to generate the containers that generate power thus already exists in Giddens' formulation, in the form of accumulated resources. Mann's historical sociology attempts to separate out such distinct 'sources of social power', but provides no more than a study of its variable composition, since the elements he focuses on are already powerful by definition.

For all these formulations, organized violence is *a priori* a resource of power, directing attention to the effects of the deployment of force in historically variable social contexts conventionally aligned on an axis with modern state centralization at one pole and early medieval feudalism at the other. Enquiry into the processes by which violence becomes instrumentalized as force is then unnecessary, since its sociological significance is assumed to consist in its instrumental deployment. However, the whole point of studying 'military power', to get nearer to the source of social domination, is thereby displaced into the *a priori* conceptualization of an already-utilizable 'force'.

The reduction of bodies of violence to instrumentality is already given, an unexplained subjection preceding and enabling the explanation of domination as the basis of society. There are three possibilities within these formulations impinging upon this problem, two of which are 'black boxes' (i.e. devices that perform a function but conceal the actual workings) into which the condition of subjection is displaced. The idea that organization itself instrumentalizes and subjects already assumes, like Giddens' 'containers', both power to organize and

2

subjection to authority, while the concept of discipline similarly presupposes both capacity of command and obedience to orders. These preconditions are often referred to Max Weber's 'forms of legitimation', but there, Weber, like Giddens, ultimately refers this capacity to resources, with the implication that obedience is given in the commander's control of the means of need-satisfaction, invoking infinite regression to explain command over those resources. Another possibility is simply to argue that these relations of domination over the instrumental forces of domination are not themselves social in any case.

This is the solution taken by Georg Simmel, who delimits the scope of his enquiry by arguing that absolute domination which reduces the subordinate to pure means for the dominant party, as in the *societas leonitas* of the Roman jurists, 'annuls the very notion of society'.[2] Implicitly following the development of the Roman legal order,[3] Simmel introduces the idea of a third party, mediating the tendency of dyadic relationships to absolute, asocial domination, but thereby reduces the foundation of society to the normative model of the contract. This is quite the opposite of Weber's view, which firmly located the foundation of society in relations of original immediate domination. De la Boétie had pursued this problem in his *Discourse of Voluntary Servitude*,[4] first published in 1577 amidst the French Wars of Religion, by reversing the order of the problem, asking not how domination could be achieved, but why obedience is achievable. De la Boétie dispensed with second-order phenomena such as legitimation and ideology to argue that civil obedience is an effect of the inculcation of a 'natural' subjection (a rational cowardice) to an original violence that is maintained as a parasitic form supporting itself from the spoils of domination. However, these forces of domination (which are the instruments of power) must be maintained in a state of constant insecurity, a condition which cannot reproduce itself. Referring the infinitely regressive question of the obedience of the forces of domination to their share in the spoils simply does not explain the condition of military discipline which enables the instrumentalization of violence; obedience unto death. As Simmel shows, we cannot evade the problem of obedience without relinquishing the idea that society is ultimately based upon violence, but the problem is also irreducible to the terms of a material exchange that would posit a contract within the original constitution of the forces of domination.

Another perspective is provided by Norbert Elias' work on the 'civilizing process', in which a correlation is drawn between the historical development of affect-management, especially self-control of a violence given in embodiment, and state monopolization of means and opportunities for its instrumental deployment. However, these two empirical trends are traced through a narrow range of studies and remain no more than a questionable correlation. His theorization of the 'civilizing process' rather relies on a metaphysical model of structures and forces drawn from Sigmund Freud. The later theorization of a 'de-civilizing process'[5] attempts to disembed his theory from the particular historical narrative traced in the *The Civilizing Process* and *The Court Society*, which severely compromises Elias' project to develop universal theories and models of social relations and processes.[6]

The methodological premises of historical sociological treatments of 'military power' thus seem to foreclose their own object, and demand a normative definition of society as constituted by a monopoly of violence. Rather than providing an explanation of society's foundation in violence, they show how it is founded upon the *use* of force, presupposing a presocial set of relations that must be excluded from consideration, inadvertently replicating the object of their critique of the contractual version of the story. This book pursues the problematization of the category of military power, which macro-sociology substitutes (via the state) for the juridical concept of sovereignty and uses in its explanations, but which itself evades explanation. Instead of assuming the instrumentality of violence as given in sovereign command, I draw on historical texts as maps of the effects of political technologies and practices of government, defining and providing knowledge of the terrain and identifying objects for strategy in their practical engagement with the problematics of the conduct of violence.

Quentin Skinner's methodological premises for the history of ideas[7] provide a guide to reading primary texts as sources of historically embedded concepts and models for historical sociology as an alternative to *a priori* abstraction, conceptualization and theorization, and the uncritical utilization of secondary historiographical constructions. Skinner methodologically rejects 'textual' and 'contextual' analysis, on the grounds that both apply criteria from outside the discourse in which the text operates. 'Textualism' refers its analysis to concerns and meanings which are the canonical construction of the reader's own discipline, anachronistically interposing ahistorical criteria. 'Contextualism' reads the text as an expression of its social and political context, but thereby interprets it in terms of the theoretical concerns of historiography.[8] Restoring the constraints and determinations of its contemporary discourse to the historical text would produce methodological validity in the history of ideas. Rather than attempting to construct what the author 'really meant', Skinner is concerned to read the text in terms of what the author (or the text) has done.[9] Similarly, instead of referring the organization of violence to *a priori*, inferred objectives or to ahistorical tendencies, we can use Skinner's precepts as a guide to read historical texts as formulations of the problematics of military power. These do not provide 'real' descriptions of historical conditions of violence, but they are the ideal-types of their time, informing political action.

Historically, the organization and conduct of violence was not the sociologically unproblematic technical speciality to which these issues are consigned by modern assumptions of a civil–military divison and a state monopoly. Medieval and early modern European political thought addressed itself directly to these problematics in what we could describe as politico-military treatises. Skinner's methodological postulates provide us with a way of reading such treatises in terms of the operations and conceptualizations they perform, as a guide to contemporary perceptions and to projects and options for the organization and conduct of violence, rather than evaluating them in terms of criteria deriving from the reader's own projections, or 'reading-off' what they 'really mean' by contextual inference. While Skinner's own analyses are concerned with the genealogy of constitutional thought, Gerhard Oestreich argues that the conventional assumption that instruments of the state such as military and fiscal organization, 'evolved by themselves in response to the requirements of the real world' neglects 'theories of practical government' in favour of constitutional treatises.[10] The practical discourse of government focused in particular on the question of obedience to discipline, the condition of the instrumentality of violence itself. This book traces the genealogy of the organization and instrumentalization of violence through neglected, practical chapters of texts in the history of political thought which grapple with the historical problematics of 'military power'. These are also problems fundamental to the constitution of society, however it is conceived.

Rather than studying the conduct of violence in abstract terms, we need to recognize that it is simply not always the same thing, and so cannot be measured by its progressive development or regression in terms of any abstract ideal-typical conception, or reduced to an instrumental role as a resource accumulated and called upon by a power that originates elsewhere. Taking up Foucault's project to trace the *genealogy* of the legion, the sword, the army, as well as the discourse informing their deployment, reveals historically distinct modalities of violence which operate quite differently, with economies that are irreducible to a common denominator since they have different objects, different ends and comprise very different forces. There is no singular mode of military technique, government or deployment that could be the object of progressive perfection or accumulation.

However, in order to address itself critically to the grand-theoretical tradition of historical sociology, this book takes the form of a narrative, enabling comparative studies to be made and taking account of the dimensions of time and space in which military power is produced in the exercise of bodies. The body provides a recurrent point of reference, referring military discourse to other forms of knowledge, since the organization of violence lies at a crucial juncture between the physical and the collective body, as well as (at least historically) being both embodied and effecting its operations in and upon bodies, a juncture articulated in the exercise of discipline. The army is well known as a primary site in which modern techniques of discipline were pioneered,[11] but this study shows how these techniques developed in the Middle Ages over subjects who were raised up, liberated from, prior subjection to domestic discipline. We must thus add to techniques of discipline exercised over bodies in an architectonic space, the regulation of bodies maintained in a permanent transit, for which I have used Virilio's notion of 'dromology'.[12] Furthermore, Foucault extended his work on power through the recognition that discipline required free subjects to act upon, but points out that: 'There are two meanings of the word, subject to someone else by control and dependence, and tied to his own identity by a conscience or self-knowledge',[13] the latter sense indicating theories of government which address the condition of obedience. This perspective helps us to be able to see how the shifting relation between violence and society is a matter of organization, but also of conduct and the order of subjectivity.

The organization of the book

The book is divided into four parts, roughly corresponding to conventional historical periodizations of ancient, medieval, late medieval and early modern Europe, but, rather than treating these as self-enclosed systems of relations between warfare and society, it traces transformations of the order of violence through historically contemporary problematizations of military power.

In ancient Rome, the shift from individual combat to hoplite warfare empowered the plebs[14] in the military order of the city mobilized for war, and the old right of command was broken in the *secessio plebis*. However, new modes of government developed in the displacement into strategic space of the subject of liberty and the military order of the city in which political identity was invested. Later again, under the empire, further forms of government of the self emerged in the administrative space created by the monopolization of patronage in the emperor, for which the conduct of violence became a functional performance.

In contrast to the organization and conduct of violence of the Roman republic and empire, early medieval feud constituted an entirely different social order, but cannot be reduced to a correlation between unconstrained affective violence and political atomization as the negative polarity of a 'civilizing process'. The castle, a tactical innovation in feud, is shown to have produced not one but three new modalities of violence, each of which had its own identity, economy, and rationality; knighthood, the retinue, and itinerant hired bands excluded from the settled order of society formulated in the socio-theological project of medieval Christianity. The struggle between these forces produced a new political order, the body politic, and a new mode of kingship operating upon this terrain to establish the rule of law, reconstituting the subject of political-military obligations in its administrative programmes. Unintegrated elements were incorporated in royal military household organization to comprise a force which could be unleashed upon the body politic, in a new mode of warfare between princes that contrasted radically with the feudal conduct of violence, invoking a struggle that contested not the control of resources, but the very constitution of violence itself. This struggle, conducted in the pre-political and extra-legal dimension of war itself, produced military organizational means of circumscribing an army against its environment in the field and of regulating bodies in transit on the road.

Such proto-disciplinary techniques were most fully developed not in any direct line in the formation of a future nation-state, but in the precocious Duchy of Burgundy, where they fatefully encountered other forms of organization, with their own mode of conduct of violence, in the particular liberties of the Swiss cantons and the early modern city. The late medieval deployment of forces liberated from domestic and political discipline against the body politic led into the great crisis of early modernity and the formulation of new problematics of military power in both early modern treatises on the art of government and the practical projects of reformation. Limited by the particularity of urban identities, this discourse adopted the model of the army and its order for the project of government and reformation in general. The army alone provided subjects liberated from particularity and from domestic discipline, a vehicle in which new modes of government could be pioneered. The final chapter of the study traces the development of the organization and conduct of violence in relation to social and political order in early modern France, England and the Netherlands.

This book pays much attention to military administrative and disciplinary codes in their development from the ordinances of war of the late Middle Ages through to the articles of the armies of early modernity. These articles provided for the integration of military administration, economy and discipline, operating over subjects displaced from the social and political order. They circumscribed the army as a domain of prerogative right, but are not simply a form of 'special law' in Weber's sense.[15] They can be read as the codification of the practical operationalization of political technologies. Beginning as a negative circumscription of the medieval host against its environment, they address the peculiar conditions and the liberty of their subject from other disciplines and orders. Finally, in the great series of annual English Mutiny Acts, from 1688 into the nineteenth century, we can trace the definition of the parameters of civil society in the modern constitution of violence.

Notes

1. M. Foucault, *Power/Knowledge: Selected Interviews and Other Writings,* ed. C. Gordon (Hemel Hempstead: Harvester Wheatsheaf, 1980), p. 77.
2. G. Simmel, *The Sociology of Georg Simmel,* trans. and ed. K. H. Wolff (New York, NY: Free Press, 1950), pp. 181–2.
3. P. Stein, *Roman Law in European History* (Cambridge: Cambridge University Press, 1999).
4. E. de la Boétie, *The Politics of Obedience: The Discourse of Voluntary Servitude,* (trans. H. Kurz) (Montreal: Black Rose Books, 1975).
5. N. Elias, 'Violence and Civilization: The State Monopoly of Physical Violence and its Infringement', in J. Keane, (ed.), *Civil Society and the State: New European Perspectives*, pp. 177–98 (London: Verso, 1988); J. Fletcher, *Violence and Civilization: An Introduction to the Work of Norbert Elias* (Cambridge: Polity Press, 1997).
6. N. Elias, *The Court Society,* trans. E. Jephcott (Oxford: Blackwell, 1983), p. 7.
7. Q. Skinner, 'Meaning and Understanding in the History of Ideas', in J. Tully, (ed.), *Meaning and Context: Quentin Skinner and His Critics*, pp. 3–53 (Cambridge: Polity Press, 1988).
8. Ibid., pp. 29–68; M. Van Gelderen, *The Political Thought of the Dutch Revolt* (Cambridge: Cambridge University Press, 1992), pp. 5–7.
9. Skinner's methodological object thus appears similar to that of Foucault's method in *The Archaeology of Knowledge* (trans. A. M. Sheridan, London: Tavistock, 1972), though Skinner's concept of 'ideology' is different from the Foucauldian concept of 'discourse'.
10. G. Oestreich, *Neo-Stoicism and the Early Modern State* (Cambridge: Cambridge University Press, 1982), p. 36.
11. A. Giddens, *The Nation-State and Violence: Volume 2 of a Contemporary Critique of Historical Materialism* (Cambridge: Polity Press, 1985); M. Weber, 'The Meaning of Discipline', in H. H. Gerth and C. W. Mills (eds), *From Max Weber: Essays in Sociology*, pp. 253–62 (London: Routledge Kegan & Paul, 1948); M. Foucault, *Discipline and Punish: The Birth of the Prison*, trans. A. M. Sheridan (London: Penguin, 1977).

12. P. Virilio, *Speed and Politics: An Essay in Dromology*, trans. M. Polizotti (New York, NY: Semiotext(e), 1986).
13. M. Foucault, 'Afterword: The Subject and Power', in H. Dreyfus and P. Rabinow (eds), *Michel Foucault: Beyond Structuralism and Hermeneutics*, pp. 206–26 (Brighton: Harvester, 1982).
14. I have used the term 'plebs' to indicate a collective in a sociological sense and 'plebeians' to indicate individualized actions.
15. M. Weber, G. Roth and C. Wittich (eds), *Economy and Society: An Outline of Interpretive Sociology* (Berkeley, CA: University of California Press, 1968).

PART ONE: ANCIENT

1

Ancient Rome and Historical Sociology

Foundational mythology and the myths of modern sociology

Two foundational myths alternate throughout the history of Rome.[1] An older, Latin story recounts how the twins Romulus and Remus were cast out of their patrimony as heirs to the kingship of Alba Longa and founded a new city on the augural site of Rome, where Romulus murdered his brother and enclosed the city. An alternative, Greek story, attributes the foundation to Aeneas, a leader of refugees from the fallen city of Troy. A common cult among the Etruscan cities, the Greek myth declined during the first two centuries of the Roman republic's struggle for local hegemony, but was reasserted from the time of the Second Punic War, when Rome had displaced the Etruscan Federation as the dominant power in the Latin peninsula, bringing it into conflict with both Carthage and the Greek cities. From this time, the republic entered a progressive cycle of crises culminating in the last century BC, when Cicero reworked the foundation yet again, eliminating Aeneas and the Trojan lineage from his account of the evolution of the republic, but rationalizing the older story into an explanation of Rome's greatness in terms of its Latin identity, its strategic location, and above all the evolution of a mixed constitution, conditioned by the legislation of the early kings, constituted by the creation of a patrician republic and mediated by plebeian tribunician power. The mixed constitution sustained a unique balance as a platform for men to achieve the virtue of public recognition in service to the political community, glorifying their names beyond mortal death. Cicero's foundational myth thus posited the *res publica* as the means by which the tension between *fortuna* and *virtù* could be resolved in favour of the latter via the laws, institutions and customs of the republic, providing a vehicle for personal glorification.

After the civil wars which destroyed the republican political order, Caesar Augustus' *res publica restituta* constituted his own claims to

13

glory, but effectively monopolized to his own patronage the political offices by which others could achieve greatness. Under the principate, the foundational myth was reworked once again in a revision of the Greek story, exemplified in Virgil's *Aeneid*, which attributed the foundation of Troy to Latin colonists, so that Aeneas' foundation of Alba Longa is elaborated as the revival of the Latin historical destiny to become 'lords of the world', thereby recentring the Greek myth on a Latin Rome that is from the outset worldly, while contrasting Rome's imperial destiny to the Greek policy of colonization. By contrast, Livy's *Histories*, composed in the same era, present all versions as alternatives, but in reiterating many of Cicero's theoretical embellishments throughout, privilege constitutional evolution over foundation. However, Livy was already writing an obituary, the story of the decline of the republic, a task he could only undertake as a depoliticized, professional historian in the conditions of the new imperial order.[2]

Modern accounts, which present social and economic foundations as the 'real' conditions of the Roman constitution, simply repeat the mode by which the Greek version was reasserted over the Latin, positing determinant prior conditions which were mediated by the political process, advancing their own myth of a modernity to which the underlying tragic *fate* of the past is transparent. In using Livy's account of the origins of Rome, in contrast to modern philosophical anthropology, my intention is not to reassert a primordial significance of myth over rational sociological analysis, or to assert a hidden determinant structure in mythology, but merely to show how stories taken at face value can provide us with illuminating historical concepts.

Livy tells us that Romulus founded Rome by drawing up an enclosure, and killed his brother Remus for leaping over the half-completed wall in mock escape. The structure of enclosure and the terminal sanction of its transgression provide recurrent themes for the studies of this book. Similarly, the theme of predatory violence and its recruitment of dependants outside the law is prefigured in Livy's account of how Romulus, himself a cattle-thief, populated the enclosure with vagabonds and outlaws from other dominions, to whom he offered protection, forming a city which reproduced itself primarily through seizure, in the abduction of the Sabine women and continued predation on the cattle-herds of other settlements. Livy also provides an originary account of the consequences of the creation of law by Romulus' successor, Numa, which demanded that time be divided between war and peace, that law itself then be duplicated in laws for war, and that prison be created for the criminality consequent on the blurring of the line between right and wrong inherent in this

14

artifice. The political constitution of society through its relation to forces of violence is also prefigured in the story of how the next king advanced as his successor Servius, the son of a slave woman, who instituted the census, ordering Rome on the basis of the capacity of subjects to volunteer themselves for public service in times of war, establishing the principle that, 'every man's contribution could be in proportion to his means'. The poorest were to be exempted from contributions, but not from the principle of service itself, and so retained their political privilege. Servius was overthrown by Tarquin the Proud, who instituted a programme of public works to occupy the idle poor, a burden upon the state, in utilitarian labour usually performed by slaves. The eventual overthrow of this last king of Rome was justified by citing his family's transgressions against public law, sacred custom and social convention, mythologizing the natural justice of revolt, and also its effect, since Roman political liberty was asserted in this act of popular deposition and the republic instituted so that Romans would never again have to submit to kings. Thus, Livy tells us, were the Romans prepared for liberty by legislators and commanders.[3]

In attempting to side-step social and political foundations, historical sociology supplants these ancient myths with its own, presenting us with a tragic narrative of the occlusion of political possibility by economic determination. The subject of this tragedy is universally divested of symbolic values, either disembodied as a bearer of interests, or reduced to a biological body as the source of essential needs or drives. Sociology thus projects its myth of modernity back upon history in rigorous narration, with ideology to fill in the interstices of the story, enabling increasingly sophisticated modulations of emphasis and combinations of elements. 'The state' and sovereign power are favoured supporting actors, which can always be guaranteed to provide a spectacle that never fails to bring in the crowds, while the structural parameters of the historical stage are given independently of the cast in economic determinations delineating the range of action.

Rome in Marxist and Weberian historical sociology

Since the 1960s, Marxist historical analysis has sought to reinstate the political and the cultural against tendencies toward economism. This effected a bifurcation of Marxist historiography into, on the one hand, micro-histories which tend to concern themselves with cultural aspects of class formation, as in the work of Christopher Hill and E. P. Thompson, and, on the other, structuralist macro-histories, which focus upon state formation, as exemplified in the work of Perry

Anderson.[4] The Roman republic and empire provide Anderson's case-studies on the interrelation of economic and political relations in 'the slave mode of production'. Since military service permeated the elements of Roman society engaged in the political forms of class struggle, Anderson includes an account of military organization and the fortunes of war as another aspect of the superstructure, though he does not accord it any formal conceptual autonomy.

By combining juridical analysis and sociological reasoning, Weber was able to specify the interrelation between military and economic organization and between political struggle and military tactics.[5] However, Weber seeks to assimilate the Roman republic to a 'feudal' model to show how its configuration of legal property relations and political-military forms ultimately succumbed to economic limitations on viable extensive colonial settlement by a peasantry competitively disadvantaged by slave production. Weber's focus on peasant smallholdings, and the subjectivity effected by independent production as opposed to proletarianization, as the source of compulsory military service to the state, transposes onto ancient Rome the concerns of the German state in the late nineteenth century with the erosion of the conditions of the Prussian military-political constitution, which Weber had earlier investigated himself.[6] Thus, the (virtuous) republic could be characterized as primarily a political formation and the (decadent) empire as economic, though it was still dependent upon the military form of the legions that had originated under the republic but that were now deprived both of their sociological basis in the 'yeomanry' and of their dynamic in the peasants' desire for land against the competitive incorporation of their farms by the estates operating slave production. The contemporary concerns reflected in Weber's structural model are usually overlooked by its axiomatic deployment in historical sociology, providing, for instance, the hidden hand which connects the lines and fills in the spaces left by the stencil of Anderson's historical materialism.

Weber and Anderson both read in their own histories of the republic the occlusion of politics, of human possibility, by economics. This is history as tragedy, a salutary and repetitive story which we assume, if we tell often enough, with sufficient precision, we might eventually be able to overcome. However, other approaches, which begin not from centring our attention upon apparently fundamental, essential properties but in decentring our attention by directing it to the margins, might suggest that this historical tragedy is a perspectival effect, a myth, perhaps the favoured myth of modern social and political critique. Side-stepping foundation and entering after the act of enclosure, Weber and Anderson seek the key to the tragedy of history in a 'Rome' already structured by the order of their analyses. Against the division of Roman time between peace and war, each with its own laws, divisions and cycles, their structural narratives posit Rome within a continuous, economic time of production. In contrast, the time of early republican Rome in Livy's history is repetitive, distinguished by the named persons holding annual consular office. It is also a time in which peace and legislative reform were repeatedly deferred by war and mobilization. Only when the people refuse military service, step *outside* the civil order and encamp *outside* the walls, effectively suspending the cycle of time and its return, does change break into this cyclical repetition.

For both Weber and Anderson, Roman military service was primarily an economic negative, its effects operating through the neglect of economic function, through the absence of 'peasants' (Anderson) or 'yeomen' (Weber) as economic agents on their land, and only secondarily a political negative, since while they were away they were unable to participate in the political community. However, every enclosure also constitutes an outside, an exteriority, which Weber and Anderson neglect – the space beyond the walls, the excluded terms, the banished social categories. Absence from the land and from the city was equally a *presence* elsewhere, in different social relations, in a different space and a different time, in which the citizen–soldiers were not merely passive material for a military machine operating independently of them. Rather, the security of enclosure produced a marginal condition of absence in military subjection which mutated and returned to the centre in the fall of the republic.

However, prior to conceptualization, both Karl Marx and Weber also engaged in their own foundationalism, from which we can sketch two philosophical anthropologies of primitive European military forms. Firstly (after a Nietzschean Weber), a *predatory form*, in which a cattle-owning aristocracy of castle lords organized into rival familial clans, engaged in raids of seizure against other communities and lords. Since raiding precluded dependence upon extensive economic property, the warrior-caste provided protection to peasants on an arable domain around their strongholds as law-givers rather than as owners, and came to exercise political functions of authority and justice in exchange for these political-military services. Their household fortresses attracted warrior retinues subject to fraternal, customary codes rather than to the law exercised over the lord's domain. Weber draws a lineage to feudalism from this anthropology, but in the history of Rome's resultant 'agrarian' society, he posits the economic corruption of political relations in the accumulation of wealth around slave production, a corruption which leads to the collapse of Rome and a long, slow process of cultural recovery in the West that is persistently problematized by the influence of economic relations.

Secondly, the Marx of the *Grundrisse* sketched a *communal form*, in which whole communities held land collectively, periodically relocating *en masse* to newly cleared, fertile land, which would be conquered if necessary, driving out or enslaving the inhabitants. Shares of collectively held and sometimes collectively tilled land were allocated by the assembly of the whole community, which had political and juridical functions. In this anthropological form, the strategic axis runs not from raid to protection, but from defence to conquest. The whole community was mobilized for war service, so political participation and military obligation were dual aspects of membership of the community of free men subject only to its own laws and jurisdiction. While the predatory form was constituted by a social and spatial division of military–political and economic functions, in the communal form these functions were divided in time, so that the community was dualistic, organized quite differently for war and for peace.

These anthropologies provide ideal-types, often existing within the same community. Rome's foundation can be seen as a synthesis of the two forms.[7] However, they both posit a singular essential unitary subject through which the nineteenth-century romantic historical tragedy of Rome's rise and fall has been reworked into historical sociology as the displacement of functional political unity by destabilizing structural economic forces. Critical historians have recently pointed out how nineteenth-century historiography of ancient Rome constructed an ideological metaphor for contemporary nationalism and imperialism. In response, they have increasingly made a reflexive return to ancient sources as an alternative to grand-narrative reconstruction.[8] Focusing on the constitutive role of the order of violence, like Livy and philosophical anthropology, but, in contrast to the narrative tragedy of historical sociologies, this approach has identified a series of Roman military constitutions in which distinct forms of warfare are related to the transformation of society.[9] These studies also problematize the question of whether Rome's wars were essentially defensive or predatory.

In the first stage, the early republic allied itself as a local power with other Latin plains cities against pastoral mountain tribes relocating on to the plains. Such wars were undecidable, routine and ritualized. The second phase differed in intensity from the first, producing both outcomes and organization, marked by the introduction of legionary pay (406 BC) and the final defeat of Rome's local rival, the Veii, with the destruction of their city and the enslavement of its population. The sack of Rome by the Gauls, however, produced acute insecurity and enabled erstwhile allies to turn against the now singular dominant Latin power. In this phase, warfare became both an opportunity for plunder and a struggle for security. Roman political order was structured around an annual cycle of war as the customs of the first phase became institutionalized, but political relations remained poised between internal and external domination.

The beginnings of the slave economy may date from the defeat of the Veii, but economic slavery also problematized the status of freemen, as indicated in Livy's record of the plebeian struggles against debt bondage between 389–342 BC, and in the formal recognition of distinct statuses implicit in the tax on the manumission of slaves (357 BC). Freedom and subjection only became formally distinct with the social reforms instituted from 367 BC. This shift also marks the inception of a third stage in the internal relation between Roman warfare and society. The debt problem was resolved in part by a new policy of colonization. Coupled with an end to aristocratic monopoly of access to the *ager publicus* (state lands, continually expanded through appropriations in military victory), colonization offered land settlement to impoverished plebeians. Additionally, the institution of *nexum* (debt bondage) was abolished, and from 296 BC, freedmen were enlisted as full citizens in the legions. In this era of annual warfare, between 343 and 264 BC, Rome achieved domination of the Italian peninsula south of the Po valley. In this period, the policy of obliging conquered peoples to cede land to the *ager publicus* and to become allies providing forces (*socii*) to serve in Roman campaigns was substituted for mass enslavement, as slaves were taken in the course of war rather than conquest. Though the republic had become a military vehicle engaged in annual wars of predation for land, booty and slaves, expertise in military command was not a function of the state, but a quality of the political nobility, whose emergent internal competition for personal status differentiation provided a further spur to engagement in war. A fourth phase, and a further transformation of Rome's military-political constitution, is marked by the Punic Wars against Carthage, with massive and protracted, but intermittent, campaigns and a new need for strategic garrisoning of legions at a distance. This transformed the annual militia into an effective standing army, serving fixed periods of military duty in permanent legions which were replenished by individual substitutions, under prolonged appointments of command over provincial stations.

Historical sociology traces transformations from the centre outward, and sees the military constitution and spatial expansion of Rome as an effect of endogenous social forces in the context of relations with other military-spatial formations, on the model of modern states in international context. However, the new historiography of Rome enables us to see how the appearance of strategic space in this period constituted a virtual republic in the military provinces, in which there developed new relations and economies of domination (military clientage and patronage). This also enables us to trace a genealogy of the military subject into the late republic in the fifth phase of Cornell's periodization, characterized by internal conflict, in which the transformations that had appeared in the provinces returned to the centre, reconstituting the political order of the republic. The new regime of Caesar Augustus, Cornell argues, represented the final working-through of this revolution.

These serial transformations cannot be understood purely in macro-structural terms. New historians such as Cornell and Rich, following Harris,[10] argue that the common state structure of the Latin plains communities predisposed them to war, so that Rome itself was both structurally driven to war and compelled to engage in war as a hegemonic power to provide an outlet for the similar structural drives of its *socii*. However, this mode of argument simply elevates the reductive model of the body of the 'agent' of sociology on to a collective category, positing a simple identity between state and subject which fails to recognize transformations at the 'micro'-level, or in subjectivity, and thus cannot explain the other face of power, obedience. The following chapters trace this theme through the transformations of ancient Rome.

Notes

1. H. Tudor, *Political Myth* (London: Macmillan, 1972), pp. 65–90.
2. Unlike the earlier, more overtly partisan, writers of Rome's mythic foundations, Livy's authorship was not embedded in a political career; he was, rather, the first 'professional' Roman historian. His narration of the greatness of men's actions realized the Ciceronian promise of the republic in recording them for posterity, but this was only accomplished under conditions that precluded the pursuit of those virtues in Livy's own time, since historiography became 'objective' by becoming divorced from political rhetoric in the same process that monopolized virtue to the *princeps*.
3. T. Livy, *The History of Rome, Books I–V, The Early History of Rome,* trans. A. de Sélincourt (Harmondsworth: Penguin, 1971).
4. P. Anderson, *Passages From Antiquity to Feudalism* (London: New Left Books, 1974), P. Anderson, *Lineages of the Absolutist State* (London: New Left Books, 1974).
5. M. Weber, *The Agrarian Sociology of Ancient Civilizations,* trans. R. I. Frank (London: New Left Books, 1976).
6. M. Weber, 'Developmental Tendencies in the Situation of East Elbian Rural Labourers', *Economy and Society,* 8, 2 (1979), pp. 177–205.

7. Whether the foundational myth is true or not is irrelevant here. Little is known of Roman social and political organization before the Servian constitution, and the foundational myth, rather than any true origin, has been historically decisive. The political history of the republic could be written as a struggle between the two forms latent within Roman society. Though neither was fully realized, they enable us to identify tendencies (to predation and security) in tension with one another, which provided objects for the struggles of social groups or classes within the republic.
8. S. Oakley, 'The Roman Conquest of Italy', and T. Cornell, 'The End of Roman Imperial Expansion', in J. Rich, and G. Shipley, (eds), *War and Society in the Roman World* (London: Routledge, 1993), pp. 9 and 141–2, respectively.
9. Cornell, 'End of Roman Imperial Expansion', pp. 155–9.
10. W. V. Harris, *War and Imperialism in Republican Rome* (Oxford: Clarendon Press, 1979).

2

The Roman Republic

The military constitution

One of the most far-reaching developments of the ancient Mediterranean world was the transformation of its military culture from the individual combat of heterogeneously armed warriors, attended by their retinues or clients, to collective hoplite warfare with uniformly equipped men on foot who were tactically organized into a phalanx that could withstand cavalry or missile attack, and had the impetus in concerted motion to crash through less cohesively disciplined lines of forces. The hoplite form redistributed violence from an elite aristocracy onto a mass, but the shift in the constitution of violence indicated by this tactical transformation is not simply a matter of military technique reflecting social forms, as in Otto Hintze's model,[1] since it required the constitution of a collective body on to which war could be transposed.

Rome may have adopted the new military culture from its more powerful neighbour, the Etruscan confederation of 12 cities, from which the term *legio*, is derived. Three Roman tribal districts made up ten sub-divisions, each of which contributed 100 men (a century) toward its 1,000-strong contingent, commanded by the tribunes (tribal officers). These units in turn comprised the 3,000-man force of the legion. In addition to these levies, the Roman clan aristocracy, the *equites*, served as mounted warriors.[2] The new order of warfare was effected by the institution of a *census* under the king, Servius Tullius, which divided people into classes indexed to tactical categories according to the kind of weaponry with which each class could afford to equip themselves. This organization of armed public service in defence of the city was distinct from the Athenian and Spartan models. Livy declares Servius' military census as the establishment of the principle 'that every man's contribution should be according to his means' and as the anticipation of the republic.[3] The Servian constitution precluded the monopolization of force by any particular caste, producing military interdependency across the orders of the census, which also included a sub-class of the population as *infra classem*, a residue too poor to be able to arm themselves, the *capite censi*, 'those counted by heads', who had no military duties, but were still subject to military service in principle and hence entitled to some reduced political privileges as citizens,[4] so that the political order was constitutionally identical with military formation and technique.[5] Servius also divided the tribes into centuries for voting, a political privilege accorded to the military classes. The political space opened by the Servian constitution was thus already irreducibly identical with the military organization of Rome.

Roman royal succession required the assent of the people in arms in their centurial assemblies, and of the aristocracy, politically organized as the Senate for which Servius built a permanent House.[6] The Senate provided the king's counsel, but he held the authority of *imperium*, which comprised command in war and jurisdiction over life. With the overthrow of the monarchy and institution of the republic, these military and juridical prerogatives were invested in the office of *consul* to which two members of the nobility, the senatorial class, were elected for each year. There was no functional division of labour between the two consuls; each held military command as well as civil jurisdiction, but in time of emergency, a *dictator* could be appointed to hold the *imperium* alone for a strictly limited six-month term.[7]

The secessio plebis

Collegial *imperium* in the two consular offices and the senatorial status of candidates ensured that the Senate could exercise more influence in the republic than it had been able to under singular kingship. However, the foundational synthesis of insecurity and predatoriness embroiled Rome in constant warfare, so that the military–political constitution carried over into the republic from Servius endowed the plebeian classes eligible for military service with an extra-constitutional power in the capacity to refuse consular war-orders. The *secessio plebis* was first exercised in 494 BC, when the plebs walked out of the city and encamped beyond the walls. Their liberty within the republic had been rendered insecure by the prospect of debt bondage, in which insolvent debtors could be held to labour for their creditor. The consuls were divided on the issue, and the plebs took it upon themselves to free debtors, holding meetings across the city.[8] When the Senate advised the consuls to clear the streets by enlisting the plebeian mob for military service, the plebs took refuge in collective identity, refusing to answer to their names when called. Nevertheless, they enlisted for the annual wars under the *dictator* appointed by the Senate, since they had previously received favourable judgements under such emergency mediation, and exhorted their commanders to join battle so that they could return home to Rome to press their case before the term of the dictatorship expired. After the annual wars, the Senate attempted to use the soldiers' oath of allegiance to their consul-commanders to order them to march out of the city again, even though there was now no enemy to fight, but the plebs responded by encamping themselves in military order on the Sacred Mount three miles from Rome in an assertion, not a refusal, of their soldier–citizenship, thereby independently establishing the *res publica* in its military form outside senatorial jurisdiction. Denied their right to liberty in the civil sphere of the public realm, the plebs could assert it in the camp, demanding recognition of their liberty in public protection against judgements which would have removed it for a mere private debt.[9]

The *secessio plebis* marks a revolution in the pre-political order of ancient Rome, a shift in the *moral* constitution of power, breaking the old right of command by noble patricians over the plebs, which was constitutionally sanctioned in the senatorial class's monopoly of consular office. From this moment on, the condition of obedience was problematized and command no longer guaranteed, even though the military order of the republic itself was maintained by the plebeian encampment.

The Senate sent as its spokesman, Menenius Agrippa, to address the legions with a fable of the body politic in which the members of the body 'had each its own thoughts and the words to express them'. In Agrippa's fable, the other parts resented providing food for the belly, which did nothing, and so conspired to deprive it of food, as a consequence of which all wasted away. The fable is not an allegory of production; rather, Menenius argues that this illustrates the necessity of the aristocratic political function of distribution:

> ... the belly has no mean service to perform: it receives food, indeed; but it also nourishes in turn the other members, giving back to all parts of the body, through all its veins, the blood it has made by the process of digestion; and upon this blood our life and our health depend.[10]

This allegorical representation of the republic as an organically integrated body communicated the Senate's recognition of new realities of power in the face of plebeian secession. Ensuing negotiations led to the institution of annually elected popular tribunes, constitutionally empowered to veto consular decrees and to protect and represent the plebeians against the civil law and debt bondage by physical and immediate powers of *intercessio*, that is, bodily interposing themselves between the magistrate's officer, the *lictor*, and the plebs, a physical presence sanctioned by the plebeian oath of blood vengeance against any who laid hands upon the tribunes.[11] The tribunes rapidly extended their political scope by calling assemblies of the tribes in military order to sanction or reject their own legislative proposals (though it was not until 287 BC, after another secession, that tribunal proposals ratified by *plebiscite* were established as law) and their campaign for legal equality eventually led to the codification of the laws of Rome in the Twelve Tables.[12]

However, these political advances by the plebs are usually seen as having been negated by economic factors. For Anderson, the growing economic power of rich peasants and patricians, who had been able to enlarge their land-holdings and now farmed them with slaves, undercut any advantages gained in the political field, since the general position of the plebs had declined insofar as material deprivation rendered them dependent even as they extended their political liberties. Plebeian struggles in the political sphere for agrarian reform were increasingly confounded by the competitive exclusion of peasant farmers from the land and by manipulation of the urban mob in a political process of exclusion led by the cross-class fraction of slave-owning agri-culturalists. By the late republic, the plight of the plebeian peasants had become depoliticized and was transferred on to the military relationship between the legion and its commander.

> The bond between legionary and commander came increasingly to resemble that between patron and client in civilian life: from the epoch of Marius and Sulla onwards, soldiers looked to their generals for economic rehabilitation, and generals used their soldiers for political advancement.[13]

This interpretation, however, imposes a material valuation upon the Roman culture of patronage and clientage, reducing it to the terms of a contract between economically competitive agents motivated by individual self-interest. The transformation of military relations does mark a great shift in the constitution of the republic, but any account of this has to recognize that the conditions of the military subject were quite distinct and increasingly isolated from economic relations. Rather than looking to the supposed centre of Roman society upon the land, in legal relations or in political struggles, we can trace this transformation in the legions and the space of insecurity outside Rome.

The space of insecurity

After the *secessio plebis*, military command was mediated by constitutional terms of negotiation, while the political struggles of the plebs were inextricably bound up with their military identity, with the space of the camp, the time of the levy and the campaign, and with imperatives of Roman policy deriving from the city's foundational insecurity and predatoriness. Both Weber and Anderson reductively conceptualize these factors as epiphenomenal effects of structural economic and political processes at the centre. For them, the transformation of military relations is produced by the quantitative variation of these functions: the increased duration of enforced economic inactivity of the peasants on military service and the increased physical distance of Roman domination from the centre. However, the campaigns of the legions projected the military order of the republic into the conditions of a space and time entirely distinct from the centre and the interests generated there.

The legions of Rome did not occupy territory, but traversed a space which was perceived in linear rather than territorial terms. Roman military surveying techniques were grounded in the practice of centuriation, which had originated as a function of military road construction and only secondarily became concerned with territorialization. Its grids cut indiscriminately across communal lands and their allocations, as well as across the *ager publicus*.[14] The roads were more like low walls, built for the speed of legions on the march, while trade was mostly conducted by water. Plans based on such techniques were used only for land division, while Roman commanders used itineraries that marked routes measured by the standard pace of march, but not topography, since terrain was of significance only in its immediacy, in terms of the disposition of forces upon it, and the intelligence was gathered locally *in situ* and not codified. Ethnography rather than geography represented the Roman world, and ethnographic classification comprised the categories of knowledge, organized by linear measurement into a concentric space of the world with Rome at the centre, and barbarism increasing with distance, and mapped not onto territory, but onto linear distances calibrated by a standard day's march by a legion. Even for Caesar in his extensive conquests, the prime concern was movement, rather than territorial occupation, and his conquest of Gaul was undertaken without prior knowledge of its geography. Only crossroads on the network of itineraries were subject to centuriation when colonies were founded at such points as military–ethnographic outposts of Rome.[15]

Up to the mid-third century, slave raiding and even land seizure were secondary to the establishment of hegemonic alliance as the Roman object of war. Early Roman practice was to enfranchise other peoples where possible, so they became citizens of the republic, bound to pay taxes and subject to military service, with rights of intermarriage and private contractual relations.[16] When this policy shifted to one of federation in perpetual alliance from the mid-third century BC, Rome did not destroy the property relations and political institutions of the vanquished, or ordinarily enslave whole populations, but wherever possible imposed binding treaties which exacted tribute in military contingents rather than material wealth. The *socii* served alongside the legions on campaigns, implicating subjected allies in Roman actions and thus constituting common military interests with the security of Rome. This policy enabled Rome to call upon dominated peoples in its own defence, but required ever more extensive lines of communication linking the allies to Rome itself.

Rome thus existed in a linear and ethnographic space that it sought to reduce not through occupation, but by traversing that space with its own interests, projecting them onto others. It did not need enemies, but allies, and practised military policy, rather than strategy. The two major incursions into its interiority by other strategic actors caused profound upheaval and invoked exceptional measures.

Incursions and transformations

The Gallic incursion of 390 BC was the high tide of a wave of conquest by the surplus population of a barbarian community assembled in war order. Livy describes the shock of their appearance at the Italian town of Clusium in ethnographic terms: 'strange men in thousands were at the gates, men the like of whom the townsfolk had never seen, outlandish warriors armed with strange weapons, who were rumoured already to have scattered the Etruscan legions on both sides of the Po'.[17]

Clusium called on Roman assistance, but the envoys were unable to accord recognition to this Other appearing in its hegemonic domain. In the ensuing campaign, Rome was confronted with an entirely alien mode of warfare. The sheer speed of the Gallic advance was terrifying to those whose perceptions were based on the marching rate of the hoplite phalanxes of the Italian peninsula; the legion fielded against the Gallic invaders fled in terror at the sight of 'this strange enemy from the ends of the earth'. The Gauls entered Rome and killed the noble patricians where they sat like disbelieving statues in front of their mansions. Exiled from their own city, the Romans assembled fresh forces at their garrison in Veii. The Senate appointed a *dictator*, who led the Romans to victory in battle, but then had to extend his dictatorial authority to ensure that the city was rebuilt and not abandoned by its citizens – an imperative reconstruction, undertaken without design, producing a Rome 'more like a squatter's settlement than a properly planned city', resembling an artefact which its citizens occupied, rather than a city in which they lived.[18]

The same kind of internal transformation was also imposed on the legion. In response to the unprecedented and disastrous encounter with the Gallic mode of warfare, which relied on speed rather than the coherent disciplined grammar of the Mediterranean hoplite formations, the Roman legions were reformed internally into *manipuli*. These were smaller, more mobile sub-units, which provided gaps in the battle order between units in line, overlapped by lines of subsequent units in depth. The manipular battle order was more capable of flexible response, enabling the legions to overcome the phalanxes of the Greek world to the east,[19] but transforming the principle of military constitutional representation into an order determined by the imperatives of its tactical function. The *manipuli* now comprised the units of tactical order, while the legions became purely administrative units.

Roman expansion in search of hegemonic security also brought it into conflict with another expanding Mediterranean power. Carthage was primarily a commercial rather than a political city, employing mercenaries to fight its wars, and it was thus not possible to extend the principle of hegemony to this encounter. The protracted First Punic War (264–241 BC) was indecisive, but the armed truce, which prevailed until the Second Punic War (218–202 BC) amounted to an extension of war, without battle and without resolution, in the virtual space and time of strategic deployment opened by the stalemated confrontation, in which the military condition of the republic was transformed. In the Second Punic War, the Carthaginian forces under Hannibal sought to undercut Rome's hegemonic dominance by invading Italy through Spain and Gaul to establish its army in the peninsula and realign the allies of Rome. Carthage was able to undertake this long-range strategic mode of warfare by employing mercenary forces, rather than levying a political community, and Rome was thus once again confronted with a military configuration alien to its perceptions. At Cannae (216 BC) Hannibal defeated the Italian legions, precipitating emergency military measures that were to impel long-term processes of Roman military transformation.

To substitute for the losses at Cannae, the property qualification for the Roman military levy was suspended to enable enlistment of the *capite censi*, prisoners and even slaves, in defence of the republic.[20]

After these emergency enlistments, the census property threshold separating the *classis* from the *infra classem* was lowered further, creating another tactical grouping – the *velites*, unarmoured skirmishers who were drawn from the newly added, poorest social category.[21] This reduction of the threshold of military citizenship was part of a long process throughout this period in which the property qualification would remain as a formal census category, but would lose its constitutional significance. The plebs' military contribution to public service also formed the basis of their political force. They were not merely citizen voters, but citizen-soldiers. Roman political order was constituted not by economic stratification, but by the census classification of capacities for military service. The erosion of the property qualification thus offered to the very poorest the same sense of political identity and self-legitimation which had hitherto been the privilege of the propertied peasantry.

The army was neither a passive structural transmission belt nor simply a variable quantitative factor, but appears as a particularly complex knot, at once the form of plebeian political identity and effectively the exteriority of Rome itself. During extended services in the strategic provincial garrisons required after the First Punic War, the army became something exterior to, rather than of, Rome – a virtual military space in which political relations underwent radical transformation. Livy notes that during the First Punic War, a 'bad precedent' had been set when a *praetor* had been elected to command for an extended term by his own legion 'in their camps abroad', a novel procedure usurping 'the proper sanction of law and official control' by the consulate and Senate.[22] The election was quashed, but it indicates that service in the field was beginning to establish an autonomy from the constitutional centre that could invest novel authority in its condition of command. This autonomous usurpation was adopted as a formal measure to govern the space and time of strategic protraction, when the annual limit on consular office was extended into proconsular offices of provincial command.[23] Constitutional constraints were further outweighed by necessity after two legions were destroyed in Spain in 211 BC. The Senate voted provincial command to the formally unqualified, but militarily adept Scipio the Younger, who in five years destroyed the Carthaginian forces there and returned to Rome to secure a consulship, again unconstitutionally.[24]

Lesser offices were also transformed in this time. Military tribunes were not originally offices of command, but had political duties to protect the interests, health and welfare of the soldiers in the legions. Like the plebeian tribunes, they were *equites* who were required to have served a minimum of five years to qualify for the office. However, as legions came to be deployed separately in distant parts of strategic provinces, at a distance from consular command, the tribunes began to exercise command by proxy. The new field of command opened by this *ad hoc* arrangement was colonized by the patriciate when the tribune's role of proxy command was formally substituted by *legates*, senior senators appointed on commission by consuls to exercise delegated authority in their name over part of a province and the legion stationed there. The path into a political career via the military tribunate for *equites* was now closed, displaced by a new opportunity for consuls to acquire senior patronage and for nobles to pursue political careers through personal commissions in the army without any direct experience of political responsibility to the soldiers or the legions.[25] The effect was profoundly to destabilize the Roman constitution, which was based upon the identity of political and military aspects of citizenship, by displacing public with personal accountability for subordinate military office. The commission of *legate* as an office of command without political responsibility marked the first fissure in the Roman constitutional identity of the military and the political.

In substitution for the military tribunes, the *legate* was commissioned to exercise delegated *imperium* over the order of the legion in the field. Legions were not identified with the province in which they served, but were maintained in isolation from 'local' territorial relations. Regulations forbidding marriage during service, for instance, clearly indicate the danger perceived in localization. In its traversal of linear space, the legion remained enclosed against the environment, encamping every time it halted in a pre-assigned and exactly regulated order of survey, delineation, entrenchment and deployment. The standard plan of the camp replicated the Roman model town-plan, and conformed to the military–constitutional order of the legion. This design never varied, since marches were calculated by *itineria* to enable the camp to be constructed by nightfall. Within the fortified enclosure the legion was deployed in order, with clear lines of communication along roadways of a standard width.[26] Over-winter quarters for the legions in the field and for permanent garrisons were laid out in precisely the same form. Polybius refers to the camp as a 'mobile city',[27] and for the Romans, the camp was identical with the city in its military order. It was in this order that the secessionary plebs had encamped outside Rome, establishing for themselves another, virtual city in which their liberties were inscribed in the grammar of the camp itself. In the extension of the legion in strategic space, however, the syntax of the military order was to undergo a fundamental shift even as that grammar remained unaltered.

Within the camp, discipline was exercised inexorably, but even its harshest customs must be understood as a mediation of the full juridical authority of the consulate, which was invested in the field with the *imperium*, comprising command in war and discretion over life.[28] In camp, therefore, capital punishment became almost the only formal sanction. Offences against military order were definitively capital offences in a military law which could know only an absolute sanction that could not be ameliorated in law, but only in custom. Military justice was thus arbitrary in a juridical sense. The severity of decimation, for instance, was merciful in its proportion, while lesser, peer-administered customary punishments, such as the gauntlet, established a complicity between subjects and the consular *imperium* which held their very lives in its hands as a gift of the consul to the soldiers, customized in military procedure.

Excursus: The sociology of domination and obedience

With the transformations of the Punic Wars, the genealogy of the Roman military subject begins to enter another phase. It may be useful to reflect upon how these two phases are usually conflated, which can be seen most clearly in the work of Max Weber. There is a purposeful tendency in Weber's work to draw analogies between feudal and ancient Roman society (rather than its formal political institutions). Such analogies are scattered throughout the incompleted fragments posthumously edited as *Economy and Society*, where their elevation to the level of conceptualization effectively displaces the Roman political order from Weber's account. For instance, speculating on the origin of clientage in the auxiliary military service rendered by dependants to their patrons in heroic combat leads Weber to conceptualize the Roman military order of peasant legionaries as 'a stratum of plebeian war fief-holders'.[29]

Weber's elevation of analogies into concepts separates the political and the military order *a priori*, since the formal institutions and identities of the political order are not subject to the analogy. When Weber presents the thesis of a general historical tendency toward increasing rationalization in the economy, resulting in the differentiation of 'civil' and 'military' subjects, he is merely attributing to economic processes a division he has already established *a priori* through his analogical reduction of Roman military relations to the medieval feudal order. He can then argue that the historical development of imperial patrimonialism and 'military monarchy' (another anachronism) is a result of economic rationalization, as well as of the geostrategic implications of frontier protection resulting from quantitative territorial expansion. Weber's sleight of hand in establishing the feudal order as an analytical norm thus goes unnoticed, producing a neatly deterministic sociological law of wide utility in the construction of historical narratives, since we can vary the emphasis between the economic and the geostrategic to produce new accounts, eliding the political concepts and identities that shaped Roman political action.[30]

This elision in modern sociology correlates with Weber's conflation of domination and obedience, which again can be reviewed critically through the historical sociology of the Roman republic. In defining domination for the purpose of his sociology, Weber first excludes indirect domination, reducing the concept to the result of the juridical formulation of sovereignty (the one-dimensional idea of power as power over) which commands unconditionally, thus consigning the problem of obedience to a black box. Weber qualifies this carefully, acknowledging that his definition excludes economic domination. However, while this accommodates Marxist objections, it reduces the scope of the theory of domination to juridical and economic categories.

> In the following discussion we shall use the term domination exclusively in that narrower sense which excludes from its scope those situations in which power has a source in a formally free interplay of interested parties such as occurs in the market. In other words, in our terminology *domination* shall be identical with *authoritarian power of command* ... To be more specific, *domination* will thus mean the situation in which the manifested will (*command*) of the ruler or rulers is meant to influence the conduct of one or more others (*the ruled*) and actually does influence it in such a way that their conduct to a socially relevant degree occurs as if the ruled had made the content of the command the maxim of their conduct for its on sake. Looked upon from the other end, this will be called *obedience*.[31]

Weber acknowledges the 'awkwardness' of the 'as if', but refers the condition of obedience only to modes of legitimation. Command is not something constructed in practices, but given in social codes (tradition, charisma, legal rationality) which must then have their own authority referred, ultimately, to societal functions or to interests. The normative and exclusionary effects of the delimitation can already be seen here in the way Weber ahistorically infers 'social relevance' from his own analytical construction. 'Discipline', for Weber, tends to fill the space left empty by this formulation, but, while he asserts its crucial role in history and society, it remains a 'black box'. For the Roman republic, as we shall see, discipline could not fill the box emptied of the sovereign authority of command in the *secessio plebis*, while economic domination became an increasingly distant prospect in the post-Punic legions. For the sources of obedience, we thus need to look elsewhere.

The personalization of command

Scipio, the architect of Rome's decisive defeat of Carthage in the Second Punic War, had reinstituted forms of discipline in the legions, which the annalists argue had lapsed in the years of truce, but discipline in itself does not secure obedience, and the protraction of military service was straining the viability of the republic to constitute this condition in its military subjects. The success of Scipio's military reforms lay rather in his development of a new constitution of military obedience based on the customary patron–client relations of Roman society. Scipio had accumulated political patronage in part by granting official commissions during his extended proconsulship and in part by inheriting it from the military careers of his father and uncle. In the state of emergency, however, he was able to establish mass clientage in the legions.

Refused an extraordinary *dilectus* (levy) to raise fresh legions by a Senate fearful of his influence, he personally recruited volunteers from time-served veterans and from the *proletarii*, the propertyless urban citizens who predominated in the tribal electoral assemblies of the third century,[32] armed them at his own cost, crossed to Sicily and drove the Carthaginians back to Africa. On his Triumph, against senatorial opposition, he settled veterans of this campaign in Sicily on land confiscated from renegade allies.[33] The Senate's opposition stemmed from its desire to maximize the land accruing to the state,[34] but also because soldiers settled by Scipio would continue to provide him with a colonial clientage of veterans close to the mainland, since the patron–client relation was not like a modern contract, to be completed by an exchange between Scipio and the troops who had volunteered to serve with him. Scipio's gifts of land to the soldiers, like the popular votes which had elected him against the constitution and the volunteered service of his veterans, can only be understood in terms of the peculiar nexus of Roman patron–client relations and the politically symbolic gift.[35]

Authority as right to command, constitutionally incorporated in the office of consul, had been in long-term decline since the *secessio plebis* of 494 BC. A sovereign right inhered in the military order itself, in the consul's official *imperium*, exercised and delegated as the military jurisdiction, but its composure was lost to the patriciate as an order since the *secessio*. Even Scipio is significantly credited with reinstituting *discipline* as an organizational condition of obedience, rather than simply asserting a jurisdictional right of command. The office of consul provided a form for command, but there was no constitutional means by which its exercise could be guaranteed over a people who had asserted their liberty in discipline itself, effectively co-opting it in the *secessio plebis* as their own. The plebs had marched out of Rome in military order in 494 BC, not against but '*without* orders from the consuls'.[36] The residual problem was not so much that of who could command, as of how obedience, no longer guaranteed by any right, could be secured.

Patronage as government

In his later work, Foucault formulated precisely this problem for theory in recognition of the way that his earlier work on discipline could be misunderstood as a totalizing 'theory of power', as which it would always appear inadequate. Discipline – the codes of rules, the manipulation and deployment of bodies, the architectonics of subjection – appears to require free subjects to act upon, and Foucault's interrogation of disciplinary power thus leads to the question of obedience. We can perhaps make a useful analytical distinction here between subjection, i.e. subjection to domination and subjectification, i.e. the constitution of subjects who are free to act, free to obey.[37] The subject is thus not constituted wholly in disciplinary subjection, but pre-exists it in *obedience to orders* of discipline. The plebs (including in principle the *proletarii*) were subject to military order, in which their liberty as citizen–soldiers was invested, but as the secessions had shown, this order in itself did not constitute obedience to command.

Command was, rather, vested in the soldiers' oath, sworn not to the office of consulate, but to the persons holding the office in annual tenure. Originally, this oath of personal obedience to the office-holder was synchronic with the cyclical campaigns for which the legions were raised, but as the legions' service became extended in time, so soldiers in extensive service were required to swear anew to incumbent consuls as the two forms of public service became out of synch. The personal liability of Roman public service meant that though consuls were exempt from legal indictment while in office, on the expiry of their term they could be arraigned for their acts during their consulship. The remedy was to secure further formal immunity from prosecution through the extension of office into a proconsulship, using the extra time and the prerogative of commission to build clientage in the Senate which would act as a political buffer against future threats of indictment. This strategy endowed military proconsulship with great political value and rendered the provincial military space in which it was located a theatre of political action. Proconsulship as an office of military command over legions which were themselves extended into a different time from the centre, also enabled relations of patronage and clientage to be constructed between generals and legions.

Foucault's formulation of the question of how obedience is secured as the question of government can be pursued for the Roman army of the late republic through the work of Paul Veyne,[38] who uses Weber's terms to show that the Roman conception of public office was very different from both the legal–rational conception of bureaucratic office in modernity and from the patrimonial conception of office as the property of the office-holder which pertained in early modern absolutist Europe, where the state itself was considered the patrimony of the monarch. The legal-rational, modern sense of public office and service, Veyne argues, was confined to the Stoics such as Cato, for whom the magistracies were 'missions', and for whom official obligations constituted vocational work, rather than the means to self-aggrandizement. Veyne also suggests that Cato was almost unique in Roman republican society, which by the beginning of the second century BC was based on two parallel institutions. On the one hand there were the formal public institutions, the civil magistracies and the legions, and on the other, interpersonal relations of clientage, marked by a symbolic exchange of services and gifts between patrons and clients. The formal institutions no longer effectively carried the old right to command and were yet to acquire the ethical rationality which Cato projected on to them. Public life was thus ordered by relations of patronage and clientage, which Max Weber categorized as regulated by 'special laws',

> ... which in Antiquity escaped the control of general or common law and the jurisdiction of the regular courts ... they have in themselves no formal structure of their own ... [but] were governed ... by a mixture of sacred norms on the one hand and conventional rules on the other.[39]

Veyne traces the genealogy of these relations from the Greek culture of euergetism, voluntary personal endowment or provision of services to the commonwealth as gifts which do not fit the model of an exchange economy, but rather constituted the symbolic 'political economy' of antiquity. In Greece,

... euergetism was very different from the gift as primary form of exchange. It does not enable a person to obtain goods or services through an informal exchange. It belongs to a different species, political gifts, which are bound up in a certain way ... with relations of authority ... A political gift is a symbolic gift ... from a society divided into classes there was a transition to a society in which ... the notables constituted an order, which public opinion recognized as the right to govern and the duty to perform patronage.[40]

In the third century BC, a deep ethical crisis erupted in the Roman republic around the question of what the persons holding elected magisterial office should do with money which came into their hands during their term of office, such as fines to the magistrate, or loot to the general. This ethical question was resolved by translating the Greek practice of euergetism into the already established social relations of patron and client, as gifts or largesses from those in office to their clients. This established relations which were quite distinct from the sovereign authority implied in Weber's typology of legitimate domination, since both parties necessarily retained their autonomy. Veyne uses the example of the political process to illustrate its workings. Although clients' votes could be a service which they rendered to their patron, patronage could not dispense with politics. Rather, conventional rules required the candidate to *negotiate* with clients who retained their autonomy, on the basis that both parties would gain from the relation. From the perspective of Weber's typology of legitimate domination, this appears 'corrupt', but an euergetic gift established moral relations and did not necessarily signify the price of service. Clients retained their autonomy, while an elected patron held the authority of public office not under any principle of general obligation but as his private property, with only personal obligations to his clients.[41]

Relations of patronage and clientage were not relations of domination and subjection, but can be understood as a mode of *government* in the sense that Foucault approached it – an extra-legal constitution of voluntary obedience, in which both parties were beholden to conduct themselves and act reciprocally in a particular way regardless of the content of their negotiations. The relations of obligation thus established extended over an unspecified duration and unlike the contract, they were not terminated by exchange, since the values involved were symbolic and irreducible to equivalence. Symbolic gifts constituted an affection, a *care*fully nurtured personal recognition which maintained the relation over a duration quite distinct from that of economic exchanges or formal political events. This affective aspect of the constitution of an obedient subjectification, as distinct from disciplinary subjection, thus took on a quality of love, which was not unconditional, but, in principle, unlimited.

The transposition of euergetism onto patron–client relations provided the means whereby obedience now became secured in the legions. By the time of Scipio, whose command provided the model for subsequent military reforms under the republic,[42] this 'state of relations' had been substituted for the right to command as the mode of military government in the Roman legion. On campaign in Africa, Scipio became renowned for his *liberalitas*, his noble generosity toward his legions with gifts and shares of booty. Scipio was not buying his soldiers' allegiances, but affirming that as soldiers they were his clients; settlements and donations to his veterans can thus be seen as further symbolic gifts. However, this constituted neither the kind of sovereign domination which we are accustomed to think of as the condition of military discipline, nor a form of mercenarism which would be circumscribed in extent by the terms of a contract: 'The personal bond between soldiers and their chief came to acquire features not very consistent with that passive obedience which may be thought essential where military discipline is concerned.'[43]

Administrative rationalization

Anderson acknowledges that the army had become governed by the patron–client relation, but interprets this in economic and contractual terms, so that the legions' motivation is attributed to economic self-interest mediated by the power of military commanders to make donations to their soldiers, as if soldiers served in exchange for veteran settlement in land. Where the legions involved, like Caesar's, were not of Roman origin, a purely mercenary motivation is imputed to them, divorced from even legal land relations.[44] This reductive approach reiterates the modern myth of the tragedy of Rome: the confoundation of plebeian democracy (Anderson) or constitutional politics (Weber) by the *depoliticizing* effect of economic motivations and interests. However, such economistic explanations require us always to re-interpret the historical record, to reduce the subject to material economic determinants through the theoretical construction of extensive mechanisms of mediation, particularly to explain why men were prepared to give up their lives in obedience to commands. It is difficult to explain the harsh discipline exercised in the legions by these terms, as a perversely mediated self-interest. In contrast to this materialistic economism, the symbolic economy which Veyne identifies in Roman patronage provides a dimension of the political which can explain obedience in Roman military relations without elaborate mediation or the reduction of the military subject to imputed interests.

> Political power consists in reigning over men's hearts, in being loved. The colonel who 'knows how to make himself loved' by his regiment is kind because his role as colonel involves this: he is not kind in order that he may be promoted general by his men. The idea of depoliticisation is thoroughly anachronistic.[45]

While the reductive economistic explanation of voluntary military obedience is problematized by the increasing alienation and hardship of legion service, these trends provide conditions which actually prepared the way for patronage to invest the military subject. A subsistence allowance for military service (*stipendium*) had been introduced as early as the wars against Veii, and state provision of arms and clothing instituted in the time of the Gracchian tribunes enabled the property threshold for military service to be lowered. However, tribunician proposals to reduce the maximum years of service and to adhere to a minimum age for conscription were obstructed because keeping time-served soldiers on reserve duty in the provinces was less politically contentious than raising new levies. In lieu of substitution, these veterans were settled on expropriated land in Spain and Sardinia, thus providing self-supporting colonial garrisons.[46] These piecemeal developments were administratively rationalized by the commander, Marius, when he secured successive re-elections as consul from 104–101 BC after his victorious African campaigns with an expanded army in the Jugurthine War, which had enabled him to build huge patronage in the Roman political system.

The property qualification had progressively been reduced tenfold from the Servian level, falling well below that necessary for peasant subsistence, and as the legions were now armed out of state funds, Marius was able to regularize the voluntary enlistment of urban *proletarii* regardless of property. Soldiers became economically dependent upon a state which in this respect at least was no longer identical with the state of public representation, but was becoming an administrative domain. The obliteration of political representation in the state was pioneered in military space by Marius' administrative isolation of the legions from social ties other than the patronage of the commander and their economic maintenance by the state. Serving soldiers were barred from marriage and camp-followers (who had hitherto provided informal domestic services) were reduced to official quotas. Henceforth, the men were to carry their own cooking equipment and emergency rations as well as their arms, becoming known as 'Marius's mules'.[47] The citizen–soldiers thus became (like women in Roman society), subjects of domestic bondage, with profound implications for their political identity. According to Livy's formulation, plebeian military service under the Servian constitution had been a constitutionally equivalent public service to the senatorial duties of the patricians, but now legion service became qualitatively differentiated from patrician military office, degraded not by clientage, which was quite distinct from political identity, but by administrative reforms that required the soldiers to perform *domestic, non-political* service.[48]

The military order was also transformed in Marius' administrative counter-revolution. The old tactical division of the legions, inscribed in the space of the camp, had originally represented the plebeian order of liberty, the practical representation of the principle that each contributed an equivalent service to the republic proportionate to their means. With the state provision of arms to enable the admission of the *capite censi* as volunteers, all that the plebs contributed were docile bodies in subjection to discipline, rather than the subject of liberty. Marius rationalized this homogenization of plebeian service in reforms of the internal organization of the legions, as represented in the standards they bore. In the old legions, each tactical group of the *census classis* had its own distinctive standard (often the head of an animal), but under the Marian reforms these disappeared as the legion, an administrative rather than tactical entity, became the only differentiated military unit.[49] The old divisions had represented the Servian principle, translating class distinctions into an interdependent tactical order in the discipline of the legion. In the state-equipped Marian legions, however, the divisions of *manipuli* were reduced to their tactical functions and reformed as *cohorts*, after the organization of the *socii* tribute–contributions of subjected peoples, while the legion itself no longer represented the unity of the different classes assembled for a campaign, but became a virtually permanent administrative unit extended in a time of continuous war-readiness and terminated only by its obliteration in battle or disbandment in disgrace.

While the *socii* provided the model whereby the contribution of the Roman classes of liberty was substituted by the institution of tribute from subject masses, the hegemonic allies' tributary contingents also bore an increasing burden of the military demands of strategic security from 200 BC.[50] The burden of military service fell increasingly upon those who benefitted only from Roman hegemony, and not from the privileges of citizenship, and were thus denied senatorial representation, intermarriage and contractual rights as private individuals in civil law.[51] The Latin allies' demands for full citizenship (which would have equalized the military burden) eventually led to the Social War (90–88 BC), in which the republic faced troops trained and organized in Roman discipline, and was forced to concede citizenship to those allies who had rallied to its authority. The devastations of this war left many homeless, destitute and without patronage, for whom citizenship offered only the opportunity to enlist in the legions as a means of life, boosting the proportion of propertyless, dependent volunteer soldiery, which formed a mass fraction that preferred service to settlement, as war became their way of life and the legion virtually their home. Commanders such as Sulla made their name with such troops, for whom military patronage provided their only political identity.

The opportunities for patrician patronage had been vastly expanded by the extensions of office and commissions in strategic provinces. These suspensions of constitutional limits returned to the centre as political crises resulting from inflated patronage were met by emergency commissions, further extending opportunities for ambition and creating conflicts over preferment to extraordinary offices that offered further opportunities to build patronage. Thus, external threats now divided rather than united the political community, while military office enabled commanders to establish colonies of personal clients, displacing citizens in the peninsula and threatening the strategic security of the republic in the provinces.[52] Patronage inflation created a spiralling crisis of the republic that was not resolved, but merely banished when the Senate ruled that consuls be restricted to Italy during their term of office and excluded from the peninsula during their proconsulship as provincial military governors. This legislation aimed at once to separate rivals, demarcate the centre and the margins, and divide rights of command, but in effect both exiled and institutionalized the provincial commander–army nexus independently from senatorial control, opening avenues for new strategies, which Julius Caesar was to exploit to the full by instrumentally developing this nexus in the provinces before returning it to the centre in laying claim to a 'right of coming home', to claim his Triumph (a state procession through Rome) with his army.[53]

Patronage and political rationality: A new theory of obligation

In the provinces, the campaign had become autonomous. In distant, vast conquered Gaul, the proconsul Julius Caesar used the structural division of powers given in the Senate's legislation as a political means,

40

rationalizing its reconstitution of senior provincial military office as an independent authority and the reconstitution of plebeian military service as subjection in patronage to produce a new military policy. He used proconsular prerogative and commander-patronage to raise forces for provincial defence from local, hegemonically allied peoples, enlisting them directly as his own legions, while incorporating recognition of the patron–client relation into the tactical order of march and camp by prioritizing the security of the baggage train, which carried the personal possessions, the booty, of the soldiers under his command.

Incorporating clientage into the tactical military order had important implications for the relation of commander to legion (which Caesar later implemented at constitutional level when as *dictator* he instituted automatic land settlement for all time-served veterans). In his exploration of the origins of the patron–client relation, Weber pointed out that the original form of the symbolic gift, the grant of land by patron to client, had established reciprocal duties governed not by the public or civil law of the city-state, but by religious sanction and conventional rules; civil courts resolved contested ownership of such allotments by equating them with the allotment of land to a legitimate son.[54] However, since the authority of the public state ceased at the threshold of the patriarchal domain, Romans were subject to the magistrates only as citizens. As sons and the recipients of such a gift, they were subject to their fathers.[55] This decision illuminates the status of soldiers *vis-à-vis* their commanders, for although military law did develop in the legions, it never had the status of civil or common, public law, but remained, like the conventional rules governing patron–client relations, a category of 'special law'. Such rules were not necessarily codified and were constituted by cultural evolution rather than formally legislated.[56] In the army of the late republic, then, the clientary soldiers of proconsular patronage were in a sense equivalent to the sons of fathers, infantilized subjects of patriarchal authority for whom booty, and later land settlement, thus invoked something of the son's pre-political dependence upon the patriarch. Caesar's third-person memoir of the civil war shows the sense of personal propriety in both provincial governorship and military command of the legions:

> It was unfair that Pompey should require Caesar to leave Arminium and return to the province, while he himself kept *his own province* and *another man's legions* as well.[57]

Caesar's rationalization reveals how the military identity of the soldiers was now enfolded with proprietorship and patriarchal authority through the investment of command in patronage as the mode of military government. This divorce of the military subject from the political had crucial implications for government and discipline within the legions. Caesar presents as exemplary the text of two speeches by Curio, one of his commanders, which show how government, morale and the security of obedience were not given immediately in command, even in Caesar's rigorously disciplined legions. Curio emphasizes the *sensitivity* the commander must have toward his troops. Any insensitivity is purely instrumental, since the commander must always act as though his troops are honourable and never give his men reason to think that he doubts their trust in him.[58] To neglect to subject them to the most rigorous discipline or to privilege their safety over the chance of victory in battle would make them believe that they were not thought honourable.[59]

This identity of honour in the patron–client relationship, rather than materially articulated economic relations, provided the value-economy of relations of command and obedience in the legion, even during the civil war. It demanded action in 'good faith',[60] a condition that could impel its subjects into a decisive and unwavering enactment of an ethos of conviction, rather than the ethos of responsibility of military 'professionalism'.

Summoning troops recently captured from another commander, Curio formulates 'a new theory of obligation'. Their old commander, in abandoning his men by running away without their knowledge, 'threw away the symbols of office, abandoned command and became a private individual', thus nullifying the oath of obedience they had sworn to him. The distinction between the public person and the private individual is evidently powerful here. The patron–client relation, though not a formal constitutional relationship, pertained to public persons and was thus very different to the contractual relations pertaining between private individuals in civil law. Curio's new theory of obligation simply rationalizes the superimposition of patron–client relations onto the public oath which soldiers swore to their commanders. It does not substitute the terms of private contract for the original constitutional relation between consuls and their legions. Caesar is not contrasted as a private individual to the commander who ran away, but as a commander who will fulfil his function as patron of the legion through his public office. The obligations on both sides are not contained in an abstract concept of office or duty, but in the functions of commander as patron and legion as *clientela*. The commander is held to his official duties not by conscience or a sense of mission, but as a necessary condition of his personal government of his men. No obedience is owed to the commander who does not fulfil his office; not because he is dishonourable by abstract ethical standards, but because he thereby treats his men as personally dishonourable, and thus forfeits the condition of patronage in which command is invested, not by official military order, but by the military subjects themselves.

> We are left with a new theory of obligation, that you should ignore the oath by which you are bound and uphold the one which was cancelled by the surrender and loss of rights of the general ... I indeed chose to call myself a soldier of Caesar's; you have hailed me as imperator. If you have changed your minds, I return your gift. Give me back my own name, in case you should seem to have bestowed the honour upon me by mockery.[61]

This mode of government of command and obedience is also built into Caesar's tactical practice. He argues against battle by night because the light of day subjects the soldier 'to the gaze of everyone'. However, this gaze of disciplinary surveillance does not operate juridical values given in either the 'professional' or constitutional identity of the soldier, but through an internal value-economy which Curio has shown to be carefully constructed in recognition by the commander as a dutiful, morally obligated patron of clients who are valued as honourable. This constructed interiority is a far more necessary condition of obedience than the exterior *restraint* provided by the presence of disciplinary officers in camp and field.[62]

Paul Veyne has shown that the condition of military command was very different from that which we assume to be the essence of military order, 'that passive obedience which may be thought essential where military discipline is concerned'. The commander of the republic had to negotiate the condition of obedience and govern his men as the condition of command. Obedience to command was thus far from automatic. Soldiers argued with their commanders, shouted at them, had to be pleaded with by weeping generals who had neglected, 'to court the favour of the common soldier, and thought that everything that was done to please one's command only dishonoured and undermined one's authority'.[63] In such a relationship, negotiation did not entail any loss of authority, but was its condition. As Curio shows, by the time of the late republic, the *imperium* was still a function of office, but effective command was only vested in the office-holder as a gift from the soldiers, establishing a relation of honour and reciprocal moral obligation between the ranks and the commander, rather than making them his subjects. The substitution of this moral economy for a right of command given in nobility, also had other implications. 'For an authority which was more paternal than governed by regulations, winning respect meant winning love',[64] an axiom that was all the more so in the post-Marian legions, where domestic maintenance of life and body was imposed upon the soldier, and still more so when veteran land settlements equivalent in civil law to grants to a legitimate son became a regular distribution from the commander's Triumph. In Rome, 'obedience was always somewhat like a family relationship', but whereas those bonds had been fraternal in the city's original military order, they became increasingly patriarchal in the later republican legions. These bonds contained the soldier's freedom, which for the secessionary plebs of 494 and 297 BC had been constituted in the liberty of their military order, but was now transposed onto the relationship with the commander. The soldier was then free only in his relation to the commander, not in the military order *per se*. A client veteran of Caesar's rallied his company to battle at the end of the first civil war thus:

> 'Follow me ... and give your general the service you promised. Only this one battle remains; after it, he will recover his position and we our freedom.' Looking at Caesar, 'General,' he said, 'today I shall earn your gratitude, either dead or alive.'[65]

The soldier is thus not in bondage to his commander, but his liberty has become identical with the commander's political position. This is not because the commander owns him (he is still virtually free), nor through any relation of contract (there is no mention of reward, only gratitude), but because he is enmeshed in a net of reciprocal moral and personal obligations, even unto death.

The reconstitution of the republic

Caesar's military autarchy in Gaul did not represent any fundamental break, but simply organized existing practices, identities, relations and economies in the virtual conditions of strategic and hegemonic provincial space. In returning these transformed military relations to Rome, Caesar rationalized the divorce of politics from the order of the constitution. As well as the mass mutation of military subjectification in the provinces of the later republic, patrician military office in the legions had also been transformed. Commanders stood to gain personally not only through opportunities to establish patronage in the army and throughout the provinces, but in material wealth as well. The commander's share of booty and the public Triumph, both offered great material incentives. However, if we were to see investment in generalship as motivated only by material calculation, we would again misunderstand the collapse of the late republic into civil war. Just as the motivation of the soldiery of the legions was more complex and mediated by moral rather than material values, so too was the motive of command.

The reform of commandership after Sulla operated on a very different subject to that of either the right of command or the fraternal Roman constitution of men's public identities, but is also irreducible to either a Stoic ethos of public service or to private, individual self-interest, neither of which secured obedience in the legions of the late republic. Political mastery in the late republic came to consist in the capacity 'to make the machine [of state] work', which required the resources and preparedness to expend private wealth in political office. Similarly, military command had come to depend on the capacity to make the war-machine work regardless of personal expenditure. Military costs and even the provision of men themselves seem to have become an expectation of military command. Defending the republic in Spain, Pompey had pleaded to the Senate for money only when his own resources were exhausted.[66] Anyone who could not raise forces and maintain them of their own initiative could not command. As the legions increasingly became clientary retinues of their patrician patrons, Rome slid into civil war.

At this time, the patrician Cicero articulated the new political conditions in a reformulation of the republic, where the *res publica*, the public space of the city in its political and military order, becomes an *abstraction*, the virtual city. He elevates the welfare or security of the state over and above the representation of the city's order, but the portion of his text where he begins to translate this abstraction into military order is lost. However, in his letters, Cicero regarded the original content of the republic (the outlaws attracted by Romulus), as a mere instrumental necessity, thus reconfiguring the Servian constitution as a means rather than as an end. The essence of Cicero's republic lies in its function as a vehicle for the personal attainment of glory. Cicero is attempting to ground an ethics for political life, and so does not oppose patronage to the constitutional order, but seeks to assimilate its political realities to the Stoic tradition by reflecting on how his advisee might live his ambition ethically in relation to the means available to him.[67] The essence of the republic in the mythic foundational moment is thus transposed on to the self of ambition.

Notes

1. O. Hintze, *Historical Essays,* ed. F. Gilbert (Oxford: Oxford University Press, 1975).
2. L. Keppie, *The Making of the Roman Army from Republic to Empire* (London: Batsford, 1984) p. 15.
3. T. Livy, *The History of Rome, Books I–V, The Early History of Rome,* trans. A. de Sélincourt (Harmondsworth: Penguin, 1971) I.43, p. 81.
4. P. A. Brunt, *Italian Manpower, 225 BC–14 AD* (Oxford: Oxford University Press, 1971), p. 404.
5. Although a formal distinction between the orders of the city in times of war and peace persisted, the doors to the temple of Janus were only to be closed for one year in the next 600. Livy, *History of Rome, I–V,* I.19, p. 54.
6. Ibid., I.30, p. 67.
7. The term *praetor* is sometimes used alternately with *consul,* to denote the military aspect of the office. Despite the increased power of the Senate, republican maintenance of the primarily military constitution of political community is evident in the use of the term *imperium* in both a narrow and a wide sense, as indicated in the military function of the office alongside its civil functions of *coercito* (executive) and *iurisdictio* (jurisdiction), but used also to refer to consular power in general. W. Kunkel, *An Introduction to Roman Legal and Constitutional History,* 2nd edn, trans. J. M. Kelly (Oxford: Clarendon Press, 1973) pp. 15–16, 54.
8. Livy, *History of Rome, I–V,* 2.23–28, pp. 129–35.
9. The social implications of credit continued to create a major dilemma in Roman republican politics into the final years, when Cicero advanced much the same argument against concessions as had been used four hundred years earlier.
10. Livy, *History of Rome, I–V,* 2.32, pp. 142–3.
11. P. A. Brunt, *Social Conflicts in the Roman Republic* (London: Chatto and Windus, 1971), p. 52.
12. M. Weber, *Agrarian Sociology of Ancient Civilizations,* trans. R. I. Frank (London: New Left Books, 1976), pp. 289–90, 296–7.
13. Anderson, *Passages From Antiquity,* p. 68.
14. Weber, *Agrarian Sociology,* p. 300.
15. R. Syme, *Roman Papers Part III,* ed. A. R. Birley (Oxford: Clarendon Press, 1988); N. J. E. Austin, and N. B. Rankov, *Exploratio: Military and Political Intelligence in the Roman World from the Second Punic War to the Battle of Adrianople* (London: Routledge, 1995).
16. Brunt, *Social Conflicts,* p. 3.
17. Livy, *History of Rome, I–V,* 5.34–36, pp. 379–81.
18. Ibid., 5.55, p. 402.
19. A. H. M. Jones, (ed.), *A History of Rome through the Fifth Century, Vol. II: The Empire* (New York, NY: Harper & Row, 1978).
20. Enlistment of the *capite censi* was only a breach in convention, since as citizens they were bound by the principle that each should contribute according to his means. Even when the legions were comprised of self-armed citizens, poor freemen were levied as an unarmed following to take up the weapons of those who had fallen in battle. Brunt, *Italian Manpower,* p. 404.
21. Keppie, *Making of the Roman Army,* pp. 34–5. Unlike the three main groupings of the Servian *classis,* the *velites* were not formed into manipular

tactical units, but took their place in the battle order at the very front, a vanguard of military–political society which ventured ahead of the masses into the space of chaos, the no-man's land between the lines of military order.

22. T. Livy, *The History of Rome, Books XXI–XXX: The War with Hannibal,* trans. A. de Sélincourt (Harmondsworth: Penguin, 1965), 26.1–2, p. 366.

23. The old annual consular commanders returning from the provinces on the expiry of their terms brought with them the time-served men, who were replaced by new recruits from the year's *dilectus*, who in turn marched out with the new consuls to reconstitute campaigning legions, which over-wintered in the field. However, when legions had to be maintained as permanent strategic garrisons, consular commands were extended beyond their year's elected office, as *proconsul* or *propraetor*, effectively sanctioning a *virtual time* for the military republic in the strategic provinces. Keppie, *Making of the Roman Army*, pp. 55–6.

24. Ibid., p. 31.

25. Ibid., p 40. Interpreting this as the 'professionalization' of the Roman army imposes a modern normative civil/military distinction upon a Roman order in which these functions were constitutionally united, as in the office of consul. A differentiation of functions and jurisdictions does not necessarily require the institutional division which modern functional rationality imposes. Similarly, Roman public office was not divorced from the person holding the office, and the issue of commissions was understood in the Roman context as personal acts of the consul for which he could be held personally accountable and open to prosecution on the expiry of his office.

26. Ibid., pp. 36–8.

27. Polybius 6.31.10, quoted in N. P. Milner, 'Introduction', in R. F. Vegetius, *De Re Militari (Epitome of Military Science)* (Liverpool: Liverpool University Press, 1993), p. 22, n.2.

28. Kunkel, *Introduction to Roman Legal and Constitutional History*, pp. 15–16 and 54.

29. M. Weber, ed. *Economy and Society: An Outline of Interpretive Sociology* G. Roth and C. Wittich (Berkeley, CA: University of California Press, 1978), p. 1356.

30. Furthermore, this reductive conception of the ancient republic provides support for the modern (liberal) presumption that its universal concept of civil identity and liberty is quite distinct from the constitution of violence, and that the separation of the two is underpinned by a process of economic rationalization inherent in the conception of civil subjects as pacific economic agents.

31. Ibid., p. 946.

32. Brunt, *Social Conflict*, p. 63.

33. Brunt, *Italian Manpower*, p. 392.

34. Land accruing to the state through conquest would be sold to increase the treasury or added to the *ager publicus*, which the slave-owning agriculturalists who were increasingly represented in the Senate could occupy more competitively than the plebeians.

35. In the face of the unpopularity of legion service, the explanation that economic necessity propelled the urban *proletarii* to vote and volunteer in a tacit contract with Scipio simply does not hold, since they were supported by the great houses of their patrons and had hitherto preferred the poverty of social clientage to the prospect of economic insecurity as subsistence smallholders or legion service. Brunt, *Social Conflicts*, p. 123; *Italian Manpower*, p. 410.

36. Livy, *History of Rome, I–V*, 2.32, p. 141.
37. A. Barry, T. Osborne and N. Rose (eds), *Foucault and Political Reason* (London: UCL Press, 1996).
38. P. Veyne, *Bread and Circuses: Historical Sociology and Political Pluralism*, trans. B. Pearce (London: Allen Lane, 1990).
39. Weber, *Economy and Society*, p. 839. However, Weber assimilates Roman patron–client relations to a *feudal* type of domination by positing an anthropological origin in the immediate domination of economic producers by individual warriors who exercised a jurisdiction over life which they collectivized by aggregating in a fortified enclosure, constituting the city and the law, in which they monopolized jurisdiction as a class translating physical protection into the legal representation of clients (Weber, *Agrarian Sociology*, pp. 272–88). Even the origin of the republic is attributable to the quasi-feudal *original nature* of Roman patronage (Weber, *Economy and Society*, pp. 1356, 1285–7), the plebeian tribunes appear as merely 'a surrogate for patronal protection' (Weber, *Agrarian Sociology*, p. 283).
40. Veyne, *Bread and Circuses*, pp. 69–70.
41. Ibid., pp. 207–16.
42. Keppie, *Making of the Roman Army*, pp. 28–40.
43. Veyne, *Bread and Circuses*, p. 217. We could understand this more fully by asking, in what kind of love a commander could decimate his legion? This is conventionally reduced to a utilitarian function which requires that 'he who loves also chastises', but in terms of the rigour of Roman military law, decimation appears as an amelioration, a voluntary symbolic gift of the commander's personal mediation of his office, to spare nine-tenths. It can also only be explained within this order of symbolic economy, since without the maintenance of military order, the legion could not be sure of its commander's patronage, while in order to kill every tenth one, the commander would have to have secured their unlimited obedience in clientage.
44. Anderson, *Passages from Antiquity*, p. 68.
45. Veyne, *Bread and Circuses*, p. 261.
46. Keppie, *Making of the Roman Army*, p. 61; Brunt, *Italian Manpower*, p. 400.
47. Keppie, *Making of the Roman Army*, p. 66.
48. Patrician perceptions further attest to the degradation of the soldier. Cicero referred to the soldiers of the legions as 'beasts' (Veyne, *Bread and Circuses*), and associated the *egentes* (the needy homeless who now volunteered for the legions) with the *perditi*, the criminal, establishing an association which has characterized perceptions of common soldiers throughout European history.
49. Keppie, *Making of the Roman Army*, pp. 63–4.
50. Brunt, *Italian Manpower*, p. 392.
51. Brunt, *Social Conflict*, p. 3.
52. Powerful patricians also began to subsidize the state in order to gain the advantage in preferment. For instance, when the Macedonian king, Mithridates, seized the province of Greece, Sulla and Marius both put forces under arms as rivals for command of a campaign against him.
53. J. Caesar, *The Civil War*, trans. J. F. Gardner (London: Penguin, 1967), p. 78.
54. Weber, *Agrarian Sociology*, p. 275.
55. P. Stein, *Roman Law in European History* (Cambridge: Cambridge University Press, 1999), pp. 5–6.
56. Weber, *Economy and Society*, p. 839.
57. Caesar, *Civil War*, p. 41 (emphasis added).

58. Ibid., p. 96.
59. Veyne follows Weber in placing the value of the concept of honour at the heart of the investments comprising the patron–client relation. The subject of this 'special law' remained outside the development of *ius civile*, Roman civil law, and the grounding of patron–client relations in the mutual recognition of *fides* (honour) was not equivalent to the grounding of civil contractual relations in the rights of citizens as private individuals. The services owed by each party in the patron–client relation were not always the same, but, 'What one owed to another according to *fides* depended on the peculiar nature of the concrete relationship'. The sanctions of the patron–client relation rendered the tie personally and politically binding upon both parties, but did not translate into economic power for the patron (Weber, *Economy and Society*, pp. 703, 1355).
60. Weber, *Economy and Society*, p. 703.
61. Caesar, *Civil War*, p. 98.
62. Ibid., p. 69.
63. Plutarch, *Life of Lucullus*, quoted in Veyne, *Bread and Circuses*, p. 217.
64. Ibid., p. 267.
65. Caesar, *Civil War*, p. 152.
66. Veyne, *Bread and Circuses*, pp. 246–7.
67. Marcus Tullius Cicero, *De Re Publica* trans. C. W. Keyes (London: Heinemann, 1928), p. 281.

3

The Imperial Order

Although the transformation of the Roman political regime from republic to principate appears to refer us to sovereign power, Roman imperial power cannot be explained away by reference to command of resources or to categories of legitimation. Rather, the basis of subsequent imperial rule was formed by the constitutional and administrative assemblage of the regime of Caesar Augustus, requiring us to trace the diverse deployments of heterogenous political technologies through which the new order was constructed.

Imperium personified

Senatorial control of the Treasury had traditionally enabled the class as a whole to pull its members back into line, since the consulate, in which the *imperium* was vested, was ultimately dependent upon the Treasury to supply the army it commanded. However, for the proconsulate to which successful political actors ascended at the very height of their influence, 'the provinces were a reservoir of money and resources, an arena for the conquest of glory', enabling men to act independently of senatorial control.[1] It was not considered corrupt to exploit office for personal benefit, an integral aspect of the Roman political system that Cicero elevated to the essence of the republic itself. Magnates simply funded themselves to be patrons of their own careers. Hence, patricians such as Pompey and Caesar raised forces to defend the republic, the vehicle for their self-aggrandizement, regardless of whether they actually held the appropriate office, while *in* office they regarded themselves as free to exploit the *imperium* for their personal credit.[2]

Caesar and Pompey set the practice for those who followed them, building temples for the public, not palaces for themselves, from their own fortunes. Veyne shows that the distinction between public and private funds was scrupulously maintained; the 'principal citizens' (*princeps*) did not dip into the public purse to fund buildings in their own honour, but produced their honour by providing public buildings at personal cost. Caesar Augustus secured his singular principate in part by reserving the privilege of such euergetism in Rome to himself alone.[3] Monopolization of privilege by the *princeps* seems to have proceeded initially through the translation back into Rome of extraordinary military-provincial *jurisdictional* capacity to exercise clemency, a right denied to ordinary magistrates. In provincial office, Caesar and Pompey had exercised the *imperium* as an absolute right over life and death in the military order, where clemency was granted as a symbolic gift of the patron-commander. Caesar's 'right of coming home' brought with it the discretionary, extra-juridical practices of provincial military government, and the right to exercise clemency was grafted on to the joint triumviral office instituted after the dictator's death.

Julius Caesar's adopted son, Octavian, inherited his clientage and political practice. After the disorder that followed his father's assassination, Octavian appeared to contemporaries as the saviour of the state. Popular by virtue of his patronage, powerful by virtue of the absence of any single rival, he succeeded in restoring constitutionality by further rationalizing the *de facto* power that had arisen in the provinces and the legions, at the level of the constitution itself, renaming himself Caesar Augustus, as singular 'principal citizen'. The nexus of command and obedience, patronage and clientage, personal obligations and public liberties provided the imperial constitution of Caesar Augustus' principate, constituting a new political subjectivity and transforming the social condition of knowledge. Before this regime, military technique was uncodified, and has to be reconstructed from the personal memoirs of military patrons, the histories of authors such as Livy, and archaeological remains.[4] The identity of political liberty and the military order of the republic suggests that republican Rome possessed no specifically military science because military expertise was common knowledge, vested in the public sphere, in the regular exercises in which citizens had to participate. In the first century AD, however, a text by Frontinus claims to have founded just such a science. It is only here that we find the complete instrumentalization of organized violence in the concept of military technique as distinct from politics.

The conditions of this epistemic shift can be traced in the institutionalization of the transformations traced above in Augustus' imperial regime. Augustus' personal testament, the *Res Gestae*, inscribed on two bronze columns in Rome and other public places throughout Italy, does not provide any (re)new(al) myths. Its claim to provide the foundations of the state is a personal one, in the tradition of the Ciceronian subject of posterity. Augustus' personal honour is recorded as consisting not only of his euergetism but also of the legality of his *imperium*, and is reflected in a listing of the offices he held in person and his deference to constitutionality as demonstrated by his refusal of, 'any office inconsistent with the custom of our ancestors'.[5] This plurality of offices, however, effected a singular authority through the medium of monopoly patronage. To contemporaries, Augustus as first citizen restored the republic; only to later writers did the new regime appear to have established monarchical power.

Initially, he held dictatorial authority with two others, as a *triumvirate*; by the end of the civil wars, he held it alone, and the honourability of his subsequent abdication of this office was recognized in his official acclamation as 'Augustus *princeps*'. He then held consular office from 31–23 BC, with *imperium* in Rome and Italy and over all provinces deemed strategically insecure, governorships which he was to retain as *proconsul* if he should vacate the consulate. The precedents were military and provincial: Marius had served as consul continuously from 104–100 BC, and Pompey had governed Spain through *legates* while consul in Rome. In 23 AD, Augustus resigned his consulship and received instead the tribunician power as 'annual and perpetual', with 'the right to count the years for which he held office', establishing the constitutional form in which the *imperium* was held by the *principes* until the death of Nero.[6] Tribunician power consisted in the right to present bills to the plebiscitary assemblies, to veto decrees of the Senate or consulate, to coerce compliance, and to intervene and investigate the oppression of citizens by other magistrates, enabling the *princeps* to act as the patron of the Roman plebs.[7] Augustus and his successors, however, also retained the office of provincial governorship as a 'greater' proconsulate (*imperium proconsulare*), by which they could exercise provincial *imperium* and overrule other provincial proconsuls while residing within the city of Rome itself.[8]

Engineering the new order: The construction of 'charisma'

Weber's typologization of the imperial power as a 'patrimonial monarchy' assumes that the emperor owned the state as a personal resource, but Veyne's analysis of the euergetic programme of public building by the principate shows, against nineteenth-century interpretations, that the *Res Gestae* can be taken at face value to show that Augustus did not consider himself to own the state, as a patrimonial ruler, but rather sought to achieve honour for himself as its patron. The *princeps'* private funds were accounted separately from the state coffers.[9] This reflects upon the political sociology of the power of the *princeps*, which was not simply given as sovereign authority, but was carefully constructed through the exercise of personal patronage in constitutional offices. Thus the personal quality of the *princeps'* rule, which we might call charisma, was not at all mysterious or ideological, as in Weber's formulation,[10] but was rather constructed by specific political technologies which did not require patronage of the whole empire, but only of those in close proximity (including the plebs of Rome) and those in military commands.[11]

In *Economy and Society*, Weber lists the typical forms of legitimation as charismatic, traditional and legal-rational. Drawn from Christian soteriology, the concept of charisma is anachronistic in the case of republican and even early imperial Rome, where a deifying emperor-cult did not develop in the army until the third century. The authority of Augustus and the Julio-Claudian dynasty was also certainly not grounded in tradition, and their claim to juridical constitutionality merely provided channels for the exercise of patronage. Through senatorial nominations, Augustus secured for his clients the administration of the roads of Italy and of the water supply, grain provision and fire precautions of Rome itself.[12] Once a political order of public persons, the city now became reconstituted in terms of physical spaces and flows, as the administrative province of an engineering regime which had as its model the camp of the legions, where order was manifest in the architectonic of the survey, the imperatives of rule were given in logistical supply, and authority derived from personal patronage. Augustus also appropriated for himself the right of Triumph, an occasion for donations to the legions.[13]

Augustus' military reforms simply rationalized and institutionalized developments which had occurred in the course of the civil wars. He had already followed Scipio's example by settling his client–veterans on land allotments within Italian cities, displacing citizens to accommodate them. Like Scipio's, Augustus' military patronage extended beyond the term of service, providing personal client colonies within the peninsula itself. Many men now had no other home but the army, and the extension of the term of service from six to 16 and then to 20 years was politically mediated by the *princeps'* personal underwriting of their wages, thus securing the conditions for life careers in the army ranks.[14] The donation on retirement which had once been paid by the patron was now replaced by a cash gratuity from a special state treasury funded by revenue from taxes on inheritances and auctions, but under control of the *princeps* rather than the Senate, thus substituting the commander's patronage by state provision under the *princeps*, who guaranteed its provision by personally underwriting the funds. Donations avoided the fiscal complexities involved in a regular pay increase, and served to maintain the personal relation between *princeps* and soldiers. In Tacitus' view, the provision of pay and benefits to the army was an essential function of the principal powers in execution of the state's statutory obligation to the legions, but this function was underwritten by their *personal* resources and fortune.[15] The *princeps* was both paymaster and patron, and only this combination ensured that the legions were maintained in physical and moral order, in body and in obedience. The soldiers' allegiance could not be bought by money but required a moral bond, in which the donation and the personal guarantee of their wages held symbolic rather than material value.

Senior patronage was managed closely and military commissions under the *imperium proconsulare* were kept short even as legion service was extended, and came to be linked to a progressive career structure in public administration, accessible only through the *princeps'* patronage.[16] As political levers against senatorial oligarchy, Augustus thus monopolized the army and the city of Rome itself. Using the appointment of his clients to administrative posts, he secured the military and urban administration which enabled him to extend largesse to the legions and the urban citizens. Veyne argues that Augustus' monopoly of Rome's urban administration closed the city as a theatre of politics to the oligarchy; we could add that the theatre of the army and its operations which had been opened in the civil war were similarly closed by reservation to the *princeps*. By virtue of the same closure, however, the city 'ceased to be an autonomous commune',[17] and the army and provinces also ceased to have a political identity autonomous of the imperial office. The army was now identical not with the republic, but with the office of *imperium* in its monopoly of military patronage.

Principial tribunician power in the city was more than juridical, and similarly the *imperium proconsulare* meant more than the formal right of command. The two powers or offices bound the plebs and the army to the *princeps*, but also bound the *princeps* to them. By making a legacy to the people in his will (the *congiarium* to the plebs and the *donatium* to the soldiers), the *princeps* affirmed his personal protection of them and provided a vehicle for succession, since in ensuring this legacy, the successor inherited patronage. *Donatii* and *congiarii* imbued office with the moral charge necessary to establish patronage, and simultaneously sealed the person of the *princeps* to the offices of the *imperium*, fusing person with office.

The moral economy of the army under the principate

The *princeps* managed their personal relations with the army through rhetoric as well as largesse. Campbell has traced the use of the term *commilitones* (which he translates as 'fellow-soldier') in the addresses of the *princeps* and emperors to the legions.[18] The term had been used in preference to the more objective *milites* since the time of Caesar by patron-commanders in their addresses to their legions, but Augustus reserved it for private conversation, affirming that he was the patron of soldiers not by virtue of his public offices, but in a personal capacity – a distinction continued by his successors to identify themselves as the personal patrons of the legions. Tiberius publicly referred to himself as their *imperator*, but when the legions mutinied he appealed to them personally as their representative, and sent his son Gaius (Nero) to be brought up in the camps. The peculiarly familial aspect of military patronage was clearly expressed by Nero (37–41 AD), whose self-stylization as 'son of the camp' and 'father of armies' indicates the persistent extra-legal dimension of military patronage, beyond both civil law and the public codes of relations between equals. The term *commilito* came into use once more during the civil wars after Nero's suicide, but thereafter its use seems to have been restricted to the emotional aspect of the commander-legion/patron–client relation, occurring only in the soldiers' oaths and in letters of appeal from emperor to legions. The quality of the relation it signified became merely rhetorical, suggesting that it was no longer negotiated and maintained, but inherent in the honour of the *princeps*. Pliny's *Panegyric* to Trajan asks, 'how many are there to whom you have not been a *commilito* before a commander?', indicating the institutionalization of this relationship and showing that *commilito* in its later affective sense signified an abstract, given relation between *imperium* and the army, which became less personal and increasingly reified as a structural relationship independent of persons.

The issue of booty again illustrates relations of subordination in the army. Under the principle of *patria potestas* in Roman law, sons were subject to the legal authority of their father and could neither own property nor make contractual agreements in their own right while their father was alive. Augustus introduced a privilege for serving soldiers by excepting property acquired in military service from this principle.[19] However, rather than liberating the soldier from paternal authority, this privilege substituted the *imperium* of military command for the authority of the father, since the acquisition and retention of booty was dependent upon the commanders' discretion of 'load discipline' – the inspection and enforced jettison of baggage to maximize mobility.[20] The *princeps* as patron now protected the soldiers' booty against the law while reserving jurisdiction over its disposal to his office of command.

Rhetoric and military administration both show how the personal relationship of military patronage became institutionalized and reified under the principate, ultimately transforming both the *princeps* and the army into transcendent objects, the one to be worshipped, the other given in its order. However, this metamorphosis of military patronage into a new right of command was not so much an evolution as a genealogical transformation of political technologies and the conditions of obedience. Even as the *principes* consolidated their regime of military patronage, it ceased to operate as a mode of government and became displaced in a new military order dependent upon immediately exercised discipline and regulation under bureaucratically delegated authority.

This transformation can be traced in the soldiers' oath and in the *adlucutio*, the *princeps'* formal address to the legion. Under the republic, the citizen-soldiers had made an oath to each new consulate to assemble on its orders, not to leave military service without its authority or desert their posts in battle, and to obey its orders to the best of their ability.[21] Under the principate, this oath named not the commander of the legion, but the *princeps*, who was also the guarantor of the soldier's pay (in office) and benefits (as patron), thus enfolding in the oath a given, rather than achieved, identity of patron, office and person. The *adlucutio* was a formal address by the *princeps* or his adopted heir from a platform to the camp tribunal, where the soldiers assembled in military order. Augustus regularized this institution, which came to be used by the *princeps* politically as patrons to privilege their troops by explaining the current political situation to them.[22] This formalized platform for the affirmation of patronage secured its political dimensions and was particularly useful in crises of constitutional legitimation. It made use of the tribunician power which Augustus had appropriated to the *princeps* through the traditional, constitutional identity between the tribal assembly and the military order of the legion, but now provided a means whereby the identity of a permanent army with the *princeps* could be secured over and above the constitution. In the *adlucutio*, we see how the security of obedience, or the government of military subjects, came increasingly to depend upon administrative routine and structured space. Similarly, the exercises of discipline by which the collective body of the republic had maintained itself in military order became less a purely technical function *exercised by* military subjects in their order of liberty, and became increasingly a means whereby the legions could be *subjected to* an authority which no longer referred itself to the republic but to the security of the *imperium*. In the imperial monopolization of patronage, the soldier came increasingly to be identified by particular privileges which were dependent upon the *princeps* in office, and the army became less the legions of Rome in their liberty and increasingly the legions of the *princeps* in his *imperium*.

The order of the self and the organization of violence

In *The Care of the Self*, Michel Foucault charts the transformations of the Roman 'political game' from the beginnings of the crisis of the republic through to the second century AD, which marked the same period in which patronage first became the route to a public career, and then a career in itself under the *princeps'* monopoly of strategic public offices. Against conventional interpretations which see the patriciate withdrawing from politics as civic life declined and the imperial state monopolized military power, he argues that we can see a problematization of political life, rather than its cessation, leading to the emergence of a new moral relationship between the self and public office and status, an ethic which displaced the laws, institutions and customs of the republic as the determinant of political action.

For the first two centuries, Roman imperialism did not seek to substitute central administration for civic authority, but preferred to operate through municipal agents. Thus, the regime of the *princeps* pursued extensive power by a similar mode of policy to that practised earlier by the republic, seeking allies in hegemony rather than subjects in bureaucratic domination, while representing Roman/imperial dominion as the city writ large, in which all subjects shared advantages and authority as though they lived in a single city.

> Rather than imagining a reduction or cessation of political activities through the effects of a centralized imperialism, one should think in terms of the organization of a much more complex space. Much vaster, much more discontinuous, much less closed than must have been the case for the small city-states, it was also more flexible, more differentiated, less rigidly hierarchized than would be the authoritarian and bureaucratic Empire that people would attempt to organize after the great crisis of the third century.[23]

The conventional thesis about the emergence of Stoicism as the private creed of elite political abdication and withdrawal into the self is problematized by Foucault, who argues that the rise of Stoicism is much more complex.[24] He relates changing techniques of self-government (from the traditional patrician ethic of self-mastery to the

Stoic ethic of self-monitoring) to the structural transformation of a class (from noble patriciate to service aristocracy), and to the shifting conditions of power (from the patrician's alternation between command and obedience to a simultaneous subjection and domination). This establishes a correlation, at the level of conditions of emergence, between a mode of ethical practice emerging in the early empire which still provides us with terms by which to mediate the separation of the self from social functions, the appearance of a class which both commands and obeys, and the state as strategic engineer of a moral order through policy and administration.

> ... the most important and determining phenomenon for the new emphases of moral reflection did not relate to the disappearance of the traditionally dominant classes, but to the changes that could be observed in the condition of the exercise of power. These changes concerned recruitment first of all, since it was a matter of addressing the needs of an administration that was both complex and extensive.[25]

The numbers of those whose status could lead to a political career increased in the first centuries AD, but such public careers were now constituted by new social relationships, no longer those of the Ciceronian republic, the ultimate end of which lay in their production of public virtue, but in offices granted by revocable principial patronage, producing a 'managerial aristocracy'.

> Changes also affected the role they were led to play and the position they occupied in the political game: with respect to the emperor, to his entourage, to his councilors, to his direct representatives; within the hierarchy, where competition played a major part but in a different fashion from that found in agonistic societies; in the form of revocable offices which depended, often quite directly, on the pleasure of the prince; and nearly always in an intermediary position between a higher power whose orders must be conveyed or carried out, and individuals or groups whose obedience must be obtained.[26]

At the same time, since public careers were dependent on monopolized patronage, the identity between self and status was broken, so that entry into political life became a matter of personal choice and not axiomatic with status. The relation of self to public office now displaced the laws, institutions and customs of the republic as the *moralized* determinant of political action. Exploitation of the opportunity of the status of one's birth, which for Cicero had been unquestionable, was no longer given in the end of virtue for which the republic provided a singular vehicle, but in a carefully nurtured and monitored inner ethic that ultimately denounced the pursuit of public recognition even in the exemplary performance of the functions of office which it demanded. This meant that the government of men had to proceed very differently, according to a different rationality to that which the older, plural and competitive mode of government through patronage had tapped into by establishing relations of mutual obligation in the recognition of honour. Government now had to appeal not to a subject of 'special law', but to a subject of *internally* mediated moral rationality.

> Such a modelling of political work – whether it concerned the emperor or a man who exercised an ordinary responsibility – shows clearly how these forms became detached from status and appeared as a function to fill; but ... that function was not defined in terms of laws belonging to an art of governing others, as if it were a question of a 'profession' with its own particular skills and techniques. It ... depended on the relationship he established with himself in the ethical work of the self on the self.[27]

The dissociation of the old identity of self-mastery with the exercise of authority meant, in Livy's terms, the dissociation of liberty (consisting in self-masterful voluntary subjection to the disciplinary forms of one's classical contribution to the republic) from power. 'Self-mastery had implied a close connection between the superiority one exercised over oneself, the authority one exercised in the context of the household, and the power one exercised in the field of agonistic society.'[28]

Similarly, techniques hitherto related to an art of governing others in their liberty increasingly became a functional performance quite distinct from the self, an ordering of objects by an objectified functionary, removed from ethical considerations. From the time of the *princeps*, the art of military command could thus be learnt independently of mastery of the self, so that gradually the technical function of military command came to displace almost entirely the concept of command as necessarily the ethical government of men as articulated in Julius Caesar's autobiographical historiography and Livy's retrospective account of the military–political virtuosities of the early republic. In the bureaucratic construction of late empire, this displacement finally reached the point where men became bodies to be fitted into forms of discipline that produced their own order quite irrespective of the content. Obedience then ceased to appear as a problem for military thought.

A systematic Roman 'military science' only appears with the empire. Until then, military order and operations appear as *political* activity in the field beyond the walls of the city, an aspect of the art of politics in which all men aspiring to a political career were expected to have expertise, drawing knowledge for the government of citizen-soldiers from the city's institutes, laws and customs, and for relations with other communities and peoples from the history of the city. History thus provided the criteria for public recognition of military command, but there was no independent *military* discourse of the republic.

The appearance of such a discourse with empire may be explained functionally in Augustus' formal integration of military and senatorial careers through the identification of personal principial patronage with the imperial administration, absorbing provincial administration and military appointment as well as those offices relating to the administration of the city itself. Augustus effectively institutionalized the structural linkage of military and political career-patronage for *equites* and nobles that had emerged in the provinces and the distantly-stationed legions. With this rationalization, individual appointees to military office as a first step in an imperial career required an abstract source of knowledge of military technique and function quite distinct from the self-aggrandizement of late-republican political memoirs. The work of Sextus Julius Frontinus marks the precise point at which an empirical and operational body of knowledge related to independent political careers translates into a discourse, an art of war or military science independent of the careers of political personages.

Frontinus' own career followed the structure of imperial patronage institutionalized by Augustus. He was preferred for election as a consul in 73–4 AD and then assumed the provincial governorship of Britain, where he undertook a military engineering campaign against the Silures of Wales, constructing the Via Julia to give the legions ready access to their lands. After returning to Rome in 78 AD, he spent the next 20 years of his life writing his 'Art of War' (which has not survived), the *Stratagemata*, and works on surveying and land law which served as standard sources for Roman state employees for many years.[29] In 97 AD, Frontinus continued his public career with his appointment as water commissioner of the city of Rome, a commission which Augustus had secured for the *princeps'* patronage by creating an administrative government of Rome independent of the Senate. During his tenure in office, Frontinus wrote his *De Aquis*, an account of both the technical aspect of the Roman water supply and of the reform of its administration as an exemplary exercise in depersonalized public service and economy.

Under the republic, public office had provided an opportunity to build up patronage and secure clients to oneself. However, in holding the *imperium* of army and the provinces and controlling appointments in the administration of the city's utilities and supply, the principate monopolized this personal function of public-service opportunities. The water commission offered the author–administrator of *De Aquis* little personal opportunity beyond performance of the technical functions of the office. As an exposition of the administrative mentality, *De Aquis* shows a Stoic approach to public service as primarily a duty rather than a personal opportunity, effecting the transposition of the concept of honour from person to office. The imperial constitution of the rationality and the subject of public service also enabled Frontinus to objectify recorded military experience as the source for a science. Hitherto, there had been no object for military discourse in the abstract, since service in military command was performed by particular persons in particular situations. Now, however, that service had become a transitory individual occupancy of office, identified with the performance of particular public functions, rather than with the personal office-holder. Effective functional performance had always been necessary, even to build up patronage in office, but standardization of performance would have negated the very import of public office under the republic, which was to win the virtue of public recognition and to construct patronage. Only with the Augustan monopolization of administrative and military patronage and a career structure for clients in the imperial administration, did it become valid to provide standardized administrative manuals. The scope of such a mode of discourse extended far beyond merely functional aspects of official performance, since it had both to construct its subject of imperial patronage in public office and provide the means whereby subjectification could be accomplished.[30] The technical, administrative manuals of Rome, whether civil or military, are thus also manuals for government of the self and others.

The works of historians such as Livy and Polybius and of veteran commanders and patrons such as Julius Caesar, offered an archive of military empirical knowledge that was at once particular and recurrent. Military thought in the Western tradition has always emphasized the need to treat each scenario as a particularity; but at the same time, it also aspires to transcend the tendency to remain a mere compendium of historical events. This problem of military discourse is inherent from the very beginning of the science, as Frontinus constructed both his 'Art of War' and the *Strategemata* by abstracting categories of military situations from the archive of historiography and personal testaments which thereafter served as sources of exemplary illustrations.

A military science

Frontinus explicitly claims that his 'Art of War' originates an *abstract* discourse of military science: 'I alone of those interested in military science (*militaris scientiam*) have undertaken to reduce its rules to a system.'[31] The 'Art of War' is lost to modernity, but reductive abstraction alone perhaps presented too radical a discontinuity with previous modes of military knowledge, and to complement the earlier work he sought to provide in the *Strategemata* 'specimens of wisdom and foresight' readily abstracted from 'the body of history' for busy, practical men. In this origination of Roman military discourse, the past is used both as an empirical archive of abstracted experience and as a repertoire of possible deployments of force. Rather than reproducing masses of particular instances, the task of the *Strategemata* is to provide ready examples of the classifications of military operations and their categories already developed in the earlier work;

> ... setting forth, as if in response to questions, and as occasion shall demand, the illustration applicable to the case in point. For having examined the categories, I have in advance mapped out my campaign, so to speak, for the presentation of illustrative examples.[32]

Readers would be able to supply other examples themselves, and the author restricts himself to only a few for each category in order that the system of classification remains clear and is not overwhelmed with the mass of possible examples which could be compiled under its headings. The *Strategemata* is a manual for practice, not an exercise in historical classification.

Frontinus distinguishes 'strategy' from 'stratagems', which include tactics to evade as well as to defeat or annihilate the enemy. Through the classified examples, he shows *how* strategies may be achieved, how to 'determine the character of the war' by tactical deployments, by military government and by the programmatic schema of Roman hegemonic policy. The *Strategemata* thus illustrates techniques which instrumentalize a field of subjects and objects of war, producing the means for an imperial military strategy out of a mass of particular and personal accounts ordered by a system of classification.

The means available include speeches as well as deeds, reminding us that for the Romans, rhetoric was an effective force in itself, with the capacity to move properly constituted bodies like those of Cicero's republic through its operations upon them as subjects of moral order. In the *Strategemata*, however, rhetoric is a resource for military deployment, not a value in itself. Though utilizing the moral appeals of rhetoric, the discourse of the *Strategemata* is purely instrumental, upon which moral considerations do not impinge. Tactical objectives may be instrumental for strategic designs which have hegemony rather than annihilation as their object, but the outcomes do not figure as ends and no moral considerations impinge upon the operation of stratagems. (Frontinus recommends, for instance, using prisoners as a human shield to enable an army to pass through hostile territory.) Nevertheless, this does not mean that commanders are free to pursue a purely functional rationality. As we shall see, the order of the army itself introduces moral considerations into Frontinus' military science.

The resources and means which Frontinus deploys can be listed: knowledge, utilized as secrecy (and its obverse, intelligence); appearance, utilized in dissimulation; cognition, utilized by distraction; terrain, utilized by modification; and reason, utilized to effect an economy of force. All these elements are relativized in Frontinus' discourse. For instance, the manipulation of appearances to produce effects, to cause movement, blurs or diffuses the distinction between appearance and reality. What can be made to appear real is real in effect, by virtue of the force produced, so this military science already constitutes a virtual reality. The entire policy of hegemony, and its accomplishment in the construction of clientage, depended precisely upon recognition of this force *in the abstract*.

The most important part of Frontinus' text is where he deals with the effect of the rationality of the art of war that he has constructed upon the military subject. We can read this in the examples comprising the fourth book, where he provides illustrations 'rather of military science in general than of stratagems'.[33] The first three books concern what can be done with an army, divided into the classification of things which provide the means by which strategy can be realized – stratagems for the guidance of command before battle (Book I), in battle and after (Book II), and when besieging and besieged (Book III). The fourth book alone concerns the constitution of an army, its *disposition* rather than its deployment. Furthermore, this book is distinct from the others because the categories by which Frontinus organizes historical examples here do not fit into the system of classification applied to organize the means of strategy.

The army as a moral order

In contrast to the republican government of the army reconstructed from the memoirs and histories on which Frontinus draws for his anecdotal illustrations, his organizing principle shifts the focus from practice of patronage (now monopolized in the military by the *princeps*) to techniques which operate directly upon and through the body of the soldier to constitute the body of the army. The army in this discourse is thus a *corporate*, rather than a collective body, comprised of bodies which are given only as inert material, but are produced as instrumental agents in the army's moral order.

Again in contrast to the military expertise practised and recorded by commanders such as Julius Caesar, a disciplined army is a preferred instrument for a commander to an army constituted by personal patronage. We can understand this shift as effected by the Augustan regime's displacement of the commander, who can no longer build his own clientage in the legions since military patronage has been monopolized by the *princeps*. However, this displacement opens new options for command. Rather than the scope for command being narrowed, constrained by subordination to the emperor, as a sovereign model of military power would suppose, Frontinus' text reveals the way in which military science has become refined, its instrumentality sharpened and focused rather than constrained by the displacement of ends through the impersonalization of command. His technical discourse enables us to see how in this new military constitution, functional effectiveness is increased without any intervention by a 'grand strategist'.

The first illustration establishes the productive effect of military isolation from domestic order and military preoccupation in Publius Scipio's reformation of a demoralized, fragmented army by dismissing camp-followers and instituting daily routine. All bodies and equipment surplus to the needs of the campaign are to be expelled from the camp, and the significance of these measures 'against indolence and timidity' spelt out to the soldiers, so that the effect is seen to proceed directly from the will of the commander. Frontinus thereby introduces the *modus operandi* of Book IV; that the government of the army according to abstract, functional principles, rather than particular relations, can *produce* order and force. The intention or will of discipline is to operate upon and through the raw elements of individual bodies, selected for their size, to produce bold soldiers knitted together into the collective body of the legion, a corporate body which bears its own honour and shame, the values of the economy upon which the government of men may operate. Other measures available include dietary regulation, the formal and obligatory oath of *ius iurandum* (which replaced the voluntary oath of *sacramentum* that soldiers had pledged *to each other* before the Carthaginian Wars), the burden instituted by Marius, and the spatial order of the camp.

The body is to be kept occupied, even if the product of its labour has no utility in the plans of the commander, since such preoccupation operates not through the object produced, but effects moral order through exercising the body of the labouring soldier, 'in order that ... troops might not become demoralized by idleness or inflict harm on their allies in consequence of licence resulting from leisure'.[34] However, this economy can also be negatively applied. The body itself may be reduced, to the same end, by amputating the hands of soldier-thieves or bleeding them, by the sale of deserters into slavery or by their summary execution as enemies on the battle field, and even by the infamous practice of decimation. Such punishments, however, no longer presented even a perverse gift of recognition to restore honour and relations of patronage between the commander and his men.

Desertion presented a will opposed to the functional rationality of command, usurping the prerogatives of movement and reduction of the body of the army, eliciting absolute punishment. Similarly, unordered (and hence, by definition, disorderly) plunder also usurped an instrumental function, and was to be dealt with uncompromisingly, by mass executions of perpetrators. Frontinus' military code of discipline thus constrains or places beyond limits acts that partake of the instrumental function of force itself – autonomous movement and expropriation. By contrast, a refusal to serve under orders or provide the body as an instrument, was in itself a lesser order of offence, its severity contingent upon circumstances rather than absolute, warranting only reduced rations, menial labour, or some form of military banishment, sanctions designed to produce a positive effect, since soldiers banished from the camp or those banished to Sicily during the Punic Wars, could redeem themselves, regain interiority and reincorporate their bodies into the space and time of the camp or the Latin peninsula through feats in the field into which they had been banished. Their banishment was positive, in contrast to the disincorporation of the four thousand soldiers executed for looting the federated town of Rhegium, whom it was forbidden to bury or mourn. Usurpation of the instrumentality of the army was uniquely irredeemable, subject to only a negative, deductive moral economy of exclusion transcending even death itself.

Understanding such a code as an *economy* enables us to see that these negative operations did not merely operate by invoking constraint in the reasoning subjects of the ranks assembled to witness their execution, but also constituted a corporate body with its own inherent processes, its own internal logic, its own mechanics. Furthermore, these mechanics, this law of the army as an economical body, did not follow from contingencies, but derived from the functional instrumentality of the army as an absolute determinant, as its own end, effecting an economy that operated mechanically, irrespective of particular conditions. Its absolutes applied even if the losses incurred through executions seriously weakened the numbers or the position of the army, and irrespective of familial, personal or official relations, transcending time and eventuality. Frontinus cites the example of Manlius, who executed his own son for attacking without orders, even though his attack had been successful and the army had petitioned for his pardon.

Despite the distinction of Frontinus' schema from the orders of the legions of the early and late republic from which he draws the examples to illustrate his classifications, function and order are still integrated in his early imperial army. In the second section of Book IV, rigorous discipline enables the elements of bodies and equipment to combine *faster*, imbuing the function of military engineering with a speed which conquers its adversaries by enabling it to use *time* to appropriate *space*. Discipline also effects a kind of counter-number, as its mechanics will triumph over the arithmetics of merely superior numbers.

However, if discipline is primarily deductive and functions to establish a distinct mechanical body with its own economies and qualities, the Stoic virtues of continence, justice and constancy produce a positive effect in this body, represented in the third section's succession of illustrations of exemplary commanders, headed by Fabricius, who refused proffered gold with the retort that he preferred to rule those who had gold than to have it himself. But Stoic continence was not self-*sacrifice*. Instead, Ciceronian virtue is re-situated in the context of a transcendent, global empire. In imperial public recognition, the impoverished but victorious commander gains glory transcending the transience of worldly riches, a personal recognition in the annals of universal history closed to those who opt for worldly enrichment. A massive shift has thus taken place from the late days of the republic, when enrichment and glory could go hand in hand and indeed *necessarily* complemented each other in the use of public office for euergetism. Stoicism, under the empire, has now divided these into an either/or. Self-restraint is thus productive, not sacrificial, for those who must command as well as obey. The army, too, can practise such a productive economy of self-restraint and thereby increase itself, as in Frontinus' own experience during the campaign in Gaul, when the army refrained from plundering the temples of a rebellious tribe and was consequently augmented by seventy thousand tribal *auxilia*. Such augmentation, like imperial public recognition, is neither a mechanical reward, nor fate. It is rather, an economy which can be instituted, its precepts followed in practice.

Similarly, following the abstract principle of justice also proves productive. In the fourth section of Book IV, Frontinus illustrates the military application of this maxim with the example of the commander who refused to detain hostages taken by treason from a besieged city, instead returning them to their city. Having proved his honour, the city then surrendered to him voluntarily. The commander's actions are not determined by morality for its own sake, since he exercises justice for ulterior ends, and the principle of justice is not valuable in itself, but nor is it to be deployed as a ruse, a mechanical stratagem. Rather, its instrumentality may only be realized in its practice as an absolute, whereby its effect surpasses other stratagems, since the commander's ends are realized by constituting others' voluntary compliance.

Constancy, however, seems a virtue of a different order in Frontinus' discourse, operating through and upon the self, constituting a quality beyond the mean, calculable limits of the body. Stoic refusal of despair in apparently hopeless circumstances can effect an army's escape against all odds if it is affected as an absolute, without limit, even unto death. Frontinus cites as exemplary the Spartans' assertion of the capacity to die honourably even when faced with certain defeat, presenting their enemies with the prospect of a bloody fight to the death rather than their surrender. The determinant power of the ethical relation of the self to the function described by Foucault as an effect of the new regime could not be more starkly illustrated, but Frontinus also shows how the Stoa, as a means of managing this relationship, produces a military rationality, rendering the prospect of defeat an opportunity for instrumentalization. Death need not constitute the limit of this will, since even the management of death can be instrumentalized for the self's relation to external functions, thereby asserting the will as an ultimate value even over life.

Notes

1. P. Veyne, *Bread and Circuses: Historical Sociology and Political Pluralism* (London: Allen Lane, 1990), p. 250.
2. Ibid., p. 247. The mediation of power by honour and its investment in the person meant that Caesar and Pompey, first in provincial and then in extra-constitutional 'triumviral' authority, came to exercise authority in such a way that they no longer regarded themselves, but their clients, as responsible for the consequences of their actions in office, since their command was secured by patronage. We can see this clearly in Caesar's address to his troops: 'The setback we have received is anyone's fault rather than my own. I gave an opportunity for battle on favourable ground; I took possession of the enemy camp; I drove them out and overcame them in fighting. But whether through your own agitation, or from some mistake, or by some stroke of fate, the

victory that was as good as in our grasp was lost; so you must all make an effort to repair the damage by your valour.' J. Caesar, *The Civil War,* trans. J. F. Gardner (London: Penguin, 1967), p. 143.

3. Veyne, *Bread and Circuses,* pp. 251–8.
4. R. W. Davies, *Service in the Roman Army* (Edinburgh: Edinburgh University Press, 1989).
5. P. A. Brunt and J. M. Moore (trans. and ed.) *Res Gestae Divi Augusti: The Achievements of the Divine Augustus* (Oxford: Oxford University Press, 1967), pp. 21, 27–9.
6. Ibid., pp. 38–40, P. A. Brunt, *Social Conflicts in the Roman Republic* (London: Chatto & Windus, 1971), p. 147.
7. Z. Yavetz, *Plebs and Princeps* (Oxford: Clarendon Press, 1969).
8. Brunt and Moore, *Res Gestae,* pp. 10–13.
9. Veyne, *Bread and Circuses,* pp. 253–8.
10. M. Weber, *Economy and Society: An Outline of Interpretive Sociology,* ed. G. Roth and C. Wittich (Berkeley: University of California Press, 1978), pp. 241–6.
11. R. P. Saller, *Personal Patronage under the Early Empire* (Cambridge: Cambridge University Press, 1982).
12. Brunt and Moore, *Res Gestae,* p. 14.
13. There seems to have been an attempt by Augustus here, as in relation to the accounts of public expenditure, to clarify the distinction between personal largesse and official function in order to maximize his own honour. He held many Triumphs up to 29 BC, but then declined further honours of this kind, as a largesse to the state which paid for them. J. B. Campbell, *The Emperor and the Roman Army: 31 BC–AD 235* (Oxford: Clarendon Press, 1984), p. 139.
14. L. Keppie, *The Making of the Roman Army from Republic to Empire* (London: Batsford, 1984), pp. 129, 132, 146.
15. Campbell, *Emperor and Roman Army,* p. 160.
16. Keppie, *Making of the Roman Army,* pp. 147–9.
17. Veyne, *Bread and Circuses,* p. 340.
18. Campbell, *Emperor and Roman Army,* pp. 33–41.
19. Ibid., p. 229.
20. E. Luttwak, *The Grand Strategy of the Roman Empire from the First Century AD to the Third* (Baltimore, MD: Johns Hopkins University Press, 1976), p. 72.
21. Keppie, *Making of the Roman Army,* p. 78.
22. Campbell, *Emperor and Roman Army,* pp. 69–87.
23. M. Foucault, *The Care of the Self: The History of Sexuality,* vol. 3, trans. R. Hurley (London: Penguin, 1986), p. 82.
24. Rather, *The Care of the Self* enables us to see Stoicism as an active, political philosophy, but one that produces a politics which operates through the avenues of administration, the domain of the Renaissance *populo mediocri* and of the modern professional middle class, whose manifestos are not to be read in the overtly public domain, but in their construction of a moralized norm of the self in the realm of expert knowledge, a knowledge which Foucault had exposed so incisively as constitutive of its subject in his much earlier work on medicine and psychiatry. We can see both continuity and reflexivity in his critical endeavours if we read *The Care of the Self* as concerned with tracing the genealogy of those techniques of construction back through the subject of desire, which earlier modern critical theory had counterposed to the implicated subject of reason as the domain of an essential freedom.

25. Ibid., p. 83.
26. Ibid., p. 84.
27. Ibid., p. 91.
28. Ibid., p. 94.
29. Sextus Julius Frontinus, *Strategemata,* trans. C. E. Bennett (London: Heinemann, 1925), p. xviii.
30. The conventional proto-sociological concept of 'professionalization' usually applied to characterize the development of Roman military and civil administration under the empire, reduces the nuances of the economy of self that provides the condition of authorship and readership of these manuals to rationally regulated self-interest, transposing a distinctively modern governmentality upon ancient Rome. It is unable to explain how such techniques developed beyond asserting a correlation of techniques with structural (bureaucratic) forms. The conception of this correlation as 'functional rationalization' at once posits an evolutionary tautology *and* a universal rationality to which all 'successful' historical forms and processes must be seen to conform. In addition to the theoretical problem of verification thus invoked, this position makes it difficult to employ the same sociological explanation for the extraordinary successes of pre-rationalized republican Rome.
31. Frontinus, *Strategemata*, I.1, p. 3.
32. Ibid., I.1, p. 5.
33. Ibid., IV, p. 267.
34. Ibid., IV, p. 270.

4

From *Pax Romana* to the Order of Feud

Roman imperial policy continued to require tribute in the form of troops, *auxilia,* to serve alongside the legions, which could comprise up to half of the army in the field. Auxiliary service also incorporated individuals by recognition of marriage, which enabled their progeny to inherit the Roman citizenship awarded for 25 years' service, thus providing the basis for a generational reservoir of auxiliary forces. The proportion of Italians in the legions declined throughout the first century, until by the second they were comprised mostly of provincial citizens.[1] Veterans were now usually allotted land outside Italy, in colonies of militarily qualified citizens. Roman imperial policy was thus still based upon hegemony, according recognition in *ius gentium* (the common law of peoples) of an equivalence between citizens of Rome and other communities. However, this recognition required a sovereign authority, and the political irreducibility of the Germanic tribes of the Teutoburg Forest confronted Rome with a limit to its hegemony.

The regime of the *princeps* also encountered political limits to the government of its forces by the patron–client relation, appearing at the juncture of imperial succession. The *donatium* provided an uncertain continuity of patronage, and when news of Augustus' death reached the legions on the Rhine and in central Europe in 14 AD, mutinies ensued, prompted by complaints of the extension of service, poor pay and corruption. The new principate was only able to suppress the mutinies by conceding a 16-year maximal term of service (soon restored to 25 years by Tiberius), in combination with deployment of the privileged imperial household Praetorian Guard.[2] Military enlistment had become entry to a world apart with the assignment of legions on an effectively permanent basis to particular provinces and only a 50 per cent survival rate to receive the 25 service gratuity.[3]

Withdrawal to the Rhine shifted the efforts of Rome away from the military–political search for security in hegemony by ever-extensive alliances, toward a new, military–diplomatic security strategy, which created a chain of client tribes around a core of peoples who were reduced in hegemonic subjection to imperial administration. Techniques of treaty, military tribute and patronage were sanctioned by a range of measures from subsidy to punitive warfare, in order to construct sovereign tribal authorities that could recognize imperial patronage, upon which they became dependent. The Flavian imperial dynasty, emerging from the succession crisis of 68–69 AD, rationalized the provincial order by consolidating an increasingly perceptible margin over the late first and early second century through intensified military engineering campaigns and administrative organization for revenue collection. The consolidation of the margin in turn reconfigured hegemony as an object, rather than as a process. Rome was now an empire and from the second century on, the legions were deployed in a succession of distinct patterns within its clearly defined space.

By the time of Hadrian, the limits of empire were demarcated by a chain of marginal clients. The *limes* now indicated a system of horizontal roads linking permanent garrisons as elements of a great surveillance and communications system. This 'frontier' was not yet a horizon of interception, and the legions were distributed through an ascending hierarchy of concentration in signal posts, watch towers, auxiliary forts, and legion headquarters, along lines of march running perpendicular to the frontier, from which they could move rapidly to make preclusive strikes against major threats. In the second century, the forts of the western and African spheres of the Roman empire were moved up to a perimeter.[4] Later still, the system evolved into one of 'preclusive defence', in which outpost forts were constructed far beyond a definite front line, in space previously secured by hegemonic policy. Finally, in late antiquity, the army was divided between those stationed in permanent frontier forts and mobile forces barracked in cities deep within the empire.[5]

Military occupation

These distributions of force effected a military order very different from the old mobile legions. No longer a virtual city traversing 'empty' space, the legion now *occupied* the empire, permanently quartered in stone garrisons. Maintaining static forces was an entirely different enterprise to the direction of independent, mobile legions, since the soldiers were permanently isolated from the political order, with little prospect of booty or contact with their commander. Permanent bases constituted bodies whose regulation was given neither in the order of mobilization of the republic, nor in the patronage of a commander. Issues of static bodies, such as sanitation, had to be dealt with *administratively*, rendering previous modes of government through political identities and moral economies superfluous.

This is again illustrated in terms of address. Where Caesar's speeches to his troops repeatedly emphasize the *moral* government of the legion, for which discipline was a means, Hadrian's speeches and Roman military practice in the empire emphasize discipline as an end in itself. His speech to troops in North Africa[6] refers not to the *loyalty* of the legion, but to their fulfilment of strictly military *duties*, and not in battle, but in drill and labour. He praises the soldiers for having fulfilled their obligations to his office, not to his person, and refers to the care of the *legates* for the men as their official function, not as his own delegated patronage. Hadrian presents himself to the soldiers not as their patron, but as *imperator*, and the legion is evaluated in technical rather than moral terms, making 'allowances' for its technical disposition (the number of times it had to move camp, the administrative discontinuities entailed by the imperial rotation of proconsuls and its depletion by absent cohorts). There is little trace of moral judgement, in which commanders could 'allow' for the virtuous record of the legion. Hadrian's speech thus reveals how the moral economy of military relations had been displaced by technical assessment of the legion as an administrative order.

Military administration did not originate in a bureaucratic project emanating from some great political strategist. Under the republic, records had only been kept while the legion was in existence, and the governors had taken their day-books home with them at the end of their office as a source for their memoirs. The administration of permanent legions, however, required provincial governors to maintain records on every soldier in the province in order to authorize recruitment, transfers and discharges. Modern archaeology shows that these records could be updated, circulated and retrieved, and a number of soldiers were permanently assigned to the tasks of legionary administration in the camps and the governor's office.[7]

In the absence of a moral economy to mediate relations between the *princeps* and the functional order (as opposed to the personnel) of the army, these techniques had developed to sustain continuity of operations across the discontinuities of brief personal commissions. Though structural determinations (such as the length of plebeian and auxiliary service) played a part, the independent function of this uncentralized, pre-bureaucratic structure was nevertheless predicated upon a standardized and abstract mode of knowledge, establishing depersonalized principles for functional performance which was integrated with a mode of subjectification that operated to constitute a self morally autonomous of external recognition and hence able to fulfil functional requirements independently of the mediations of patronage. A military structure thus emerged independent of the occupants of office and increasingly unaffected by the deployment of patronage.

Incursions

From the end of the second century, the destabilizing effects of Roman policy in its marginal contacts with loose tribal kin-associations resulted in waves of barbarian incursions into the empire. Roman policy had constructed a new political model for the Germanic peoples, in which war-leadership became a permanent institution, enabling imperial patronage to be established over clientary warrior-retinues. But fixing the tribes in their form of mobilization for war created a condition of interminable conflict within the German forests (the 'Marcomannian Wars'), from which successive waves of 'invaders' fled into the empire.[8] In containing these incursions and the opportunistic rebellions that broke out, the emperor Marcus Aurelius applied Stoic ethics as a guide for self-conduct in strategic fulfilment of the function of the *imperium* itself.

> From the emperor Antonius ... Marcus Aurelius recalls that he received three lessons: first, not to identify with the political role that one plays ('see to it that you do not become Caesarized, or dyed with that colouring'); second, to practice the virtues in their most general forms ('treasure simplicity, goodness, purity, dignity, lack of affectation, justice, piety, kindliness, graciousness, and strength for one's appropriate duties'); third, to hold to the precepts of philosophy such as that of revering the gods, protecting men, and being mindful of how short life is.[9]

Self-restrained distantiation of the self from the gratifications offered by power regulated its exercise by maintaining an equilibrium of the soul, 'carefully planning one's projects and seeing them through', irrespective of the terrors of functional performance, the ostentation of fame and the infuriations of the world, enabling Marcus Aurelius to admit the barbarians to the empire as settlers while dealing decisively with plots within his own family to usurp his legitimate authority.[10]

In the context of murderously internecine palace politics, the army's increasing independence as a political actor, and the pressure of destabilization beyond the Germanic frontier, Marcus Aurelius' death precipitated the 'crisis of the third century' that saw more than 20 emperors and usurpers contest the *imperium* between 192 AD and 284 AD.[11] In this context, the army of the provincial legions constituted a continuity relative to palace politics, and for the first time independently acclaimed an emperor in Septimus Severus in 193 AD. With a static and socially stable base, the armies on the Danubian and Rhine frontiers emerged as major political players. Severus' son, Caracalla, positively fostered his own political dependence upon the army, funding a 50 per cent rise in soldiers' pay by debasing the imperial coinage and vastly increasing the flow of revenue to the public coffer that Augustus had established independent of senatorial control.[12]

As the soldiers' income rose above subsistence, settlements grew up around the permanent garrisons in the frontier zones, where the distinction between the military camp and the civil environment became increasingly blurred. Military operations were infrequent and soldiers had time and capital to engage in local agriculture and industry. Each legion held huge tracts of land as a reservoir for veteran settlement, which was leased to locals or farmed by the soldiers themselves. The prospect of land settlement enabled soldiers to form local attachments and even families, with their sons entered on the roll and receiving rations,[13] reinforcing the tendency to irreversible static deployment, as it invested them in the defence of their own sector. Only new recruits could be detached to reinforce other parts of the frontier, draining the standing garrisons of the mobile elements on which the Hadrianic defence system depended for interception. By the time of the barbarian incursions of the third century, the Roman army had become a highly efficient administrative and logistical structure defined in terms of its functional performance and imbued with multiple mechanisms of motivation, but no longer functioned effectively as a frontier defence force. With the means for preclusive tactical offence depleted, the third-century empire became vulnerable to attack by tribes who were able to make use of the Roman road system designed to carry legions to intercept them, and raiders penetrated hundreds of miles into the empire.[14]

Under Diocletian, who had risen through the army to become emperor in 284 AD, civil and military administration were separated by creating frontier zones administered directly by military officers who took over from the civil governors and by reforming civil administration in parallel with the army.[15] In this period wastes appeared in the space of the interior, the *ager desertus* abandoned by peasants fleeing impossible burdens of taxation or serfdom imposed by landlords, and brigands appeared on the roads. The provincial aristocracy formed itself into a civil class divorced from the military aspect of empire, defined by its special legal status, its land-holdings and fortified rural *villae*, and with its political interests invested in the sub-provincial government of the urban *civitates*.[16] However, localized civil security was enframed by Diocletian's redistribution of imperial military forces in depth in new defensible forts guarding granaries and roads, creating zones of military control which were increasingly dependent upon barbarian *foederati* in tributary military service to the empire, who were incorporated into the Roman army and came to occupy high office within it.[17]

Between 250 AD and 300 AD the number of treaties between the empire and the tribes had increased enormously, and barbarian clientage had shifted into a relation of service as Rome supplied grain to tribal war-leaders to secure their authority and the provision of *auxilia*, who were deployed within the empire itself.[18] Some barbarians were admitted to settle the *ager desertus* as *laeti*, hereditarily obligated to serve in the Roman army, but others remained outside the *limes* as client tribes, 'imperial Germans', whom the Romans sought to isolate from the influence of the Germanic interior. The implications of permanent military service transformed the barbarian political order, producing a permanent state of war-mobilization under a warrior-king (*rex*) who had originally only held authority during communal emergencies. In military service, the barbarians were implicated in a moral economy which trapped them in their war-order as reservoirs of violence. Barbarian military service was no longer a means of escape from domination, but now cemented the authority of the *rex* and locked the tribal grouping into subjection to an empire with which they increasingly identified themselves.

The militarization of empire

In the fourth century the army was restructured into dual bodies when Constantine (324–337 AD) institutionalized the *de facto* tactical order by finally dispensing with the legion and dividing the army formally into two; the *comitatenses*, regionally based mobile armies barracked in towns within the empire, and the *limitanei*, garrisoned in the permanent camps and forts along the frontier. Distinct comtal and ducal orders of command were instituted respectively for these interior and frontier zones. The strategic and functional division of the army also had internal political effects, since the *comitatenses*, quartered within the empire on public routes, had greater opportunity to represent their grievances than did the *limitanei* on the frontier, at the mercy of their tribunes, *praefects* and the *duces*. By a mid-fifth century petition to the emperor, the *comitatenses* even deprived their junior officers of the traditional right pertaining to all Roman governorships, to flog and reduce them in rank.[19]

The army by this time comprised a world of its own, maintained and equipped as a distinct military-industrial complex. Soldiers and their dependants also held distinct privileges, such as tax exemptions. Their regular wage (*stipendium*) had been eroded by inflation, but the *donatium* could amount to ten times its value. In addition, Diocletian reorganized the fiscal system on a logistical basis to pay soldiers in kind (the *comitatenses* were supported by the compulsory services of guilds to grind their corn and bake their bread). As the army became increasingly the profession of those who had no other means to support themselves, so it became effectively hereditary, tying generations in economic dependence to its independent logistical administration and privileged exemptions. The imperial administration could do little to reform the structural bifurcation between the military and the civil empire. Diocletian attempted to reinstitute conscription, but by the fourth century, special sanctions had to be introduced against families who cut off their sons' thumbs to invalidate them, recruits had to be imprisoned during transit to their stations, and laws were enacted to punish and recover deserters. Money commutation of conscription assessments, however, was facilitated by the increasing employment of *foederati*,[20] barbarian forces serving under their own commanders and discipline, with forms and techniques often difficult to reconcile with the historical repertoire of Roman strategy and military science.

Vegetius: The military thing

Form and technique had thus become the major problematics for military practice in late antiquity. Vegetius' text, *De Re Militari*, reconstructs the forms and tactics of the armies of the early principate in an attempt to recover a rational military order for the exercise of war.[21] However, the conditions of this discourse were very different to the conditions of Frontinus' military science.

In contrast to Frontinus, *De Re Militari* presents us with 'the military thing', rather than with a discourse of war. From the dedication onwards, the text refers us to a concept of authority as given in the forms themselves, so that obedience no longer appears as a problem. The Vegetian programme to recover the condition of military science proceeds by reconstructing abstract forms of military order, where Frontinus focused upon the conditions of order. Technique similarly figures as a function of its object, military formation, and not as a *practice* which must refer itself to *principles* of order rather than to their forms. The discourse of *De Re Militari* itself lacks the underlying principle of order which can be read in the *Strategemata*'s organization of historical and material examples. Instead *De Re Militari* tries to assemble a war-machine without a guiding principle for the assembly of its mechanical components.[22] The figure of the grand strategist fills the place of such a unifying principle, but this produces a war-machine as a pure instrument without a subject. Discipline is thus conceived as a mode of conforming bodies to a programme that is inherent in the abstract forms themselves.

Vegetius begins by asserting the counter-numerical quality of his programme of selection, instruction, exercise, preparation and subjection to capital sanctions, where Frontinus had carefully established counter-numeracy as an effect of discipline, rather than as a quality inherent in military forms. This example reveals the distinction between two different relations to knowledge; that of Frontinus' methodologically reflexive discourse, in which the army is something to be constructed, and that of Vegetius, for which the form of the army already exists and to which material must be made to conform. Again, the substantive aspect of the text mirrors its discursive technique. For Frontinus, military science was to be carefully constructed from historical records by first classifying the material and then selecting exemplary illustrations for organization into categories. For Vegetius, however, military science already exists as an abstract formal truth which has been misplaced and must be recovered through the 'painstaking and faithful labour' of reconstruction. Frontinus does not lay claim to such authenticity, but to an authorship which Vegetius expressly denies. For Vegetius, Frontinus' sources have become authorities, including Frontinus' own texts.

Vegetius' programmatic reconstruction of the Roman war-machine takes us through a narrative which begins with the body of the recruit and ends with its consumption in battle and siege. Original motive force is no longer constituted in the republic (as it is in Cicero), or in the self (as in Stoic thought), but is diffused from the sun, corresponding to the diffusion of force from the emperor throughout the empire. This singular source conditions the body, which has finite capacities for absorption, so that it is more intelligent, but with less blood, where more exposed to the sun's heat in the south, but less intelligent, and with more blood, in the north. Because its capacities are finite, the body is also imbued with a natural economy of blood, so that those of the south are less useful for war since they are more averse to the loss of blood through wounds. Temperate climes condition bodies most suitably for war, with both ample blood and intelligence, along with other naturally given conditions for selection, so that even though the proper forms of training can produce mental and physical vigour in bodies naturally unsuited to a life in arms, the norms for this corporeal production are already given in nature. Military practice, which for Frontinus was a distinctive art and for the republic a form of political action, is thereby reduced to the level of fabrication, reproducing the natural world.[23] The same shift from art to reproduction occurs with respect to war itself. In Vegetius, war is not an operation constituted in applied techniques, but exists, like the military object, as an abstraction, *a priori*. Stratagems are not means to create the character of war and strategy, but war and strategic space appear as given fields to and in which stratagems may be applied. War is no longer artificial, but a natural state with its own truths, to be recovered in the reconstruction of its forms.

Rather than providing means whereby empire may be realized, Vegetius offers only its reflection, so that the 'natural' forces he reads in the historical record mirror the actualities of the empire: energy is diffused and the dispositions of bodies are conditioned by trades (which had become hereditary by the third century), and by breeding. Space is similarly given, and can be related to the fixity of imperial deployments, since the legion no longer constitutes space by traversing it, but occupies a space already constituted as empire. Knowledge is similarly determined, reposing in the person of the emperor, a prince who is already invincible, to whom Vegetius dedicates his text.

Whereas for Frontinus Stoic military philosophy ultimately enabled the command and the legion to overcome overwhelming odds by will, for Vegetius, training operates not through subjectivity, but upon the external body of the soldier, which is treated as though without will, as natural material. The *instrumentality* which Frontinus' military Stoicism produced as an active quality thus becomes a passive *instrumentation* in Vegetian discourse. For example, habituation to burdens was an operation originally designed to produce a disciplined soldier, but now produces only bodies habituated to burdens which themselves become the formal preconditions of an army. Similarly, menial duties are not imposed to produce a moral effect in the soldier or the army; rather, the formal figure of the soldier is defined by his menial service.

The ultimate utilitarian value of the bodies of infantry formed in training lies in stasis, enabling (or constraining) them to form a *wall* which can withstand any attack. The analogy of the wall figures again in Vegetius' description of the camp, which no longer traverses insecurity, an enclosure from which the soldiers march out to face the enemy in the field as *agonistic* warrior–citizens, but comprises a security for the soldiers to retreat within. It has become 'a place to stay' and the mass of bodies enclosed within it produce sanitary and supply problems which the marching camps of the republic did not encounter. The health of military bodies thus becomes problematized in the same moment in which they are reduced to natural bodies without will, and exercise also translates from a moral economy into a 'natural' one, becoming a sanitary measure to maintain health. The problematized health of the body in the security of its encampment constitutes a new, second-order insecurity, reducing the mobility that was essential to the republican legion to a sanitary necessity, since the health of the inert body must be ensured 'by frequent changes of camp'.

Naturalized and sanitized, the will-less bodies of Vegetius' soldiers are over-determined not by tactical function, but by forms of discipline which are ends in themselves. They must be exercised in lines composed with arithmetic and geometric precision so that the area may be calculated abstractly, enabling their reconfiguration into squares, wedges, and even circles. Mathematical abstraction of the collective body can then substitute for the moral order as the condition of battle, an order derived from simulation and requiring no political action. Obedience appears only as an issue of administration. Half the donative given to the soldiers by the emperor is deposited with the standard to ensure that soldiers will defend it in the field. The gift in itself no longer secures anything; only withholding it from the soldier can ensure his adherence to the standard, indicating not so much a political practice as the absence of a mode of government, producing a self-interested will that must be constrained, and undermining the very object of training and geometric determination. Finally, Vegetius' abstract reconstruction of military instrumentation must always have a *reserve* at hand, building anticipated mass attrition into its programme.

The regime of the city in late antiquity

While the formal Vegetian programme was probably never realized, it nevertheless articulated the concerns and terms of military thought in late antiquity. The 'military thing' formed a parallel to civil administration in the division of the interior of the empire into military regions to which *comitatenses* were permanently assigned, effectively militarizing the empire and shifting the focus of deployment and the object of military *imperium* from the frontier to the towns of the interior, where they formed a parallel to the civil order. 'Constitutionally and administratively ... the cities were the cells of which the empire was composed.'[24] Self-governing urban communities, the *civitates*, administered the empire outside the capitals. Imperial expansion since Augustus had systematically pursued a policy of leaving annexed communities intact wherever they could correspond to this administrative model, boosting township, so that by the time of Diocletian the empire was thoroughly urbanized. The imperial urban constitution required council assemblies to elect civic magistrates and enact decrees and law in keeping with those of the empire, and for those eligible by age, property and origin of birth, council service was compulsorily co-optive. Its elected officers performed both local and imperial functions (administering local services such as corn and bread supply, sanitation, and games, regulating the market and maintaining public works, including the town fortifications, administering imperial communications and roads, managing mines, and collecting taxes and the levies of provisions and men for the army), but they were also personally responsible for underwriting shortfalls in tax collection. During the fourth century, this constitution was completely transformed, establishing a new, Christian episcopal power in the cities which further alienated the provincial aristocracy, who retreated to their fortified *villae* in the countryside.

Care of the poor had traditionally been practised by the notables of the urban councils as a form of *euergesia* that established them as the head of a social hierarchy, relieving the principate of the need to maintain a military presence to control the lower strata within the provincial towns,[25] though *euergesia*, like patronage, did not *ensure* mass obedience, which still required local political work if protest was not to escalate into violence. Within this urban order, the Christian Church had only been able to establish itself in charitable administration to poor strangers outside urban membership. However, imperial anti-vagrancy legislation from the second century on indicates a progressive erosion of the basis of imperial order in civic identity defined by urban origins. Increasing displacement of plebeian populations by barbarian invasions and flight from debt, tax and clientary obligations, severely strained the distinction between strangers and the poorer members of the city, until the scope of Christian charity shifted to include all dependent clients, severing the original identity of the urban poor with the civic order. Church administration of charity obliterated the personal element of *euergesia*, but the role of the bishops in poor relief made them the new patrons of the cities. As a new medium for imperial control, they consolidated their political advantages by no longer treating the violence of the urban poor as part of a local dialogue, as it had been under the old order, but as the voice of the Christian poor, to be articulated by the bishop for transmission to the emperor. Already responsible for organizing supplies to the poor urban masses, the bishops also took on the function of defenders of the cities, a role that translated literally into the administration of fortifications. As urban Gallic notables withdrew to their fortified rural *villae*, the bishops, in alliance with the *comtes*, consolidated their authority in cities isolated by the expanses of *ager deserti* that opened up around them. Against dispossessed peasants who had turned to banditry (the *bacuadae*), their alliance offered security to the communities which supported them in a new military-episcopal relationship independent of the functions of imperial administration.[26]

With imperial attempts to regulate the disastrous social mobility of late antiquity by making all occupations hereditary legal categories, military service became a hereditary male obligation marked by a tattoo to differentiate these from other bodies, whose obligations could be commuted for money. Additional numbers could only effectively be recruited beyond the frontiers, and the policy of cultural hegemony through Romanization was used to enlist forces from barbarian *foederati*, who now provided a hard core of the field armies. These 'imperial Germans' actively sought permanent incorporation into the imperial military system as a means of accessing the relative security of the empire. To the military administrators of the *imperium*, their territorial settlement repopulated the *ager deserti* and provided a reservoir of force. As hereditary military citizenship was gained on completion of service, so they settled not as conquerors, but as subjects of a military empire providing security to the civil zones.

The 'barbarian' order

Nineteenth-century historiography saw the 'barbarian' regimes of late antiquity as corrupted forms of the Roman order, a mere transitional phase between the ancient and medieval forms of juridical power. However, more recent research shows that rather than imitating the formal categories of Roman juridical order as conquerors attempting to appropriate the glory of Roman *imperium*, they took over the empire and its military administration by default through their provision of military service. The Franks first appear as 'imperial Germans', a grouping of clans providing military service under a *rex*. The Merovich clan established itself as a new form of dynastic regime in the province of Gaul by allying itself with the bishops when the *rex*, Clovis, converted his personal clients and kin to Catholicism, rather than the Arian Christianity of the Goths who had previously settled in the empire.[27] The urban episcopacy controlled vast funds bequeathed by displaced Gallo-Romans who had sought its sanctuary. Through this alliance, the Merovingians were able to take over the military administration organized around the ducal and comtal town palaces.[28]

Although Merovingian law took Germanic form, its codification as the Salic law was authorized by the *imperium* of the military administration. Its main element was the old tribal constitution of political association around universal military obligation and the permissive regulation of internal violence in feud by fines and penalties.[29] Tribal mediation of feud had been vested in the assembly, but the synthesis of Salic law with the Roman form of *imperium* translated this role on to the *rex*, enabling Clovis to use feud strategically, destroying rival Frankish kings in brutal and personally targeted campaigns of elimination, and territorializing a Merovich clan domination now encoded in legal authority.

Wallace-Hadrill's sociological analysis of the Frankish institution of feud shows that it constituted a horizontal network of social relations quite separate from the vertical rule of kings.[30] Royal codification of the Salic law actually acknowledged feud as a parallel legal order beyond its jurisdiction. Instead of legal regulation, Salic law provided objective terms and conditions for the negotiation of composition (settlement by symbolic recompense in blood or money) under royal arbitration, but the king and his officials had no sanction to enforce these agreements. The particular interpretation of the case in arbitration could be contested, and the feud continued in search of more favourable grounds for composition. The concentration of political relations in the court did not imbue the *rex* with a public role; feuds between courtiers ignored royal reconciliatory proposals and flouted their judgement in the very precincts of the palace. The prohibition on drawn weapons in the immediate presence of the *rex* was a function of the arbitration role, not a sign of subjection to sovereign power. Though Salic law took Roman form and established the *rex* as inheritor of *imperium*, it did not follow Roman law in precluding private violence, but created a court of arbitration around the *rex* that depended upon the institution of feud itself.[31]

The institution of feud was a crucial integer of the Frankish regime. It demarcated the Franks from other groups, while linking them across their highly irregular pattern of distribution. With no characteristic mode of life of their own to sustain, the Franks did not seek out any particular topography, but settled in multiform sites; abandoned rural *villae*, new upland ranches, and Gallo-Roman towns. Differentiation from their social environment thus depended upon the institution of feud as a focus for kin associations dispersed across heterogenous spaces with different orders of time. The instrumentalization of the custom of feud in the new synthesis may also explain the apparently unusual role of women in the Merovingian regime, indicated by the 'reverse' dowries paid by the husband's family to the wife's. Geary ascribes their value to the function of bearing heirs,[32] but this explains neither the Frankish adoption of monogamy nor widows' inheritance rights. However, marriage conjugated associations between households, precluding feud between them and establishing a mutual obligation to revenge injury by outsiders. As feud became a political instrument, women took on a *political* value, and some played their own parts.

Feud also constituted an economy of violence, involving not only blood-vengeance, but covering many other infractions of rights, such as theft, cattle-rustling and accidental injury. It provided the only societal sanction available to the Franks, with the exception of outlawry, and the Merovingian kings thus fostered and protected the institution, since even though it delimited the authority of the *rex*, its arbitration was their main political function in time of peace.[33] However, Frankish dispersal in the space of empire also transformed feud, and in turn transformed Frankish society. Firstly, composition (the mutual agreement of a blood-price) seems to have become more difficult to establish with the dispersion of kinship across disconnected and heterogenous settlements. Secondly, feud had originated in the space of the tribe, where it was conditional upon the *public* exaction of vengeance by the blood kin of the wronged party. However, as personal pursuit of exaction was impossible to maintain in the mosaic space of late antiquity, so the use of retinues became conventional, with hired, covert assassins as a regular means of pursuit. Nevertheless, feud was *not* the obverse of peace. It did not invoke the radical division of time between war and peace instituted in the foundational *imperium* of Rome, which became the prerogative of the *rex*, endowing him with authority to levy the tribe and its resources. Since feud constituted a social order in itself, the ruler-function of the Merovingian inheritance of the *imperium* was restricted to war. Kings themselves undertook feud and the Merovich dynasty had established itself in a series of bloody feuds, instrumentalizing the institution in its definition in Salic law.

The Merovingian dynastic regime was established in the mid-fifth century in the towns and shaped by the concentric spaces around them, where it utilized the dual technical remains of the Gallo-Roman administration; the imperial military order of the *duces* and *comtes*, and episcopal authority over the residual legal and fiscal administration of the *civitates*. Within the imperial territorial legacy in Gaul, Merovingian consolidation thus proceeded by, 'the acquisition and defence of as many fortified cities and castra as possible',[34] drawing on the late Roman military legacy of siege techniques, severance of enemy communications and supply, and military control of surrounding populations and their resources, which were passed on through the work of Vegetius (available to the regime through its association with the urban bishops) as a compendium of techniques rather than as a source of formal concepts of public military service or discipline. Their tactical flexibility was conditioned by the historical formation of the Franks as *foederati* in imperial service, unencumbered by tribal traditions.

Beyond Gaul, the Merovingians conducted raids with the object of seizing removable wealth, rather than of establishing territorial dominion. They sought neither to subject nor subjugate, but replicated their own mode of rule over the Gallic provinces by marital conjugation. Frankish *duces* appointed from the *trustis* to govern conquests according to their own laws were required to make marriage associations with the king's new subjects. Clannic conjugation, however, excluded the Gallo-Roman landed aristocracy and rendered the regime dependent upon the bishops in the towns of late antiquity.

The ruin of the towns and the refoundation of imperium

Working from an abstract norm of centred sovereign power, the urban and ducal investments of barbarian late antiquity appear to historical sociology as 'centrifugal tendencies', but anthropological approaches suggest that the source of insecurity of the Merovingian *rex* lay in internecine palace plots. In the context of the chronic uncertainty of authority dependent upon the embodiment of kingship in blood succession, the bishops and *duces* provided a structural security against palace factions. It became deliberate royal policy to cultivate kin appointments to the bishoprics and seventh-century appointments of new Merovingian provincial *duces* can be correlated against the rise of the Pippinid clan faction, which threatened to dominate the regime through the offices of the palace *maiores domus*, who managed the military retinue and controlled access to the king.[35]

As *maior*, Charles Martel mobilized the royal retinue as a campaigning force. His grandson Pippin acceded to the kingship in 751 AD through a combination of new alliances, election by the Frankish landed nobility and the sanction of the papacy, which was anxious to assert its authority over the episcopacy. The urban bishops thus formed the main obstacle to the new regime. As the main remaining authorities in the towns, their administration of the local levy and city fortifications enabled them to raise forces and dominate the surrounding regions.[36] The Carolingians, after Martel, transformed the royal retinue of followers from a palace guard into a highly mobile force for annual military campaigns in which they subdued the bishops and other major aristocratic rivals. Their piecemeal, tactical victories produced a new model of Carolingian kingship as decentred rule, in which only the personal, embodied presence of the king ultimately guaranteed authority, so that when not engaged on campaign, the king had to engage in a continuous itinerary of the kingdom.

The rise of the Carolingian dynasty to imperial dominion under Charlemagne became a crucial referent for subsequent medieval kingship through the medium of clerical chroniclers who sought to identify kingship with the sacral authority of the church. Reduction of the urban episcopacy as a political power established a new secular-hierocratic alliance through the great abbey of St Denis, which protected its rights to widespread property while confiscating the huge episcopal estates.[37] This alliance of secular kingship with the monastic network provided the Carolingians with access to the material, technical and authoritative resources of the church while opening the way for the Gregorian project of a universal social order modelled on the rule of St Benedict, a new way of life pioneered in the monasteries.

Carolingian warfare took the form of predatory raids for slaves and plunder by hosts of followers assembled for short and even seasonal campaigns of continuous mobility, focusing upon fortified strongholds in which people took shelter with their removable goods when invaders entered the land.[38] Timothy Reuter's study of the capitularies (royal ordinances)[39] shows that the Carolingian forces were not levied, but made up of 'unbeneficed warrior followings', heavily armed by their magnate leaders and concentrated in expectation of booty and the honour of fighting, in the Germanic tradition of the war-band, rather than as defensive mobilizations. The retinues were complemented by professional horse-warriors maintained, trained and equipped as monastic military dependants (*scarae*) by the abbeys as their contribution to the new alliance.[40]

In contrast to the negotiable service of retinues, the levy of free men was severely circumscribed by its institution in law, effectively precluding its use for anything other than local defence. The renowned Carolingian capitularies for the levy proliferate only after the phase of expansion, from around 800 AD, when the regime's consolidation of the space of conquest as tribute and plunder from its campaigns transformed the Frankish kingdom into an empire and shifted the object of war from plunder to defence.[41] These capitularies provided for particular forms of force for quite separate objectives, instituting different relations of subjection to those of conquest and constructing a distinct model of kingship, authorized in office, which governed through written laws and orders and produced documentary archives. Juridical approaches through these sources trace the translation of the ecclesiastic *benefice* into a political system of 'feudalism', which enabled a sovereign power to maintain military forces in the condition of dispersal necessitated by low levels of economic and administrative resources, from the reign of Charlemagne, around the year 800 AD, where the term appears in documents establishing warriors of the king's personal retinue on lands near the frontiers. However, more recent, decentred approaches to the documentary archive show these as *ad hoc*, contingent measures contemporary with others of more comprehensive scope and politically integral to the regime's alliances, such as the creation of the *scarae*, the institution of levies and the regular clerical monitoring of comtal administration.

Notes

1. P. A. Brunt, *Social Conflicts in the Roman Republic* (London: Chatto & Windus, 1971), p. 150.
2. J. B. Campbell, *The Emperor and the Roman Army: 31 BC–AD 235* (Oxford: Clarendon Press, 1984), pp. 176, 370–1. In Rome itself, the Praetorian Guard had been formed as a permanent personal bodyguard by Augustus out of the clientary career soldiers he had inherited from Caesar. The Guard continued as a military elite, with conditions very different to those of the provincialized legions, becoming a crucial actor in Roman palace politics.
3. L. Keppie, *The Making of the Roman Army from Republic to Empire* (London: Batsford, 1984), p. 182.
4. In the east, the desert formed a marginal space, while towns by their very nature constituted defences, built compactly around water sources with narrow streets that would trap nomadic raiders.
5. E. Luttwak *The Grand Strategy of the Roman Empire from the First Century AD to the Third* (London: John Hopkins University Press, 1976), pp. 74–5.
6. A. H. M. Jones (ed.), *A History of Rome through to the Fifth Century, Vol II: The Empire* (New York, NY: Harper & Row, 1978), pp. 154–6.
7. N. J. E. Austin and N. B. Rankov, *Exploratio: Military and Political Intelligence in the Roman World from the Second Punic War to the Battle of Adrianople* (London: Routledge, 1995), pp. 156–61.
8. P. Geary, *Before France and Germany: The Creation and Transformation of the Merovingian World* (New York, NY: Oxford University Press, 1988).
9. M. Foucault, *The Care of the Self: The History of Sexuality, Vol. 3*, trans. R. Hurley (London: Penguin, 1990), pp. 89–90.
10. It was not ironic that this philosopher-emperor was engaged in warfare

throughout his *imperium*. There is no essential hiatus between philosophy and war; rather, the Stoa provided the perfect foil. Marcus Aurelius' commemorative column thus records his military accomplishments as an engagement with humanity, rather than as the simple and personified triumph of civilization over barbarism.

11. Geary, *Before France and Germany*, pp. 10–11.
12. Ibid., p. 18.
13. A. H. M. Jones, *The Later Roman Empire, 284–602: A Social, Economic and Administrative Survey, Vol. 2* (Oxford: Blackwell, 1964), p. 631; Geary, *Before France and Germany*, p. 15.
14. Luttwak, *Grand Strategy*, pp. 129–32.
15. Jones, *Later Roman Empire*, pp. 43–5.
16. Geary, *Before France and Germany*, pp. 20, 94.
17. Luttwak, *Grand Strategy*, pp. 132–4, 159–61.
18. Ibid., pp. 115–16; Geary, *Before France and Germany*, p. 21.
19. Jones, *Later Roman Empire*, pp. 647–8.
20. P. Contamine, *War in the Middle Ages*, trans. M. Jones (Oxford: Blackwell, 1984) pp. 7–9.
21. Renatus Flavius Vegetius, *De Re Militari: Epitome of Military Science,* trans. and ed. N. P. Milner (Liverpool: Liverpool University Press, 1993).
22. Such an underlying principle of military science was only to be formulated again with the Renaissance and neo-Stoicism.
23. Even the civil–military distinction, unknown to the political republic, is for Vegetius already a natural truth given in sex, and thus all men who have dealt in trades associated with women are to be rejected. The expulsion of women from the camp which Frontinus recommended as a means of moral economy thus translates in Vegetian discourse into a naturally gendered identity of the army, which can be contaminated by habitual association with women.
24. Jones, *Later Roman Empire*, p. 712.
25. P. Brown, *Power and Persuasion in Late Aniquity: Towards a Christian Empire* (Madison, WI: University of Wisconsin Press, 1992).
26. Contamine, *War in the Middle Ages*, p. 7.
27. J. Le Goff, *Medieval Civilization, 400–1500*, trans. J. Barrow (Oxford: Blackwell, 1988), p. 21.
28. Geary, *Before France and Germany*, p. 86.
29. Ibid., pp. 90–3. Whether Salic law applied to the Franks only, or to all, is contested by modern historians.
30. J. M. Wallace-Hadrill, *The Long-Haired Kings and other Studies in Frankish History* (London: Methuen, 1962).
31. The *fisc* of the imperialized *rex* could profit from composition, but by a share in the composition as a fee for arbitration services, rather than by levying a fine as symbolic recompense for the disturbance of a public royal order.
32. Geary, *Before France and Germany*, pp. 105–7.
33. P. S. Barnwell, *Kings, Courtiers and Imperium: The Barbarian West, 565–725* (London: Duckworth, 1997).
34. B. S. Bachrach, *Merovingian Military Organization, 481–751* (Minneapolis, MN: University of Minnesota Press, 1972), p. 127.
35. Barnwell, *Kings, Courtiers and Imperium*, pp. 32–40.
36. Geary, *Before France and Germany*, pp. 210–11.
37. Le Goff, *Medieval Civilization*, p. 30.
38. These fortification were merely adaptions of the natural terrain, uninhabited

on a regular basis and offering protection to large numbers only in time of danger, belonging to the village community mobilized for its common defence, rather than to any lord.

39. T. Reuter, 'The End of Carolingian Military Expansion', in P. Goodwin and R. Collins, *Charlemagne's Heir: New Perspectives on the Reign of Louis the Pious, 814–840* (Oxford: Clarendon Press, 1990), pp. 391–405.
40. J-P. Poly and E. Bournazel, *The Feudal Transformation, 900–1200*, trans. C. Higgit (New York, NY: Holmes & Meier, 1991), p. 21.
41. Reuter, 'The End of Carolingian Military Expansion', p. 404.

PART TWO: MEDIEVAL

5

Medieval History and Historical Sociology

Excursus on feudalism: Learning from and against historians

Nineteenth-century theses that feudalism originated in the Carolingian regime were largely based upon juridical models and etymological analysis of the formal terms of legal documents. These theses have been refuted in the field of cultural history, most notably in the work of Georges Duby, whose micro-historical research into the medieval Maconnais area shows that the *subjective* conditions of *feudalism as an order* (a necessary condition for the use of enfeoffment as a governmental strategy) only appeared in the socio-theological reformulations of society in the Peace of God movement of the tenth century.[1] The idea of an objective order pre-dating any consciously strategic use of its forms by enfeoffing agents rests upon a conception of a protective ruler-function inherent in domination itself (as the necessary condition of legitimation), which was only subsequently rationalized and articulated in the ideology of the Church.

The offensive of recent military historians such as Bachrach, Reuter, Bradbury and even Contamine[2] against the imputed predominance of mounted, armoured warriors in early medieval France has profound implications for historical sociology, whether it posits a continuity of development through the Middle Ages to the modern West,[3] or whether it uses 'feudalism' as an antecedent type of 'pre-modern society' against which to define the historical singularity of modernity.[4] Structural historical sociology has depended to large extent upon nineteenth-century analyses of formal juridical terms, tracing the evolution of the category of the fief as a military function on the assumption that since the medieval era had no sovereign power, authority was given in law, in which the sovereignty of a formal *imperium* was immanent. The early medieval period is thus consigned to 'feudal anarchy' preceding the recovery of a systemic discourse of sovereignty in law in the eleventh-century medieval renaissance. Against this 'idealist' juridical perspective, Norbert Elias began from the point of early medieval 'anarchy' to develop his sociologically 'realist' conceptualization of a system constituted by a precarious balance between forces of centralization and decentralization.[5] However, his 'civilizing process' reproduces normative logocentrism, since the social-evolutionary formation of lengthening 'chains' of economic interdependency and the political concentration of hierachic relations produce a progressively centralizing tendency within this historical process. While rejecting the concept of feudalism as a stable system along with the 'stages' model of vulgar Marxist evolutionism, the grand-narrative of Elias' 'civilizing process' nevertheless effectively reproduces the 'vulgar Weberian' grand-narrative of an historical process of objective rationalization.

Both the grand-narrative of historical evolutionism and the concept of feudalism can be traced to the same intellectual origin. The historian Elizabeth A. R. Brown has mapped out the deconstruction of the concept of feudalism in historiography,[6] beginning with F. W. Maitland's dismissal of an English 'feudal system' as a construct of nineteenth-century historians on the basis of work by the seventeenth-century antiquarian Henry Spelman. J. G. A. Pocock traced the substance of Maitland's allegation to Spelman's reference to a sixteenth-century edition of a twelfth-century text, the Lombard *Libri Feudorom*. The Huguenot editors, Hotman and Cujas, provided a 'precise and detailed' definition of *feudum* as abstract, formal criteria of heritable land tenureship, which Spelman used to classify English and Scottish medieval legal records as evidence of a uniform '"feudal law", an hierarchical system imposed from above as a matter of state policy'. The legal definition was expanded by eighteenth-century writers, who reified the social and political relationships of medieval Europe under this conception, rendering it, 'an "ism" ... reflecting on its essence and its nature and endeavouring to fit it into a pattern of general ideas',[7] a shift which was complemented by Montesquieu's characterization of medieval society in terms of a general form of law, as *feodalité*. By the mid-nineteenth century, the term 'feudalism' was being used as a totalizing conception of pre-modern European society which henceforth dominated the study of medieval history.[8]

The definition of feudalism as a formal, constitutional formation thus appears as an integral element in the early modern normative project of political thought (Huguenot legitimation of resistance to absolutism) that traced a progressive evolution in the development of normative legal concepts, and which Skinner identifies as establishing the discursive condition of political modernity in its reworking of medieval concepts.[9] Sociology, emerging in the nineteenth century as a distinctive discipline, aimed to substitute descriptive, objective analysis for such normative projects, but grounded this substitution in its own radical differentiation of modern from pre-modern social forms and relations, for which the concepts and vocabulary of the tradition of political theory were deemed analytically inadequate. Ironically, sociology's self-legitimizing disciplinary justification is thus itself grounded upon the very concept of 'feudalism' that was developed by the critical methods of the Huguenot project, which provided sociology with a conceptualization of the pre-modern as a contrasting totality or systemic formation, against which the discipline defines its own task of developing a vocabulary for the analysis of modern society. This conditional totalizing dichotomization paradoxically requires modern sociology to reformulate the concept of 'feudal society' in its own normative terms, as an integrated system.[10]

Structuralist approaches which seek to interpose other societal formations between the medieval and the modern continue to rely upon systemic concepts of 'feudalism', providing various combinations of a normative juridical conception of sovereign power with a normative concept of societal function, i.e. to theorize the medieval world in terms of systems and social integration. Perry Anderson, for instance, grounds his totalizing formulation in the conception of medieval war and the military function of the feudal manor as a mode of extraction of an economic surplus.[11] Other approaches continue to posit the functions of sovereign power as the normative terms of their analysis, so that 'feudalism' appears as the fragmentation of sovereignty, a counter-tendency to the longer term historical process of the concentration of sovereign power in the state. Medieval society can then be totalized in terms of feudal 'centrifugal tendencies'.[12] For Poggi, 'The main trend through most of the feudal period was fragmentation of each large system of rule into smaller and more autonomous units.'[13]

Mann's attempts to reconfigure the subject of historical sociology in terms of power processes rather than structures reduces itself in its encounter with 'feudalism' to normative juridical categories, structural functions and material resources (in a passage in which the conceptual slippage between forms of state and society to which systems analysis is prone is also clearly evident). Mann describes the early medieval polity as 'a weak feudal state' emerging out of the relation between the castle and warrior knighthood, where 'supreme power' conventionally rested in a singular, lordly ruler, whose position in turn rested on some form of contractual exchange of land or protection for military services, provided by vassals who also exercised the functions of sovereign power at the local level. The 'military nature of the feudal state' and the social differentiation of the nobility further rested upon,

The overwhelming superiority of the armed mounted knight and the fortress over the peasant and urban infantryman until the fourteenth century, and the functional necessity of knights and fortresses in areas threatened by invasion, increased the yield of 'protection-rent' exacted by knights. Only a relatively wealthy man could keep a horse and equip himself with body armour ... in a fairly primitive economy, no lord could generate the liquid wealth to pay a large number of mercenaries. The only solution was land grants, which gave the vassal soldier a potentially autonomous power base.[14]

This formulation presents us with three core descriptive/explanatory elements which sociological discipline substituted as objective, social terms for the normative, ideal categories of political thought in its adoption of the concept of feudalism. Firstly, an inherent tactical military superiority of mounted, heavily armoured warriors; secondly, functions of social and systems integration of the form in which these warriors were maintained in given medieval economic conditions; and third, an immanent sovereign power.

The thesis that feudalism emerged as a functional system out of Charles Martel's need to procure large numbers of heavy mounted warriors against the Muslim advance in Gaul was first developed by the nineteenth-century German historian Brenner.[15] Brenner argued that the Carolingian institution of *beneficium* provided warriors with the means to support themselves in military readiness, mounted and armed, on estates granted from the king in exchange for his right to their military services. The ecclesiastic institution of the *benefice* was thus fused with the institution of vassalage, constituting the military-political system of feudalism. Brenner's thesis has been elaborated in historical sociology into a functionalist characterization of the entire medieval period as a feudal system which enabled the maintenance of expensively armed and economically unburdened individual warriors for the simultaneous defence and domination of a society with relatively low levels of uncentralized economic production and poorly developed communications.

The Brenner thesis depends upon a typologization of early medieval warfare as dominated by heavily armed mounted forces, a tactical superiority that White and others have grounded materially in the invention of the stirrup, which enabled a 'shock charge'.[16] This thesis usually situates the 'origin' of feudalism in the Carolingian era, when mounted forces enabled the reduction of rival powers and imperial expansion of the Frankish regime. However, Carolingian campaigns were punctuated by serial sieges against fortified enemies who did not meet them in open battle where the stirrup might have proved decisive.[17] Their relatively small forces, armed and gathered as a following around the personal leader of the palace guard, used horses to traverse the space in which their enemies were dispersed, but *in situ*, the Roman legacy transmitted through Vegetius provided them with a compendium of techniques to re-organize the space and the resources of a locality for siege, with the warriors dismounting to fight.[18]

The sociological adoption of this conception of feudalism further requires the formation of a distinct status, defined not only by a monopoly of superior means of violence, but also differentiated by a social order which enabled warriors to maintain these means as economic non-participants providing defence and protection to the economic producers from whom they extracted their maintenance on a regular basis, an order legitimized in an ideological representation of this role that placed them under certain social constraints. However, micro-sociological historical work dispels the abstract functionalism of these macro-level conceptualizations. Georges Duby, in his study of the medieval society of the Maconnais region of France (part of the area where indicators of feudalism first appear), concluded that the identification of the knight as noble, i.e. the monopoly of the means of violence to a definite status, did not take place until the thirteenth century, and then as a primarily cultural rather than a military or political process.[19] The knight became noble and knighthood became a self-identifying social formation, he argues, through the adoption by lower-status warriors of noble practices such as lineage-identification and encastellation. This usurpatory self-aggrandizement was accomplished on two conditions.

Firstly, the Church's formulation of a theological order of society, which it attempted to substitute for the order of feud. This ascribed to all those designated as *miles* a sacral monopoly of violence in defence of the other two orders, the clergy and the poor. In this socio-theology, one order prayed for grace (*oratores*), one order defended justice in arms (*bellatores*), and a third worked to support the first two (*laboratores*). By ascribing to the *miles* a monopoly *right* to fight and to conduct *werra* (feud), the Church was able to subject their violence to regulation by truce, to demand that it comply with certain criteria of just cause, and to delimit its usage against the poor and the clergy. The new order was thus defined by a monopoly of legitimate violence. Secondly, this order displaced the residual Carolingian distinction between the free and the unfree: henceforth, all *miles* would be considered as free equals in the socio-theological order of knighthood. The conceptual distinction between the nobility and the *miles* was thus eroded just as the *miles* were actively usurping the prerogatives of the older nobility. The distinction eventually disappeared, constituting a singular unitary caste of knighted aristocracy, just as did the distinction between the free peasant and the serf. Furthermore, the concept of nobility was itself transformed in this process: the *miles* did not simply raise themselves into a cultural and political status hitherto occupied by a smaller group. Against the noble *domini* of the eleventh century, the kings used the institution of enfeoffment to tacitly encourage the knights to usurp the nobles' privileges while at the same time seeking to secure the homage of the *domini* and the military service of all knights. This thirteenth-century transformation, according to Duby, thus comprised an unspoken alliance between kings, who sought to monopolize war, and the *miles*, who sought to usurp noble status, in a field mapped out by the Church's socio-theological order of society. This historical schema has been referred to as the 'mutationist' thesis.[20]

However, more extensive historical research has shown that the fief was just one sign, enfeoffment one kind of link between men. It was not identical with the knighted status which *miles* came to designate, or even with vassalage, which required rites of fealty quite distinct from the right to *fief-rent*, or the 'knight's fee'. Fealty was sworn, and could only be rendered in person, a symbolic entrustment between vassal and lord, a customary relationship of honour, rather than services, between living men, that did not pass through generations as an inheritance. Enfeoffment, by contrast, was legally sanctioned, secularly codified and deemed to be a legal aspect of the patrimony, thus enabling an individuated lineage,[21] while vassalage only rendered an identity with the lord to whom it was sworn. Vassalage could be sworn to more than one lord, a means of asserting mutual recognition of equable honour between two men, and had a standard formulation from the outset. Enfeoffment, however, was not even a singular, uniform category in law.[22] Rather, the fief of 'feudalism' is an abstract conceptual generalization which depends upon the interpretation of a heterogenous plurality of particular legal agreements as indicators of relations of an exchange of tenanted land and jurisdictional rights for military services, anachronistically projecting the Roman legal concept of contract onto such agreements as a universalistic conception of all agreements in law.

The general conceptualization of the fief as an *exchange* of landed livelihood for military service was definitively formulated by Ganshof,[23] but military service was not the only form which such a relation could take and enfeoffment was not the only provision that could be made for armed services. There was no intrinsic or necessary connection between enfeoffment and knighthood; rather, the typological norm of an enfeoffed and independently-equipped knight appears as an effect of sociological abstraction. Of the knights provided by lords as a legal obligation, at least some would be equipped by them, some only being provided with arms when an array was summoned. The land-holdings of many 'knights' would have been insufficient to maintain them in arms and recent historians have tried to develop a stratified model of knighthood itself based upon plural criteria of land-holding, arms ownership, legal status and the variables of contingent, independent and dependent military obligation.[24] Not all knights held fiefs, and it was not unusual for knights to buy themselves freedom from the obligations of the fief, or even to abscond with the arms provided by their lord, becoming a part of the large number of unenfeoffed, wandering knights available for hire who comprised an important element of the actual forces gathered and deployed in medieval warfare, a reservoir of force which the English barons in particular used to fill the quotas established in royal inventory surveillance of vassal obligations, and which also comprised a large part of the French royal host.[25] Indentured or mercenary service was not precluded by vassalage or enfeoffment and those owing service to the lord themselves or serving as a part of a baron's quota might also serve for the king's money.[26]

Enfeoffment thus appears as one among a range of means open to medieval lordship to procure military services, rather than constituting a functional military system around the armoured, mounted warrior as the effective monopoly of the means of violence. Enfeoffment was not used primarily to maintain forces for war, but was one among several *strategies of alliance* available to lords, such as marriage, diplomacy and unenfeoffed vassalage. Furthermore, the array of feudal obligations was not the favoured means of territorial contest, but was rather deployed as a last resort, and even then the function of the array was not to make war, but to provide a symbolic display of alliance.[27] The major Anglo-Norman barons used sub-enfeoffment among themselves, for social, political and even economic purposes, rather than as a means of retaining warriors in independent arms, which was more usually achieved by an non-heritable land-grant. Sub-enfeoffment proliferated from as early as 1050, and effected not so much a ready provision of military force as a legal *corpus* accruing around definitions and restrictions on particular obligations, a massive and unwieldy body of individually variable obligations, rather than a system, making the feudal host almost intractably difficult to array.[28]

Recognizing the fief as the form of a legal and a social network, rather than as an indicator of a hierarchical military system based on contractual exchange, enables us to understand the feudal host in terms of its medieval representation, as a symbolic function in a regime of signs, rather than as a military function in a structurally integrated system. The appearance of the arrayed host was often sufficient in itself to bring enemies to negotiation. The formula of threat used by William II to the Count of Maine in 1096 provides a typical illustration;

> ... at the earliest opportunity I will visit the city of Le Mans; I will show them a hundred thousand lances with banners before their gates and will not leave you unchallenged in the enjoyment of my inheritance.[29]

The banners were to signify that this was a host constituted in feudal array, rather than in indenture or household authority. However, such an array was severely circumscribed; the obligation to serve under feudal summons was limited to 40 days, response tended to depend upon the particular circumstances, and the lord could do little to command it against the culture in which knighthood was embedded. Rather than enfeoffment constituting a functional order in the sense that Mann theorizes, there is little evidence that the feudal array *ever* provided the military function which the various systemic theories of feudalism posit for it.[30]

In this context, we can re-examine the martial culture of knighthood, free from preconceptions about its putative social function. Research into medieval knightly culture shows that the lance, which would have given the greatest advantage to the 'shock charge', had a primarily symbolic role in differentiating the knight by his arms, rather than as an instrument for killing. The special skills with lance and mount, which the feudal nobility supposedly required economic exemption to acquire, thus had little *military* value outside ritualized combat with other, similarly-equipped knights who could be engaged in elaborate lance-fencing, with the object not of killing or even necessarily of removing the opponent from the field, but of unhorsing them for ransom.[31] The tradition among the knights of the king's household, whom one would expect to form the nucleus of a shock charge, was to dismount to fight.[32] In any case, battle was rare. Uncertain in outcome, and with limited command over the deployment of forces, it was generally avoided. The final claim which could be made for the technical 'superiority' of mounted knights is their mobility, but in the field, the mounted warrior only had an advantage over good roads and in clear places. Since much medieval warfare took place off the main routes, it could be pursued almost as easily by troops on foot.[33]

The conceptualization of knighthood as a military function thus collapses when we begin to abandon *a priori* assumptions, and with it the hypostatization of feudalism as a social system. This is not to say, however, that medieval society was any the less formed around violence, but while the concept of feudalism is taken up by historical sociology to advance a standard case for the gradual monopolization of violence under the legitimate sign of the sovereign (and its reduction outside this sign to transgressive violence), the invalidation of feudalism as a military system presents us with the prospect of a *struggle* over violence, a struggle for and against its monopolization and instrumentalization, a struggle which constitutes a rather different body politic to one neatly divided between dominant aggressors who hold the means of violence, and their victims, who are excluded from yet subject to it.

A debate in the journal, *Past and Present*, invoked by an article by Bisson,[34] revolved around precisely the question of the distribution of violence, its role in the emergence of the medieval world and in modern constructions of 'feudalism'. Barthélemy sets Bisson's contribution in the context of two successive theories of the emergence of medieval society.[35] In the old historiography, from about 1840–1940, feudal society emerged as the seigneurial economic structure of society around the villa developed local defences against marauding renegade counts, thus localizing the defence function of Carolingian kingship. In this schema, a continuity of legal forms can be traced through their transposition onto local lordship, leading to a social order characterized by Weber as 'patrimonial domination' in the household or fief: 'domestic authority decentralized through assignment of land and sometimes of equipment to sons of the house or other dependants'.[36] In later twentieth-century historiography, Duby and others showed that early medieval society was not primarily 'seigneurial', but consisted in patronage networks, rather than territorial lordship. In place of a continuity of legitimate forms of authority, the new historiography traced a long-term mutation into an entirely new order, discontinuous from the Roman *imperium*. For Duby and his fellow scholars, the 'feudal revolution' led to new economic and social relations, i.e. new relations of production and exploitation. In both theses, however, seigneurial 'feudal' violence is contrasted with legitimate regalian rule, which is assumed to constitute the only possible restraint of that violence, so that 'feudal society' appears as the antithesis of the state and social order, as immediate, predatory, violent domination. However, Barthélemy argues that feud also constituted an economy of violence.

> In reality, regalian authority was never the only curb on the 'violence' and 'oppression' of the nobility. Violence can also limit

itself, and neither it nor oppression destroyed the social fabric. Both suffered from the weakness of their means and met resistance.[37]

White follows this up by pointing out that we need to be very careful when reading medieval accounts of 'violence', canonical terms which were specifically deployed by clerics to portray the Church as victim.[38] Their discursive strategy abstracted violence from the physical body onto a moral and political body, so that some acts would no longer appear as violence, while others were inscribed in the records of the eternal Church. The clerical record of violence was thus part of the struggle over its monopolization and instrumentalization.

An inventory of early clerical sources reveals that the categories comprising violence were not merely the resource of the seigneury, but elements of feud, which could be practised by individual and corporate bodies. Violence could thus be used by any group, served multiple functions and took on different meanings in different contexts. In tenth-century Francia, violence was 'institutionalized within as well as outside the legal order', and its constitution contained no traces of a sense of delegated sovereign power.[39] The institution of feud did not operate as a *post facto* justification of affective violence, since it was carefully delimited and confined in both custom and law. Rather, both before and after the 'watershed' of the year 1000, feud was the mode by which violence was meaningful, controlled and directed, and thus cannot be characterized as unrestrained, however extreme the practices.[40] In the emergence of medieval society, then, violence was far from the exclusive prerogative of knights, and, although over the next centuries they would attempt to monopolize many of the forms of violence as their collective prerogative, that attempt and the means by which it was conducted must be seen as a constitutive struggle, rather than a precondition, of medieval society.

Notes

1. G. Duby, *The Chivalrous Society*, trans. C. Postan (London: Edward Arnold, 1977).
2. P. Contamine, *War in the Middle Ages*, trans. M. Jones (Oxford: Blackwell, 1984), pp. 181–4.
3. M. Weber, *General Economic History* trans. F. H. Knight (New York, NY: Greenberg, 1927).
4. A. Giddens, *The Nation-State and Violence. Volume Two of a Contemporary Critique of Historical Materialism* (Cambridge: Polity Press, 1985).
5. N. Elias, *The Civilizing Process* (2 vols), trans. E. Jephcott (Oxford: Blackwell, 1994).

MEDIEVAL HISTORY AND HISTORICAL SOCIOLOGY

6. E. A. R. Brown, 'The Tyranny of a Construct: Feudalism and Historians of Medieval Europe', *American Historical Review*, 79, 4 (1974) pp. 1063–88.
7. J. G. A. Pocock, *The Ancient Constitution and the Feudal Law: A Study of English Historical Thought in the Seventeenth Century* (Cambridge: Cambridge University Press, 1957), p. 249.
8. Brown, 'Tyranny of a Construct', pp. 1064–5.
9. Q. Skinner, *The Foundations of Modern Political Thought* (2 vols) (Cambridge: Cambridge University Press, 1978).
10. For example, see Giddens, *The Nation-State and Violence*, pp. 7–11. This disciplinary condition of sociology is replicated in the many late twentieth-century attempts to develop a distinctive sociology of post-modernity, which similarly define their historical subject against totalizing, reductive conceptualizations of modernity.
11. P. Anderson, *Passages from Antiquity to Feudalism* (London: New Left Books, 1974), p. 31.
12. B. Downing, 'Constitutionalism, Warfare and Political Change in Early Modern Europe', *Theory and Society*, 17 (1988), pp. 7–56.
13. G. Poggi, *The Development of the Modern State* (London: Hutchinson, 1978).
14. M. Mann, *The Sources of Social Power*, Vol. 1 (Cambridge: Cambridge University Press, 1986), pp. 391–3.
15. B. S. Bachrach, *Armies and Politics in the Medieval West* (Aldershot: Variorum, 1993), Ch. XII, p. 49.
16. L. White, *Medieval Technology and Social Change* (Oxford: Clarendon Press, 1962); R. L. O'Connell, *Of Arms and Men: A History of War, Weapons and Aggression* (Oxford: Oxford University Press, 1989).
17. J. Bradbury, *The Medieval Siege* (Woodbridge: Boydell Press, 1992), pp. 21–9.
18. Archaeological and documentary evidence also refutes the 'Ross–Brunner–White thesis'. Despite attention to the technical details of warfare, the first Western representation of a stirrup only appears over a century after Charles Martel launched his campaigns in 733 AD. Contemporary literary sources do not mention it, and stirrups have been found in only 1 per cent of the archaeological record of equestrian remains of the time (Bachrach, *Armies and Politics*, XII, p. 59–69).
19. Duby, *Chivalrous Society*, pp. 158–70, 180.
20. D. Barthélemy, 'Debate', *Past & Present*, 152 (1996), pp. 196–205.
21. R. Bartlett, *The Making of Europe: Conquest, Colonization and Cultural Change, 950–1350* (London: Penguin, 1993), pp. 49–50.
22. Though medieval secular law centred around particular disputes over rights and obligations pertaining to fiefs, providing the terms for early modern critical analysis, legal feudalism does not imply a military function.
23. F. L. Ganshof, *Feudalism*, trans. P. Grierson (London: Longman, 1952).
24. S. Harvey, 'The Knight and the Knight's Fee in England', *Past & Present*, 49 (1970), pp. 3–43.
25. J. Scammel, 'The Formation of English Social Structure: Freedom, Knights and Gentry, 1066–1300', *Speculum*, 68 (1993), pp. 591–618.
26. S. Morillo, *Warfare Under the Anglo-Norman Kings, 1066–1135* (Woodbridge: Boydell Press, 1994), p. 24; J. H. Baldwin, *The Government of Philip Augustus: Foundations of French Royal Power in the Middle Ages* (Berkeley, CA: University of California Press, 1986), p. 279.
27. Morillo, *Warfare Under Anglo-Norman Kings*, pp. 32–3.
28. Ibid., p. 71; Contamine, *War in the Middle Ages*, pp. 47–9.

101

29. Orderic Vitalis, quoted in Morillo, *Warfare Under Anglo-Norman Kings*, p. 33.
30. Ibid., p. 55; Baldwin, *Government of Philip Augustus*, p. 303.
31. G. Duby, *The Legend of Bouvines: War, Religion and Culture in the Middle Ages*, trans. C. Tihanyi (Cambridge: Polity Press, 1990).
32. Morillo, *Warfare Under Anglo-Norman Kings*, p. 157.
33. Ibid., p. 113.
34. T. N. Bisson, 'The Feudal Revolution', *Past & Present*, 142 (1994), pp. 6–42.
35. Barthélemy, 'Debate', pp. 196–205.
36. M. Weber, *Economy and Society*, ed. G. Roth and C. Wittich (Berkeley: University of California Press, 1978), p. 1011; S. D. White, 'Debate', *Past & Present*, 142 (1996), pp. 205–23.
37. Barthélemy, 'Debate', p. 203.
38. On the basis of a canonical record which sought to marginalize, discredit and delegitimize the institution of feud in favour of its own order of society, modern historians have 'depicted an interlude of turmoil, insecurity, disorder, violence, anarchy and lawlessness between more respectable periods of law and public order by portraying aggressive, restive and violent warriors and local strong men who practice usurpation, coercion, exaction, rapine, pillage, depredation and endemic brigandage'. (White, 'Debate', p. 217.)
39. Ibid., p. 218.
40. T. Reuter, 'Comment', *Past & Present*, 155 (1997), pp. 177–93; S. D. White, 'The Politics of Anger', in B. H. Rosenwein, (ed.), *Anger's Past: The Social Uses of Emotion in the Middle Ages* (New York, NY: Cornell University Press, 1999), pp. 127–52.

6

Encastellation

The appearance of the castle

In the year 1000, during an obscure but protracted feud with Fulk Nerra, count of Anjou, the count of Blois in the Loire valley built a *motte* around his existing fortress[1], grounding the insecurely dispersed forces by which feud was conducted in a new form that was to revolutionize the organization of violence in medieval society. Blois' son expanded his father's dominions in a campaign of aggressive castle-building, establishing a technology of territorialization which rapidly disseminated itself through northern France and spread across Europe in the ensuing centuries.

These castles of the new millennium, comprised of a small keep upon a raised mound and surrounded by a ditch (the *motte*), were of an entirely different order from the urban episcopal fortifications besieged by the Carolingians, and from the defensive fortifications erected in their subsequent programme of localized defence as strategic elements linking fortification with legitimate authority to raise the levy.[2] By contrast, the *castella* were quite explicitly tactical. They did not offer defence as their primary function and were not integrated with authority. Rather than adapting existing topographical features, they were constructed by radically reconstituting terrain, even in their rudimentary form of a simple *motte*. Castles assembled and transformed not simply the advantages of site and the human, livestock and food contents of a contiguous area, but also traditional authority, local labour services, the personal following of the war-band, forestry resources and the earth itself. The castle grounded an immediate domination which did not require legitimation.

The castle as technology was more than a material construction. It was an assemblage of elements, incorporating the human and the non-human (earth, wood, stone, water), and embodying the activity of domination itself in a discrete, non-systemic technology – a medieval machine. Conceptualizing the castle as technological enables us to separate it from the medieval regime of signs. It did not originate in a grand strategic design to establish 'feudalism' as the expression of a sovereign power, or as the function of such a system. It was not a strategic instrument, but a tactical innovation. The *motte* castle was defensible rather than defensive, and embodied domination rather than attack or raid, thus producing forces and an economy of violence quite different to conquest and seizure. Unlike urban defences, it could be built quickly and easily at little or no cost by a hundred men in ten days by exercising immediate, local domination.[3] Castle buildings, 'in themselves were worth little more than a cottage of one of the peasant tenants: they could be quickly demolished and almost as speedily rebuilt and equipped'.[4]

The building of fortifications was the jurisdiction of the king, an aspect of the *imperium* which had been revived to consolidate the Carolingian regime by creating strategic defences against incursive raids. The new type of castle simulated the *effect* of sovereign authority, reproducing what had been inimitable before. However, conceptualizing this new phenomenon in terms of the *fragmention* of sovereign authority ontologizes the juridical model of power. Castle lordship did not usurp the function or privileges of an ahistorical category of 'the sovereign', but constituted an entirely new mode of power. 'What itinerant rulership was deprived of between 1073 and 1080 was legitimacy and logistics, not a hold on public power which it never possessed.'[5]

The very attempts by kings and duces from 1000 AD to assert royal control of what had hitherto been their unproblematic and unremarkable prerogative of defensive fortification attests to the transformation of authority effected by the castle; lordship was new, but kingship too was transformed into a contestable and relative title, requiring its reformulation, but also opening on to new strategies. Kingship became identified and projected in its prerogative of fortification, as in the decrees of both Anglo-Norman and French kings. Norman ducal injunctions appearing from 1091 prohibited digging a ditch deeper than a man could throw the earth out of, or setting up a palisade,[6] while in France, the royal prerogative was reformulated as the king's right of access to any castle within the realm. In Norman England, control of fortification became the means to establish a new dynasty and an entirely new mode of rule.

Seeking to trace a continuous historical line of authority, as something 'reasserted' through royal control of castles, simply throws us back upon a sovereign model of power, in an attempt to explain something by reference to what needs to be explained. Primarily, the castle and its forces were not defined in their relation to an exterior, sovereign power, but in their relation to each other. These relations were formalized in vassalage, which operated horizontally as much as vertically;

> ... the majority of these castles were built by great landholders to support the exercise of power which was 'neither a continuation of old patterns of patronage, nor a substitute for the weakened regalian duty to preserve peace and uphold justice (the *ban*)'. In other words, there was no continuity with previous practices.[7]

The castle effect

In its effective sense, we need to look at how the castle reconfigured the space of the early medieval world, at the new forces it constituted, at the options it opened up for the deployment of force, and at how it transformed war and the techniques by which violence was organized and governed. The focus then shifts from feudalism, or the delegation and usurpation of sovereign power, to the *effective* power of the castle itself, which already appeared as 'modern' in the eleventh century, when Alpert of Metz described the struggles of the lords of the lower Rhine.

> There is a marsh 200 paces from the Meuse, within which was a little hill, very hard to reach ... For anyone eager for a change it offered the chance to build a castle.[8]

This short quotation illustrates the tactical relation of the castle to its environment, compact, elevated and inaccessible, privileging defensibility over defence; but it also shows the new perception which its technology had effected in the gaze of the author who sees not just a hill, but a possible site for a castle, not just natural terrain, but a virtual field of force. This revolution in perception also indicates new ways of life, since the marsh in which Metz envisages a castle would have previously been considered uninhabitable. The 'deserts' of uninhabited lands had grown since late antiquity, transfiguring settlement from public space into enclaves, but they were now transfigured by the castle into a resource, not merely as economic value, but as a social space for assemblages of force.

Jacques Le Goff[9] provides us with a conceptual map of the medieval forests and wastes, which served as a refuge for the *fuga mundi* in the tenth century, heterogenous extro-social elements in flight or exile from hierocratic, domestic and legal authority: hermits, lovers, brigands, outlaws, younger unlanded sons of warrior families, clerical apostates, all the subjects of the exclusions against which medieval community formed itself.[10] The desert deterritorialized and decoded, and was thus at once a space of freedom and of enchantment.[11] The castle colonized this space, recoding it as a zone of domination constituted by the visual surveillance afforded from the tower, a military gaze watching for movement, for encroachment by other retinues upon its space. From this location in the space of enchantment, the castle took on a mysterious, enchanting quality itself, effecting a magical transformation of the space which it invested with new value. Appearing suddenly in the emptiness of the desert, looming in the mists of the marsh, it transcended the division of space between settled and waste lands, interposing its cellular form and transformative effect upon all spaces, ubiquitously and indifferently, since terrain was instrumentalized in its technical capacity to actually reconstitute the physical contours of the earth.

Bartlett notes how Alpert's phrase manifests the castle in contemporary discourse as a complex revolutionary force, 'reshaping the rules of both military and political life'.[12] The castle's transformative capacity operated across the thresholds of formal legitimate authority, refigured tactical options and constituted new subjects. Its potentiality opened space to 'anyone eager for a change', marking a transformation as fundamental as that produced by the vehicular republic of the legion and its camp, converting currents of migration and flight, stabilizing the immediate domination of semi-nomadic warrior-bands. In Alpert's articulation of these *new* possibilities, time itself is opened.

The castle liberated fortification from its function of protection, but also liberated domination from the need to engage with the economic reproduction of the communities off which it lived, so its force was not rendered void by the disruption of economic production and interruption of the life of the community. Though some were built within or overlooking towns and villages, others were built in the wastes; the castle had no necessary connection with the community, but proceeded as indifferently of social space as it did of terrain. It reoriented the direction of domination, severing the connection to settlement, and could be quite separate from lay or ecclesiastic communities of economic production.[13] The castle was thus able to colonize new territories without need of administration. Settled lands could be terrorized and subjected, and reterritorialized and recoded by the castle, but it could also territorialize and encode the vast emptiness of the deserts which enclosed medieval settlement.

By the middle of the twelfth century, when castles had spread across all of Europe, medieval society had become a settled society. 'To begin with, wanderers had been the normal people, whereas later on the normal people were the stay-at-homes. From the fourteenth century onwards, only vagabonds and wretches wandered.'[14] This settlement of the 'continuous yet irregular "Brownian movement" of medieval society' is often associated with the growth of ecclesiastical and pontifical control of pilgrimage and social mobility, as clerical encryption of relics, prescription of penances, and hospitalization of alms to travellers channelled the search of grace away from apostolic abandonment of the world into regular itineraries of pilgrimage and crusade,[15] but the castle played a different part in this settlement, as a block rather than a way-station on the road. It gathered within its space fugitive elements; bands of brigands, couples of unauthorized liaisons, wandering landless warriors, outlaws, war-bands. In its narrow, confined space, these elements were fixated and compressed, engendering a new way of life and a micro-society enclosed within itself, but replicating itself dynamically. Its mystery was thus invoked not only by its appearance, but in its transformation of the bodies that entered it. The dynamic of early medieval society is not to be found in its economic capacity, its legal forms, or its religious code, but in the new social formations produced by the castle. Robert Bartlett suggests that, 'Perhaps the key to the aristocratic expansion of the eleventh, twelfth and thirteenth centuries lies neither in the dynamics of war-bands alone, nor in the structures of kindred alone, but in a fateful conjuncture between the two.'[16] Focusing on lineage-kinship and the war-band as the social forms conjoined in the castle directs our attention away from the legal relations in which persons (the identifiable individuals of a juridical order) are invested, to the body.

The bodies which first inhabited the castle were not encoded in orders of chivalry, lineage, legal relations or customary obligations of vassalage, but were bodies of men of war maintained for the institution of feud, in which the value of kin relations was invested. These bodies were not the subject of any formal codified order.[17] Rather than the castle functioning to produce the forces of feudal obligation, it produced retinues of men who were not contractual mercenaries, but appear in the documentary record as *milites gregarii*. The retinue was a horizontal, not a vertical, formation. The warriors defined by their relationship to the castle, the '*guerriers du chateau*', were, at once, a family under the 'fathership' of the master of the castle; a clan amongst themselves, depending upon concepts of loyalty and friendship reinforced (perhaps to the point of strain) by communal living in the castle hall; and corporate possessors of the seigneurial authority. The 'master' or lord thus seems defined less by formal authority and more by his embodiment of the object of feud. He could not even marry his son or daughter without the assent of his warriors, and required their advice in all his actions as master. The mounted warriors rode out to raid and intimidate the tenanted peasantry as co-embodiments of castellar power, not as authorized representatives of the master, who was lord over the land alone, but not over them. An indissoluble investment of the body of the retinue in the castle is evidenced in the customary mutilations of the bodies of retained warriors captured in feud; blinding them, amputating their right hands, or casting them from the tower of the keep.[18]

The castellany also provided for other bodies living within and receiving specified revenues produced in its zone of domination for part of the year, but provided for within the castle itself for a specified annual number of days of castle-guard. Again, however, we need a model other than that of the modern contract to understand these more liminal relations. The direct provision of bodily shelter and sustenance in castle-guard can be referred to the ancient practice of largesse, securing obedience by symbolic gifts.[19] It appears that these warriors were often ex-members of the garrison who were settled outside the castle, individuated by a proper rather than a minor name, appearing in written documents.[20] In diverse ways, the castle operated as a hydraulic social machine, with unmarried peasants incorporated into the castle as servants and married peasants provided with the arms and mounts that made them into *milites*.[21]

In the colonization of Europe by encastellation and its way of life, military equipment, service and expertise was not confined to or monopolized by a nobility. Attention to the micro-politics of castellar life shows that the castle's transformative effect cannot be reduced to the creation of lordships in juridical records, whether these are classified as an economic or a political order. Its micro-society and its expansive technology generated pressure for individuation, actually producing the order of feudal signs which it is conventionally assumed to express, but encastellation neither directly constituted nor precluded a political system. Rather, it produced new technologies of government and control which were used in Norman England to assemble a new regime controlling its bodies of violence within a bureaucratically monitored distribution of obligations and jurisdictions, enabling a new mode of kingship in deployment across an integrated circuit of royal castles.

Norman England – the castle, strategy and 'integration'

By the mid-eleventh century, the Norman dukedom had assembled a serial lineage-network of castellar formations across Europe, but its authority was insecure, mainly, because of the technology by which this expansion had been achieved. The early castles were materially insubstantial and subject to predatory usurpation. Landless warriors still wandered without roots, providing ready forces for any who could pay them. Enfeoffment and its sub-forms grounded local domination by creating a legal identity with land, but this grounding could also discharge authority since the very identity it instituted enabled autonomous usurpation of the privileges of legal jurisdiction. The Norman regime developed special techniques to fix this identity and its relationship to the duchy in a written archival inventory of the juridical obligations identified with named persons and castles,[22] but the development of these inventories cannot be explained by their military function. Firstly, by the end of the century, *scutage* (money commutation of military obligations, a practice more highly developed in Norman domains than elsewhere) opened the possibility of hiring mercenaries instead of depending on inventoried military obligations.[23] Secondly, for its military forces, the Norman dukedom depended primarily on its household retinue, rather than levied bodies. Thirdly, the inventories' emphasis on the duty of castle-guard suggests that they provided a means of containing subordinate rivals in a network of obligations to the duke, rather than functioning as a means to maintain and raise forces for expedition. Inventories enabled Norman enfeoffments to be carefully calibrated against castle-guard obligations, so that no surplus capacity was left to provide for independent forces. In the space of conquest, this political technique became the very fabric of a new domain.

In William I's preparations for the invasion of England, the inventories were not used to raise expeditionary forces. Rather, a sweeping review and reform of inventoried obligations substituted members of the duke's personal retinue for uncooperative castellar lords, thus enabling the invasion by ensuring Normandy during the duke's protracted absence. To raise forces for the field, William liquidized his own patrimony and even stripped the churches for money to hire mercenaries, and utilized kin-networks across the far-flung Norman castle-colonies to attract unpaid adventurers from as far south as the Mediterranean.[24] The temporary force of landless, wandering mercenaries and adventurers around a core of his own household was sufficient to break into relatively unencastellated England, where defence depended on the new King Harold's personal retinue and the unwieldy levy, offering little effective resistance to the latest techniques of colonizing warfare developed around the castle. England was not conquered by 'feudal' forces, but by a heterogenous assembly seeking loot and personal individuation in enfeoffment, both of which were dependent upon the duke's personal patronage.

The encastellating Norman colonization deployed castles in entirely new ways. Up to five hundred were built in England between 1066 and 1100, but the mode of conquest was not a strategic, integrated plan developed *a priori* and operationalized by a sovereign commander; William had hoped to negotiate an alliance through vassalage with English magnates and the ecclesiastical establishment.[25] When negotiations failed, he invoked feud to exercise the sanction of *werra*, laying waste to the land and sweeping away property and customary rights, to partition England among his followers and establish a circuit of castles within which they would be preoccupied by obligations subject to the administrative surveillance pioneered by the Norman ducal clerks. The expedition had been well-prepared, but the actual domination of England and the formation of a new regime only proceeded *ad hoc*, as an effect of applying available technologies of domination and government to contingent conditions. The 'strategy' of the new regime was an emergent, rather than an operationalized project. As Colin Gordon puts it, 'The concept [of strategy] only becomes pertinent as an instrument for historical decipherment at the point where the instrumentalization of the social terrain interacts with its formation by programmes and technologies of power.'[26]

The political principle and organizing technique of the new regime first appeared in the order of William's tactical deployment and government of his invasion force, the war-machine-without-a-state created by his liquidization of ducal assets. A prefabricated castle bailey transported across the channel with the invasion forces provided the vehicle through which William, encastled first at Pevensey, then Hastings, exercised authority over his assembled forces as over a personal, household domain, without the constraints of juridical legitimation. He thus forbade plunder, issued regular pay, and arranged markets to supply his forces, while laying waste to the surrounding land, so depriving the English king of the means to maintain a foraging army in the field and forcing him to join battle.[27] By simulating the order of the castle, William had effectively switched the relation of forces, so that Harold found himself as if an invader in his own land, without local access to the resources necessary to maintain his host in the field.

The offensive deployment of encastellation continued as William traversed England, spreading terror by his exaction of feud against the authorities that had confounded his original project of alliance. Castles were erected not according to a strategic plan, but at opportune sites throughout the land,[28] often within the course of a few days, their location determined by immediate tactical considerations unrelated to customary economic and political organization, thus transforming the spatial figuration of Anglo-Saxon England into an alien form that became the framework for a new kingship. Tactical contingency also enabled William to use the castle in a new way; rather than enfeoffing his vassals and adventurers, he entrusted castles, even to major barons, only where absolutely necessary. Where fiefs were created to supply castle-ward for smaller castles, they were secondary to, and outnumbered by, paid garrisons.[29] The order of household authority established at Hastings thus provided the model for Norman rule as military government.

Dispersed as garrisons among the royal castles, the occupying forces were subject to administration by itinerant officers of the *familia*, the constable, master-marshal and deputy-marshals, who together with the chancellor and the chamberlain comprised the *domus regis*, the body of government itself, with *magistratus familiae* (military household officers) in executive command of the castles and garrisons. William thus controlled the circuit of castles by retaining his adventurers and mercenaries as members of his household, translating the personal authority which had held the promissory order of plunder and enfeoffment in abeyance for invasion and conquest into a permanent order of military government by enabling him to subject organized forces of violence to administrative regulation that did not require particular agreements.

The *Leges Henrici Principi* detail William's construction of a codified disciplinary order for the *familia regis*, administered by special judges ('whom the common soldiers fear') with jurisdiction over the distinct domain constituted by the code.[30] Rape, murder, drunkenness and plunder were prohibited, and put the offender at the king's mercy for life and limb. The *familia* was also divided for the administration of this prerogative justice into disciplinary sub-units. This separate and administratively organized military jurisdiction, in which the king had absolute prerogative right over life and death, established a domain alienated from medieval political and legal thought. However, the chronicler, Orderic Vitalis, saw this divisional subjection to prerogative law as a source of legitimation by which the *familia* could be differentiated according to the medieval epistemic principles of similitude from a horde of *indisciplinati*, 'such as might serve under lords ignorant of the strictness of discipline of Roman warfare'.[31] The fetishized 'tactical superiority' of mounted, mailed knights and their imputed monopolization of legitimate violence are further refuted by the composition of the *familia regis*, which included large numbers of foot soldiers, unknighted mounted warriors, archers and engineers, elements essential to the medieval practice of warfare, in contrast to the symbolic function of the feudal array.

Feudal obligations did not operate within the *familia*, but were used to fund it through *scutage*, so the *familia regis* could be administered as a permanent household domain, supplemented in case of need by feudal levies and mercenaries. Mercenary service on the king's money and provisions was advantageous to many knights, whose landed fees were inadequate to support them at much more than a subsistence level,[32] as well as to the king, providing a flexible force that was not subject to the juridical constraints on feudal obligations. The *Constitutio Domus Regis* cites the conditions of service in office in the *familia* as stipendiary, with additional allowances in kind, and all *familia* service was, 'with compensation for loss of horse or equipment in service and entitlement to eat the king's bread'. Only supplementary forces in the Norman period appear to have been paid solely in money, but even then *familia* regulations provided the model for the terms of service, discipline and government by which all non-feudal supplements were incorporated, applying *en masse* to a thousand Flemish men-at-arms added to the *familia* in 1101 and 1110.[33] In addition to these formal conditions of service, the *familia* was also maintained as a moral order by the practice of largesse, with bonus payments, estates and offices as symbolic gifts, constituting a political space quite distinct from the feudal polity.

Rather than reading-off subjection and domination from social structure and juridical forms, the detailed analyses of historians working from 'archaeological' sources thus enable us to see how power was produced in the 'micro-circuits' of the *familia*, in the exercise of immediate domination in the household as discipline, producing an administration, and through the moral-political technology of the unreciprocable gift as a mode of government, constituting subjects of honour.

Capetian France – the castle, violence and 'disintegration'

In contrast to pre-Conquest England, the encastellation process rapidly reproduced its effect across almost all of the Capetian kingdom of France. Philippe Contamine usefully divides this process into three stages, each with a different dynamic,[34] unlike Elias' picture of progressive, centrifugal fragmentation. Between 888 and 920 AD, defensive ducal military commands deployed on the Carolingian model on the periphery of the kingdom independently exercised the authority previously delegated to them by kings. From 940 to 970 AD, counts usurped such authority at a more reduced territorial level, and from the end of the tenth century, even the counts were unable to hold their authority, as the military levy (the *ban*) was assumed by castellanies. Here, however, the technology of the castle intrudes upon the narrative of fragmentation. The kings of France, despite their central juridical power, were unable to maintain the sovereign division between time of peace and time of war, because the castle had transformed the practice of feud, which lay outside their sovereign jurisdiction, and in feud there was no peace, only truce.

It is from this point, as the original nadir of his 'civilizing process', that Norbert Elias maps out a connection between the spatial centralization of power and social integration.

> We see the following movement: first one castle stands against another, then territory against territory, then state against state, and appearing on the historical horizon today are the first signs of struggles for an integration of regions and masses of people on a still larger scale ... This may take centuries or millennia; however ... the growth of units of integration and rule is always at the same time an expression of structural changes in society, that is to say, in human relationships ... the 'civilizing' process, seen from the aspects of standards of conduct and drive control, is the same trend which, when seen from the point of view of human relationships, appears as the process of advancing integration, increased differentiation of social functions and interdependence, and the formation of ever-larger units of integration on whose fortunes and movements the individual depends, whether he knows it or not.[35]

In this schema, violence is conceptualized as absolute and essential. An essential body as the origin of drives forms one pole of an axis running from anomic anarchy to centralized sovereignty, along which social structures force power in history. Elias' sociology self-consciously seeks to transcend the division between 'the individual' and 'the social', and there are thus two directions for the historical process; either centrifugal, toward unconstrained affective violence, political disorganization and social disintegration, or centripetal, toward affect-constraint, a centralizing 'ruler-function' and social interdependence. This model is axiomatic, as well as axial; there is no question of other combinations, other directions. In the ninth and tenth centuries, Elias argues, social structures had 'disintegrated' to an 'extraordinary' extent, so that:

> Each small estate is under its own rule, a 'state' in itself, every small knight its independent lord and master ... there is not much

to constrain members of this ruling stratum to control their affects in any continuous way. This is a 'society' only in the broader sense of the word which refers to every possible form of human integration. It is not yet a 'society' in the narrower sense of a more continuous, relatively close and uniform integration of people with a greater constraint on violence, at least within its confines.[36]

Elias' schema, applied to early medieval Capetian France, raises the same issues as the historians' debate in *Past and Present*. Firstly, his essentialist conception of violence takes the clerically mediated sources to represent a 'real' level of violence, ignoring their discursively strategic dichotomization of 'violence' from 'force', which both colours and selects the material recounted in the chronicles. Secondly, his schema axiomatically identifies centralized authority (ultimately, the state) with order and an economy of violence, and decentralized authority with disorder and an absence of constraint upon drive affects. However, anthropological approaches to feud show that it was not comprised of an unrestrained discharge of affect, but consisted in the technical exercise of violent exaction in a customary economy of honour. Alternative contemporary sources also seem to show that emotional affect was a political technique in the order of feud, deployed strategically.[37] Furthermore, the pleasure of knights in acts of violence reported in medieval sources cannot be seen in isolation from the construction of knighthood in a code that imbued it with a sacral function, thus *producing* a joy in violence enacted as the sword of God righting injustices or 'rebaptizing' the land in blood.[38] Violence between knights was to become highly regulated from the twelfth century in the code of chivalry as an effect of the sacral valuation of knighthood, a mode of regulation which often appears in opposition to the royal centralization of power.

Abbé Suger chronicled the *Deeds of Louis the Fat* as a man of St Denis, the ecclesiastic ally of the Capetian royal dynasty.[39] His chronicle enables us to see the effect of the castle in an entirely different field to that of the Norman invasion of England. He describes how castles were used tactically in pursuit of feud, and illustrates how their technology changed this institution. In his account, castles are constructed rapidly and offensively as purely tactical devices to challenge other castles nearby, an account supported by archaeology, which reveals remains at an average density of one per ten square miles, but often much closer, up to the range of projectile weaponry. Many seem to have been only occupied temporarily and there are remains of far more than were inventoried for obligations.[40]

Abbé Suger recounts how Louis the Fat began to build territorial domination with no more than the forces of his own *demesne*. Elias ascribes the motivational force of this project to an 'acquisitive urge', implicitly invoking Hobbesian social theory by assuming, in the absence of overarching power, a ubiquitous and unrestrained competition for relatively scarce opportunities.[41] However, even early medieval kingship cannot be read-off from such a reductive conception of social agents any more than from putative functions of social structure or the juridical category of the sovereign. 'Louis the Fat' embodied not only the biological body of drive-affects and the formal concept of kingship, but also other elements. He had been crowned by the Pope, and thus his body, as the temporal body of the anointed king, was sacralized. He also embodied a lineage, which he had to perpetuate. His juridical authority was embodied in the castles held by the *ban*, and encastellation had produced an extra-juridical corporate body in his *familia*, a household that exercised its own will but was also under internal pressure from its members' desire for individuation in enfeoffment. Elias reduces both violence and social agents, so that the political and long-term historical struggles become simply a zero-sum game in which nothing is produced: 'if some of the contenders are victorious, their opportunities multiply; those of the vanquished decrease'.[42] Consistently, the same applies to bodily affects, which are not socially produced, but pre-existent and subject to progressive repression. However, the political modes of violence available to Louis had been transformed, firstly, by the castle, which transformed feud by its territorialization of domination, and, secondly, by the valuation of knighthood in socio-theological discourse, producing a new subjectivity.

Feud had never been under the control of the king, but was by definition outside the jurisdiction of the ancient *rex*, and had only been regulated by its legal recognition as the right of free men in the Salic law.[43] With the territorialization of domination effected by the castle's locality, *werra*, the violence of feud, became directed not merely at the person or even the household of the offending party, but at the territory and resources of the castellany. There was no longer any necessity to seek out the kin of the offender to exact the sanction of violence upon what was now a body corporate. The chronicles provide a litany of mutilation and outrages, but these were executed as quite precise, functional exactions and systematically inflicted sufferings against the chattels of an enemy. Feud did not unleash violence from affect-control or sovereign order, but produced it, as deliberate sanction. Feud thus became a form of war with its own techniques, quite distinct from the *bellum* of the sovereign. *Werra*, not *bellum*, was the activity for which household warriors and soldiers were retained.

The Gregorian project of the Peace of God movement could not abolish feud, since removing the right of *werra* from the *miles* would disarm them. Instead, it sought to regulate knightly violence by encoding it within the functional schema of its tripartite social orders (a society under God comprised of those who prayed, those who fought and those who laboured), in which the knights were ascribed a monopoly of the exercise of violence as the sword of God to protect the other two orders, and to right injustices, a riding clause which covered and affirmed the right of feud in order to subject it to clerically mediated regulation.[44]

Encastellation transformed feud to produce a new mode of violence, while the socio-theological order invested the knight's violence with a sacral value. From this contextualization, we can develop an explanation of the pleasure in violence which appears in the medieval chronicles without invoking an essentialist violence of bodily affect. Abbé Suger's account of the king of France's engagement in war enables us to see how pleasure in violence was produced by the sacral or moral investment of value in the profession of violence;

> ... they piously slaughtered the impious, mutilated the limbs of some, disembowelled others with great pleasure and piled even greater cruelty on them. No one should doubt that the hand of God sped so swift a revenge when both the living and the dead were thrown through the windows.[45]

While this deliberate violence was the province of the sacrally invested knight, the routine technical slaughter and destruction of *werra* was undertaken by the profane soldiery of castellar incorporation. Suger recounts how even such low-born men, assembling themselves into 'communes' without a lord, might raise up castles in liberty from juridical power, beyond the relics of legitimation; but as one of Louis' counsellors tells him, 'Hell is the only place they are fit to be.'[46] *These* bodies were beyond the limits of all community and thus suffered the same fate as an insurgent castle, to be obliterated from landscape and memory. Suger tells how one such man was hung up next to a dog, which bit at his face when it was beaten, inflicting upon him an 'eternal death'.[47]

Suger's chronicle illustrates how encastellation produced not singular, but plural modalities of organized violence, each with its own economy, subjectivity and instrumentality, engaged in a highly charged struggle with one another that was conducted on a different plane to the social and political structures traced by mainstream sociology. In Georges Duby's analysis of the Battle of Bouvines, these modes of violence are revealed as the elements comprising a highly complex 'feudal' host.

Notes

1. J. Bradbury, *The Medieval Siege* (Woodbridge: Boydell Press, 1992), p. 49.
2. R. Bartlett, *The Making of Europe: Conquest, Colonization and Cultural Change, 950–1350* (Penguin: London, 1993), pp. 65–6; P. Contamine, *War in the Middle Ages*, trans. M. Jones (Oxford: Blackwell, 1984), p. 28.
3. J. Keegan, *A History of Warfare* (London: Pimlico, 1993), p. 150.
4. G. Duby, *Legend of Bouvines: War, Religion and Culture in the Middle Ages*, trans. C. Tihanyi (Cambridge: Polity Press, 1991), p. 71.
5. T. Reuter, 'The End of Carolingian Military Expansion', in P. Goodwin and R. Collins, *Charlemagne's Heir: New Perspectives on the Reign of Louis the Pious* (Oxford: Clarendon Press, 1997), p. 191.
6. Contamine, *War in the Middle Ages*, p. 46.
7. G. Duby, *France in the Middle Ages, 987–1460: From Hugh Capet to Joan of Arc*, trans. J. Vale (Oxford: Blackwell, 1991), p. 59.
8. Quoted in Bartlett, *Making of Europe*, p. 68.
9. J. Le Goff, *Medieval Civilization, 400–1500*, trans. C. Barrow (Oxford: Blackwell, 1988).
10. B. Geremek, 'The Marginal Man', in J. Le Goff, (ed.), *The Medieval World*, trans. L. G. Cochrane (London: Collins & Brown, 1990).
11. Le Goff, *Medieval Civilization*, pp. 131–4.
12. Bartlett, *Making of Europe*, p. 68.
13. H. W. Goetz, *Life in the Middle Ages from the Seventh to the Thirteenth Century* (Notre Dame, IN: University of Notre Dame Press, 1993), p. 169.
14. Le Goff, *Medieval Civilization*, pp. 135–7.
15. J-C. Martin, 'Cartography of the Year 1000: Variations on *A Thousand Plateaus*' in C. V. Boundas and D. Olkowski, *Gilles Deleuze and the Theatre of Philosophy* (London: Routledge, 1994); Geremek, 'The Marginal Man'.
16. Bartlett, *Making of Europe*, p. 50.
17. Ibid., p. 45.
18. Duby, *France in the Middle Ages*, pp. 60–1.
19. S. Morillo, *Warfare under the Anglo-Norman Kings, 1066–1135* (Woodbridge: Boydell Press, 1994), p. 71.
20. Duby, *France in the Middle Ages*, p. 62.
21. Bartlett, *Making of Europe*, p. 51.
22. J. H. Baldwin, *The Government of Philip Augustus: Foundations of French Royal Power in the Middle Ages* (Berkeley, CA: University of California Press, 1986) p. 287.
23. Contamine, *War in the Middle Ages*, p. 38.
24. Ibid., pp. 52–4.
25. Ibid., p. 52.
26. C. Gordon, 'Afterword', in M. Foucault, *Power/Knowledge*, ed. C. Gordon (Hemel Hempstead: Harvester Press, 1980), p. 252.
27. Morillo, *Warfare Under Anglo-Norman Kings*, p. 126.
28. '*Castella opportuna per loca stabilivit*', Orderic Vitalis, quoted in ibid., p. 87.
29. Ibid., pp. 75–6.
30. '... as he restrained the people with arms, so he restrained the army with laws'. William of Poitiers, *Histoire de Guillaime le Conquerant*, quoted in ibid. p. 134.
31. Orderic Vitalis, quoted in ibid., p. 135.
32. S. Harvey, 'The Knight and the Knight's Fee in England', *Past and Present*, 49

(1970), p. 15.
33. Morillo, *Warfare Under Anglo-Norman Kings*, pp. 62–5.
34. Contamine, *War in the Middle Ages*, p. 43.
35. N. Elias, *The Civilizing Process: The History of Manners and State Formation and Civilisation,* trans. E. Jephcott (Oxford: Blackwell, 1994), p. 332.
36. Ibid., p. 333.
37. S. D. White, 'The Politics of Anger', in B. H. Rosenwein (ed.), *Anger's Past: The Social Uses of an Emotion in the Middle Ages* (Ithaca, NY: Cornell University Press, 1998).
38. Abbé Suger, *Deeds of Louis the Fat,* eds and trans. R. Cusimano and J. Moorehead (Washington, DC: Catholic University of America Press, 1992), p. 142.
39. Duby, *Legend of Bouvines*, p. 69.
40. Duby, *France in the Middle Ages*, pp. 57–9.
41. Elias, *The Civilizing Process*, p. 347.
42. Ibid., p. 347.
43. J. M. Wallace-Hadrill, *The Long-Haired Kings and Other Studies in Frankish History* (London: Methuen, 1962).
44. G. Duby, *Chivalrous Society,* trans. C. Postan (London: Edward Arnold, 1977) pp. 165–70.
45. Suger, *Deeds of Louis the Fat*, p. 80.
46. Ibid., p. 108.
47. Ibid., p. 141.

7

Three Orders of Violence

The orders of battle

Encastellation had produced plural forms in which violence was organized, elements comprising a complex medieval host when brought together in the spectacle of battle, which was the prerogative of kings to end war in trial by combat. Though the host was assembled as a body corporate, Duby's analysis reveals three distinct elements, each with its own conditions, economies, subjectivities and trajectories, fighting what amount to three different battles. There could be no mode of knowledge or singular mode of domination for such heterogenous hosts, and strategic command was thus effectively limited to the summons to array itself. Duby identifies the forces comprising the opposed hosts, arrayed as corporate bodies of Philip Augustus, king of France and Otto of Brunswick (behind whom stood the figure of John Plantagenet, king of England), each composed of

> ... actors ... caught in an intertwined tangle of multiple loyalties which weave between them the threads of a very tight-knit coherence ... family ties of filiation or affinity ... the complementary ties of vassalic homage ... the long-standing friendship initiated in childhood, during the years of apprenticeship at the court of a common lord ... territorial ties, the feeling of belonging to the same region which they need to defend together ... which assemble knights and esquires around the man who bears the comtal title or who controls the main fortress of the region and which also motivate comradeship within communal troops ...[1]

This paragraph provides us with a sophisticated picture of the heterogenous modes of 'integration' which produced the corporate host: ordered by kinship, chivalry, vassalage, law, friendship, community, and charter, but even this list neglects the camp followers, carters, servants, smiths, merchants, etc. servicing the arrayed host in the background. This is not a picture of court society, but of a battle, the other side of the sovereign prerogative of juridical power, revealing medieval society to us through the only site where its lines converge.

The moralized symmetry of the observations of the battle orders enables Duby to explore the relations between the component forces of the host through the chroniclers' critical descriptions of 'the other side', which reveal these ties as largely illusory; 'multiple solidarities hold each of the regional chivalries, cavalry corps [household knights], communal bands and mercenary companies firmly together. But there are no real ties *between* these solid granules'.[2]

The different articulations by which this host is assembled thus maintain their differentiation within the formal unity of the host and the space of battle, so at least three battles are fought between corresponding elements on either side. Even the tactics are not complementary (and if they were it would be a matter of coincidence, since there is no grand strategist). Using all the techniques at their disposal, Philip Augustus and Otto have assembled heterogenous forces, but while they have their battle to fight (the trial by combat), each element also has its own. The unitary order of battle array is only a temporary suspension of the different times and vectors of these elements, since the feudal levy's transcendence of their social differentiation cannot be maintained for any protracted time, but operates only to call the spectacle of array into appearance. It is not and cannot become indefinite time, like that of war. The different elements will not even wait for the battle to be over to resume their different trajectories. They are not integrated, but only arrayed alongside each other, and as soon as battle is engaged they will each fight their own struggle, with their own techniques, for their own ends. Strategy is thus restricted to the process of seeking battle, to belligerence, which must be joined in the limited time of *proelium* (the condition of impending battle).[3]

Battle royal

The sign of battle under which the multifarious forces are assembled does not signify war, but the remedy for war. Battle was 'a procedure of peace',[4] trial by ordeal of combat, while war, *werra*, was feud, the argument and not the settlement, which consisted either in a decision to agree or the result of battle.

> Opening on to the sacred, the battle is ordered into liturgy. Like the ordeal, the judicial duel, it requires its 'field' ... Champions confront each other on a campus; one of them must perish, run away in shame, or beg for mercy.[5]

Its time is ritually judicial; its order sacred, trinitarian, determining the deployment of the host in three formations on the field (the van, the rear and the main body). The object of battle, 'consists entirely in trying to enable the two champions to approach the other, to strike each other'. Its technique envelops each champion in a tight formation of his own followers, the *conroi*, 'each of the two adversaries uses hands other than his own, those of the knights of his house'.[6] Blows are not practically exchanged between kings, or even between kings and the servants of kings (it is deemed sacrilegious to strike an anointed, crowned head), but are rather exchanged between households, the corporate bodies of the contending kings.

> It is his knights, comrades of his own house, his team, this unit which acts as his own person, which he sends forth. The duel is then engaged according to the rules, not between two individuals but between two 'banners', two *conrois*, two bodies welded by a collective task.[7]

These were the forces of the king himself, in his household *familia*, not the king as a feudal monarch.

Bellum simulacrum

In the same historical moment and location, there also occurs a tourney, with its own space and time: again, not war, but a simulacrum of fighting which does not have death as its object. The tourney was defined by a contemporary as 'devoid of any intention of hatred, but for the sole exercise and the display of forces of the body'.[8]

Duby himself defines the tourney in functionalist terms; it serves to train the knights of chivalry in the arms and techniques necessary for their societal function of defence of the socio-theological order and is assumed to serve an individual psychological function as a cathartic outlet for the aggression produced in the body by knightly training and constrained by the order which sacralizes their arms. However, the Church consistently opposed the tourney, so the precise point at which ideology and structural requirements are supposed to come together turns out to be a moment of 'contradiction'. Another explanation could refer to the ruler-function, as if the practice of tourney ensured that trained knights were ready for the communal defence entrusted to the king, and thus functioned as an epiphenomenon of this sovereign mediation of societal requirements. However, its practice was not confined to battle and disrupted the ruler-function of peace-keeping,

121

readily spilling over from simulation into real warfare between contending knightly teams.[9]

The Battle of Bouvines provides a test case for such theorizations, since the military functions of the knights who engaged in the rounds of tourney would have manifested themselves here, in service to the king against an opponent who, if victorious, might vent his displeasure against the towns and villages as part of the corporate body of his enemy. The field of battle would have operationalized any latent social functions of its component elements. However, the chroniclers' descriptions show something entirely different. The chivalrous knights assembled do not participate in the king's combat. Their only function in the host was to provide a spectacular array of arms, indicated by the signs they bear, which might have induced the opponent to capitulate without fighting. The 'function' of knighthood is thus merely symbolic, not instrumental. In this case, the opponent does not capitulate and battle is joined, but what the knights do next fully dispels modern functionalist myths about knighthood.

The knights of chivalry do not join the *conroi* or provide it with tactical support. Their order of battle, and their symbolic function, is redundant as soon as the duel is joined by the corporate households of the two protagonists. At once, the knights are free to take up their own trajectory: to play the field of tourney. Even the exception shows this clearly. At Bouvines, Duby tells us, reading from the chronicles, a knight of the holy orders (experienced in the fighting of the Crusades, where the knightly function was not differentiated from the death-struggle) begins the battle by sending 200 sergeants, mere castle-guard men-at-arms, in charge against the Flemish chevaliers, who are scandalized into fury, since they had come to joust, not to fight against worthless opponents.[10] Their furious response is thus invoked by the affront to their own honour, not by allegiance to their king.

Such emotive investments in identity provide us with another way to look at the practice of tourney, as a means of social differentiation and even individuation. It had its own forms and its own economy, circulating symbolic bodies, values, and forces. It was a spectacular, a team enterprise to be undertaken in the open field drenched with light to reveal the actors in the splendour of their arms. The teams were comprised not of kin groups, but of voluntary associations between young men, for whom the heraldic devices of lineage were individualized, their chevrons identifying mostly minor, younger and bastard sons excluded from the patrimony by primogeniture. Such knights wandered the land in small or larger groups, coalesced around those funded by their patrimony to keep them away from the family estate once they could no longer be held as a squire-apprentice at the castle of another lord, seeking feuds, quarrels, injustices to right, in the quest for symbolic status.[11] Array for battle offered them an opportunity to capture a highly valued adversary for ransom by unhorsing him in the skilled 'ballet of lance-fencing'. The object of tourney was not killing, since the chivalric code's sacral valuation of knighthood translated into a market economy in ransoms of captured adversaries, the tournament functioning as an 'instrument of redistribution' within chivalrous society.[12] In the late twelfth century, knights increasingly affected a disdain for money and the economy of honour became more pronounced. This was not so much in response to externally imposed regulation, but to differentiate themselves from the mercenaries appearing everywhere, whose violence was not at all symbolic.

Duby suggests that the affect-structure of knightly aggression was not a drive overproduced in the body by training in violence, but was rather produced as a spark, a short-circuit at the terminus of lineage identity. Over the twelfth century, the nobility adopted primogenitural inheritance to ensure undivided transmission of the patrimony. Disinherited younger and bastard sons were thus projected into a liminal space, an indefinitely prolonged time of 'wandering the earth' in the tourneying bands of *juventes*. The continual refrain in medieval discourses on counsel to be wary of the advice of young men can thus be explained by their tendency to antagonism with their elders and their unwillingness to wait upon time. When confronted with the host which Philip has raised by feudal levy of his settled knights, the youth in Otto's councils of war, 'screamed that they should not wait for the morrow, but attack the army of old men right away', even though it meant joining battle on a day of truce, a Sunday.[13]

The practice of tourney often appears negatively in medieval records, condemned by the Church and presented as a major problem for secular authorities and a source of insecurity for commerce and property.[14] The tourneying circuit was a route of flight from such sources of social determination, a social space in which the culture of romance developed,[15] as those rejected by primogenitural inheritance could assert them*selves* independently of lineage, in the values, economy and techniques of the circuit, 'in freedom, in profanity and under threat of Church reprisals ... prowess in the tournament became the basis of freedom and self-assurance. Prowess liberated the individual from the real-life, necessary, constraining, at times suffocating hold of lineage and of friendship.'[16]

Even elder sons awaited inheritance of their patrimony on the circuit of tourney and served an apprenticeship in the culture of chivalry, and the autonomy that tourney gave to knighthood to realize an identity for itself independently of societal functions thus frustrated the Church's socio-theological construction of the order of arms. The very sacral valuation which the Church placed on the knight to channel his violence as the sword of God precluded precisely the defence function it was intended to effect, since the valued knights preferred to ransom rather than kill each other.

War

Even if the code of chivalry and the circuits of the tourney still produced a symbolic function, English kings at least had already found other ways to procure symbolic power: at Brémule, Henry I failed to capture his adversary, Louis VI, but was able to buy a banner seized by a foot soldier, purchasing for twenty marks 'a sign of the victory God had given him'. The source of his purchase indicates a third struggle, which was as distinct from royal combat and the tourney as they were from each other. Duby, like many others, relates the emergence of mercenary soldiers to money, which 'became the lifeblood of war'.[17] The term 'mercenary' already conflates soldiers and knights, but the foot soldiers traversed a different world again to those of the king's household or the tourney. In terms of the theological and chivalric orders of society, the common soldier serving for pay was by definition transgressive, outside the orders of society.

Medieval mercenary foot soldiers differed from the knights of chivalry in one crucial respect: they were useful instruments.[18] However, their mass invoked quite peculiar problematics for medieval government, which had no means for subjection to discipline, and no techniques by which to exercise it in mass bodies. Their very instrumentality for warfare consisted in their *externality* to the medieval social and political orders, and so placed them beyond any right of command or obligation. In a spatial sense, they represented the return of violence to the centre from which it was extruded; they came from the frontiers of encastellated 'civilization', such as the Welsh and the Scottish Borders, and from the surplus populations of the overcrowded commercial towns to which displaced peasants fled in search of a living.[19] The problem was not in raising such forces; they came of their own accord, propelled by displacement to the source of money, and also, perhaps more importantly, by the prospect of sharing in the *right to take*, the prerogative of *prise* which was invoked when war was undertaken by one sovereign lord against another.[20] Their economic order cannot be separated out from their tactical instrumentality, their technical specialism of laying waste, which was employed in war to inflict damage upon the corporate body of the feudal adversary embedded in the land and its resources (population, villages, farms, equipment, crops and castles). The exhaustion of either money or the adversary's resources thus invoked the greater problem of how mass forces could be dispersed after the acts of war.

However, their military function was not merely as mouths which hungrily ate up the land. Even contemporary chroniclers recounted that, 'they are not inferior to the nobles in the science and the virtue of combat',[21] thus dispelling the modern projection of a knightly monopoly of effective violence. The science of war was shared by these men who knew the stratagems of siege, had their own technique of fighting, their own weaponry, and also their own economy of violence. At Bouvines there were such men on both sides, providing the bodies killing and being killed on the battlefield, for killing was their art. For their paymasters, they could provide a wall of steel pike as a refuge from the *melée*. Their prize in battle lay not in the ransom of captured knights, or in the prospect of knighthood (as it did for the sergeants and squires), but in the enemy baggage train. As well as knowing the secrets of the castle, they also knew the secrets of armour, and killed knights who fell among them with their quick knives, finding the points at which the plates joined in the groin, or stabbing through the visor.[22] No one would ransom a knight to such men without honour, so they expertly extinguished the life within the iron carapace. Their own lives were of little accord to the other participants, and they themselves had learnt to be economical with death. If captured, they might be killed out of hand, like the 700 mercenary foot soldiers slaughtered by Philip after the battle of Bouvines as their reward for providing a pike-wall for a French noble fighting with Otto. There was no ransom to be paid for them, and their presence was considered pestilential.[23]

They traversed another space, neither that of community, nor of castle or court, but the route, the road which they lived upon when not in employment, and this motivity gave them a peculiar relation to settled medieval society. Duby and others anachronistically refer to them as 'professionals', but it would be better to think of them as embodying war and carrying it within them everywhere. War was not something external to them, in which they engaged, but constituted their reality, their way of life. For them, *all* resources were there for the taking. Beyond the regular penitential or mercantile itineraries that provided its terminals, the open road was the space of war, of bodily displacement, of continual transition, transgressing territoriality. If the castle territorialized war, the itinerant soldiers' companies deterritorialized it. And since they embodied war, it appeared that war could be eliminated by eliminating them. Thus they were subject to summary death by the orders of society, by knights who searched them out in their bands and by peasants who ambushed them on the outskirts of the villages, led by clerics. In the eleventh century, they reached the mass proportions of the 10,000 slaughtered by knights of the Peace of God at Dun-le-Roi, where several routes converged.[24]

Contamine explains the appearance of knightly mercenaries as a supply response to the twelfth-century decline of the feudal levy,[25] while Duby explains the increase in mercenary foot soldiers as an effect of monetarization on kingship and warfare. However, their explanations return us to the theoretical assumption that force is by definition instrumental to an original sovereign power constrained or enabled by the accumulation of resources, inflating Weber's analytical definition of the modern state into an axiom for general theory. The resource of money is thus assumed to provide not only forces, but the condition of obedience as well, while strategy originates with a given power. This takes us to one of the key problematics of this book, that the instrumentality of violence (and the condition of obedience) is not given in an abstract analytical category of 'military power', but is effected in particular techniques which constitute the field of strategy.

Duby's analysis of the field of Bouvines shows that the diffusion of the order of battle into its component elements was not a function of the form of sovereign power (in this case, specifically, not an effect of the corporate embodiment of kingship, which was restricted to the *conroi*). Military commentators argue that the elements assembled each fought in their own way because they were tactically specialized, assuming a rational and functional 'division of labour' in violence (which is itself undifferentiated, given in its function for a sovereign object), with each fighting separately because the resources to co-ordinate them were underdeveloped. It thus posits command as an immanent quality of force itself, for which the means of realization have yet to develop along a path leading in a unilinear progression to the standing, professional, disciplined army of modernity, with its apparently automatic obedience. More detailed sociological study, however, reveals quite distinct micro-techniques and structures of subjectivity in the 'mercenary' condition.

The order of incorporation: The familia regis

In battle, the *conroi* of the king was not formed by his chief vassals, who were drawn up with their retinues on the wings of the array, but by the royal household, which appears increasingly important in recent medieval historiography. When the *familia regis* of the English kings was first identified for modern scholarship in the household documentation of Edward I (1272–1307), within the old historiographical framework of a militarily functional feudalism, its appearance was assumed to indicate the thirteenth-century eclipse of the feudal levy by wage payments.[26] However, subsequent historical research has shown that the *familia* played an important part in the regimes of English kings right back to the Norman Conquest.[27] The relative anonymity of the *familia* often renders it invisible in non-administrative historical documentation, since medieval chroniclers recorded events in terms of chivalry and lineage, so that deeds of the *familia* are thus not recognizable as such, but are encoded under the noble names of its officers or in the name of the king. But the form of the *familia*, and even its particular conditions of service, were apparently well known to medieval military society from the time of William I, who drew his forces from across Europe, while Henry I was able competitively to advertise through the network of kin and vassalage for men of ability 'wishing to make a start in life'.[28] However, the historical-sociological significance of the *familia* lies not only in its institutional organization, but also in its composition and its particular forms of subjectification, the condition of obedience which produced the bodies and forces that shaped royal strategies.

The *familia regis* provides a continuity between the forces of the Angevin kings and those of the Hundred Years' War. The governmental technology of Henry I already had the capacity to incorporate large numbers of men whose service was given in treaty, but their obedience was secured by admitting them temporarily to the *familia* in which they would be maintained in body and compensated for any loss of horses in war. Treaties did not specify the wages for service, suggesting that wage levels were already 'usual' by the beginning of the twelfth century and that foreign knights, 'were expected to be familiar with the customary terms of service in the military household of the kings of England'.[29] The terms of *familia* service contrast with the employment of mercenaries proper, who were hired in large numbers for a limited period for simple wages, but without the king's bread,[30] though this contrast maps onto neither the order of socio-theology or status differentiation, since noble knights might serve as mercenaries, and commoners as men-at-arms in the *familia*, where nobles were retained alongside those of more 'modest families', 'almost landless' knights, and even archers and vavasours, differentiated only as tactical categories in the administrative documentation.[31]

The *familia* provided the mass force for the Norman system of military government through the administration of the *Constitutio Domus Regis* and a circuit of royal castles, supplemented by castle-guard.[32] The development of castellar technology[33] enabled the *familia* to be deployed distantly in castle garrisons as an instrument of the king independent of his individual bodily presence, but also to be assembled in the field for local campaigns. Chibnall estimates that the host of *familia* that fought at Bourgthéroulde (1124) was composed entirely of such garrisons, 'probably a hundred to each castle', including mounted archers.[34] Unlike the levy and array, this assemblage was not delimited in time and could be deployed distantly and indefinitely, a permanent field force autonomous of its social and political environment that could be circulated between castle depots supplying provision and rearmament. The vulnerable countryside traversed by the circuit could be laid waste with impunity, since its castles could be restocked independently of local resources.[35] Autonomous and interlinked, the castle circuit also constituted an independent jurisdiction in which new techniques of discipline, administration and surveillance developed.

The different subjectivity of the men of the *familia* from those of the horizontal network of vassalage is clearly marked in the speeches which Orderic Vitalis attributes to the rebels at Bourgthéroulde, who identified themselves as 'the flower of chivalry' and scorned the *familia* as '*gregarii et pagenses*'. The *familia regis* comprised a force in the field led that day by an ignoble man-at-arms, containing mounted archers and administratively indifferent to social status distinctions. Orderic has Odo of Borleng, the *familia* marshal, rally them with this axiom:

> If we stand by, trembling ... how shall we ever dare to enter the king's presence? We shall forfeit both our wages and our honour ... and we shall never again be entitled to eat the king's bread.[36]

This speech positively expresses a different order of men *against* the feudal and theological orders by which medieval society is usually typified, indicating that an entirely different regime is in operation here, which we can begin to analyze sociologically.

Commoners, who comprised at least part of the force at Bourgthéroulde to which Odo's speech is addressed, did not possess the right to face the king, and were required to bow their heads before him or prostrate themselves in obeisance at his feet, but Odo's speech suggests that this right was invested in the *familia* regardless of status. Furthermore, his order to fight on foot suggests that this common mode of resistance was positively revalued in its techniques in an alliance with personalized kings. The incorporate identity of the *familia* is crucial, since it does not mean that each man was elevated to noble status or its equivalent, or that they were individually endowed with the capacity to face the king. Rather, the *familia* acted as an extension of the body of the king, not representing his authority, but incorporating his person in their deployment in garrisons and in the field. They faced the king not as equals, but as his incorporate body. In terms of Kantorowicz's anatomy of the two bodies of the king in medieval political theology,[37] the *familia regis* appears not as an instrument of the political ruler-function of kingship (which consisted in the sacralized office of the king, a transpersonal, 'public' institution which 'never died'[38]), but as an instrument, or even an organ of his 'private' person.

We can also begin to explicate the mechanisms and effects of the political technology by which the *familia regis* was ordered and governed, by attending to its differentiation from those who served for economic or political advancement. The king's wages and entitlement to eat his bread are presented by Orderic as an honorific, a symbolic gift by which the giver bestows recognition of honour upon the recipient, rather than as an exchange for services. We are dealing here with an economy which must be understood primarily in terms of its moral rather than material values. Many of the men-at-arms of the *familia* were of noble lineage or enfeoffed, and thus not economically dependent upon wages and sustenance at the king's table. From the Norman regime through to that of Edward I, 'substantial but not sensational' fees of retainer were paid annually and wages carefully calculated to the exact number of days service on deployment outside the household and its castled extensions. Grants of land were made only occasionally, and then at the king's pleasure and only for life, though the close surveillance of routine expenses maximized the moral value of such extraordinary largesse.[39] In status terms, *familia* service in itself did not endow the wider recognition ascribed to enfeoffment or knighthood. In political terms, *familia* membership simply did not count: their appearance in the records is thus largely anonymous (indicated only by minor names, not surnames) and socially undifferentiated, sometimes even indistinguishable from *servientes*, archers, pages and others. Neither social nor material rewards, then, seem to explain why the men of the *familia regis* would be prepared to die as an instrument of the king's person; but more than social identity, more than life itself, was at stake here.

Transgressions against the extra-legal regulations of the *familia regis* placed the offender at the mercy of the king. The public law of the realm which was otherwise vested in transpersonal kingship had no jurisdiction in this personal domain, though this does not mean that the king's authority here was absolute; Duby's description of the castellan's dependence upon his retinue also applies to the relations of king and *familia*, whose interests lay in the fate of the royal household and the king himself. It would thus be inaccurate to say that their fate was in his hands, but we could say that their hands were his hands and that his fate was theirs. There is an identity rather than a transaction here, and in order to see how this identity is produced, we need to abandon the concept of social exchange altogether, a task which has been taken up in the radical philosophy of Deleuze and Guattari.[40]

The honour of the *familia* was not given in social codes, but only invested by the king's recognition in the gift of his table and his wages. The king had literally invested himself, rather than his authority, in the bodies of the *familia regis*. These men were thus already *indebted* in the sense that Nietzsche argues constitutes the source of all moral value.[41] Deleuze and Guattari point out that such indebtedness is embodied: 'Far from being an appearance assumed by exchange, debt is the immediate effect or the direct means of the territorial and corporeal inscription process. Debt is the result of inscription.'[42] They were literally written into the household, which was the extension of the king's personal, corporate body. The *familia regis* was thus one of the places in the 'recovery' of literate culture where men's bodies were first inscribed in a moral economy by clerks, in the record of wages they were given and bread they ate not as a contractual exchange in which they retained their independence, but as a gift, a *largesse* outside the law which placed them beyond all other recognition. Just as the Roman citizen was indebted in his citizenship to the city's incorporation of Romulus, who inscribed the earth, so the men of the *familia* were indebted in their bodies to the king. However, there is a subtle difference: the *familia* were totally dependent in the king's household upon his recognition of their honour, while the Roman citizen-soldier was dependent upon both the city and the legion for his political identity. The *familia* thus had no identity of their own, but were incorporated in the king. The debt of the *familia* was one in which they were honoured as dependants, and hence was irredeemable because its embodiment was inscribed in their incorporation.

Incorporation in the *familia* further substituted its extra-feudal identity for the desire for lineage reproduction. In his discussion of the *gregarii* of the castle, Duby remarked how these incorporate bodies, the social product of the castle-machine, were identified with the lord and he with them, and the *familia regis* was a similar assemblage. The sense of honour, the value which motivates Odo and the men for whom he speaks, is given only in their identity in the king as he is incorporated in the *familia regis*. They do not contract an honorific equivalent of exchange with the king, to whom they have nothing to offer but themselves. Rather, their honour as household warriors consists entirely in their identity in the *familia*. They will fight to the death not for the king, but as the extensive embodiment of the king. Their

130

identity embodies the *familia* rather than being something invested in it. Producing such bodies without interiority, unindividuated, the *familia regis* cannot really be described as a regime of subjectification. Nonetheless, it provides a genealogy of the governmental technology of the symbolic gift and personal identification throughout a medieval era in which these forms of domination are usually assumed to have been supplanted by juridical relations of land-tenure.[43] As the extensive embodiment of the king's person, rather than of a delegated ruler-function, the men of the *familia* did not perform an office, but 'did his will', as Edward I wrote of Otto of Grandson.[44]

The order of exclusion

Clear distinctions can thus be drawn between the *familia* of the Anglo-Norman kings' households and 'ordinary mercenaries'.[45] The concept of the mercenary invests identity in a contractual relationship which is anachronistic to the High Middle Ages. Nevertheless, itinerant bands for hire reached huge proportions in medieval Europe, periodized by Philippe Contamine into three waves: at the turn of the twelfth and thirteenth centuries as *routiers*, around 1375–1400 as the Free Companies, and after the treaty of Arras in 1435 as *écorcheurs*.[46] In constructing a sociology of these bands in medieval terms (rather than reading-off their social formation from structures of systems or 'long-term' historical processes), it is necessary to use sources that are already suffused with the canonical disapprobation of the Church, reports collected, written and often recycled verbatim by clerks invested in the hierocratic establishment.

The sources consistently indicate their heterogeneity and social and spatial marginality, which is more significant in medieval terms than the imposition of modern criteria. They are identified collectively in the chronicles by markers which are simple variants on their alien-nation (Brabançons, Aragonese, Navarrese, English); by their itinerancy (*routiers*); by their sacrilegious transgression (*ruptarii*); by the distinction of their dress (coterells or *cotereaux*); by stigmatized trades (*écorcheurs*); or in Vegetian terminology for their tactical function as a 'reserve' or supplementary force (*Triaverdiri*).[47] Contamine notes the problematic, uncertain etymology of the terms by which the bands were known, often word-play that constructs moral associations through negatively charged neologisms which themselves transgress the rules of language and the distinctions of languages; '*ruptores, sive raptores*' (Jacques de Vitry); the semblance of the word *route* to *ruttae*; *cotereaux* (appearing in the twelfth century), and its associations with *cultellus* (knife), *cottar* (peasant), *coterie* (sect) and *coterel* (a short chain-mail coat).[48] This transgressive order of similitude represents their marginality quite literally as an inherent affront to the moral order of the world.

The modern concept of 'deviance' has been exhausted by sociology with the realization that it is constituted in the very code from which it deviates, i.e. deviance is the necessary corollary of a normative code, and similarly, the figure of the band represents a 'deviance' which only appears as 'nomadic' movement against the background of a 'settled' society, as illegitimacy or violence against a normative social or political order, and as marginality against the integer of community. In each case, however, their 'pathology' is a necessary condition of the norm. Insofar as similar normative categories constitute the object of modern sociology, for example, in its moralization of 'social integration' and indeed in any holistic conception of 'society', it remains incapable of theorizing difference (producing only pathologies) and is unable to break from cyclical repetition of the very normativity it set out to escape (either producing enmity, or anomie).

Philippe Contamine reminds his readers that the history of the *routiers* cannot be reduced to an opposition between 'the forces of anarchy and the state'. The *routiers* played a major part in the formation of medieval moral order, community and polity, a role which offers considerable sociological insight into the process of social formation and exclusion. The medieval term, *exsilium*, one of the key concepts of medieval marginality, already conflates the spatial with the social. Just as Marx's 'alienation' and Durkheim's 'anomie' posit an essentialist integrity, so *exsilium* presupposes that: 'The natural condition was to live where one was born, where the tombs of one's ancestors provided continuity; it meant living within the context of a community of neighbours united by ties of kinship and proximity.' The 'Brownian motion' of late antiquity thus did not disappear, but became identical with the opprobrium of society. However, 'only those who made being continually "on the move" their way of life, who fled organized social life, or who had been excluded from the community felt the full effect of the processes of marginalization'.[49]

This tendency in the formation process of a *moral* order of settled society also mapped on to a clerical dichotomization of violence which confounds attempts to construct objective comparisons because it comprises the historical record. For instance, Strickland attempts to compare the violence of twelfth-century knights to that of *routiers* and Scots raiders in order to establish an objective index of atrocity in the practice of warfare against which to evaluate the degree of discrepancy between the 'real' behaviour of the knightly order and its 'ideology of chivalry'. Such an index would provide some measure of the extent to which the 'civilizing process' constrained the affectual violence of knights by their code and *habitus*. However, this attempt to construct an objective norm entirely misses the point that the terms 'knight' and '*routier*' did not merely mark differences of social status, but were *morally invested categorical oppositions*. These moralized social differentiations had real effects as 'social facts', rendering the recorded behaviour of *routiers* and knights categorically distinct and thus incomparable, encoded in entirely different terms and values. Strickland's exercise thus undoes the very construction of the violence it seeks to investigate, and we can perhaps learn more from the way these moral investments *effected* violence. Rather than trying to reduce the clerical discourse of condemnation to an objective record of comparable equivalences, we should perhaps seek to explore the way these categories were constituted and how this produced both the appearance of and the imperatives to violence.

The Scots were bestialized by the chroniclers in part at least because they contravened Roman Christian morality by practising enslavement, which was prohibited in canon law enforced by the Anglo-Normans as part of their order of conquest. But this distinction cannot be moralized, since it created its own imperative violence; captured Scots were not enslaved by Anglo-Normans, but summarily beheaded. Another marker is provided by the Norman ideology of civilization by which the conquerors differentiated themselves from the conquered, which constituted a new mode of warfare and is sometimes seen as the beginning of an Eliasian 'civilizing process' in the constraints it introduced. However, comparison is chronically problematized by the distinct economies of violence involved, which imbue the record with variable meanings. For instance, when the sources report that *routiers* did not 'spare' women and clergy, this does not necessarily mean that all were killed, but that none were exempted from extortion of the means of life.

Strickland's reasoning simply affirms hierarchical, elite-led models of linear cultural progression. In arguing that the practice of ransom between knights marked the beginning of a 'civilization' of warfare, it mistakes a specific code for a historical tendency by neglecting the basis of this practice in the differential evaluation of knighthood as the legitimate (sacralized) elite monopoly of armed violence. The Third Lateran Council decreed that *routiers could* be enslaved, because it defined them as outside the Christian community of the Church,[50] illustrating how they functioned in this discourse as a fundamental condition of the Church's construction of a functionally legitimated order of violence in its socio-theological schema, the

Other against which the knights defended the social order, their threat the necessary condition of the socio-theological valuation of knighthood. A legitimate monopoly of arms would have been an empty concept if the modern construct of feudalism actually represented medieval reality. The knightly 'conscious desire to avoid killing' did not extend to the common soldiery, since arms outside of this schema constituted the object of sacrally imperative violence. Defeated *routiers* were slaughtered *en masse* since they were already, in arms, a direct affront to the identity of knighthood in its monopoly of 'legitimate violence' and to the sacral order in which that identity was constituted. In battle they had to fight for their very lives, unlike the knights.

We can thus see *within* medieval warfare itself the moral conditions of a continuous and implacable military class-war, in which the knights kill the *routiers* without mercy in defeat, while the *routiers* actively seek out unhorsed knights to kill whenever possible. Duby cites a report from Bouvines of how an audacious *routier* attempted to kill a fallen and wounded knight with a knife through the joints of his armour, even while he was being attended as a captive by a guard of his fellows in chivalry.[51] Strickland cites how *routiers* employed to fight at sea captured a whole shipload of knights, and had to be physically dissuaded by their chivalrous lieutenants from beheading them and casting their bodies overboard. On the other side, as Strickland acknowledges, defeated *routiers* were routinely executed by decapitation. As men-in-arms who were not men-at-arms, they were also outside the community of the Church, not Christians but effectively heretics, an anti-sacral identity, which according to the chroniclers they positively embraced with their war-cry, 'There is no God.' Not only *could* they be slaughtered, but they *had to be* slaughtered, an orgy of killing in which the other non-clerical order, the peasantry, took part alongside the knights. The *routiers* were already beyond redemption, referred to by the clerical courtly chronicler Matthew Paris as creatures of damnation: 'Satan's minions', 'night-prowlers, arsonists, sons of Belial'.[52]

The *routiers'* antithetical relation to the moralized socio-theological order of violence was a necessary condition of that order. Even if the Church had intended its investment of a monopoly of legitimate violence to regulate feud between knights, it effected a social order only in relation to a non-knightly Other, an illegitimate source of violence as the object of the knight's function of defence of the other orders under the Church, the peasants and clergy. The construction of a moralized medieval social order thus depended on its production of an anti-social Other.

Medieval community implied static subjection, and there was an implicit association of the anti-social with a liberty from domination that has its condition on the road and violence in its hands; 'when a man was freed from serfdom by an act of manumission, primitive law decreed that the owner of the serf should show him the open door and the open road, and place in his hands the weapon of a freeman.'[53] Although medieval law narrowed the status of warrior to include only the nobility, arming youth with a knife commonly marked the vital threshold into male adulthood in which a man could receive liberty in his own right.[54] Such liberated men, however, were projected into peregrination on the road.

Contamine identifies a 'second generation' of *routiers* in France, operating in smaller, more readily employable groups, a form that also appeared in England.[55] This shift in form itself suggests that warfare was a resort, rather than an essential social identity, along with begging, prostitution, day-labouring, theft and violence as other means of life to marginals.[56] The medieval epistemological principle of similitude also identified the bands and marginals with itinerant friars and ascetics whom the Lateran Councils sought to dissociate from the Church as heretical, since they preached abandonment of the trappings of the world that the established Church valued as a form of symbolic exchange with God. Clerical socio-theology thus associated the bands with the mendicants, and the Lateran Councils excommunicated the *routiers* while simultaneously invalidating the poor friars' claim to be men of God. Chroniclers embedded in the Church hierocracy or settled Christian community, composing texts within the monastic network or on commission to nobles, were predisposed to see the unregulated life of the road as the antithesis of community based on exchange, settlement and functional order.

The bands were characterized by their quality of movement, which differentiated them from a society increasingly defined by place and regulated by circuits (itineraries) between static locations invested with determinate social relations: the courts of great castellans, the shrines and abbeys, and the chartered market towns. Initially appearing against the formation of medieval community in the process of settlement described by Le Goff, the movement of the bands acquired a further distinct quality in relation to the regular topical itineraries of the Middle Ages, increasingly codified from the tenth century on, which also ordered time.[57] Thus, in inverse relation to the territorialization and regulation of medieval society, vagrant bodies acquired *speed* as the *variable* quality of their relative movement. As the flows of bodies of medieval society became increasingly conjugated in the functional orders, the regimes of signs, legal relations, kin and lineage identities, so the bodies still upon the open road became forces by virtue of their liberty from such conjugations, forces which could be connected in mercenary employment that offered not just money and plunder, but temporary protection for their way of life, which became the way of war. They thus appear only in war, as an instrument, and in the public peace, as predators and outlaws.

There is little in contemporary chronicles that could be used to analyze the bands in terms of their internal relations, social identities or forms of subjectivity, because their social organization could not be recognized and thus remained uncodified. We only know of them in their definition against 'organized society' by their exclusion and marginality in socio-theological discourse and in the legal record of the mechanisms of social sanction, in which they appear as a recurrent, rather than continuous, phenomenon throughout the Middle Ages, a unitary, complicated object of social opprobrium which resists analytical breakdown, marginals whose identity seems wholly constituted in their *exsilium* and their free movement. Embodying the condition to which medieval concepts of marginality were assimilated, they did not come to stay. They did not share in the times and spaces of the medieval world. Outside all orders, they appear to embody disorder, and appear only with war, as identical with it and as its condition. Peace then appears as identical with, and conditional upon, a war against them.

The very exclusion of the *routiers* from social order and community also endowed them with a utility that enabled the development of strategies of war, rather than of battle, kin and diplomacy. With the legal circumscription of feudal obligation and the customary delimitation of the levy, early medieval princes and kings could only wage protracted war in a personal capacity. In such conflicts, the bands were the only embodied forces unrestrictedly available to supplement the *familia*. Kings often associated closely with the *routier* captains they employed, and could even incorporate them into the *familia*,[58] but did so only in their personal capacity. Personal investment did not preclude political action, and the king could turn on the *routiers* himself, or at least turn his back and allow the barons to slaughter them.

Such apparent duplicity was enabled by a new distinction between political kingship and the embodied king in his person that was produced by the employment of *routiers* themselves as mass forces independent of the feudal polity. The struggle of kings against the barons was only possible through the employment of *routiers*, since vassalage networks tended to operate horizontally to facilitate a defence of the plural political order against regalian assertions of kings' personal interests, while the *routiers'* exclusion from social order and community made them reliant upon personal employment for protection. Successive Angevin and Plantagenet kings of England, and the Capetian dynasty of France, relied heavily upon the employment of these men of war, but their very success produced a new possibility and condition of *public peace*, under political kingship, which was quite distinct from the peace of God that had invested a monopoly of violence in knighthood.

The king's peace offered the prospect of universal, public order under politicized monarchy. In the elimination (or at least mutual cancellation), of personal threats to the political order, kingship became a public, political authority to which the *routiers* represented a threat as forces of war serving personal interests. Their threat was not simply abstract, since the discharged bands lived off the country, practising the 'right to take' hitherto exercised as their tactical function. The first task of kingship in its new role of political authority was thus the elimination of the *routiers* whom the kings had previously employed in their personal capacity. This reconstitution of kingship and its relation to the forces of war did not depend upon regal victory over the barons, since both sides laid claim to the defence of the polity even as they waged war with personal forces. When King John of England signed the Magna Carta, a condition of the political kingship it instituted was that he undertook to expel the foreign men of war, most of whom were in his employ. The barons did not demand this expulsion to deprive kingship of force as a public power, but rather to deprive the king of those forces he held in his personal capacity. Where kings were victorious, the effect was the same; one of Henry II's first acts as king was to expel 'foreign' *routiers*, and in 1174 he again reasserted his public office by expelling the Flemish who had aided the rebel barons and the Brabançons he had brought over himself.[59]

The establishment of political kingship was not a singular event, but a recurrent process in the cyclical time of the medieval world. In twelfth-century France and the Holy Roman Empire, the same process occurs, in which *routiers* provided the instrument which enabled kings to assert themselves independently of the feudal lords and the order of vassalage, while their repression became the object of the new function of political kingship's legitimate use of force. They were thus fundamentally necessary to the medieval constitution of political authority, both the condition of its appearance and the object of its function, just as they were to the formation of moral order and community.

PROBLEMATICS OF MILITARY POWER
The order of the body politic

For Walter Map, writing in the reign of Henry II of England, the bands are classed among his 'Courtiers' Trifles' as 'A Certain Sect of Heretics':

> These heretics have gathered throngs of many thousands, the so-called Routiers (*Ruttae*), and arming themselves cap-a-pie, with hide and metal, sticks and swords, have reduced to ashes monasteries, granges, and towns ... at first, sallying forth as robbers, they made for themselves a law against all law ... They have now multiplied so immeasurably and the hosts of Leviathan have waxed so mightily that they abide in safety or wander through lands and kingdoms amid the hatred of God and of men.[60]

Map was a familiar of the court of Henry II (perhaps the first king of England who occupied the new form of kingship), was employed as a clerk by the royal household and served as an itinerant justice. His text is an anti-court satire from the perspective of the clerics who provided it with the expertise necessary for the new mode of government under public kingship.[61] The Church had undergone a massive shift since the eighth-century papal alliance with the Carolingian dynasty. Gregory VII had turned his back on the alliance with the old form of personal kingship. From 1050 onwards, the papacy developed administrative techniques by taking an increasingly interventionist role in ecclesiastical order.[62] On the one hand, this operationalized the Church's claim, after Gregory VII, to 'universal sovereignty', and on the other, provided technical expertise for new forms of secular government.

> The ideal church of the twelfth and thirteenth centuries was a society of disciplined and organized clergy directing the thoughts and activities of an obedient and receptive laity – kings, magnates, and peasants alike ... The new techniques of government depended increasingly on expert knowledge ... by the end of the eleventh century ... advanced scholastic training ... gave the clergy a monopoly of all those disciplines which not only determined the theoretical structure of society but provided the instruments of government.[63]

This new role, however, implicated the clergy in the organs and affairs of the new secular realm, exposing it to both political and popular

138

violence. When Thomas à Becket was murdered by members of the king's *familia* for his interference in secular government, his pupil, John of Salisbury went into hiding and undertook the task of reformulating the relationship of the Church to the new secular power of political kingship, seeking 'to extricate the clergy from the jurisdiction of temporal authorities' which exposed them to violence.[64]

John of Salisbury, like Map, had served the court, but in his *Policraticus*[65] John does not simply assert the Church as a transcendent power over the new secular modes of government. Rather, in adopting the model of the body politic from ancient sources for the new secular regime, he recovers for practical political philosophy the concept of the *res publica* as the constitutional form of the public good and as a framework for the conduct of public service. In John's *Policraticus*, Augustine's transposition of Roman Stoic military virtue on to Christian morality is translated back into the new political domain beneath the Church, enabling John to develop an ethics of service to the lawful prince. Georges Duby has argued that *Policraticus* must be read as a '*speculum curiae*' for the new officers of the public realm, whom he identifies as the court clerks in contrast to the knights,[66] but John's text also presents the soldiers of the king as a distinct category, to whom the military–ecclesiastical model of discipline applies.

John anatomizes a politically functional body of which the feet are the peasants, the stomach officials of the Exchequer, the flanks the prince's retinue, the hands the officials and soldiers, the ears, eyes and mouth the provincial governors, and the head the prince, but always, like the human head, subject to and stimulated by the soul, that is, the Church, which acts in God's place upon earth. He differentiates the king from the tyrant by his lawful administration of an office concerned with 'the burdens of the entire community', by his necessary parental affinity with his subjects, but also by his representation of the divine will in his public office, in which he bears 'the sword of the dove, which quarrels without bitterness, which slaughters without wrathfulness and which entertains no resentment in fighting'.[67] In terms of his political rule, the transference of peace from God in the Church to the prince in public kingship means that the concern of the king is no longer with securing vassalage for the feudal array, but with the government of a military formation, the *familia*; no longer with the management of private feud under the Salic Law, but with the fulfilment of public utility. Moreover, John devotes disproportionate space to the hand which wields the sword, treating it separately in Book VI, while other members of the body politic are discussed in Book V. A close reading of his text shows how he differentiates the *familia* from both knighthood in general and from mercenaries, establishing the condition of military service to political kingship as a technical vocation, rather than as a sacral function of knighthood given in a socio-theological order.

The utility of the armed hand is conditional upon 'selection, knowledge and practice,' since practice banishes fear and knowledge nourishes courage, while selection is conjugated by the oath to become the basis of an ethical economy, of the soul of the soldier. John follows Vegetius for the criteria of selection, but while freedom is a necessary qualification, the necessity to become accustomed to bearing burdens and the hardship of the road, and to maintain the soul in performance of servile tasks, suggests that these are not the conditions of service of a feudal nobility. For John, history reveals that luxuriation weakens discipline and arms, precipitating attacks by raiders into the lands of plenty. Military mobility, not feudal stability, is necessary to pursue the raiders into the space in which they take refuge. Rather than a 'civilization' of warfare, John proposes a cold, technical violence as the necessary condition of the armed hand, since pacification may require the genocidal slaughter of the enemy.

In contrast to the spectacular, boastful knight of the feudal array whose identity is invested in his name, his heraldic insignia and his adornment of arms, John's soldier is made by two things: by selection and by the oath he swears, again a model analogous to a militant of the Church, characterized by self-renunciation and dedication to the city of God through rule, which is here the technical function of the military arm. In swearing the oath, the soldier has already placed himself in an ethical relation to law in the authority of the prince. Thus, the vocational soldier produced by the oath is the instrument of God in the lawful authority bestowed by the Church upon the office of the prince: but the man in arms without a vocation in such service to an anointed prince is by definition already damned and outlawed. The military vocation is also charged with a certain asceticism, in contrast to the glitter of the chivalric host. The armed hand must not be adorned, since it is not necessary and attracts rather than repels the enemy, and continuous preoccupation of soldiers in practice and labour will maintain their strength in body and their calling in the soul. The body of the soldier also provides a means for command, since just as 'a hungry rabble does not know fear', so provisions can be used as sanctions in the military formation that is dependent upon the bread of the prince.

The *Policraticus* is not a military text or a military discourse, but seeks to situate the forces of the *familia* in the new political space opened up by the substitution of the king's peace for the peace of God. In this new discourse, in contrast to the Three Orders of socio-theology,

John of Salisbury invests the legitimate violence of the body politic in the familial *disciplinati* of political kingship, rather than in a noble knighthood governed by an independent code of chivalry.

Notes

1. G. Duby, *The Legend of Bouvines: War, Religion and Culture in the Middle Ages,* trans. C. Tihanyi (Cambridge: Polity Press, 1990), p. 25.
2. Ibid., p. 30.
3. P. Contamine, *War in the Middle Ages,* trans. M. Jones (Oxford: Blackwell, 1984), p. 48.
4. Duby, *Legend of Bouvines*, p. 110.
5. Ibid., p. 113.
6. Ibid., p. 115.
7. Ibid., p.129.
8. Quoted in ibid., p. 85.
9. R. Kaeuper, *War, Justice and Public Order: England and France in the Later Middle Ages* (Oxford: Clarendon Press, 1988).
10. Duby, *Legend of Bouvines*, p. 124.
11. G. Duby, *The Chivalrous Society,* trans. C. Postan (London: Edward Arnold, 1977), pp. 112–21.
12. Duby, *Legend of Bouvines*, pp. 94–5.
13. Ibid., p. 130.
14. Kaeuper, *War, Justice, Public Order*, pp. 200–9.
15. Duby, *Chivalrous Society*, pp. 118, 181–3.
16. Duby, *Legend of Bouvines*, p. 97.
17. Ibid., p. 77.
18. Ibid., p. 123.
19. Ibid., p 79; V. G. Kiernan, 'Foreign Mercenaries and Absolute Monarchy', in M. Aston, (ed.), *Crisis in Europe, 1560–1660* (London: Routledge & Kegan Paul, 1965).
20. M. Prestwich, *Armies and Warfare in the Middle Ages: The English Experience* (New Haven, CT: Yale University Press, 1996), p. 254.
21. Quoted in Duby, *Legend of Bouvines*, p. 82.
22. Ibid., p. 81.
23. Ibid., p. 132.
24. Ibid., pp. 81–3.
25. Contamine, *War in the Middle Ages*, pp. 99–100.
26. J. O. Prestwich, 'The Military Household of the Anglo-Norman Kings', in M. Strickland, *Anglo-Norman Warfare* (Woodbridge: Boydell Press, 1992), pp. 93–6.
27. M. Chibnall, 'Mercenaries and the *familia regis* under Henry I', *History, 62* (1977), pp. 15–23; S. Morillo, *Warfare under the Anglo-Norman Kings, 1066–1135* (Woodbridge: Boydell Press, 1994).
28. Prestwich, 'Military Household', pp. 100, 119.
29. Ibid., pp. 100–1.
30. Chibnall, 'Mercenaries and *familia*', p. 90.
31. Ibid., p. 89; Prestwich, 'Military Household', p. 86.
32. Morillo, *Warfare Under Anglo-Norman Kings*, p. 76.

PROBLEMATICS OF MILITARY POWER

PROBLEMATICS OF MILITARY POWER

PROBLEMATICS OF MILITARY POWER

33. R. Bartlett, *The Making of Europe: Conquest, Colonization and Cultural Change, 950–1350* (London: Penguin, 1993).
34. Chibnall, 'Mercenaries and *familia*', p. 88.
35. Morillo, *Warfare Under Anglo-Norman Kings*, pp. 79, 116.
36. Orderic Vitalis, *Ecclesiastical History, Vol. VI*, ed. and trans. M. Chibnall (Oxford: Clarendon, 1980), p. 350.
37. E. Kantorowicz, *The King's Two Bodies: A Study in Medieval Political Theology* (Princeton, NJ: Princeton University Press, 1957).
38. E. Kantorowicz, 'Kingship under the Impact of Scientific Jurisprudence', in M. Clagett, G. Post and R. Reynolds (eds), *Twelfth-Century Europe and the Foundations of Modern Society* (Westport, CT: Greenwood Press, 1966), p. 97.
39. Prestwich, 'Military Household', p. 96.
40. G. Deleuze and F. Guattari, *Anti-Oedipus: Capitalism and Schizophrenia,* Vol. 1, trans. R. Hurley *et al.* (London: Athlone Press, 1984), p. 185.
41. F. Nietzsche, *On the Genealogy of Morals,* trans. W. Kaufman and R. J. Hollingdale (New York, NY: Random House, 1967).
42. Deleuze and Guattari, *Anti-Oedipus*, p. 190.
43. Prestwich, 'Military Household', p. 120.
44. Ibid., p. 95.
45. Chibnall, 'Mercenaries and *familia*'.
46. Contamine, *War in the Middle Ages*, p. 243.
47. M. Strickland, *War and Chivalry: The Conduct and Perception of War in England and Normandy, 1066–1217* (Cambridge: Cambridge University Press, 1996), p. 297.
48. Contamine, *War in the Middle Ages*, p. 244.
49. B. Geremek, 'The Marginal Man', in J. Le Goff (ed.) *The Medieval World,* trans. Cochrane (London: Collins & Brown, 1990), pp. 347–9.
50. Strickland, *War and Chivalry*, pp. 312–17.
51. Duby, *Legend of Bouvines*, p. 123.
52. Quoted in Strickland, *War and Chivalry*, p. 299.
53. R. W. Southern, *The Making of the Middle Ages* (London: Arrow Books, 1959), p. 105.
54. M. Mitterauer, *A History of Youth,* trans. Dunphy (Oxford: Blackwell, 1992), pp. 56–7.
55. J. Schlight, *Monarchs and Mercenaries: A Reappraisal of Knight Service in Norman and Early Angevin England* (Bridgeport, CT: University of Bridgeport Press, 1968); N. A. R. Wright, 'Pillagers and Brigands in the Hundred Years War', *Journal of Medieval History,* 9 (1983), pp. 15–24.
56. Geremek, 'Marginal Man'.
57. J-C. Martin, 'Cartography of the Year 1000: Variations on *A Thousand Plateaus*', in C. V. Boundas and D. Olkowski, (eds), *Gilles Deleuze and the Theatre of Philosophy* (London: Routledge, 1994).
58. Strickland, *War and Chivalry*, p. 247.
59. Ibid., p. 320.
60. Walter Map, *De Nugis Curialum,* trans. Tupper and Ogle (London: Chatto & Windus, 1924), pp. 71–2.
61. Kaeuper, *War, Justice and Public Order*, p. 326.
62. R. W. Southern, *Western Society and the Church in the Middle Ages* (Harmondsworth: Pelican, 1970), pp. 104–9.
63. Ibid., p. 38.

142

64. G. Duby, *The Three Orders: Feudal Society Imagined,* trans. A. Goldhammer (Chicago, IL: University of Chicago Press, 1980), p. 267.
65. John of Salisbury, *Policraticus,* trans. and ed. C. J. Nederman (Cambridge: Cambridge University Press, 1990).
66. Duby, *Three Orders*, p. 266.
67. Salisbury, *Policraticus*, IV.2, p. 31.

8

Medieval Formations: War-State and Law-State

In contrast to approaches which attribute inherent rationalities of legitimation to the state deriving from its essential societal functions, Ernst Kantorowicz's historical legal sociology showed how the capacity of medieval kingship to make law was an effect of historically and culturally specific practices and techniques operating upon a specific terrain of domination.[1] Medieval legislative sovereignty derived neither from ancient right nor from legitimation, but was constituted piecemeal (and often inadvertently) in the transformative effects of discrete practices and techniques. The medieval discourse of the law-state was thus not determined by rationalization of the distribution and conditions of domination, nor given in a fusion of ancient concepts of *rex* and *imperium*. The practices and techniques of medieval government were not given in the technology of domination either, since the castle and its collective body of force, the retinue, were also subject to such political technologies. Rather than stasis or decay, comparative study of the political kingships of thirteenth and early fourteenth-century France and England shows that they undertook successive projects of 'modernization', deploying a variety of techniques across diverse political fields.

The castle as domain

The government of early medieval England was based upon the barony as the administrative unit organizing obligations of castle-guard and the show of arms in array of battle, but these never produced forces for prolonged or disciplined service in war, and both the baronies and these obligations were already in decline by the time they were systematically codified as general principles.[2] The castles of the Norman conquest defined a terrain of domination in which their strategic significance was given by their relation to one another, rather than to the subjected population. The Norman kings' military government divided England into military districts corresponding to the economic capacity to support major castles with warriors for castle-guard, rather than rivers or roads, which were largely irrelevant to their territorialization.[3] Anglo-Norman kingship retained the prerogative of encastellation, only delegating rights of licensed castellation and the creation of castle-guard obligations to the magnates. The period of civil wars known as the Anarchy was basically a fragmentary struggle of the kings against the baronial assertion of exclusive private rights to castles. Henry II decisively ended this contestation with a campaign which reduced the ratio of private to royal castles from 5:1 to 2:1, demolishing many and appropriating others to himself.[4] Since simple castles could be readily reconstructed, this re-establishment of royal prerogative authority required a continuous regime of reduction, for which Henry maintained a large household force of mobile, specialist foot soldiers skilled in techniques of siege and demolition, who were deployed as garrisons under the command of constables rotated on short tenure between the king's immediate household and its extension in the royal castles.[5]

Castle architecture responded to the development of siege techniques over the next 150 years, with stone castles replacing the more primitive wooden palisades and keeps, which disappeared from England under the impact of the royal programme.[6] It is usually argued that the king's singular financial capacity to develop and implement new technological assemblages already exhibits the rational-historical ascendancy of a centralizing military-fiscal state over a centrifugal feodality of barons and lords.[7] However, stronger castles did not themselves enable the reduction of smaller ones. Rather than royal success being determined by a nexus of finance and technology, the Angevin programme depended on organizational techniques and particular relations of domination peculiar to the *familia regis*. On the medieval terrain, strategy did not issue from given juridical rights such as the *fisc* or from the technological means themselves; rather, the key to Henry II's success lay in the organization of the elements, the *principle* of assemblage, which produced and shaped strategic capacities.

The tendency to centralization was itself an effect of *ad hoc*, tactical organization, not given in the systemic function of the ruler or in anachronistic concepts of kingship. Norman military government established sheriffs in the royal castles as local representatives of the king's law, as distinct from the common law and particular urban liberties. The royal castle circuit thus constituted an extended and spatialized jurisdiction of the king, in which men could find refuge and appeal against customary law, accumulating archival records, eventually reposited in the Tower of London,[8] which also became the central depot for the engines of war (another royal prerogative) and their technicians, maintained as part of the royal household and administered by the Wardrobe. This department had originated as the strong-box containing the royal treasure which accompanied itinerant kingship on its circulation about the kingdom. It had become a static entity only through the Anglo-Norman organization of military government, manifesting in the transformation of a chest and personal servants into an administrative entity the same process that transformed kingship from an itinerant authority embodied in personal presence into an abstract principle. By the thirteenth century, the Wardrobe had become a static administrative body in the Tower, supplying the king's household in its extension throughout the royal castles and integrating and maintaining them independently of local environments.[9]

The thirteenth-century French conquests of Philip Augustus and other Capetian monarchs did not undertake the programmatic reduction that produced the administrative form of public kingship in England. Different means were available to the kings of France, where royal prerogative was established by extending the practice of 'jurability and rendability' as a general principle applying to encastellations of private domains as well as those held in fief, producing a different mode of political kingship and a different form of the body politic. Rather than government proceeding through structures emergent from the royal household, French political kingship was constituted by a matrix of rights in which the king exercised the function of arbitration. As the king's peace and the principle of a public domain was secured and extended over the course of the thirteenth century, the arbitration role enabling the king to prohibit particular instances of encastellation where these would pose a political challenge to others became sanctionary, so that part or whole of a lord's castle would be demolished as retribution for infringements against the peace.[10] While English kingship was able to assert formal prerogative authority directly through its circuit of royal castles, French government of the king's peace operated indirectly through the institutions representing the great castellar lords in the body politic, and kingship was reformed around the transformation of its arbitral role.[11] French royal government thus produced neither the extensive castellar circuit of the English royal household, nor its intensive development of the *familia* and the household administration.

Medieval military subjects

The functionalist conception of an era of 'feudalism' provides a contrast enabling the parameters of modernity to be drawn in terms of historically discrete social systems. However, the medieval body politic was radically reconstituted in sweeping political reconstructions of military obligation between the twelfth and the thirteenth centuries, using techniques that restratified the social order and produced new categories of subjects, a *'programme* to make knighthood a desirable and enviable status'.[12] The particular, military-feudal conditions of land tenureship appeared absurdly anachronistic to contemporaries as early as 1300, when

> one man appeared with the terms of his tenure, equipped as an archer, with only one arrow ... fired it at the first Scot he saw, and promptly left for home; the man obliged to attend on a horse worth five shillings, carrying a stick with a bag on the end of it, was of little more use.[13]

The more general obligations which comprised armed hosts at the turn of the thirteenth century were not 'traditional', but had been created during a century of development of the mechanism of the body politic in both England and France; they were not given in the systemic function of 'feudal society', but were constructs of administrative technologies applied on a political terrain.

The techniques used can be traced back to the castle-guard inventories of the Norman dukes, but their application as a programmatic political technology dates from the accession of Henry II of Anjou to the English throne at the end of the Anarchy. While Henry II reconfigured the landscape of power in his programme of castle reduction, he also undertook a major reform of the order of government and the order of his subjects, establishing the model for subsequent Plantagenet regimes. His 1181 Assize of Arms operationalized an entirely new mode of government, concerned not with obligations couched in particular agreements such as land-tenure or particularistic legal status, but with establishing new ones on a quantitative basis. The Assize classified the king's subjects by income-bands and decreed the contribution to arms to be maintained by each stratum, enabling the crown to issue orders of distraint requiring individuals with sufficient income to become knights.[14] Particularities were thus reduced to equivalences not merely for the purposes of taxation levied upon things, but for active obligations incumbent upon embodied subjects, thus creating an entirely new, singular and political relationship between the subject and the king as head of the body politic.

The reconstruction of military-political obligation in Assize cut across the tangled web of feudal obligations, enabling numerical and impersonal calculations of potential forces, in the same manner as the administration of the *familia regis*. Assize became a regular feature of English late medieval government in serial enactments which could adjust the quantitative basis of assessment to emergent strategic perceptions. The new political order it created was administratively insulated from resistance, since its reduction of particularities foreclosed legal challenge and minimized the capacity to mobilize resistance on the basis of the old vassalic form of political relationships by cutting across these existing orders. For its subjects, assize and distraint did not necessarily require personal performance of the obligation; the principle of commutation was well established in the institution of scutage, and even distraint could be respited for a fee, while if all else failed, a substitute could be hired.[15] The Statute of Winchester (1285) formally converted these obligations into a political relation specifically between the Crown and its subjects in general. The phrase 'armed according to his status' which recurs in the re-enactments of this statute referred not to the condition of tenureship given in feudal law, but to the index of arms to wealth first established by the Assizes, down to the provision of those with less than twenty marks to serve with 'swords, knives and lesser weapons'.[16]

The new military modes of subjection also effected new problematics and produced new bodies and conditions of war. In Edward I's Welsh campaigns, obligatory service was extended by payment of expenses beyond the 40-day limit out of the royal Wardrobe on the same administrative basis as for knights, thus subjecting levied men to prerogative royal justice under the condition of maintenance at the royal household's expense. Though the Welsh campaigns proved the effectiveness of foot soldiers, existing means of recruitment to the community levy proved increasingly ineffective, as the sheriffs appointed in the localities lacked expertise in the techniques of selection necessary to produce suitable bodies for extensive campaign and frequently colluded with the communities to send the least fit (the economically expendable). Even when writs of summons were used to specify skills in arms and proper equipment as uniform criteria, the commissioners were unable or unwilling to implement these details. From 1282, they were substituted by officers of the *familia* specially commissioned to array and select free men for foot service.[17] Selective levy for extensive expeditions also opened a 'dromological' space and time of the movement of mobilized bodies,[18] as the levied body tended to numerical decay through desertion *en route* to the campaign,[19] a problematic which would invoke the development of techniques of identification in the muster.

The bodies abstracted by the selective levy into extended service were free men only in their public liability to serve, which with royal household pay and its implications ceased to be circumscribed by customary right or political membership. In their paid service they were no longer the subjects of public kingship, but merely objects, instruments in its hands. The Scot, James Douglas, either cut off the right hand or gouged out the right eye of any English archer he captured,[20] exacting his retribution through corporate liability in the body that had translated over from private war, but was now liberated from the constraints and carefully delineated reciprocations of retributive justice in feud. Under the old economy of violence, even noble violation of a serf had invoked the lord's duty of reprisal, but the violation of levied bodies abstracted from the body politic into the king's pay incurred only the 'loss' of a resource, not loss of honour or any injustice. Their bodies were simply instruments placed in the hands of the king for public purposes as a part of his private household. The cause for which he fought (the public peace) was not his 'own', not personal, so any violation incurred no personal obligation upon him and was secondary to technical considerations. The levied body in pay of the king was subject to his prerogative justice, but was also disposable, as an instrument he held. Levied men had been raised up out of political subjection into the jurisdiction of his household, but they were also less than his personal clients. He did not bear the responsibility toward them that men bear toward the things they possess.

By contrast, the thirteenth-century conquests of the Capetian dynasty in France initially concentrated on asserting particular obligations beyond the immediate royal domains, accumulating inventories of those owing particular 'host service' as successive administrative regions were brought under the king's peace. Forty days was the customary limit of the 'free service' of such obligations in the absence of immediate prospect of battle, the only condition on which the king could compulsorily retain men, and even then only within the kingdom and at his own expense. A host might thus evaporate while awaiting distant contingents. The *ban* was personally negotiated as a particular legal relation, and though thirteenth-century French kings could also call on the service of town and village under the *prise des sergeans* (a list of the foot soldiers and carts which each commune was obliged to supply dating from 1194 and revised in 1204),[21] like the service of fief-holders, the particularities of the obligation had to be negotiated 'separately at a different rate, for a different duration, and on the basis of particular rights and privileges', for 'each town, district, fief, or area'.[22] However, even such particular relations were politically susceptible, rather than an organic function of a feudal social system.

While in England military-political subjection proceeded from every man direct to the king, in the French polity, each man owed service to his immediately superordinate lord, and only via this vertical chain to the king. As part of a general move to codify customary law and thus establish some grounds for royal jurisdiction through the concept of the king's peace as guarantee of the rule of all forms of law, the 1270 *Etablissements de St Louis* attempted to establish general principles of military subjection by formalizing customary rights and constraints of the various categories of military obligatees. They formalized the 40-day limit, attempted to specify a general obligation of baronial service, and sought to generalize as a principle the service owed by customary (as contrasted to feudal) tenants to their lord. These customary tenants, like the subjects of English political kingship, were obliged to array armed according to their wealth.[23] However, in the condition of the French body politic, operation through particular relations proved more flexible and practical. After the destruction of the flower of French chivalry by the communes of Flanders at Courtrai in 1302, royal commissioners were sent into the kingdom to find rich burgers or peasants who would pay for the privileges of ennoblement, to make up the losses.[24] The particularistic basis of the *ban* thus enabled mass substitution on a personal basis, an option unavailable under Assize. Another response to this defeat attempted to re-institute the ancient *arrière ban* as a levy of all able-bodied men not subject to the feudal summons. In practice, such universal mobilization was impossible, but the innovation established the principle of universal contribution, enabling new taxes and securing a new basis for negotiating contingents from the communes.[25]

In the English domain, the political technology of Assize first co-opted customary forms of obligation, transforming them by indexing obligation to unqualified categories of wealth, and then in the Statute of Winchester finally codified them as singular, political relations of universal subjection. By contrast, in the face of resistance through the legal particularities of feudal obligation, kingship in France sought to establish itself as a new form of public authority, with a singular relationship to its subjects, through the more archaic legal forms of customary law and ancient rights. 'Feudal' military-political obligation under both the French and English modes of political kingship was thus the creation of techniques of government. As such, it was never an accomplishment, but a continuous process, which had continually to be surveyed, repeated and reformed.

The law-state and violence

The contrast between the French and English forms of public power and of public authority come together in the different constitutions of the 'law-state' which formed around quite different problematics of jurisdiction over violence. In France, the main problem around which public kingship formed was the right of feud, or 'private war', while in England, crisis around the threat to public order appeared as 'common criminality', which emerged earlier in England than in France as a problem for the administration of justice. In both cases, these problems appeared against a background order effected by specific governmental techniques. The different problematics of government of the king's peace in the two domains thus reflected their distinct forms of political kingship.

The socio-theological order of society had effectively sanctified a right of feud between knights in order to contain and regulate violence, but under the body politic this right underwent a further transformation. Jurists of the thirteenth and fourteenth centuries distinguished four possible conditions of war: *guerre mortelle* (as in trial by battle, a war to the death in which the defeated party could be killed or enslaved), *bellum hostile* (public war in which spoils could be taken but the honour of knights was respected in the ransom of noble prisoners), *guerre couverte* (as regulated by the ecclesiastical law of the peace of God, feud with licence to wound and kill but not to take spoils or prisoners), and *truce* (not peace, but a pause in war).[26] The transference of the concept of the peace of God on to the peace of the king as head of the body politic thus lent continuity to the claim that feud was a right consisting in knighthood itself, outside royal jurisdiction and only subject to royal arbitration.[27] By contrast, in England, no such right had been formally established and it was possible to bring it under royal jurisdiction as treason in the thirteenth century, so that any private warfare was deemed to be an attack on the king's peace and hence on the king, even where he was not directly involved in the dispute.

The shift of the concept of peace on to the king as head of the body politic was first operationalized in France in the programmatic codification of customary law in the *Etablissements de St. Louis*. Private war and judicial duel, as customary forms of retributive justice and adjudication, were regulated by royal edicts under this regime (in 1258 and 1260), but the charges of *port d'armes* and *chevauchée* (the means by which feud was conducted), remained baronial and local jurisdictions until the fourteenth century. Even royal edicts were particular and thus localized in scope, directed at specific feuds such as that between Armagnac and Foix in Gascony in 1296 and 1304.[28] Like the English king's repression of private unlicensed castles, any such prohibition had to be both serial and enforceable to achieve general applicability, and the absence of protracted public war seems to have precluded any effective royal prohibition of private warfare. Frequent serial regulation began only during the Hundred Years' War, using the jurists' distinction between categories of war to prohibit *guerre couverte* during the duration of *bellum hostile*.

Until then, political kingship in France operated through particularistic administrative technologies, but a general principle of royal regulation was established through systematic application of these forms, effecting a royal jurisdiction where none existed in the form of law itself by using in new ways old measures that originated in the arbitration role of personal kingship. At the turn of the thirteenth and fourteenth centuries, systematic application of particularistic edicts of safeguard under Philip the Fair enabled increasing numbers of offences to be brought under Crown jurisdiction. *Panonceaux*, pennants bearing the sign of kingship, the fleur-de-lis, were affixed to 'castles, churches and abbeys, manor houses, farmsteads, mills, ships, forests and even gallows' (the symbol of jurisdiction).[29] Attacks upon these signs enabled charges to be brought under royal jurisdiction, where the substance of the feud itself was outside that jurisdiction. Similarly, royal issue of *assurements* for peaceful behaviour between particular feuding parties enabled the number of cases for violation to be increased tenfold in the first half of the fourteenth century. This technique of operation through a regime of signs by precise and detailed exercise over particular subjects on an extensive scale also required continuous and consistent application. Thus, Philip V's ordinance of 1318 ordered all royal officers to remain in post '*continuellement et personellement*', prohibited them from acting as lieutenants to other parties, and authorized captains (provosts) for all towns to organize and command the communal defences in the cause of maintaining the king's peace, thus imposing a royal office alongside the local militia organization as a counter-authority against urban mobilization for feud.[30]

In contrast, particular measures were used executively by the English kings to enforce general principles. When, at the end of the thirteenth century, Edward I attempted to exercise royal jurisdiction over the endemic private warfare of the Welsh Marches, exemplary cases were strategically selected to establish general principles of subjection to the order of the king's peace. In England, minor feuding seems to have been no less endemic than in France, but the absence of an established right of private warfare and direct royal jurisdiction over the offences produced violence by proxy, with outlaw gangs for hire, by which the gentry hoped to escape public prosecution. New, but different, strategies of nobility also emerged under the French royal regime. The systematic and serial application of particular edicts enabled strong parties to gain prerogative exemptions which established a different order of relation to kingship: the Burgundian dynastic counts gained charters exempting them from royal orders of *assurement* and truce.[31]

In England, a 'late medieval crisis of order' appeared against the background of the king's peace, where from the end of the thirteenth century the Crown began to mobilize the reformed relations between subject and kingship of the body politic into 'the medieval military revolution'.[32] Assize and the levy reconstituted the secular medieval communities as an order of political subjection, but the communities' old condition of formation around exclusion of vagabonds now translated into formation around exclusion from the body politic under political kingship. This category of exclusion was inflated by the very means of mobilization of the body politic in time of war; by incorporation into the extended *familia* of the royal household for extended military service, levied bodies were 'raised' out of community into a condition of dependence on the Crown and displacement on the road. Desertion or discharge from this condition, however, did not return them to subjection in the body politic, but thrust them into a new condition of exclusion. They had been lifted out of community and its free status, and on their discharge from military dependency on the king appeared in the domain of the king's peace as displaced elements, the embodiment of disorder. Around this new category of exclusion, new techniques of control and technologies of government were to develop.

They joined the 'floating population' generated by the seasonally variable labour demands of the agrarian economy and the growth of urban demand for day-labour, representing a singular problem for the government of a body politic in which such elements had no place. In the regime of political kingship, the 'vagabondage' previously subject to customary law became the object of series of special commissions of arrest. These commissions cannot be explained simply as responses to the labour economy, since they explicitly associate the jurisdiction of the Crown over 'wandering malefactors' with the time of war, when authorities of the body politic (the nobility and the king) were absent on campaigns into which common free bodies were raised up, out of the discipline of domestic, domiciliary community into the domain of the royal household under the new techniques of military organization.[33] The very appearance of such extra-political and ex-communal bodies on their return (either in discharge or desertion) signified a virtual disorder, invoking the issue of general commissions for their arrest. The effect of the techniques of thirteenth-century political government and military organization thus created a crisis of government in general. As the price of legitimation of their overlordship of the body politic, English kingship had, 'accepted and even generated a volume of judicial business and encouraged a level of expectation of order which were finally beyond their capacity'. Funding the necessary judicial apparatus,

> ... would have fractured the very foundations on which the king's government had rested for centuries. Yet the king claimed a near monopoly over the serious violence and major property disputes critical to public order ... The very capacity of English government ... may have lowered the social threshold for the perception of unacceptable violence and disorder. What is at issue, then, is a contemporary English perception of crisis and a series of actions based on that belief.[34]

The limits upon fiscal extraction which provided the foundational legitimation of the state by differentiating it from brigandage, thus precluded the Crown from meeting the demands generated by legitimation, creating a medieval version of Jürgen Habermas' concept of 'legitimation crisis'.[35] Such analysis posits an essential legitimation-function, but by attending to practices rather than functions, to contingent effects rather than legitimation, and to bodies rather than ascribed interests, we can begin to see how the governmental processes which emerged did not merely recover 'legitimation' as their function in a pre-existent order, but produced that social order.

English attempts to deal with the problem by experimental development of the judicial apparatus did not effect the social or systems integration of the body politic, but reformed that body against the exclusion of unintegrated, unsettled elements, while creating its own function as a repressive apparatus by producing an extra-political domain of crime and vagrancy, as the object of specialist knowledge.[36] In the same way that practices conducted in a laboratory produce the truth of their own effects, so these experiments in judicial administration produced 'criminality' as a meaningful category charged with the violence of transgression. 'Internal' security measures thus produced insecurity in the form of an Other. Pierre Bourdieu[37] sees the productive effect of this kind of juridical codification, the 'symbolic violence' of law, reproduced in the enterprise of the sociologist. He argues that everyday social action is ordered by practical, 'principles of hierarchization, principles of division which are also principles of vision, in a word, everything which enables us to distinguish between things ... a judgement which separates.' Codification does not merely transpose these differentiations into a written form, ratifying them, but fundamentally reconstitutes the principle and its objects:

> Codification is a change of nature, a change of ontological status, which occurs when you go from linguistic patterns mastered at the practical level to a code, a grammar, via the labour of codification, which is a juridical activity ... Codification goes hand in hand with discipline and with the normalization of practices ...[38]

Bourdieu argues that practical conceptualization provides the dichotomizing model for the codifying procedure (the 'fundamental oppositions which organize the entire world-vision, night/day, inside/outside, etc.'), but codification also changes the status of such dichotomies. Thus, the association of vagrancy with violence had hitherto been a matter of linguistic practice, but now became inherent in the juridical identity of the vagrant. Furthermore, Bourdieu argues, one of the aspects of codification is formalization, which, 'enables you to go from a logic which is immersed in the particular case to a logic independent of a particular case'. For the judicial machinery, crime no longer consisted in the effect of particular acts, but was embedded in categories. Thus, codification also created a category of the 'beyond' as its jurisdiction (criminality), endowing the vagrant with ascribed intrinsic interests, for example, work avoidance and economic parasitism, whereas customary law and conceptualization had constituted vagrancy only as an exteriority, as the excluded. This process can be seen in detail in the English regime's experiments in judicial administration.

The institution of the 'general eyre' under Henry II had transformed the old mode of itinerant personal kingship into a judicial system by establishing panels of justices who visited the counties as representatives of the king's justice, a circuit facilitated by the network of royal castles which spatialized the extension of the royal jurisdiction. Beginning from the transformation of personal embodied kingship, this institution provided the vehicle whereby a more general medieval transformation of the principles of criminal justice was effected in England, from the old feud-model, 'The principle of private vengeance and of individual accusation, which requires a complaint from the victim or his family for proceedings to be instituted ... to that of the investigation or the prosecution of crime as a public obligation.'[39] The original five categories of offences which the eyre could enquire into and adjudicate proliferated during the thirteenth century into 110 'searching questions', but the system was overloaded by attempts to control feud by bringing the offence of trespass under royal jurisdiction so that the royal court could enforce its right of arbitration in property disputes. It ground to a halt by 1294, when the almost continuous campaigns of war of Edward I produced entirely new problems.

The arrest of judicial circuits, the absence of the king and the appearance of displaced bodies levied for war against the background of the king's peace created the appearance of widespread disorder and generated a level of complaint such that new mechanisms were instituted to gather knowledge of the situation. Panels of royal commissioners sent out to investigate complaints of vagabondage produced a 'picture of violence and illegality' and revealed gaols full of suspects awaiting trial.[40] The response, in spring 1305, divided England into five circuits and empowered panels of justices to enquire into the violence of 'trailbastons', veterans of the king's wars who continued to live itinerantly and practised the economy of seizure which had maintained them in the king's service. This crisis management further displaced customary local jurisdictions as juries were subordinated to report a whole range of cases to the commissions of enquiry.[41] From 1328 to 1332, more radical reforms integrated the previous measures of the period of experimentation, effectively redefining royal jurisdiction as the administration of the rule of law itself for the general order of the community and body politic. Only when this new terrain of legal relations under crown jurisdiction had been effected was power of determination (the authority to judge on the basis of evidence) settled on the local gentry as justices of the peace, replicating the dual function of law-state and war-state at local level, since they also operated as military contractors.

The domain of the king's peace thus produced a new field of knowledge, administration, judicial practice and political order. However, this field also divided perceptions of disorder into three kinds of complaint, which became categorically differentiated through the practices of judicial administration, rather than through legislation. Firstly, the internecine violence of the nobility was implicitly reduced to a question of property relations when the offence of trespass was brought under royal jurisdiction, drawing them into the polity by providing a new framework for aristocratic strategies through litigation and proxy violence, rather than feud. Secondly, complaint against royal officers became channelled into Parliament, constituting new legal relations of a political order. Thirdly, the brief and procedures of the trailbaston commissions had produced a picture of criminality which foregrounded particular forms and agents of transgression, the problem of socially dislocated vagabond soldiery providing the original object of the royal jurisdiction of criminal law, beyond the body politic.

If we follow the analysis of the crisis as a medieval crisis of legitimation, then it appears that the extension and intensification of the state takes place in the same movement as a retraction of political recognition from displaced, excluded elements, who become the figure of violence and the object of extra-political mechanisms of government. As Corrigan and Sayer put it in a more general account:

> Within England, to be active outside this 'official politics' (in terms of the central state or local state forms) was to be semi-criminal, precisely in a neat double sense an 'outside agitator'. But this system of official politics – normalized to become politics as such – requires contextualization. If this form of rule requires consensus, then justice requires coercion. And it is precisely that mythic entity, 'the law' – as discourse, practice and institution – which unifies both. Who could ever be above/outwith 'the law'? Only outlaws ... those outside the 'political nation', suffer 'justice'.[42]

Geremek shows a similar process in France, where the codification of customary law under St Louis provided the vehicle for the transformation of a system of individual accusation and private prosecution into a function of royal power to investigate and prosecute crime as a public obligation. Here, the model for the emergent public judicial system was provided by the exceptional category of 'the marginal' in customary law. Marginality was not merely a problem of the towns. Though their demand for day-labour acted as a 'magnet' for the dispossessed, exiled and voluntarily vagrant, the towns were governed by a communal regime consisting in their charters, guild regulation, militias, curfews, sumptuary laws, charity administration, and walls, gates and gaols, which made assimilation difficult. Marginal elements preferred the relative freedom of the suburbs of large towns, 'but they were also at home in the forests, in remote spots and, above all, on the road. Nomadism was their natural condition'.[43]

The new public principles of legal administration did not require proof of criminality to adjudicate the condition of marginality, but subjected the very mode of everyday life of the marginal orders to publicly instigated judicial proceedings, criminalizing the condition itself as an effective transgression of the king's peace. Judicial punishments were inflicted on the body: loss of an ear, an eye, a finger, a hand, a limb, and finally (short of life itself, but otherwise one of the heaviest penalties), the 'civic death' of banishment, in which the offenders were driven out of the town with a halter round their neck and could be killed with impunity ('like a dog') if they returned.[44] Though Geremek indexes anti-vagabondage legislation in France to economic labour shortages, it first appears in St Louis' codification of customary laws as part of a process of formation of the body politic and its new, political relations of kingship and subjection. Its development from the first direct royal decree of John the Good in 1351 through to the fifteenth-century *Ordonnance cabochienne*[45] cannot be dissociated from the appearance of a new mode of warfare, projected by English kingship on to France in the Hundred Years' War, which effectively liberated organized violence from its former constraints.

In both England and France, the peculiar duality of the moral articulation of vagabond bodies as alternatively idle and actively transgressive thus provided the subject around which the dual aspects of the medieval state as a military organization and as the keeper of the peace were formed. The architect of the final English campaign of judicial order, the Chief Justice of the King's Bench, Geoffrey le Scrope, reaffirmed its objective and impetus in Parliament in March of 1332, but in his speech at the opening of a new Parliament in September of that year dropped all mention of law and order.[46] A new mode of war was soon to transform the problematics of military power and medieval government.

The liberation of war

Edward I's subjugation of Wales was accomplished by royal subsidies to minor lords for the construction of rival castles, creating a permissive zone of contained and limited 'feudal anarchy' as a means of local subjugation without political recognition. The Scots border, however, presented the very different prospect of a vast and largely barren zone between the emergent royal domain of Scotland and the north of England, where Anglo-Norman authority had never been comprehensively established. Relatively low population density precluded any emergence of territorially comprehensive military government based on castles. Encastellation in the north thus produced only discontinuous enclaves of domination. With both kings physically distant, private warfare continued to be endemic in this zone.[47]

In this terrain of fragmentary domination, only conjugal and juridical strategies were available to medieval English kingship against persistent raiding from Scotland. With the failure of negotiations for dynastic marriage, the only alternative was to assert juridical 'overlordship' of the English Crown over the royal domain of Scotland, which would have rendered the Scots body politic beholden to the English kings for suppression of the raids, enabling English kings to levy forces in Scotland in the formal interests of the whole public domain as overlord of both. However, battle victory over the Scots proved indecisive, as English royal garrisons failed to hold castles there.[48] Since English strategy depended on recognition of Scotland as a legal domain, it could not be divested of royal authority as Wales had been, so it was not possible to create a mass of English minor lordships to hold it by encastellation and castle-guard. The object of war here could only be political, not military, but in the face of Scots resistance to negotiation, English support for the enterprise dwindled as it appeared increasingly as a private war of conquest by the king.[49]

At Bannockburn, the Scots eschewed chivalrous play of honour in open field and chose to fight on the tactical terrain of a bog. Thereafter, they avoided battle altogether, and Edward's campaign of 1322 exhausted itself in a long march through land laid waste by the Scots themselves all the way to Edinburgh.[50] The Scots' counter-campaigns developed an entirely new mode of offensive warfare, transforming the tactics of cattle raiding into a strategic means designed to force English recognition of Scots claims while deliberately evading open battle. Abandoning the devices of chivalry, the regime of signs in array, the new tactics produced a body with a different economy, a new form of force no longer dependent upon a regime of signification, a new vector liberated from the order of battle as exchange. Froissart describes how the Scots raiders integrated the mobile body as a consumption-machine into a rudimentary logistics, carrying only oatmeal-cakes as food supplies, to offset the effects on the stomach of subsisting in the field on hurriedly cooked meat of English cattle: 'Hence it is not surprising that they can travel faster than other armies.'[51]

Froissart's account of one raid in 1327 (after the source of Jean de Bel, a Hainaulter with a mercenary contingent of the mixed English host) illustrates the incapacity of 'traditional' forces and modes of deployment to deal with the new mode of warfare. The English host pursue the Scots raiders, guided by the smoke of burning farms and villages, but the Scots evade battle and are not even sighted directly. With no order of march and little knowledge of the 'trackless wastes' by which to inform their supply carts to follow, the English host have first to abandon their baggage train and then lose horses in the marshes and bogs. Exhausted by the pursuit, they have to spend a fearful night without shelter in their armour, the foot soldiers who would have provided guard straggling somewhere far behind. Rain makes the rivers uncrossable, weakening both horses and men, and when their enforced fast is lifted some days later by the arrival of traders, the English knights fight over the food that is sold to them at inflated prices. The Scots continue to elude battle, but provide surprise skirmishes to keep the English under heavy armour in pursuit. Finally, they disappear by night. When the ragged and hungry English host investigate the empty Scots camp, they find only the residue left by a consuming body that has passed at speed: cattle carcasses and, 'more than five thousand worn-out shoes'. After a further two-day ride, the English get back to Durham, where, 'they found their carts and carters with all the equipment which they had left in a neighbouring wood twenty-seven days previously'.[52]

The Scots campaign successfully used the tactics of the cattle raid on a grand scale, transforming its methods into something else, which no longer sought to take away cattle in numerical deduction, but instead lay waste to the north, evading battle while exhausting and humiliating the host of the English domain. The techniques of private war were thus applied to operate upon the body politic, by divesting it of its essential attributes of organic function, legitimation and honour. This strategic use of the mode of private war against the body politic fundamentally transformed the economy of violence. Feud, or private war, had been characterized by a cycle of the exchange of violence as a form of retributive justice, conducted through particular acts with a specific object, an economy which had differentiated it from brigandage. The new mode of warfare was no longer a direct form of reciprocal exchange, since no battle was joined for decisive exchange of blows. However, divesting the English king of the attributes of the body politic did not transfer them to Bruce. The new mode of warfare did not therefore represent a regression to retributive private war, but redeployed its techniques upon the new political terrain that had emerged in the thirteenth century, where it no longer constituted an economy of violence. Liberated from the customary constraints of feud, these tactics now opened a new space, a liberty of violence, in which new relations and new subjects were to appear. The new practice of warfare was called the *chevauchée*, a 'ride'. Only a few years later, the English carried this mode to the heart of chivalric Christendom in Edward III's raid into France.

The campaign of 1327 was the last time that a traditional feudal summons was effectively issued in England.[53] Reliance on heavy mounted armour alone had proved not only indecisive, but potentially disastrous. Extending the conditions of the *familia regis* to incorporate the levies and array enabled non-traditional, mixed tactical deployments to cut across status distinctions. It also produced a sophisticated logistical system based upon the prerogative right of *prise*, in which victuals could compulsorily be taken for the king's household at an assessed price,[54] although now that conquest was not the object, provision was superfluous since the army could live off the land. Maintenance of the host by predation transformed the capacity, mode and relations of war: dramatically reducing costs; endowing relative speed by dispensing with the baggage that hampered the enemy; liberating the vector of force from dependence on supply lines and castle depots; opening new strategic options by transforming the raid from a diversion or an incitement to battle into a means of full-blown public war in itself; opening space, which was now laden with resources rather than inscribed with rights and privileges; producing new, embodied forces, new forms of knowledge and new problematics of power. In all these ways it provided a condition for the development of entirely new technologies of organization and new modes of subjectification in government and discipline which were to shape the modern world.

Notes

1. In Kantorowicz's account, the development of medieval jurisprudence out of canon law, the particular form it took in recovering Roman civil law through the Justinian code, and the social identities available for the self-definition of professional jurists, all operated upon a given terrain to produce a new role of kingship, transforming contemporary institutions into a legislative function and constituting a legal domain upon which sovereign legislation became possible. E. Kantorowicz, 'Kingship Under the Impact of Scientific Jurisprudence', in M. Clagett, G. Post and R. Reynolds (eds), *Twelfth-Century Europe and the Foundations of Modern Society* (Westport, CT: Greenwood Press, 1966), pp. 89–111.
2. N. J. G. Pounds, *The Medieval Castle in England and Wales: A Social and Political History* (Cambridge: Cambridge University Press, 1990), pp. 44, 131.
3. Ibid., pp. 54–7.
4. Ibid., pp. 44, 75.
5. Ibid., pp. 81–7; R. Bartlett, *The Making of Europe: Conquest, Colonization and Cultural Change, 950–1350* (London: Penguin, 1993), p. 70.
6. Pounds, *Medieval Castle*, pp. 102–5; Bartlett, *Making of Europe*, p. 69.
7. B. M. Downing, 'Constitutionalism, Warfare and Political Change in Early Modern Europe', *Theory and Society*, 17 (1988), pp. 7–56; M. Mann, *States, War and Capitalism: Studies in Political Sociology* (Oxford: Blackwell, 1980).
8. Pounds, *Medieval Castle*, pp. 98, 211.
9. Ibid., p. 146; O. F. G. Hogg, *The Royal Arsenal: Its Background, Origin and Subsequent History*, vol. 1 (London: Oxford University Press, 1963), pp. 3–8.
10. R. Kaeuper, *War, Justice and Public Order: England and France in the Later Middle Ages* (Oxford: Clarendon Press, 1988), pp. 213–15.
11. Ibid., p. 222.
12. M. Powicke, *Military Obligation in Medieval England: A Study in Liberty and Duty* (Oxford: Clarendon Press, 1962), p. 172.
13. M. Prestwich, *The Three Edwards: War and State in England, 1272–1377* (London: Methuen, 1980), p. 64.
14. P. Contamine, *War in the Middle Ages,* trans. M. Jones (Oxford: Blackwell, 1984), pp. 78–88.
15. Powicke, *Military Obligation*, p. 78.
16. Ibid., pp. 119–23.
17. Prestwich, *Three Edwards*, pp. 68–9.
18. P. Virilio, *Speed and Politics: An Essay in Dromology*, trans. M. Polizotti (New York: Semiotext(e), 1986).
19. Prestwich, *Three Edwards*, p. 68.
20. Ibid., p. 70.
21. Contamine, *War in the Middle Ages*, pp. 81–5.

22. B. Tuchman, *A Distant Mirror: The Calamitous Fourteenth Century* (Harmondsworth: Penguin, 1979), p. 84.
23. Contamine, *War in the Middle Ages*, p. 86.
24. Tuchman, *Distant Mirror*, pp. 76–7.
25. Contamine, *War in the Middle Ages*, pp. 83–7.
26. M. H. Keen, *Laws of War in the Later Middle Ages* (London: Routledge & Kegan Paul, 1965), p. 228.
27. This right was originally restricted to the knighthood, but when it became a right pertaining to the political order, cities, as corporate members of the body politic, could and did also engage in *guerre couverte*.
28. Kaeuper, *War, Justice and Public Order*, p. 235.
29. Ibid., pp. 241–3, 258.
30. B. Geremek, *The Margins of Society in Late Medieval Paris*, trans. J. Birrell (Cambridge: Cambridge University Press, 1987), pp. 21–9.
31. Kaeuper, *War, Justice and Public Order*, pp. 243, 261–6.
32. A. Ayton and J. L. Price (eds), *The Medieval Military Revolution: State, Society and Military Change in Medieval and Early Modern Europe* (London: I. B. Tauris, 1995).
33. Kaeuper, *War, Justice and Public Order*, p. 172.
34. Ibid., p. 175.
35. J. Habermas, *Legitimation Crisis*, trans. T. McCarthy (London: Heinemann, 1976).
36. See P. Corrigan and D. Sayer, *The Great Arch: English State Formation as Cultural Revolution* (Oxford: Blackwell, 1985), p. 34.
37. P. Bourdieu, 'Codification', in P. Bourdieu, *In Other Words: Essays Towards a Reflexive Sociology*, trans. M. Adamson (Cambridge: Polity Press, 1990), pp. 76–86.
38. Ibid., p. 80.
39. Geremek, *Margins of Society*, p. 13.
40. Kaeuper, *War, Justice and Public Order*, p. 286.
41. Ibid., pp. 171, 160–1.
42. Corrigan and Sayer, *Great Arch*, p. 31.
43. Geremek, *Margins of Society*, pp. 7, 11–14.
44. Ibid., pp. 14–19.
45. Ibid., pp. 31–7.
46. Kaeuper, *War, Justice and Public Order*, p. 128.
47. Pounds, *Medieval Castle*, pp 170–9; C. J. Neville, *Violence, Custom and Law: The Anglo-Scottish Border Lands in the Later Middle Ages* (Edinburgh: Edinburgh University Press, 1998).
48. Pounds, *Medieval Castle*, pp. 179–82.
49. Prestwich, *Three Edwards*, pp. 52–3.
50. Ibid., pp. 54–6.
51. J. Froissart, *Chronicles,* ed. and trans. G. Brereton (London: Penguin, 1968), p. 47.
52. Ibid., pp. 47–54.
53. Prestwich, *Three Edwards*, p. 57.
54. M. Prestwich, *Armies and Warfare in the Middle Ages: The English Experience* (New Haven, CT: Yale University Press, 1996), pp. 255–9.

PART THREE: LATE MEDIEVAL

9

The Hundred Years War

The opening campaign of the Hundred Years War extended the experimental warfare of *chevauchée*. Though my concern is with the how rather than the why of the war, the terms under which it was conducted reveal the complex conjugation of both French and English kingship by late medieval lines of allegiance that were far from certain or direct, but played a major part in the intractability of the conflict. In contrast to the scenario of two emergent sovereign powers confronting one another in proximity and driven into war by structural competition or an inherent will to power, Barbara Tuchman's decentred approach through the person and lineage of Enguerrand de Coucy, a French noble, reveals shifting alliances between emergent political forces in the estates of the body politic which were eventually to transform both royal powers.[1] In addition to these forces, we can also identify a massive revolution in the constitution of violence as the new mode of warfare opened a new time and space of war as the field of a new mode of order.

The view from the tower: War's cosmology

Edward III's opening expedition of 1339 is often dismissed as a minor prelude, but the impact upon contemporary perceptions of the English deployment of *chevauchée* as a strategic instrument in the complexities of late medieval politics is illustrated most revealingly by an anecdote from the chronicler, Geoffrey le Baker. In the culture grown up around the centre of the Capetian royal domain of the Ile-de-France (containing Paris and the royal court), the French kingdom was represented as the recovery of Christian civilization in a renaissance of its own legendary origins in the empire of Charlemagne. A French cardinal, Bertrand de Montfaves, acting as papal nuncio, urged Edward III not to wage war in pursuit of his claims against the French Crown on the pragmatic grounds that an unbreakable 'silken thread' bound together the French body politic, its kingship and the medieval order of society. This silken thread was the medieval representation of the structural 'chains' of vertical dependence and horizontal interdependence which provide Norbert Elias with the analytical dimension of his 'civilizing process'.[2]

The campaign, concentrated mainly in Flanders, lasted only three months, but the English and their allies undertook one mass raid into France. Baker records how the papal nuncio was led one evening during this raid to the top of a high tower by Geoffrey le Scrope, the English Chief Justice of the King's Bench, who had been the architect of the previous year's campaign against lawlessness in England. The choice of a tower in darkness is itself revealing in a world for which 'the towers of cities grazed the vault of Heaven and embodied the celestial virtues'.[3] The view from a tower thus offered the perspective of the earth raised up into the light of medieval renaissance, revealing the closest approximation of earthly vision and order to divine truth, in which multifaceted yet unitary medieval space would appear at its most transparent, peopled by the members of Christian community in the order of the body politic, in which violence was contained by pyramidal dependence and time marked by cycles of celebration. Instead, Cardinal de Montfaves was shown a panorama lit by the fires of burning villages and peopled by creatures of the night, a landscape in the time of total war. As le Scrope pointed out to him, the thread of civilization appeared broken. His courtly sensibility overloaded with the profound shock of this radical switch in perception, the cardinal fell senseless to the floor.[4]

The common historical characterization of the Middle Ages as a state of continuous warfare cannot account for the impact of the scene. The area invaded by the English campaign of 1339 had in fact been the subject to quite severe private warfare, *guerre couverte*, in 1298, which the cardinal would have been aware of through subsequent local ecclesiastical inquests, but the devastation of the English raid was so unbelievable that a papal commission was sent to verify the reported level of destruction before charitable relief was despatched.[5] We can only begin to understand the historical enormity of the new form of warfare which Edward III had expedited to France if we recognize that the strategic use of *chevauchée* represented a profound transformation of the medieval world itself, plunging it into a condition analogous to images of Hell.

In the medieval 'world made of wood', fire had particular significance as a sign of destruction inflicted not directly upon the particular bodies of juridical retribution, but upon the collective community and the body politic. The ravage of 'waste' on a peasant agrarian economy could inflict damage over several generations as long-term investments in tools and livestock were destroyed, as well as buildings. Where the destructiveness of traditional *chevauchée* in private warfare operated as direct retribution and was thus subject to an economy of violence, its strategic use, at a remove from the ultimate object of the campaign, tended away from economy and toward total destruction. Even conquest invoked its own conservative economy when conducted over politically recognized terrain, but Edward III's objective lay in the complexity of the medieval conjugation of right: to gain ultimate seigniory over the remains of the Duchy of Aquitaine, which Eleanor had added to the domain of the English royal dynasty in her marriage to Henry II five generations before. Edward had no real intention of conquering the Capetian royal domain, but lay claim to the French throne in order to utilize the resources of the English body politic mapped out by the Assize of Arms and the Statute of Winchester.[6]

The conditions of war

Historians have recently used the concept of 'military revolution' to draw out the wider social and political consequences of the Hundred Years War.[7] However, in using Parker's revision of this thesis, these accounts tend to fall back into a fetishization of 'hard' technology which links military developments teleologically to state formation by arguing that the state provided the most efficient form for accumulating and mobilizing the resources necessary to develop such technology.[8] Such accounts complement the historical sociology of state formation, in which centralized states with a monopoly of violence over a given territory appear as the realization of an inherent structural ruler-function or as the effect of a rationality embedded in the structures of history itself.

However, the Hundred Years War began under very different conditions to those assumed by these approaches. Edward III had exhausted the coffers of the *fisc* in his serial campaigns on the margins of England, and his reliance on the Peruzzi and Bardi banks for credit led to their collapse when the first campaign in France failed to yield the gains to pay them off.[9] Accumulated wealth had proved inadequate, and war had to be made to pay for itself.[10] Money in itself did not translate into success in war, an immense hole into which money and bodies could simply disappear. Money could assemble a consumption-machine, attracting free bodies for deployment, but the same machine could consume its own assembler. Furthermore, the option of making war pay for itself, as *chevauchée*, effectively negated the territorializing function of the castle that comprised the body politic. The new mode of warfare simply derecognized territorial rights and privileges since it operated in a different space to the terrain of local domination effected by the castle, deterritorializing domination and war.

To operate on a mass scale, this mode of warfare required special techniques that were not monopolized by knighthood. Contemporary illustrations show how the army's self-provisioning, pillage, ravage, waste and arson were conducted methodically, in that order. Unlike the itinerary of Roman legions or the durability of encastellation, this machine left little geographical trace, but its effects upon contemporary domestic community were carefully compiled and recorded by papal commissions sent to verify its destructiveness, records which confirm the chroniclers' emphasis on the unprecedented extent of devastation. The English armies set out from their terminals at Calais or Bordeaux and divided along parallel routes, dispersing among villages at night to produce the panorama of fires that had stupefied Cardinal de Montfaves.[11] Their destructiveness escalated as techniques developed over the serial campaigns of the first phase of the conflict.

> We took our road through the land of Toulouse where there were many goodly towns and strongholds destroyed ... Since this war began, there was never such loss nor destruction as hath been in this raid.[12]

The strategic instrumentality of laying waste lay not in a function of retribution or deduction, but in bringing pressure to bear through the juridical and conjugal relations that constituted sovereign recognition. Battle does not appear in the records as the object of the fourteenth-century campaigns and cannot be inferred on the basis of modern strategic reconstructions.[13] The strategic application of the new mode of warfare to an *abstract* body politic liberated destruction from any immediate object, so it became maximal; whatever could not be consumed was destroyed. The 1346 expedition to Normandy finally abandoned Edward I's system of provision, so carefully built up out of the prerogative right of *prise* (compulsory purchase for the royal household), since Normandy was considered so fruitful that the army was expected to provision itself in the field. However, strategic self-provisioning required the elements of the consumption-machine to 'act corporately' and therefore needed 'principles of conduct'.[14] Obedience to orders and compliance with prohibitions were necessary for the machine to be maintained in a mechanical sense: it was not a natural, organically functional body and had no order of reproduction. Such order could not be achieved by regulating its relations with the domestic society over which it passed because its very operations depended upon derecognition of such relations. Customary constraints, the *ius gentium* of conventional warfare,[15] were thus replaced by tactical organization. The Marshal and the Constable (responsible for provisions to the extended royal household), had exclusive right to some kinds of cattle, pigs and unshod horses, but such 'principles' of seizure and distribution referred themselves to no right external to the host itself. Juridical attempts to distinguish between what was necessary to provision the army and what might have been regarded as 'excess' seizure, foundered upon the strategic purpose of destruction.[16]

Customary and juridical constraints were also obviated by the techniques and practices of the new warfare in an economy which recognized only the army, the king and an operational field of resources. Plunder was not necessary for the strategic objective of the new warfare, but provided an internal economy for the host as both a substitute for pay and a source of authority that could raise and govern bodies, securing their obedience and identity. The host in pay from the Wardrobe, with its links to the Exchequer, was administratively a part of the royal household, but with the substitute of plunder for expenses payments and the emergence of an internal economy, the host became detached from the administration of political kingship. Plunder became a form of largesse, a 'political gift' from the king in person, quite independent of the legitimate *fisc*. Beyond common and customary law, and outside the body politic, the soldiers of the new warfare were thus indebted to the king. Plunder did not offer them a luxurious living and frequently failed even to procure the necessary provisions for self-maintenance (particularly where the host had to pass over land already laid waste to avoid battle), forcing the Constable in the field to draw supplies from the coastal depots. Nevertheless, plunder provided the soldier with a source of livelihood in liberation from dependent subsistence on expense-level indentured wages. The right to loot thus became an important condition of the indentured soldiery. Both the French and the English armies looted, often regardless of orders sanctioned by summary execution.

This image of the army, with its own order and economy, was hitherto unknown to the medieval world and no customary, internal code had developed to regulate the division of spoils. Regulation of plunder effectively began when its prospect became a condition of service under competitive contractors in the indenture and retinue system which replaced the arrays and levies. In the new host, plunder functioned as an honorific, a 'moral' value producing authority over men as a quality of the contractors who maximized opportunities for its practice, while also indebting the recipients and marking them off from other social identities.

Indenture and authority

Over the course of the Hundred Years' War, the use of indenture as a means of raising and governing men displaced political obligation to military service. In 1304, the majority of English knights had still refused to accept pay, even for extensive campaigns, since it implied an entire package, with incorporation into the king's personal household, an extra-political indebtedness, loss of personal jurisdiction over their retinue and unconditional subjection to the king's will, but by 1322 pay had become acceptable to all statuses. Under Edward III there is little evidence of unpaid military service on any significant scale.[17]

Indenture was a common medieval form of retaining all manner of services, under which men were guaranteed the income from specified estates or a specific annual sum of cash, on condition of maintaining themselves, and often additional numbers and categories of men and equipment, for immediate service to the indenting party, which could be cross-indented to others. Indenture in this form did not require royal authority, did not involve fealty, and hence did not establish any feudal obligation. As a conditional grant only for life or a fixed period, it did not conjugate any juridical authority, but only connected men as retinue and retainer. It was thus a widespread and relatively stable legal form which did not change significantly in England until the reign of the Tudors.

The fourteenth-century kings of England used indenture as a substitute for summonses of assize and levy, offering monetary indentures to supply armed retinues for service abroad for a fixed duration in the king's pay to men of known reputation, who were given advances and a commission to recruit in a given area and were held responsible for maintaining the men who sub-indented to them out of the money they received. Through the recruiting captain, the retinues were thus maintained at the king's cost and under his household prerogative for a limited period. Captain's indentures specified the numbers, the equipment and the abilities of the men to be supplied, thus realizing the Vegetian principles of selection (which had failed to operate through the commissions of array and the statutory Westminster levy) through an institution of law, producing a calculable capacity of force at predetermined cost for a limited campaign.[18]

Indenture also enabled flexibiity, as the specific terms could be varied for each campaign. Military indenture included the indemnity against legal action at home while in the king's service which had been a condition of feudal service, but also offered a new package of terms, including letters of protection, charters of pardon, bonuses ('regard'), guaranteed rates of pay to the captains for the men supplied, a division of the spoils of war and a time limit: originally 40 days with the option of extension, later a quarter- or half-year, and finally for service under the king for 'as long as he desires'.[19] The time of service in war, hitherto limited by political and customary constraints, thus became subject to the will of the king, as the personal deployment of his virtual household under terms of indenture.

Indenture also obliterated status differentiation in the new military order. Formally, there was no distinction between indenture and sub-indenture, and some men-at-arms and even bands of archers indented directly with the king, thus creating a common military condition for earls and archers, an equalization that translated into tactical capacities; knights now rode with mounted archers, and since command was unmediated by status, they could be deployed in tactically mixed retinues, in ratios that could be planned in advance through control over the composition of the companies via the terms of indenture offered for each campaign.[20]

Though the English supplied disproportionate numbers of men for the field of war, since all indentured retinues and captains served under the king in his personal capacity, the new military order was indifferent to political allegiance, and men with dual vassalage or already in outlawry from the French body politic served with the English hosts.[21] Men could be raised in any domain where they were not explicitly prohibited from service to the English Crown, and serial campaigns produced a 'military labour market' extending far beyond the domain of England. In 1359, an expedition out of Calais attracted large numbers of mercenaries from Germany and the Low Countries, but the king had no money to offer them pay, only a share of plunder.[22] English kings thus required only a nucleus of captains from their permanent household retinue, and between 1369 and 1389, retinues were recruited directly under these men.

In France, too, by the mid-fourteenth century, *lettres de retenue* provided the administrative technology whereby bodies could be raised for war without political mobilization. Their terms were regularized in an ordinance of 1374, which also reveals further strategies brought into play by these new means of raising forces, decreeing retained captains to have '*gouvernment*' of the men-at-arms and soldiers they supplied, to be responsible for their conduct under the rules of the king's household, and subjecting all retinues to muster and inspection by the marshals of the king's permanent household.[23] Thus, in France,

171

lettres de retenue provided a means to create 'horizontal' subjection in a new military domain, enabling royal authority to cut through the hierarchical structure of the feudal polity.

The nobility were apparently willing to take indentures for the profits that could be made by sub-indenting men at lower wages than those at which they had indented to supply them, in addition to shares in any plunder. However, indenture was not offered on the basis of nobility, but on the criterion of 'reputation', thus breaking the feudal monopoly of domination in the order of arms. In a quantitative analysis of contemporary records, Andrew Ayton has traced the proliferation and increasing size of retinues supplied by non-noble knights and esquires indenting directly with the king to supply men for the field. War thus became a means of social mobility for those who were in contemporary terms 'hitherto of small account'.[24] Since it was extra-political and could be made with anyone, even directly with common soldiers, the preference was for captains who could supply the greatest means of destruction in balance with strategic considerations of maintaining their retinue in fitness for combat in the field (either by dispensing the wages with which they were provided or by pillage), maintaining its number against desertion and death, and producing the obedience necessary for co-ordination with the host as a whole. Serial, rather than continuous, campaigns and the expendability of forces consequent on the military labour market, enabled experimentation with different commands and forms of indenture. For instance, an 'exceptional' indenture was given to the adventurer, Sir Robert Knollys, in 1370, granting him only 13 weeks' pay to raise four thousand men to 'live by war' in France for two years.[25]

Reputation had to be twofold. To the Crown, a captain had to offer tactical effectiveness, the capacity to maximize destruction on an expedition of limited duration; while to the men he captained, he had to offer means of maintenance in the field and a generous share of plunder. For instance, John of Gaunt, the Duke of Lancaster, building up resources almost to rival those of the king, offered the same wages as he received in indenture, taking no profit, plus a two-thirds' share of plunder.[26] The tendency toward limitless violence was thus exacerbated by the interests of the indenting captains to build reputations among experienced soldiers. Strategically, *chevauchée* required the army to be kept on the move to maximize destruction, avoid battle and preclude territorialization, but the obedience of the retinues and the moral authority of a captain depended on him maximizing their opportunities for plunder, enabling him to recruit more effective forces and so enhancing his reputation with the Crown. The tendency thus appeared as one in which soldiers, 'made no count to the king or his officers of what they did get, they kept that to themselves'.[27]

The political anatomy of the expedition

Medieval chroniclers (often clerics writing on commission at court) utilized the discourse of knightly chivalric monopoly of violence as a legitimizing codification of war to decry the enemy forces for employing ignoble elements, in keeping with the dichotomy between sacrally invested violence of knighthood and the implicitly unGodly violence of others. However, the Hundred Years War gave rise to a new form of 'realist' historical discourse which was concerned to *authenticate* events, rather than authorize them by reference to a sacral code of right. In this genre, the king's peace is no longer indexed to theology, but becomes a practical accomplishment, establishing a new criteria for the legitimation of force. For Froissart and other such chroniclers of the Hundred Years War, propaganda value could be achieved by portraying the English forces not as ignoble or sacrilegious, but as criminal, a charge which could be authenticated by evidence and testimony. This produced a new mode of historical knowledge, in which English atrocities are explained by secular, political factors such as the mode of recruitment, the consequences of which cannot be contained by either the code of chivalry or the office of marshal;

> ... there were many ugly cases of murder and pillage, of arson and robbery, for in an army such as the King of England was leading it was impossible that there should not be plenty of bad characters and criminals without conscience.[28]

Such political analysis was based in the practical conditions of the conflict. The indenture system laid no necessary premium on knighthood. As the criterion of indenture, reputation, depended on routine mobile devastation, the value of knighthood became increasingly devalued and the host became a technical order: 'no attempt was made to achieve a standardized proportion of knights among the men-at-arms ... when deficiencies occurred, esquires were substituted to make up the contractual total'.[29] Nor was the other tactical component, the mounted archers, regularly comprised of skilled and sturdy English yeomen. The political margins of the realm, Wales and the borders, were favoured recruiting grounds for commissions applying Vegetian principles to select bodies for sub-indenture. 'Hard' bodies were valued in this discourse: proven sources of energy, habituated to exposure to the elements and subsistence on meagre provisions, with an ecological proximity to dirt. To the emergent courtly sensibility of the civilizing process, dirt was already acquiring the function of a sign, and cleanliness was beginning to form a mark of social distinction in the late Middle Ages.[30] This courtly code of cultural sensibility corresponds, as Eliasian analysis would argue, to the extension of the king's peace as a political code, and with it the distinction of law-abiding from 'criminal' elements. We have seen how in the years preceding the Hundred Years War, a wave of 'criminality' had appeared in the extensive exercise of royal judicial administration as a mode of knowledge, and how the campaign against this new appearance had co-ordinated and unified disparate judicial forms and institutions, filling the gaols of England. With the expeditionary campaigns, this political detritus of the king's peace was extruded *en masse* into the new space of war. Charters of pardon or expiation for murder or other crimes leading to outlawry were offered on the condition of service in the king's host abroad. Hewitt's detailed analysis of the *Calendar of Patent Rolls* shows over 850 such charters granted between 1339 and 1340, the beginning of a series corresponding to successive expeditions. He calculates that somewhere between 2 and 12 per cent of the English armies consisted of outlaws (a figure including some knights who were later to obtain indentures).[31] These formal indicators mark only the extremes of a spectrum of marginality, to which war offered an escape from the narrowing parameters of normalization.

However, the effects of the campaigns in France cannot be seen simply as the predictable consequences of the strategic extrusion of already deviant bodies. The new conditions of war did not merely mobilize bodies which were structurally and discursively identified with violence, but produced violence by invoking a structure of subjectivity in which the cultural codes and structures of relations that Elias characterized as sources of affect-constraint were directly implicated.

A culture of violence

The necessity for soldiers in the field to take food for themselves and their horses and to replace any losses of equipment and transport did not in itself derecognize natural rights of possession, but could be referred to the customary prerogative of *prise*. However, orders of march decreeing the destruction of settlements, stocks and crops disregarded not only property and natural justice, but also negated the concept of societal function that had provided the criteria for an economy of violence in the peace of God. The explicit object of *chevauchée* was destruction of the very means upon which life depended, while French counter-tactics sought to deprive the consumption-machine of its subsistence by destroying resources in its path or simply allowing it to exhaust itself in expending its energy in destruction. Froissart records the French king's council advising him to,

> 'Let them go on. They cannot rob you of your heritage by fires and smoke. They will grow tired and crumble away to nothing. Sometimes a great storm cloud passes over the country, but it later passes on and disperses of itself. So it will be with these English soldiers.'[32]

Courtly sensibility translated royal authority from an embodied presence into an abstract quality, and the king himself rationalized refusal to engage in battle by reducing the realm to an abstract quantity: 'I have no intention of marching out and hazarding my knights and my kingdom for a bit of farming land.'[33] The new space of warfare was thus bereft, from both English and French perspectives, of the very qualities which enabled men to live in the sacral order that had been translated into the king's peace and the body politic. Even the function of the king in that order became discreditable when the violence of *chevauchée* was used as a strategic instrument to bring pressure to bear upon the conventional relations in which power was embedded.

Units of force in static dispersion are highly vulnerable to local resistance or reprisal, as well as to major threats. Furthermore, the army had to co-ordinate its movements and ensure that it procured sufficient provisions by keeping on the move, which required systematic pillage. The intensity of destruction was thus calibrated to the speed of its passage, and the variability of that speed was used strategically. For instance, in Gascony the Black Prince made deliberately slow progress through the lands of the neutral Count of Foix to pressure him into alliance. On the days arranged for negotiation, truce was observed and operations suspended.[34] *Chevauchée* could thus be deployed with some precision as an instrument for conjugal and diplomatic strategies on the late medieval terrain of plural and negotiable vassalage. This was particularly apparent to the soldiers themselves. Though war appears in the passive voice of the chroniclers as an affliction from God, the soldiery knew it as a deliberately directed technical application that was bereft of ethical sanction, since their weapons were blessed for battle, but not for the regular, monotonous routine of laying waste.

Their *unconscionable* violence was not inherent in their criminality, but was effected by their extrusion from any code which could have offered them an ethic of practice. Medieval customary laws of war provided a code of conduct for situations such as the siege and surrender of towns, the treatment of noble captives and conditions of ransom, but these objects were displaced by the new kind of warfare, which consisted of everyday routine operations unrecognizable to the 'laws of war'. The imperative economy of violence of the Peace of God applied only to knights, not to the mounted archers comprising an increasing proportion of the English armies, who were caught in a fateful double-bind. On the one hand, violent extortion was necessary for survival in the field in lieu of wages, in the hostile environment of a peasantry who did not hesitate to exact their reprisals on the soldiery. On the other hand, the indentured host was in effect the king's domain, with summary execution for disobedience of orders, as the juridical order of a host comprised of nobles each with jurisdiction over their own retinues was displaced by 'the general jurisdiction in the host of the constable and marshal'.[35] The soldiery were thus in bodily peril beyond the protection of law, while their actions excluded them from Christian community. Regardless of 'criminal origins', 'lust for plunder' or licence of affect, they were culturally and structurally constituted as bodies 'without conscience' in Froissart's terms – without independent will and beyond salvation.

Knightly championship of customary, civilized laws of war remained within the particular qualifications of that law. The chroniclers represent knights saving noblewomen from rape, or seeking to intercede with the king against his orders to slaughter surrendered townships, or to protect their own order from the soldiery,[36] but these examples were significant as exceptions to the knightly behaviour emerging in response to the erosion of their sacral monopoly of violence (as well as their cultural status) by the tactical combinations and indentured conditions of the new military organization. Froissart shows how the knights rejoiced in war, but their pleasure was no longer the twelfth-century realization of a sacrally invested identity as defenders of justice and the weak, nor can it be ascribed to licence from the 'civilizing process' of affect-repression. Rather, an unrestrained knightly violence was positively produced in the new mode of warfare. The discourse of the Peace of God had constructed knighthood as a repository of violence soteriologically invested in the fulfilment of a function within the socio-theological order, an order of construction that developed into the code of chivalry which had particular significance for those who had no investment in conjugal identity or the form of land-tenure and who now comprised the knights and knight-errants available for indenture and retainder. These new relations of service displaced them from their old conditions of chivalric constraint, reducing their status to a tactical capacity and stripping their identity of its codified investments, so that it reposed only in their capacity for violence; however simply to see this as violence *unleashed* from constraint would actually *underestimate* the production of affect. In order to prove himself worthy of the honour of knighthood in a competitive order of reputation in which men could be raised to knighthood even from the commons and in which knighthood lost all other meaningful value, the knight's exercise of that violence became imperative, especially for those who had been raised up to it in war, and who had no dynastic legacy or other source of self-value.

The Great and Free Companies

The French body politic responded to the initial English campaigns by shadowing the English forces, allowing them to depredate the countryside while the host assembled, and then trying to entrap them in battle. With no territorial basis and leaving no garrisons behind it, the English consumption-machine, 'knew nothing of the enemy's movements and had no way of knowing', while territorial intelligence enabled the French to anticipate English movement, destroying resources and bridges in its path.[37]

French tactics in this early phase still oriented upon the object of battle, in which they deployed the conventional array of a regime of signs, seeking to engage the English piecemeal, in small-group, tourney-like combat in open field, where other elements of the host became an encumbrance: at Crécy (1346), King Philip ordered his knights to cut down the Genoese crossbowmen he had employed when they inadvertently blocked the charge of knightly battalions. At both Crécy and Poitiers (1356), however, the English used the local terrain to deny the French the open space required by such tactics, while the absence of status distinctions within the English host enabled tactical co-ordination of mixed deployments that contained and destroyed the French attacks. The traditional depiction of a mass French charge cut down by English arrows is a fiction, romanticizing the English 'yeoman army'. At Crécy, King Edward released the war of the margins upon the centre, destroying the French forces of chivalry in falling darkness.

> They took no prisoners and asked no ransoms, acting as they had decided among themselves in the morning when they were aware of the huge numbers of the enemy ... among the English were pillagers and irregulars, Welsh and Cornishmen armed with long knives, who went out after the French (their own men-at-arms and archers making way for them) and ... whether they were counts, barons, knights or squires, they killed them without mercy.[38]

The slaughter of the common levies was carried out the next morning, a Sunday, and the local community was given three days to bury the mountains of corpses before the army recommenced its warfare. The French losses were huge, but many knights had exercised particular feudal rights to quit the field. At Poitiers, again manoeuvred into battle, the English used a vineyard as a trap to draw the French attack down deep, narrow lanes.[39] An English survey of the dead at Crécy had suggested that ransom might be used as a lever in royal strategy, and at Poitiers the French nobles were taken prisoner as a matter of policy, even by archers, including the French king himself. The unransomable mass levies were slaughtered at the gates of the town, which saved itself by refusing to admit them.

Ransom had developed in the contest of tourney, where it related to an economy of honour, but in the new mode of warfare it became both another form of plunder and a strategic instrument. The noble estate of France and its provinces was ruined by ransom payments inflated beyond all customary limits by trade in prisoners between their captors. Similarly, the conditions set by the English Crown for a treaty with the captured French King Jean far exceeded what could have been demanded through the conventional strategic channels of conjugal or juridical relations. However, strategic use of ransom required a unitary French body politic to operate upon, and victory slipped away as that body disintegrated under the inflated demands into internecine conflict. The peasants rose in rebellion against the nobility's attempts to raise their ransoms and the city of Paris refused to accept the authority of the Dauphin or even of the king himself to negotiate and sign conditional treaties while he was in captivity.

After Poitiers, the Black Prince returned to Bordeaux and released the indentured retinues from their paid service, but the liberation of these bodies did not dispel the charge of violence with which they had been invested. Rather, the moral economy of the new warfare had created a dynamic which now became liberated from any end. From the sovereign perspective, the fourteenth century appears as war interrupted by outbreaks of truce, but the discontinuous war of the kings could equally be seen as parasitic, epiphenomenal and dependent upon the forces and processes that kings intermittently co-opted to their projects. Releasing these forces from their incorporation in royal pay unleashed war itself from political ends, as they continued to live by armed extortion. Some English knights, particularly those raised into knighthood in war, whose identity and value was thus invested in it, became their captains. Association with the discharged companies enabled knights to build reputations, a form of military 'capital' that could translate into profitable indentures. The companies also provided space for self-elevation. The services of a captain known only as Bacon were bought for 20,000 crowns by Philip VI to serve him as his usher-in-arms, equipped and apparelled 'like an earl'; a 'poor page' by the name of Croquart rose to such repute that he was later able to decline the French king's offer of triple incorporation through knighthood, marriage to a rich wife and an annual fee to retain his services.[40]

The discharged bands operated by short, rapid marches 'by covert ways day and night', avoiding other forces and taking towns and strongholds by surprise, or else spreading terror, impelling flight from their path and enabling them to plunder at leisure. They became large bodies, attracting or abducting women and ruined labourers to incorporate a range of services independent of domestic and political relations, existing in the deterritorialized space of war in which they recognized no community or polity, no place or right.[41] They lived by the same means for which they had been raised into the hosts of kings, to whom they compared themselves. Aimerigot Marcel boasted from the scaffold after 30 years of this way of life, that 'All was ours ... we were provisioned like kings.'[42]

In addition to the depredations of the English campaigns and the ruinous ransoms after Poitiers, the activities of the free companies further displaced knights, commoners and even clerics in a countryside laid waste, who joined their bands. However, this does not indicate the breakdown of a 'social contract', since the chivalric and religious codes which held medieval society in its various orders operated in the companies themselves, though now in an apparent inversion of societal function. The activities of knights with the bands were thus recorded as 'feats of arms', recognized and valued in chivalry just as they were recognized and valued in their tactical utility by kings and princes. Sir Robert Knollys, son of a Colchester tanner and minor landowner, had been raised to a knighthood in the wars and served with the Duke of Lancaster's retinue in Normandy in 1356. He had scant incentive to return to England, where his knighthood would count for little in the intensive status and legal network of a political society rapidly gentrifying under royal judicial administration and thus remained to captain a large and growing force of discharged men. During 1357–58, his company seized 40 castles in the Loire valley, which it used as a base for raiding the countryside and extorting fees from travellers. The operations of his company were well ordered, and paid so that 'they followed him eagerly', but Knollys did not aspire to independent legitimation. When the Truce of Bordeaux expired in 1359, he put his castles at the English king's disposal for war. Thereafter, he moved back and forth between independent operations in time of truce and royal service in time of war.[43] This oscillation between independence and service in times of truce and war was typical of the military entrepreneurs who remained in France, but Knollys' example also illustrates that they did not simply and unproblematically constitute a resource for the Crown as head of the body politic. Rather, the Kings of England and France had to treat them as an externality in times of peace, while incorporating them into the jurisdiction of the royal household in time of war.

Victory in battle at Poitiers, ransom of the nobles and even possession of the king of France had failed to produce a determinate result and the expiry of truce in 1359 required further English expeditions. However, the destruction of the French body politic had negated the necessary object of English strategy, while the ruined land no longer provided the conditions for mass *chevauchée*. When English forces set out again from Calais late in the year, they entered a land already ravaged by the companies, depleted by exorbitant ransom demands, and finally emptied by the French under the Dauphin, who did not seek battle but withdrew into fortified towns and castles. The countryside could not yield the means of life to the English host, and the consumption-machine could not realize its dual functions of self-maintenance and strategic utility. The fate of subsequent English expeditions followed a similar pattern, as the French developed the strategy of emptying the countryside in their path, withdrawing the body politic upon which *chevauchée* sought to operate in fortified towns or castles, and even laying waste themselves to deny the raiders their means of subsistence.[44] The Duke of Lancaster's campaign of 1373 again found itself in a denuded land, while the French king prohibited engagement in battle and ordered the population to take refuge in the towns. Harassed, ambushed, their horses dying, the duke's army finally reached Aquitaine in November, begging for the food it no longer had the strength to extort. The warfare of *chevauchée* seemed to have reached an inherent limit.

Treaty: The life of war in time of peace

After 1360, the English and Welsh retinues returned to England, but not to the discipline of domestic domination out of which they had been raised into service in the king's pay. The road continued to offer them the means of life, as they formed companies like those that had stayed in France. '"Arrayed for war", they robbed and assaulted travellers, took captives, held villages for ransom, killed, mutilated and spread terror.'[45] As a problem for the king's peace, they invoked the measures developed in the previous century; a statute of 1362 ordered justices to collect reports, 'on all those who have been plunderers and robbers beyond the seas and are now returned to go wandering and will not work as they were used to do'.[46] Increasingly, however, companies returned to England without plunder, forming bands who were alleged to,

> ... ride in great routs in divers parts of England ... beat and maim and slay the people for their wives and goods ... sometimes come before the justices in their sessions in such guise with great force whereby the justices be afraid and do not hardly do the law.[47]

War was not the only source of such displacement, and the returning soldiers converged with the flow of labour, which was liberating itself (also beyond the law) from the constraints of domestic economy. The Statute of Labourers had been enacted to regulate the escalating price of labour after the Black Death, but it had been difficult to implement and the magistrates' response to its ineffectiveness by escalating the sanctions which could be imposed, up to outlawry, merely extended the problem beyond economic parameters, since it impelled transgressive labourers to keep permanently on the move. The statute thus opened on to an indeterminate space between the classifications of work and crime, and between economic and legal structures, in which moral values were relativized and regulation contested. Attempts to subject common labourers to the discipline of place and local domination created an imperatively migrant and free labour force, disinvested from customary and juridical rights of property and possession by outlawry, a new form of vagrancy identical with the returning companies, 'people who no longer had a clear place in society, who were accustomed to showing little respect for property and human life, who knew how to use a weapon, and who retained certain elements of organization and cohesion'.[48]

In France, the term *Tards-Venus* ('late-comers') appears in the wake of the Treaty of Brétigny and seems to indicate as much a condition as an entity. Propertyless knights who had been raised up in war, like Sir John Hawkwood, joined the *Tards-Venus*, establishing relations akin to those of the castellany, in which the lord did not so much command by right as by virtue of a corporate identity. Hawkwood always ensured his men were paid and provisioned, and they remained loyal to him whether in indentured service or independent operations.[49] Under knights like Hawkwood, some of the companies made their way into Italy, where German companies had lived freely by extortion since mid-fourteenth century. In the context of a plurality of rival states prepared to employ them, their way of life became regularized in the *condotta*, a contract for military services (at first made with the company as a corporate body, and only later with the commander as contracting individual, whose employees the soldiery became). These companies assumed the dimensions of fully-fledged business enterprises, hiring themselves out to the warring city-states whose wealthy strata maintained their political hegemony by employing mercenaries to defend the city rather than arming the urban plebs. The companies comprised not only men-at-arms and soldiery, but a whole range of services, provided by those dispossessed or alienated from the domestic discipline of household or guild.

Contrary to the Weberian and Giddensian sociologic whereby immediate domination becomes legitimized and then politicized by virtue of a rationality inherent in simple repetition, the tendency here was not toward legitimation. The *condottiere* who established themselves in the political bodies of the Italian city-states did so by marital conjugation of associations built up over successive contracts and did so later, in the fifteenth century, when such commanders of companies were no longer popularly elected leaders of a *societas societatum*, a voluntary association, but effectively the owners of a permanent establishment,[50] entering into political relations as individual magnates, businessmen, equivalent to the other members of the city elite, and not in their capacity as military commanders. In France, the *appatis* system for the protracted maintenance of armies in the field, whereby communities paid regular and negotiable contributions for immunity from arbitrary extortion, provided an institutional route for legitimation but there the violence of the companies hypertrophied into apparently orgiastic excess, 'destroying the very means they lived by',[51] rather than stabilizing in regular extortion. Such violence resists explanation in terms of needs, interests, or a logic of accumulation, but is irreducible to the asocial category of *anomie*, since the codes of chivalry and Christianity continued to operate. Rather than consigning it to pathology as the breakdown of a 'social contract', attention to the terms under which the companies operated shows that their violence was very much a product of the social order.

'Abandoned to desire': The correspondence of chivalry and violence

Far from functioning as a code of conduct conducive to public order, or bearing the values and practices of progressive 'civilization', the ethic of chivalry now operated to actually engender violence in the new terrain of destratified and deterritorialized France. We can see this clearly in the case of Sir Eustace d'Aubrecicourt, a knight of Hainault and companion of the Black Prince at Poitiers, who made himself 'virtual master' of Champagne, able to assemble 700–1,000 men at a day's notice, living by raid and extortion.

The whole of the low country was at their mercy, on both sides of the Seine and Marne. This Sir Eustace performed many fine feats of arms and no one could stand up to him, for he was young and deeply in love and full of enterprise. He won great wealth for himself through ransoms, through the sale of towns and castles and also through the redemption of estates and houses and the safe-conducts he offered. No one was able to travel, either merchants or others, or venture out from the cities and towns without his authority. He had a thousand soldiers in his pay and held ten or twelve fortresses.[52]

The object of d'Aubrecicourt's love was the young widowed Countess Isabelle of Kent, a niece of the Queen of England. Froissart reports that 'She had fallen in love with Sir Eustace for his great exploits as a knight, of which news was brought to her every day', and responded with gifts and letters, 'by which the knight was inspired to still greater feats of bravery and accomplished such deeds that everyone talked of him'.[53] D'Aubrecicourt's violence was thus not only sanctioned by the code of chivalry, but positively driven by romantic reputation. Chivalry thus engendered violence as a sign of love. Violence became *desirable*, and thus limitless.

This positive affinity of the code of chivalry with violence appears perverse against the Eliasian thesis of a progressive 'civilizing process', just as the hypertrophy of relentless extortion appears perverse against the theoretically inherent rationality of legitimation and state-formation. There was, however, still an object and hence a potential end in Knollys' alternate subjection to royal service in time of war and in d'Aubrecicourt's chivalric trajectory; Knollys retired to England on his wealth to become a member of the political body and a charitable benefactor, while d'Aubrecicourt conjugated his desirability in marriage to Isabelle. The value of a violent reputation could thus be redeemed in an exchange: Knollys' for membership of community and the political body, d'Aubrecicourt's for a conjugated identity in land and dynastic establishment. In eschatological terms, however, the companies' violence was irredeemably negative, without exchange value. Rather, violence in the terms of Christianity became a military nihilism of revelation without redemption.

'If God were a soldier, He would be a robber'[54]

A noble of Perigord, Regnault de Cervoles had once held a benefice, but had become a knight in the service of the king of France. Captured at Poitiers, like many noble French knights he had ransomed himself and thereby took leave of his indebtedness to royal service, recovering the honour of independent nobility, but only by ruining his estate, rendering his recovered identity empty, since he had no means by which he could support himself. Returning to France in 1357, he took,

> ... command of a large company of men-at-arms from many countries. These found that their pay had ceased with the capture of King Jean and could see no way of making a living in France. They therefore went towards Provence, where they took a number of fortified towns and castles by assault and plundered the whole country as far as Avignon under the sole leadership of Sir Regnault.[55]

The company called itself the *Società dell'acquisito*, and de Cervoles was known as 'the Archpriest' (similarly, the company of *Tards-Venus* under Sir John Hawkwood who crossed into Italy became known as 'The Scourge of God'). In Avignon, Cervoles was invited to dine with the Pope and his cardinals, was received 'reverently', had all his sins remitted him, and was given 40,000 crowns to distribute among his men. To see such companies as simply sacrilegious, however, would again underestimate the charge of their violence. The Pope had categorically excommunicated the companies in 1364, but they continued to actively seek absolution,[56] affirming the Church's claim to a universal capacity for soteriological intercession, while simultaneously reducing that sacral capacity to the corrupt order of a world in which anything could be gained by the sword.

This devaluation had a particular impact on the lower monastic orders, the repository of an ascetic, other-worldly tendency of Christianity which was thus always in tension with the worldly hierocracy.[57] Jean de Venette (head of the Carmelite order), blamed the ruin of the sacrally sanctioned order of the Christian community in France on the political nobility, but less hierocratically complicit monastic sources excorciate all the orders – nobility, commons and clergy – for the ruination of God's order on earth, in a discourse which radically revalues violence as the revelation of their fallen condition in the corruption of the flesh.[58] In the context of such other-worldly denunciations, the companies could even lay some claim to operate as the sword of God's vengeance upon the corrupt world. In the mid-fourteenth century, the company of Fra Monreale, a renegade prior of the Order of St John, was one of the most prominent. When finally captured and tried as a 'public robber', Fra Monreale contrasted his violence to the corrupt illusion of the world, thus converting into an ethic his way of life, 'in carving his way with a sword through a false and miserable world'.[59]

Such self-identification with the world-rejection of Christian asceticism imbued the companies' activities with a sacral charge that was given some authority by their incorporation of ruined, apostate and renegade clerics, even bishops and abbots.[60] In a pastoral letter of 1360, the Pope lamented the violation and profanation of churches and the participation of clerics in the companies,[61] but preservation of the papal establishment had taken precedence over spiritual propriety when a Pope had administered the sacrament to the companies' own 'Archpriest'. In a world where absolution could be extorted through violence, revealing the emptiness of its redemptive claim, the sword became a truth, and terror a vocation charged with revealing the corruption of the world.

The medieval sociologist and the military subaltern

If the apocalypticism of such counter-theology of violence represented one extreme of the spectrum, the routine of the companies' alternation between free action and royal service comprised a much larger sociological formation, recorded by Jean Froissart. Elias' neglect of Froissart as a source is odd for a sociologist concerned to write the micro-history of courtly culture with special focus on France. Froissart himself, as 'a product of the merchant class', occupied a peculiar place in late medieval court society. He was engaged to collect materials for a work of history commissioned by the Count of Blois, actively producing the very discourse of late medieval courtly 'civilization' which provides Elias with the vehicle for his thesis. He writes from the cultural perspective of the 'colonizers', the bearers of civilizing values and manners, in an environment which he, like his masters, perceives as alien, particularly when describing the *Jacques'* (peasants) rebellion, where the villeins figure as 'small and dark' and are slaughtered 'like cattle'.[62] Nevertheless, Froissart's perspective is not purely that of the masters. As his documentary style developed, he included interview material illustrating the view of those who, like him, served their masters as instruments, partaking in their victories and sharing the threat from peasant rebellions. Analysis of one of the subaltern interviews Froissart included in his history provides a rich source of insight into the subjectivity with which the crucial art of governing bodies of men outside community, juridical relations and the body politic had to contend.

The 'Reminiscences of Bascot de Maulein, Freebooter',[63] were collected in a courtly context, when Froissart recognized the squire's name at a Christmas gathering at the court of the Count of Foix in 1388–89. Though Bascot narrates his life in the context of chivalry, the deeds he recounts are those of *a man with a master*, not a free, formally equal subject upon whom the etiquette of manners could operate to effect internal *self*-restraint. Bascot thus provides the subaltern's story of fourteenth-century warfare. The tale is told (as such tales are) in a 'hostelry' where he and Froissart are both staying, in the space of transit, of the road rather than the castle.

Behind the recital of events which he was commissioned to produce, Froissart is a sociologist of court society. His compendious knowledge of the names and associations of the society in which he interposes himself enables him to identify key interview subjects at crucial junctures in the social structure. His methodically applied familiarization with the nodes of circulation of late medieval courts and their Goffmanesque front and backstages, enables him to pursue his interviewees and engineer encounters as an 'insider', creating the ideal framework for 'naturalist' qualitative research into the actors self-understandings behind their presentation of self. Froissart already has all the information which Bascot relates to him, but urges his respondent to tell his own tale, simply because he is 'very interested to hear you talk of deeds of arms'. Throughout the interview, it is Bascot, not Froissart the supposed historian, who is concerned to verify the events by reference to historical authority. The narrative of Bascot's tale has little sociological or cultural importance in itself, but a number of significant factors emerge which enable us to see into the construction of the subaltern military subject in the new space of war. He is, sociologically speaking, representative of the rising military class of the late Middle Ages.

Only a squire, Bascot has a master, yet unlike the retained men of the twelfth-century *familia*, he operates for himself. Nevertheless, when he hears that his master is assembling a force, he 'has to see him again', even though he is not summonsed or drawn by hope of gain. With the exception of this personalized and traditional subalternity, Bascot tells of what his captures 'brought him in', a tale in which value is expressed in monetary terms. Only when he speaks of knights does honour enter the drive-economy in his discourse. However, in battles and fights, Bascot the squire, too, is sought for capture alive, not for reasons of chivalry, but because he is a captain and can thus be expected to yield a ransom, an instance which illustrates how the custom of ransom had become juridicalized, since the money had to be sent to Paris, to the *parlement* where the lawyers were, and be certified by a receipt. However, although Bascot speaks continually of his losses and gains, of the cash incomes he has been able to extort by holding castles as a freebooter in 'command' of varying forces of companions, his talk is all about *acquiring* money, never about accumulating it; about holding, not owning. He has no title to anything permanent in the world, except his name.

Froissant reports verbatim Bascot's claim that his most recent escapade, in which he seized the castle and town at Thurie with his men by deceit, yields him 'greater profits and income yearly ... than the castle and all the dependencies of this place [the castle of the Count of Foix] would fetch if they were sold at their best price. But now I don't know what I ought to do with it.' Accumulation presents a dilemma to the new military subjectivity because it is inherently subaltern and so cannot be legitimized. Despite the income, Bascot has come to the count's court to find out if he can surrender it to the king for money in hand. The attraction of the court for these subalterns is thus not the opportunity it presents for cultural or political investment, but the information which circulates there. The new subalternity is interested in circulation, rather than in any accumulation of capital, whether cultural, political or financial. These sergeants are trapped in the economy of the war-machine which produced them as free agents and their subjectivity is invested in its economy of consumption, not reproduction; but unlike those whom Duby dubbed the 'proletarians' of war, Bascot is not criminalized. A 'freebooter' in illegitimate possession of a castle, who has customarily served the English Crown against that of France in defiance of its juridical claims (he was from Bourdeaux), he is nonetheless free to attend the court of the French king's officer and vassal, the Count of Foix.

In contrast, Contamine cites the tale of a '*laboureur des vignes*', Regnaut de Saint-Marc, traced in the *Registre Criminel du Chatelet* of 1389–92,[64] records which constitute an index of normalization and exclusion. Regnaut, (married with three children), was unable to find work to sustain himself and his family in his home town of Dijon in 1383 and so followed bands of men-at-arms, serving a succession of masters as a '*gros valet*', following them to the Low Countries, Spain, Germany, Italy and Hungary, before arriving in Paris penniless and in search of a new master, where he was arrested as a vagabond and tortured to extract his confession to ransom, horse-stealing and even theft from the masters he had served. Regnaut was hanged as a criminal.

The limits of expedition

In Italy, contractual hire to the warring city-states transformed the companies into personal retinues of leaders who came effectively to own the enterprise of war, but in the interior of France, most notoriously in the Auvergne, the *Tard-Venus* persisted in the form of free associations, *societas societatum*, proving resistant to suppression. They were thus not amenable to government by the authority of knighthood, but required techniques operating upon their particular way of life. English kingship was able to expedite its compound problem of vagabondage and the liberty of violence to France, and Charles V on his accession attempted a similar solution to the endemic problem of the *Tard-Venus*, who had proved resistant to suppression by knights. Serial late medieval attempts to organize the companies into crusading expeditions foundered on the twin problems of government and provision. The companies were not self-provisioning extensions of economically independent households, but could only live off the land, while authority over them as bodies of consumption consisted in the permissive management of this way of life. Crusade intended to expedite their violence in Christian vocation on the frontiers of Christendom thus became a passage of war conducted by apostates, devastating the lands they had to pass through and raising the cities against them. Much the same reasons precluded their use as strategic instruments in deployments to Spain and against the Austrian Habsburgs.[65]

Attempts to deal with the problem of the companies by strategic expedition were thus counter-effective, simply affirming the companies' world-cynicism and negating the very values which these projects attempted to invest in the companions. The instrumentalization of violence was not given in the condition of violence itself, or in forms of authority, but required modes of government which addressed the subject of violence through the specific economies in which it was produced and invested. These late medieval problematics of military power were thus conceptual as well as practical.

Notes

1. B. A Tuchman, *Distant Mirror: The Calamitous Fourteenth Century* (Harmondsworth: Penguin, 1979).
2. N. Elias, *The Civilizing Process*, trans. E. Jephiott (Oxford: Blackwell, 1994).
3. H. Lefebvre, *The Production of Space*, trans. D. Nicholson-Smith (Oxford: Blackwell, 1991), p. 267. In Lefebvre's account of the dialectical emergence of modern spatiality, sovereign power suddenly appears in early modernity as violence from outside the urban parameters of organic spatiality, out of another time, another history.
4. R. Kaeuper, *War, Justice and Public Order: England and France in the Later Middle Ages* (Cambridge University Press, 1988), p. 81.
5. Ibid., pp. 82–3.

6. Tuchman, *Distant Mirror*, p. 72.
7. A. Ayton, and J. L. Price (eds), *The Medieval Military Revolution: State, Society and Military Change in Medieval and Early Modern Europe* (London: I. B.Tauris, 1995).
8. G. Parker, *The Military Revolution: Military Innovation and the Rise of the West, 1500–1800* (Cambridge: Cambridge University Press, 1988); C. J. Rogers (ed.), *The Military Revolution Debate: Readings on the Military Transformation of Early Modern Europe* (Oxford: Westview Press, 1995).
9. Kaeuper, *War, Justice and Public Order*, pp. 41–55.
10. The *Secretum Secretorum*, an arcane text of medieval governmental knowledge, contains a diagram representing the connections between the king, money and war, reproduced in A. Murray, *Reason and Society in the Middle Ages* (Oxford: Clarendon Press, 1978). However, these follow the model of personal kingship's embodiment of power, which circulates rather than accumulates. In economic terms, the source of medieval wealth was similarly located in circulation in trade, and rather than relying on banks, Edward III came to seek a source of financial security from duties charged on exports, particularly to Flanders, trade that was itself a major source of tension.
11. Tuchman, *A Distant Mirror*, p. 83; H. J. Hewitt, *The Organization of War under Edward III* (Manchester: Manchester University Press, 1966), p. 102.
12. Avebury, quoted in Hewitt, *Organization of War*, p. 111.
13. Ibid., p. 99.
14. Hewitt, *Organization of War*, p. 93; Tuchman, *Distant Mirror*, p. 82.
15. M. H. Keen, *The Laws of War in the Later Middle Ages* (London: Routledge, Kegan & Paul, 1965).
16. Hewitt, *Organization of War*, p. 102; N. A. R. Wright, 'Pillagers and Brigands in the Hundred Years War', *Journal of Medieval History*, 9 (1983), pp. 15–24.
17. M. Prestwich, *Armies and Warfare in the Middle Ages: The English Experience* (New Haven, CT: Yale University Press, 1996), p. 97.
18. Prestwich, *Three Edwards*, pp. 124–5.
19. A. Ayton, 'English Armies in the Fourteenth Century', in A. Curry and M. Hughes (eds), *Arms, Armies and Fortifications in the Hundred Years War* (Woodbridge: Boydell Press, 1994), p. 82; Hewitt, *Organization of War*, p. 34.
20. Ibid.; A. Ayton, 'Knights, Esquires and Military Service: The Evidence of Armorial Cases before the Court of Chivalry', in Ayton and Price (eds), *Medieval Military Revolution*.
21. Hewitt, *Organization of War*, p. 93; J. Sherbourne, 'Indentured Retinues and English Expeditions to France, 1369–80', in J. Sherbourne, *Politics and Culture in Fourteenth-Century England*, ed. Tuck (London: Hambledon Press, 1994), pp. 5–6.
22. Prestwich, *Armies and Warfare*, p. 155.
23. P. Contamine, *War in the Middle Ages*, p. 153.
24. Ayton, 'Knights, Esquires and Military Service', p. 82.
25. Prestwich, *Armies and Warfare*, p. 93; Sherbourne, 'Indentured Retinues', pp. 6–7.
26. Hewitt, *Organization of War*, p. 31; Prestwich, *Armies and Warfare*, pp. 93–5.
27. Jean de Venette quoted in Tuchman, *Distant Mirror*, p. 83.
28. J. Froissart, *Chronicles*, ed. and trans. G. Brereton (London: Penguin, [1389] 1968) (1389), p. 77.
29. Sherbourne, 'Indentured Retinues', p. 27.
30. Elias, *Civilizing Process*, pp. 50–2.

31. Hewitt, *Organization of War*, pp. 29–30.
32. Froissart, *Chronicles*, p. 188.
33. Ibid., p. 190. In reporting these speeches, Froissart may be indulging in anti-courtly, bourgeois-materialist polemic, but the important thing for our purposes is that he was able to do so because royal strategy appeared as he depicts it.
34. Hewitt, *Organization of War*, p. 96.
35. Ibid., pp. 94–5; Keen, *Laws of War*, p. 40.
36. Hewitt, *Organization of War*, p. 123.
37. Froissart, *Chronicles*, p. 126.
38. Ibid., p. 93.
39. Ibid., p. 133.
40. Tuchman, *Distant Mirror*, p. 223.
41. Ibid., pp. 163–4, Froissart, *Chronicles*, pp. 280–94.
42. Quoted in Tuchman, *Distant Mirror*, p. 223.
43. Froissart, *Chronicles*, p. 149; Tuchman, *Distant Mirror*, pp. 165–6.
44. Tuchman, *Distant Mirror*, pp. 185–90.
45. Ibid., p. 195.
46. Quoted in Hewitt, *Organization of War*, p. 175.
47. Statute of Richard II, quoted in Tuchman, *Distant Mirror*, p. 285.
48. B. Geremek, *The Margins of Society in Late Medieval Paris* (Cambridge University Press, 1987), pp. 64–5. Wat Tyler was a veteran of the king's wars, who had come to make a living by itinerant services, not a peasant or even a settled artisan. The relation of such bodies of the road to the solidarity of settled community in England was to remain ambivalent throughout early modernity.
49. Tuchman, *Distant Mirror*, p. 225, Contamine, *War in the Middle Ages*, p. 159.
50. Contamine, *War in the Middle Ages*, p. 160.
51. Tuchman, *Distant Mirror*, p. 164.
52. Froissart, *Chronicles*, p. 161.
53. Ibid.
54. Contemporary saying, quoted in Tuchman, *Distant Mirror*, p. 225.
55. Froissart, *Chronicles*, p. 148.
56. Tuchman, *Distant Mirror*, pp. 163–5, 224.
57. M. Weber, *Economy and Society: An Outline of Interpretive Sociology*, eds G. Roth and C. Wittich (Berkeley: University of California Press, 1968), pp. 1164–70.
58. Tuchman, *Distant Mirror*, p. 167.
59. Quoted in ibid., p. 164.
60. Contamine, *War in the Middle Ages*, pp. 240–1.
61. Tuchman, *Distant Mirror*, p. 224.
62. Froissart, *Chronicles*, p. 294, see also G. Brereton, Introduction to the *Chronicles*, pp. 20–1.
63. Ibid., pp. 280–94.
64. Contamine, *War in the Middle Ages*, p. 239.
65. Tuchman, *Distant Mirror*, pp. 201–2, 270–81.

10

A Military Domain

The problem of military subjection

Medieval military thought was unable to recognize the dimensions of the subject produced in the new warfare. For medieval thought, the subjection of violence was embodied in the knight, whose moral and technical dimensions were encoded in the 'discipline of chivalry'. It could provide no mechanisms to deal with the disintegration of this normative subject and the liberation of violence from its economic constraints.

Philippe Contamine notes the appearance of 'didactic treatises' on war at this time, which can be divided into three kinds. A juridical discourse of war, exemplified by *L'arbre des batailles*, attributed to Honoré Bovet, a Benedictine prior.[1] This genre is concerned with the legitimation of war, effecting a dichotomization of violence by reducing practices to their ends, and was thus unable to provide any technical means to regulate violence that recognized no external limits. Treatises on chivalry provided a more operational discourse, a code of practice which could be disseminated as a means to construct oneself as a knight. Originally developing out of the effective constitution of knighthood as an autonomous domain in twelfth-century socio-theology, these treatises assumed an entirely new function with the construction of the body politic and its reconstitution of knighthood. Political knighthood was a more arbitrary relation to others, a title which could be acquired, but to be invested with value it had also to be recognizably accomplished, requiring a standard authoritative codification. Caxton's 1480 English translation of the much earlier *Le libre del ordre de cauayleria*, by the knight-turned-apostolic Ramon Lull, as *The Book of the Order of Chivalry*, provides a manual for the education of an aspirant squire.[2] For Lull (*c.* 1235–1315), the passage from squire to knight was dependent on investment in the ethical order itself, while for Caxton's readers, knighthood might proceed from investment in wealth, patronage or reputation, preceding the cultural investment mapped out in the text. Texts such as Christine de Pisan's

Le livre des fais d'armes et le chevalrie (also translated and printed by Caxton), recovered Vegetius as an authority for practical conversion to knighthood by men raised up from low status. These texts are pedagogical and technical manuals for constructing knighthood that also reconstruct it, operating in the context of the body politic as realized by the practices of assize and distraint to recover and reform chivalry in new conditions, under the prince in the court.[3] However, the subject of this discourse is still monadic. The texts do not concern themselves with the government of others as a military function, but outline a cultural medium for the management of political relations between knights themselves.

Only when the military function of subordinate command finally appears is the discourse of violence transformed into something more recognizable to us as a discourse of war and of the 'military thing'. Around 1460–70, Jean de Bueil wrote *Le jouvensel avancé par la guerra* as a systematic compendium of his military experience. De Bueil focused on the factors which were producing a new world, rather than attempting to deploy old concepts in the transformed context, attending to 'the machines devised by men which change the way in which things are done ... clever devices which were neither known nor used in former times'.[4] De Bueil's text is divided into three parts, '*monosticque, yconomicque et politicque* ... the first speaks of the government of a single man. The second about oneself and others. The third of the government of princes and captains, who have the charge and governance of countries and peoples.'[5] The movement from the government of the self, the prince, to the government of all is thus accomplished by de Bueil not through the model of the household, but through the government of the sword. For Christine de Pisan, who had already radically revised John of Salisbury's theme in her *Le livre de corps de policie* (1406),[6] the government of the sword was quite distinct from the government of knighthood, a separate part of the body politic. The knight governed himself, but the sword was an instrument of the royal household. There are four figures of violence in de Pisan's text: the officers of the prince, the common soldiers, the knights, and the prince's external enemies. The book's three parts correspond to the first three parts of bodies politic and how they are to be governed. The violence of royal officers, the soldiers and the enemies figure under the section on the prince, while that of the knights is contained within their self-government.

It is conventional to contrast the immediate connection of subjective interest and objective function in knighthood with the more complex subjectivity of the modern military profession, in which interests are mediated by exchange, but de Pisan's text reveals a complex constitution of the subject of late medieval chivalry that produces its social function as an effect of its own internal operations. De Pisan's pedagogical chapters on knightly self-government provide a guide to establish a *habitus* (the inner shape and quality of the form of the soul in its earthly embodiment), combining 'public and private behaviour, the world of morality with the world of law'.[7] Multiple moral and practical conditions of knighthood are integrated to constitute this *habitus* as an ethical economy, so that the duties of a knight are in accord with his reason. Thus, love of arms and their art is achieved by practising the discipline of chivalry, which consists in moral and behavioural precepts as well as physical exercises, but physical strength can be overcome by boldness, which reposes in the soul, not in the body, and is qualified as a calculative rationality, as 'things that are possible and reasonable to do'. And since the *habitus* is constructed pedagogically, so instruction ('exhortation, example and practice') can *produce* this constancy of affect. The third condition consists in the knights mutually supporting one another in maintaining the rules of chivalry, i.e. in practising pastoral peer surveillance and counsel. It is by this means that the knight may lead an army, bearing the

> ... heavy responsibility to provide for so many people, that is, thinking about what their needs might be. This means governing a large number of people for the will and good order of all, one's own honour, and the benefit of the sovereign.[8]

As a mode of operation in this task of governing other bodies, the knight should allow no moral considerations other than the monitorship of his fellows to obstruct him in his duty. If necessary, he may use deceit and ignore the law. His expertise in arms similarly includes 'stratagems' of dissimulation against the enemy. In relation to himself and his fellows, however, good manners, the renunciation of evil and faithfulness to oaths are imperative, since vice, lechery and avarice can undermine honour by establishing a rival internal economy of desire. The knight must 'love and desire honour above all things', since this provides the value which the other conditions mobilize in the ethical economy of the *habitus*.

The context of this reformed chivalry thus reveals a latent struggle between the pseudo-monastic conception of knighthood, dependent upon its self-insulation, and the worldliness in which it had to operate, a struggle that exploded in the Hundred Years' War into the military nihilism of the knights of the Free Companies. The text also reveals the problematics of knighthood as an instrument of command. Since its capacity for the government of others is conditional upon the corporate condition of knighthood as a whole, it is difficult to see how de Pisan's knighthood could mobilize its *self*-government to govern over a mass body which had no code, no ethical value, no soul, without inverting itself in military nihilism. It is against such corruption that knighthood is to retain and maintain in itself the discipline of chivalry which has become conditional upon closure against the world. In Caxton's translation of Lull, the knight's armour figures as a *moral* insulation which has become an end in itself.

The shepherd and the flock, the dogs and the rod of iron

However, other means of mass government were available. In the section of the book on the Prince, Christine de Pisan treats 'the sword' as an instrument, while her allegory of princeship as the pastoral role of the shepherd transposes the problem of mass government onto the Judaeo-Christian tradition, mobilizing an alternative to the Graeco-Roman tradition's discourses of government by patriarchal, household right and of political rule of the city.

De Pisan argues that if we consider the prince as the shepherd of his flock, then the soldiers are his dogs, held by skilled, carefully chosen *personal* servants 'who will prefer his interest', keeping the dogs leashed to their belts by day and unleashing them at night or if some danger threatens. The servants have iron staves to hit the dogs if they worry the sheep and to train them to chase away wolves. The prince-as-shepherd (and thus pastoral secular government itself) is dependent on the dogs, who also have to return the common people to the right path if they rebel, just as sheepdogs return stray sheep to the flock, a task they accomplish 'either by threats or by taking good care of them'. The dogs are clearly the *retinencia regis*, the military household of the prince, and thus provide an alternative model of the subject of violence to the knight of chivalry.[9] The dog's loyalty consists in unconditional love for his master, in which he is prepared to 'expose himself to death' in his assigned guard, in contrast to de Pisan's humanist qualification of the knight's prudent self-regard in his duties. The dog's ability to differentiate friend from foe is not mediated by any technique of knowledge, but is categorically given in the dog's constitutive identity with the prince who feeds him. The conditions of service of the *retinencia regis* thus produce, in de Pisan's allegory, an alternative mode of executive governmental knowledge to that of the judicial apparatus, which is mediated by normative criteria. The dogs' sense of territory, along with their love of the master, is grounded in the household, where they are given their food, as the bread of the king.

That bread once constituted a political gift, indebting the subjects of the household in an economy of honour, but de Pisan subsequently shows how the political gift has become problematized by acquiring an exchange value.

In a world in which honour is no longer common currency but only acquires value through work upon the self such as elect knights must perform, the king must carefully gauge his gifts to the recipient, calculating their value in relation to the individual in terms of his wealth. Such gifts, furthermore, must be given at the king's own expense. If these conditions are not carefully calibrated, the effect may be worse than useless.[10] The immediate moral effect of the gift, which demanded nothing in return but operated in an economy of honour to annul the will of those on whom it was bestowed, now operates as a medium upon the calculative will of the recipient, producing a conditional subjection, while the obedience of the dogs of war has become a *natural* function of the bodily maintenance of the dog, which is no longer a gift, either political or moral. The spoils of war, similarly are to be granted to the soldiers simply because they followed orders, rather than as a largesse. In de Pisan's discourse on the subject of violence, the allegiance of the soldier thus does not need to be achieved, but is given in the prince's logistical maintenance of his body. Discipline, too, has become transformed. Soldiers must be more afraid of the prince than they are of death, but the source of fear now lies in the iron rod as a threat of physical punishment that would operate upon their bodies, not in the threat of exclusion from identity in the city or the king's household.[11]

Projecting the body of violence: Control over space and time

By the end of the fourteenth century mass *chevauchée* had negated its own condition, transforming the French domain from a series of particular jurisdictions around the castle and represented in the body politic, into a de-territorialized zone of material resources for the war-machine, a de-stratified terrain of immediate domination which could not be represented politically. However, a space and time of the circulation of bodies, a 'dromological' dimension,[12] had begun to open up between the domain of peace and the zone of war, as the means of royal household familial governance extended to incorporate bodies in states of transition, already abstracted out of community. The space and time of transit from the point at which men were levied or recruited to the coastal points of embarkation opened on to this new dimension, in which the practices of the royal household were transformed into new techniques, providing a means of regulating the force of these bodies on the road.

Prior to 1344, English levies were accompanied by writs specifying the pay that was to be supplied to them by their local community for the journey to the point of muster at which they entered the king's service, but petitions to the Crown in Parliament had protested at the disorder of men in transit to muster. Liberated from domestic discipline in service as members of the body politic, the men often resorted to living by seizure on their way to the muster, but their arrest by local authorities was prejudicial to kingship in its rightful exercise of the levy. Complaints were couched in terms of categories of offence over which the king claimed jurisdiction, such as 'felonies, trespasses and oppression' committed by men travelling to embarkation points,[13] while offenders blamed their actions on lack of transitional support from the communities from which they were levied.[14] This jurisdictional problem was resolved by a 1344 Ordinance providing maintenance at the king's wages for men selected for service from the day they left home to the day they returned, instituting their immediate incorporation into the royal household and the king's personal jurisdiction.

This resolution opened up the heterotopic, indeterminate space of the road to *positive* regulation over liminal bodies, in contrast to their negative criminalization in terms of the customary exclusions of medieval community. In this dromological condition, men were subject to order by number rather than place of origin, status or lineage, in hundreds and twenties under an officer appointed directly by the Crown to 'deliver' selected bodies to the marshal of the household at the rendezvous. Once incorporated in royal pay, it was possible to control the *speed* of these bodies; the auditors allowed pay for a rate of march of 20 miles per day, far faster than contemporary armies in the field.[15] In the royal household retinue obedience was obtained by virtue of an identity in the person of the king, but the transitional condition constituted new subjects, neither political nor patrimonial, neither clientary nor legal, a new subject of regulation by royal prerogative.

At the embarkation rendezvous at Portsmouth in 1346, the deputy marshal lodged the men delivered up to him, 'outside the verges of the king's household',[16] a threshold over which the Provost exercised power of life and death as executor of the royal prerogative in the king's private domain, a proxy power extending to campaigns from which the king was absent.[17] The constable of France performed a similar function, but also had to negotiate the particular military obligations comprising the host, so that his office was effectively a political appointment and his death could paralyze the military order of the French body politic.

Extended English royal household administration of forces in the field constituted a mode of government of free bodies liberated from domestic discipline in their condition of displacement, but without establishing a permanent 'container' in which power-resources accumulated. Rather, in producing military power by the extension of practices and techniques originating in the royal castles over transitional spaces and indeterminate bodies, the authority of the offices of provost and constable became dissociated from the territorial jurisdictions from which they had emerged. The imperative speed of this dromological dimension also produced a new mode of resistance: the refusal to move, mutiny, first recorded in 1338 at Norwich, where men awaiting ships to the embarkation rendezvous at Yarmouth were accused by the Crown of 'conspiring to withdraw from the army without licence, dishonouring us and hindering our business'.[18] Desertion was nothing new, but in this case the men had simply refused circulation, resolving to stay put.

Ordering the body of violence

From 1385, under Richard II, royal prerogative over the new bodies became codified in ordinances providing for the domination of these subjects in their liberty from law, community and the body politic. By then, the speed of *chevauchée* had to be accelerated, as the land through which the army passed was already denuded by the depredations of Free Companies, by the withdrawal of the wealth-bearing population into fortified towns and by the destruction of resources in its path by the French Crown. These ordinances had a purely tactical intent, an attempt to codify and stabilize the functioning of the consumption-machine, rather than to civilize warfare. Such 'standing orders' also provide a medium for *generalized and continuous* command, enabling *chevauchée* to be directed beyond the immediate presence of royal authority. The 1385 Ordinances became 'a kind of ur-text, serving as the basis for subsequent orders of royal hosts throughout the Hundred Years' War', and beyond.[19] Since indentures were particular to each expedition and limited in time, new ordinances were required for every campaign, but though their clauses and proscriptions form a series which proceeds according to its own internal consistencies, their operation produced new subjects of violence and new capacities which enabled entirely new strategies, transforming the function of the ordinances despite their repetition.

The political and social displacement of men in time of war suspended all customary relations of domination; instead they were now subjected to the prerogative authority of the king and his household officials that was not given in the time of war itself, like the old right of command of the war-chief, but in terms of indenture, with government operating only through the largesse of plunder. In codifying prerogative, the ordinances constituted a new subject and a new jurisdictional domain articulated by the offices of the royal household. Richard II's ordinances for his host begin by mapping out his prerogative jurisdiction: 'First, that all manner of persons, of whatever nation, estate or condition, shall be obedient to our lord the king, to his constable and marshal, under penalty of everything they can forfeit in body and goods.'[20] The radically equalized administrative and legal subjection of indentured bodies in the royal household thus provided a new condition of governance which did not refer itself to law, but to the absolute reducibility of its subject to a mere body and goods held on the sufferance of the king.

The company, the indentural unit, now constitutes the basis of the order of march, order and forage, becoming the unit to which men 'belong'. The captain of the company, whose relation to the men in law is purely contractual, and who might be of common social status, becomes their singular 'lord and master', but is obliged to provide the constable and marshal with knowledge of his company's condition and deployment, not only for battle but also for routine operations in the field, such as lodging and patrol. The company and household office thus formally displace custom and status, creating a vertical structure of domination and subordination in universal subjection to prerogative under the ordinances, enabling tactical deployment according to the strength of units available.

In the context of the mode of warfare which had produced them, we can also see a struggle for command and a strategy for domination in the ordinances, which positively undercut the captain's capacity to govern his companions by *largesse* in opportunities for plunder and its distribution, subjecting this economy to uniform regulation. In chivalry, the 'traditional canonical immunity' from violence of the Church, unarmed clerks, common labourers and women had been enforced by sanctions enacted on knightly status. Universal subjection to prerogative power over the body enabled the ordinances to extend sanctions to all, regardless of status, but as these proscriptions were now effected by royal ordinance, not by custom, they could be suspended by royal command. Henry V's ordinances proscribed the usual technique of *chevauchée*, arson, 'without the king's orders'.[21]

The military economy that had developed in the space of war was similarly subjected to codified, rather than customary, regulation. The king's public war, 'could legitimize criminal acts and create a legal title to goods whose taking in other circumstances would be considered robbery.'[22] This legal title to booty (*prise de bonne guerre*) exempted its taker from legal proceedings for restitution, but its regulation in the ordinances reduced it to an allowance by the king or his officer in the field. The law regarding ransom was even more finely codified. To ensure these rights did not generate conflict over the division of spoils of war, another group of clauses specified the general custom of division, stipulating the 'rule of thirds' by which captains were entitled to a third of the soldiers' gains, and the king to a third of the captains'. The ordinances thus decisively undercut the capacity of captains to achieve independent government of the men sub-indented with them, extending royal jurisdiction over the military economy which had appeared with public war's 'liberation' of goods from all other rights in law.

In operating through and upon the very economies that constituted the subjects of violence, secular military government by ordinance thus intervened in the minutiae of the lives and conduct of men, not according to their social status, as sumptuary law did, or through particular relations, but by universally reducing its subjects to equivalences in the body and the conditional right to material goods. If the monasteries were the 'laboratories' of economic and productive discipline, then the armed host as it emerged at the end of the Middle Ages was a parallel site in which techniques of *political* subjectification and discipline were pioneered. These ordinances were designed to deal with specific problems emanating from the indentured condition and tactical operations of the hosts of fourteenth-century warfare, but also constituted a distinct jurisdiction, with its own order of subjects over whom a discipline could be exercised, as in the monastic order. Just as monastic discipline provided a model for legitimate conditions of accumulation, so military discipline too came to appear as the legitimate condition of force.

Redeeming the body of violence

Under political kingship in France, other modes of government responded to the devastations of *chevauchée*. The resumption of public war in 1369 coincided with the successful conclusion of an expedition to Spain, where du Guesclin had conducted war by proxy against the English over succession to the Spanish Catholic thrones through an internecine struggle between the monastic-military Orders of Calatrava and Santiago.[23] The military orders had originated during the Crusades, 'born of the need to garrison troops in the territories that had been won in order to defend pilgrims, to assist the weak and the sick, and to extend 'permanently' ... the mobilization that had made the crusades possible'.[24] They provided an organizational ethos ideally suited to the needs of the French body politic in 1369, which required a force motivated by impersonal, non-particular imperatives to fight injustice and the despoilers of the Church while practising a rigorous code of ascetic self-renunciation in their deployment of the sword in the world.

The medieval military–religious orders were a product of the Gregorian project to reform the world on the model of the monastic orders following the Rule of St Benedict. Gregory VII had reprehended the warriors who renounced the world for a life of penitence, exhorting them instead to a Godly deployment of force against worldly infamy, but knighthood had failed to fufil this ideal. Instead, the exclusive military–religious orders established a vocation of violence against evil in a fusion of the orders of *bellatores* and *oratores* by redefining war 'in terms of prayer and ascetic experience'.[25]

Such an ethos offered the military nihilism of the Free Companies the prospect of redemption. Du Guesclin apparently used this prospect to organize some of the Free Companies into royal service in 'lances' of man-at-arms, mounted bowman and squire. These units operated independently in small mobile formations to harry English foraging parties and garrisons, forcing the enemy to concentrate its expeditionary armies, and dramatically reducing its capacity to live off the land and precluding the development of any depots.[26] The zone of war, a destratified and decoded space, thus became a 'desert' in which the ethos of the orders translated into a secular, military asceticism, imbuing the new royal companies with the techniques of self-discipline to renounce opportunities for free living in the field and to dedicate themselves to a technical vocation in reconquest of the kingdom of France.

The order of conquest

By the late fourteenth century, English disillusionment with warfare had become general across settled society, with petitions in Parliament protesting abuse of purveyance, peasant rebellion against taxation levied to fund war, and declining participation by the nobility as they developed new litigious and political strategies for local hegemonic domination in the king's peace. The English Crown thus faced forms of resistance not amenable to domination by its castellar network, while across the Channel, the tactical success of *chevauchée* campaigning had actually negated its strategic object. When Henry V resumed the Hundred Years' War in 1415, the struggle was fundamentally transformed, both internally, in terms of the mode of warfare, and externally, in terms of its object. The need to secure the dynasty of the House of Lancaster projected the insecurity of the regime onto a divided, anarchic France in Henry's announcement that in invading Normandy he came 'into his own land, his own country, his own kingdom'.[27] The new object of war was conquest, investing the security of Henry's political kingship not in defence of the king's peace, but in the extension of dominion.

For this new object, old adventurist forms of raising forces were temporarily revived between 1415 and 1422 by the promise of lands in conquest.[28] During the Agincourt campaign of 1415, the captains of all great and most small companies were knights, but this was a temporary reversal of the long-term trend; companies for subsequent expeditions tended to be smaller and were increasingly captained by squires, while their ratio of composition shifted from three archers to every man-at-arms in 1415, to between 10 and 14:1 by 1429.[29]

The order of the 1415 expedition initially attempted to use indenture to solve the logistical problem of maintenance that had emerged in the space between recruitment and embarkation, requiring captains to provide the men they supplied with provisions for two months. While this proved inadequate, it may also, ironically, have forced the English expedition to accept battle at Agincourt. English provisions were exhausted in the siege of Harfleur at the beginning of the campaign and the countryside yielded little. The force that was finally confronted by the French at Agincourt was sick and desperate in a denuded land.

The English campaign had not intended to seek battle, but a direct encounter in the field offered the nobility of the beleaguered French body politic the opportunity to reassert the predominance of the noble political order against both the communes and the Crown. The Constable of France rejected 6,000 crossbowmen from the city of Paris and French bowmen were placed at the rear of their battle order to provide a clear field for the charge of chivalry.[30] The English victory does not need recounting, but two years elapsed before another expedition was launched. Normandy had proved incapable of supporting an army in the field, especially since the object was to territorialize rather than to lay waste, and the prospect of already apparently ruined lands held little attraction for the nobility, whose participation declined once again.

Rather than adventurers, the project of conquest demanded forces assembled under the ordinances that had undercut the 'reputation' of captains and transformed royal household authority into a general jurisdiction over the host, enabling Henry V to regulate the self-provisioning of forces in the field by prohibiting unnecessary pillage, so that military economy became an instrument of strategy rather than an automatic function of the war-machine.[31] Within the host, soldiers' private interests were now governed by the ordinances, rather than by the captains' need for reputation, enabling the king to use the indented companies for entirely new, delimited purposes, to the direct end of conquest, as instruments of a military strategy unmediated by diplomatic and conjugal channels.

The Ordinances of War for the expedition of 1419 extended protection to women, children, labourers and draught animals, and restricted arson to the explicit order of command, regulating the function of the consumption-machine and demarcating the host from the field of resources in which it operated. This demarcation was social as much as spatial, part of a wider trend of categorical normalization in the late medieval world. It also engendered a moralization of bodies in the organization of violence. 'Harlots' were to be expelled from the vicinity of the army, the ordinance again operating upon the body: any such woman found within two miles of the host was to have her arm broken. The regulations also instituted a sanitary regime of the collective body which had to be maintained in health within its spatial definition, beginning with the removal of 'carrion' from the camp.[32] A distinct military order was thus establishing itself in the liminal spaces of the medieval world, the marginal dimension of socially and spatially displaced, indeterminate itinerant bodies, the background against which the perimeter of the camp emerged. This regulation of the war-machine's essential functions also transformed tactical into moral imperatives. The means of differentiating the army in a devastated land constituted the host as a moral order, albeit one in which bodies were now defined in terms of their military function rather than social and political status. Its functional order provided the categories for a moralized empirical mode of knowledge which proceeded by immediate intelligence; as for Christine de Pisan's 'dogs' of pastoral kingship, who know what it is that they sense without need of mediating forms such as law to provide categories for perception.

However, the space of the new order was extensive, since it had the road, rather than a fixed perimeter, as its domain, subjecting military bodies to its jurisdiction and regulation beyond the army itself. Members of the host given leave to return home were provided with a 'billet' to distinguish them from deserters, an original passport. Its bearer was dependent upon its stamped, empirical verification of identity of the body and its vector for protection *from* law (which would take the soldier for a vagabond), the subject of a dromological state which operates through control of the speed of bodies in space.

The policy of conquest also reformed the terms of military service.

After the two-year pause, expeditions were launched into the *pays de conquette* almost annually,[33] but the protraction of war necessary to secure rather than lay waste to territory disinclined men with domestic commitments in England from taking part. Landed income and personal investment in the legal order for the gentry (as proprietors, litigants and justices of the peace) proved stronger than the prospect of land and plunder in war, predisposing recruitment to the 'subaltern' classes. Demand for men-at-arms in any case declined throughout the fifteenth century as siege replaced *chevauchée* and battle as the characteristic mode of warfare. Archers were also cheaper and easier to recruit on the military labour market, which was now centred on London.[34] Relatively few recruits returned. Some stayed on in colonial settlements, but other veterans remained to live off the land, providing 40 per cent of the English armies fielded in the 1430s and 1440s.[35]

A new military domain

The policy of conquest attempted to replicate the royal encastellation system which had constituted public kingship in medieval England, but its strategic use in conquest invoked entirely new problematics. The Crown could not afford to garrison these strongpoints permanently. Instead, the royal household retinue was maintained in the field to provide mobile forces which could respond to both French incursions and to possible rebellion by English lordships established in the conquered territories as an attempt to create colonial castle-guard obligations. However, most of the settlers drifted back to England after 1420. The system was unenforceable, since the only available sanction was to divest the settlers of the Norman land-holdings they had abandoned; by the period 1449–50 it had collapsed completely.[36]

War of conquest in its old, Norman form required relations of dependence that no longer pertained to the English nobility, which was securely embedded in the stable structures of the king's peace in England. The alternative was to garrison the castle circuit by displaced elements, which invoked the opposite problem of maintaining them in differentiation from the local domestic terrain to ensure their continuous availability. However, delegated command to captains with only a contractual relation to the Crown could not be extended indefinitely and precluded the interchangeability of personnel required for garrison duties, while expansion of the royal household to incorporate them permanently would have required taxation in England. Opportunities for fraud were also no longer constrained by the exigencies of the field. A highly bureaucratic system thus evolved to administer the garrisons, beginning with financial surveillance, but increasingly taking on the control of men and their indenting captains. Under a system of 'muster and review', a minimum of 19 documents per year were required to ensure payment (in arrears) which the captain distributed to the men, whose numbers and condition were verified by inspection at quarterly musters, while the performance of the duties specified in the captains' annual indentures were reviewed by submission of quarterly 'counter rolls' recording the activities and gains of the garrison.[37]

Deceit, displacement and desertion

Ordinances had developed as a means of providing a disciplinary code for bodies of violence in the discontinuous warfare of expeditionary *chevauchée* and were issued anew for each expedition, but the protraction of war of conquest and the need for continuous garrisons had transformed the indentured host into a bureaucratic terrain of permanent, internal military relations of domination over subjects who could be posited abstractly, enabling legislation for their continuous regulation. In 1439, two statutes were enacted to provide the means for exercise of government over the new general space of military service.

The first statute, 18 Henry VI c.18, addresses the 'Great Deceits and Falsities' of indenting captains who kept the wages they should have paid to their soldiers, causing them 'to fall into Robbery and Pillage this side of the Sea before their going as beyond the Sea'. Since the object was no longer to lay waste, abatement of pay appeared to be a further cause of the war's protraction, driving the soldiers to pillage. The statute established fixed rates for wages and forbade captains from witholding pay 'except for clothing', but this in turn problematized recruitment by removing the profit opportunity which motivated indentural captainship. The second statute, 18 Henry VI c.19, took up the problem of what would come to be called desertion, complaining of the widespread 'decay' in all stages of the companies' deployment, which imperilled the enterprise of war and demeaned the legitimacy of the king. By establishing definitive conditions for the soldier's licensed departure (sickness or other 'reasonable cause' subject to verification by the Provost), the statute makes the soldier's subjection to service otherwise unconditional. Departure from his subjection to the king's prerogative jurisdiction renders the soldier who returns 'within his term on this side of the Sea' without 'letters testimonial of the Captain' a felon, arrestable and punishable by determination of a Justice of the Peace. The statute produces the subject of an entirely new domain, who, in acceptance of wages, muster and enrollment, can be only either a soldier (and hence beyond recognition in law) or felon (subject to punishment in law), establishing juridical relations which provide the model for the legal condition of the soldier through the long series of subsequent military statutes into the nineteenth century and demarcating a peculiar extra-legal space – the army.

The marginal condition of the soldier refracted the social conditions in which the emergent figure of the army was embedded. With the host in the field no longer able to live off the land, expeditions became a logistical exercise, with an enormous train for baggage, provisions and the means to process food for what were effectively mobile cities. The ordinances against 'harlots' implicitly acknowledged the vast numbers of followers providing services to the army in the field. The Hundred Years War created and favoured but also incorporated an entire alternative social order into its companies, constituting both a problem and a field of experimental development of new administrative and political technologies.[38]

The recovery of France

The French kingdom which Henry V invaded in 1415 and 1419 was, politically, very differently constituted from his own. The cultural, legal and administrative centralization of the French body politic around the court in the king's peace had not 'civilized', in the sense of curtailing private warfare, but simply produced a figure of public authority as an object for contested control by noble factions. Power was actually produced elsewhere, in spaces of circulation and manoeuvre rather than of position and stasis. Henry's campaigns took advantage of feud between the Burgundian and Orleanist (or Armagnac) factions vying to control, but not usurp, central authority, internecine conflict which precluded resistance to conquest until the appearance of the visionary Jeanne d'Arc enabled the Orleanists and their candidate for the Crown, the Dauphin, to represent themselves as bearers of the will of God. The delivery of Orleans in 1429 marks the turning point of the war, not merely in morale but also in a massive shift in strategy by the Dauphin (sacrally anointed as Charles VII in the same year), from the pursuit of battle to a systematic campaign of reduction through siege, utilizing gunpowder weaponry and the siege trains developed by the Bureau brothers of the royal arsenal.[39] This strategic reorientation was not merely organizational and technological, but part of a much wider reconstitution of the French domain involving spatial reconfiguration, moral reformation and new political modalities. The towns became the *foci* of an entirely new order of territorialization, with new techniques and forms of regulation, around which new problematics of government appeared and new strategies of power emerged out of a juridical-military coalition forged in the contemporaneous crisis of the towns and the monarchy.

This crisis was invoked not by sovereign or internecine war, but as an effect of the treaties of Arras (1435) between the French king and the House of Burgundy, and of Tours (1444) between the French king and the English, which together displaced vast forces from military employment onto the roads, where many became *écorcheurs*, free pillagers, continuing a way of life that had no place in the new order. Geremek notes the reign of Charles VII as marking a new approach to vagabondage, enacted simultaneously at the level of the towns themselves and in royal *ordonnances*, as the problem of public order displaced concerns with labour shortages. The appearance of 'criminal organization' was an effect of the demarcation of towns against the zone of war and of the anti-vagabondage campaigns of the authorities. The Parisian bourgeoisie proposed a special force under their own authority in the districts of the city, to direct the activities of the municipal watches in conjunction with royal commissioners, whose presence they had previously resisted. Provincial urban authorities began to circulate information about specific individuals, constituting a new field of judicial knowledge in France in which confessional testimonies of criminal association produced by torture were correlated with reports of movement and crimes, producing the appearance of organized criminal fraternities and even guilds.[40]

On the other side of the emergent monarchical–urban alliance, Charles VII's 1439 ordinance 'to Prevent Pillage and Abuses by Soldiers', ordered the abolition of all companies raised without royal authority, and appropriated the right to authorize captains to raise men for the field exclusively to the king. The retention of retinues within castles was made accountable to the king, and lords were prohibited from levying or appropriating taxes to pay them. Prohibition of the means of *guerre couverte* rendered these retinues useless for feud, since they could only be governed by providing opportunities for plunder and ransom. The ordinance charged all offices of the kingdom and the law actively to investigate abuses by soldiers within their jurisdiction and administer punishment accordingly. Victims were empowered to call upon any available men-at-arms for the pursuit of offenders, who could be killed with impunity, their horses and belongings to be forfeited to their captor or killer. The ordinance also operated with renewed vigour upon relations established by legitimate *lettres de retinue*; captains were to be held responsible for their soldiers' abuses, and would be prosecuted themselves if they did not deliver offenders to justice, a principle extended to the soldiers, who shared in collective responsibility with their companions, and who would be held responsible for any offence they did not act to prevent.[41]

Criminalization may have reinforced the companions' collective commitment to their way of life, partly constituting the organized solidarity of crime which Geremek (following normative sociological convention) refers to as social *dis*organization. However, those measures were already grounded in the effect of the mobilization of the exclusions of settled society under the rubric of the king's peace and the emergent public domain, which constructed its own enemy as a coherent entity.[42] It did so by codifying the customary association of 'free' bands of men with transgressive violence and subjecting extra-economic movement not only to local popular fear and suspicion, but also to active surveillance and investigation by a widely dispersed and manifold military-juridical apparatus which already perceived it as illicit. This reconstruction of the 'antisocial' also reflected a transformation of the epistemological principles by which it could be known. The epistemic principles of similitude[43] which had identified the bands in terms of a cosmological chain of associations now functioned differently, to signify a clearly demarcated social object, around which the properties, relations and identities previously linked by multiple orders of similitude became rigorously demarcated against a background norm arising from the co-ordinated activities of hitherto plural and merely contiguous orders of bodies, places and acts. Where before there had been a series of conditional and variable distinctions between violence and force, there now appeared a singular dichotomy that would take firmer shape as the development of political institutions and modes of surveillance produced an increasingly clear definition of this social bifurcation. At this level, then, we can trace on the one hand an interrelation between the condition of knowledge and the archaeology of modern institutions of political organization, administrative and judicial surveillance and repression, and, on the other, a genealogy of moral order and the ethical subject.

At another level, we can identify the conditions and options of strategy, or strategic agency, emerging within this constellation. The association of vagabondage with brigandage and of the latter with war, enabled royal authority to obtain the voluntary compliance of the towns in a new order, subordinating municipal jurisdiction to royal military policy. As part of this new alliance, royal authority took on the function of highway surveillance, effecting a general jurisdiction of the king's peace, which had hitherto concerned itself primarily with the management of noble feud at the level of the body politic. In one sense, 'the king's war became the kingdom's war' as jurisdictional elements were integrated into a public programme that served to produce and maintain forces for war or defence,[44] but in another sense, the new public condition and integrated organization of these forces of public war also became the condition of public peace.

Practical policy: The creation of the compagnies d'ordonnance

The way was thus open for the surveillance and executive regulation of bodies on the highway (constituting the first modern public space), with powers of arrest of movement rather than expulsion and exile. In 1439, Charles VII summonsed a general *parlement* at Orleans, which voted a local levy of taxes to support armed patrols to be lodged in the 'good towns' throughout the kingdom. This vote provided the Crown with the means for an integrated solution to a number of aims, a *policy* linking quite disparate problems together to produce the perspective of a 'state'. By combining the measure created by this vote with new techniques of regulation developed in the wars, it was possible to achieve a number of goals in one move: to remove the means of noble feud; to provide a standing force for defence after the model of du Guesclin's mounted commandos; to eradicate the *écorcheurs*; to patrol the highways to arrest the 'free action' of marginal, transitory bodies; to ensure the safety of commercial traffic between towns, and to regain royal legitimation.

The truces of Tours in 1444 magnified the appearance of the nomadic predatory bands, swelling the numbers already at large and reducing France once again to a condition in which many saw portents of the end of the world. The chronicles that provide Tuchman's sources, closer to the old order of knowledge through the principle of similitude than to the new municipal perceptions, depict the French countryside from the time of Henry V's invasion as a kind of Boschian Hell, with entire peasant communities hiding on river islands or even in tunnels under the earth to escape predatory detection, and the towns closed upon themselves, admitting no one. Cannibalism was rumoured and represented in mystery plays and wolves were reported roaming the Paris suburbs. Other sources show municipal authorities alarmed by the possibility of depopulation, as starving, desperate and unemployed citizens abandoned towns beleaguered by the companies to try their own chances at survival by brigandage.[45] Other historians present different pictures, in which rural extortion became regularized in a system that the companies took over from the royal prerogative of appropriation to maintain forces in the field, while smaller municipal authorities appealed to the captains' need for reputation among their men by providing spectacular receptions and gifts.[46] But despite the capacity of the bands as military 'mobile cities' to develop internal structures of domination and a division of labour, there seems to be no evidence of a tendency toward legitimation. Rather, they appear as transitory predators, or associated with great lords who maintained them as clients, available for feud and sustaining themselves on the lands of others, or else adopting the disciplinary form of the cities as 'guilds' and 'confraternities', seeking to establish customary particular rights, rather than aspiring to legitimate sovereign domination.[47]

In 1445, representatives of the body politic met to debate a proposal of the 'private council' of the royal household, that the provisions of 1439 be used to select the most honourable of the bands themselves to form armed patrols lodged in the towns, which would enable a concerted campaign to rid the land of the rest and provide a standing force on which the king could draw for war without needing to resort to mercenary indentures. The account of the chronicler, Mathieu d'Escouchy,[48] provides us with an insight into the political mechanisms by which the Crown was able to use the particular provisions voted by the parliament as the basis for wider policy, co-opting the interests of powerful subjects despite themselves. Two problems were raised in the great council. First, that the 'soldiers of mean estate, who were very numerous in several of the companies', might learn of the plan and 'assemble in great numbers and power as in times past', making them difficult to remove. Second, that the kingdom, 'in great ruin and poverty', might be unable to pay the new forces. These problematizations, however, provided the basis to extend a simple proposal into a far wider political strategy, an example of the way that late medieval kingship began to develop positive 'governmentality'.[49]

Under this policy, the lords were to be deprived of the right to maintain forces in the field, and allowed only their domestic retinues, to be supported out of their own revenue and not out of taxation, and subject to royal inspection, but they were faced with a double-bind: either exert their influence to obtain the voluntary transfer of their clientary retinue into the new force, or else lose favour at court and perhaps also lose their retinue to the combined forces that would be gathered under the policy. If the policy succeeded and they had not enabled their clients to be incorporated, their own lands would probably suffer violence, as they would have failed their clients' trust. To the *écorcheurs*, the proposal offered the freedom of the town in exchange for the vagabondage of the road, legal incorporation into the royal dominion and an exchange of dependence upon the lord for the security of dependence upon the king. The captains of the new *compagnies d'ordonnance* were personally chosen by the king. The *lettres de retenue* under which they served gave them responsibility for recruitment, enabling the principle of selection to be applied by those who already had knowledge of their men, subject to regular royal inspection by muster and personal liability for their conduct. Dispersion of the *compagnies* among towns in different parts of the kingdom (which were to support them at fixed rates of pay and provision) ensured that their small numbers could be subject to local authority supported by communal force.

A permanent force endowed with the highway-patrol function also rendered the communal forces of the town strategically redundant, reducing their function to internal order in a new strategic terrain, a military-political or dromological landscape in which the town's significance was reduced to the fortress, which did not provide for the defence of its inhabitants in war, but acted as a strongpoint upon the state highway, the point from which circulation could be controlled. The 'citadel', a military fortress within but not of the town, definitively sealed off from it, became possible from this time. The *compagnies d'ordonnance*, stationed in the towns at the crossroads of arterial routes, did not function to repress the town's independence directly, but nonetheless effectively reconstituted it as a mere point in a wider strategic landscape.

According to d'Escouchy,[50] the remnants, the rejects and the lesser companies, 'went off to many and diverse places and dispersed ... so that in fifteen days there was no news of them in all the king's dominion'. The details of the fate of the companions are obscure. No longer the necessary Other of medieval social and political order, even their negativity effectively disappears from history. Marginality was reduced to the problem of vagrancy in a new mode of knowledge which drew relations between things very differently. In practical terms, the problems of urban order could now be removed from the political agenda and reposed in terms of the nexus of labour, poverty and welfare, distinct from concerns with violence.

A new order and new problematics

At the end of the Hundred Years' War, then, new spaces, new objects and new subjects of war had appeared. The primary question facing the prince under whom armed forces were assembled and deployed in the field was not how to *pay* the assembled host, but how to order these

210

bodies and how to secure their positive obedience, order for which the ancient figure of the army came to provide a model. Though the *compagnies d'ordonnance* could be maintained at local costs, their administrative connections to the court aligned them in its intrigues so that rather than providing a cohesive force in dispersion, they tended to fracture along the lines of allegiance in patronage. The problematic of military power at the end of the Middle Ages was not a question of the state and its finance, but of the military order of massed bodies and the government of men and things. In 1471, Jean de Bueil, author of *Le Jouvencel*, formulated this problem for King Louis XI in his council of war against the duchy of Burgundy:

> War has become very different. In those days, when you had eight or ten thousand men, you reckoned that a very large army; today, it is quite a different matter. One has never seen a more numerous army than that of my lord of Burgundy, both in artillery and in munitions of all sorts; yours is also the finest which has ever been mustered in the kingdom. How do you prevent disorder and confusion among such a multitude?[51]

Late medieval ordinances of war operate primarily through proscriptive clauses, enabling them to demarcate a body against its environment, instituting limits where there were before indeterminate margins. They address the security, spatial demarcation, health and provision of the host, but as means for the government of conduct they can only prohibit, and continue to depend for any positive effect upon the management of military economy of plunder and ransom, with their jurisdiction and authority vested in the particular assembly. Their proscriptions operate upon their subject by transforming the threshold at which the army would become something else into a limit, a terminus for the transient body, marking-off prerogative jurisdiction by gallows at the perimeter of the camp. Successful deserters are no longer their concern, having passed over the limit into the margins where they are vagabond outlaws. Within the army, command of obedience became dependent upon a novel kind of patronage which Edward IV had gained in the internecine struggles of the Wars of the Roses that ensued upon the English expulsion from France, by aligning himself in the military class-war latent within medieval warfare, with the common soldiers: 'King Edward told me that, in all the battles he had won, as soon as he could sense victory, he rode round ordering the saving of common soldiers, though he ordered the killing of all the nobles, few if any of whom escaped.'[52] Those spared would owe their very lives to him.

However, the order of things was becoming as important as the order of men. The shift in strategy consequent upon the exhaustion of *chevauchée* and the transformation of household government and dromological order into a strategic capacity of conquest had produced new military-logistical formations, most evidently apparent in the huge trains necessary for fifteenth-century campaigns through emptied lands. The French policy of reconquest reduced the English strongholds one by one through systematic siege, requiring the capacity to maintain an army in stasis, since the secure blockade of a town required circumvallation (entrenched external defence by the besiegers against counter-attack from without), creating a fortified military suburb around the besieged city. Vast numbers of followers to provide all manner of services to the body of the army were thus necessary, above all bearers, labourers and pioneers. The military-logistical formations of the late fifteenth century were thus far more extensive than a focus on the technology of gunpowder weapons can allow. Deployment of such weapons in the field (organized by the Bureau Brothers for the French king at the end of the Hundred Years War) required a whole range of supplementary organization (transport, ordnance supply, siting, entrenchment, etc.). Moreover, cannon were not the only way in which fortifications could be breached: since the time of Henry II, miners had been recruited to tunnel under the walls at carefully chosen points, until the edifice was supported only by timber props which were then set alight. Pioneers provided specialist labour for entrenching and fieldworks. These developments, of which gunpowder weapons were only one element, produced strategic systems that were maintained in peace as in war. Together with the host as a distinct jurisdiction of moral order, the military–logistical train in the field produced the camp as a virtual city. The classical sources which had provided only tactical ploys for medieval warfare now appeared to offer technologies of government for the new military bodies.

Notes

1. M. H. Keen, *Laws of War in the Later Middle Ages* (London: Routledge, Kegan & Paul, 1965), p. 21; P. Contamine, *War in the Middle Ages* (Oxford: Blackwell, 1984), pp. 119–20, 210–19. Froissart's work also had an effect on military thought. Although by the mid-fifteenth century, Frontinus' *Strategemata* was being translated and recopied, Froissart's *Chronicles* also provided a wealth of near-contemporary material from which a military science could be assembled, much as Frontinus' histories of Rome and biographies of its consuls had done earlier, thus becoming a staple item of military men's libraries.
2. W. Caxton, *The Book of the Ordre of Chivalry*, ed. A. T. P. Byles, Early English

Text Society, Original Series, no. 168, (Oxford: Oxford University Press, 1971). The 1480 edition of Caxton's translation was produced in Bruges in large print for Edward IV of England, intended to be read aloud to the court.

3. The Orders of the Garter and of the Star were founded by the kings of England and France respectively, as means to produce authority, but their politicization of chivalry enabled the knights to use its court as a space and its code as a constraint on the prince's authority.
4. Quoted in Contamine, *War in the Middle Ages*, p. 138.
5. Quoted in ibid., p. 218.
6. C. de Pisan, *The Book of the Body Politic,* trans. and ed. Langdon Forhan (Cambridge: Cambridge University Press, 1994).
7. K. Langdon Forhan, 'Introduction', ibid., p. xxii.
8. Ibid., p. 71.
9. Ibid., p. 17.
10. Ibid., pp. 26–9.
11. Ibid., p. 52.
12. P. Virilio, *Speed and Politics: An Essay in Dromology* (New York: Semiotext(e), 1986).
13. *Calendar Patent Rolls* 1345–48, 113, quoted in H. J. Hewitt, *The Organization of War under Edward III* (Manchester University Press, 1966), p. 44.
14. M. Powicke, *Military Obligation in Medieval England* (Oxford: Clarendon Press, 1962) p. 201.
15. Hewitt, *Organization of War*, pp. 42–3.
16. *Calendar Patent Rolls* 1345–78, quoted in ibid., p. 45.
17. R. A. J. Tyler, *Bloody Provost: An Account of the Provost Service of the British Army and the Early Years of the Corps of Military Police* (London: Phillimore, 1980), pp. 7–8.
18. *Rymer* II ii 1045, quoted in Hewitt, *Organization of War*, p. 84.
19. M. Keen, 'Richard II's Ordinances of War', in R. A. Archer and S. Walker (eds), *Rulers and Ruled in Late Medieval England* (London: Hambledon Press, 1995), pp. 34–5.
20. Quoted in ibid., p. 36. See also Henry V's Ordinances for War (1475), reprinted in P. L. Holmer, 'Studies in the Military Organization of the Yorkist Kings' (unpublished PhD, University of Minnesota, 1977), Appendix G, p. 239–54).
21. Ibid., p. 38; T. Meron, *Henry's Wars and Shakespeare's Laws: Perspectives on the Law of War in the Later Middle Ages* (Oxford: Clarendon Press, 1993), pp. 143–4.
22. Meron, *Henry's Wars,* pp. 40–1; Keen 'Richard II's Ordinances', pp. 65–70.
23. D. Seward, *The Monks of War: The Military Religious Orders* (London: Penguin, 1995), p. 176.
24. F. Cardini, 'The Warrior and the Knight', in J. Le Goff, (ed.), *The Medieval World* (London: Collins & Brown, 1990), p. 85.
25. Ibid., pp. 87–9.
26. Contamine, *War in the Middle Ages,* p. 168.
27. Quoted in B. A. Tuchman, *Distant Mirror: The Calamitous Fourteenth Century* (Harmondsworth: Penguin, 1979), p. 583.
28. N. Jamieson, 'The Recruitment of Northerners for Service in English Armies in France, 1415–50', in D. J. Clayton, R. G. Davies and D. McNiven (eds), *Trade, Devotion and Governance* (Stroud: Alan Sutton, 1994) pp. 102–15.

29. A. Ayton, 'English Armies in the Fourteenth Century', in A. Curry and M. Hughes (eds), *Arms, Armies and Fortifications in the Hundred Years War* (Woodbridge: Boydell Press, 1994), p. 21–37; M. R. Powicke, 'Lancastrian Captains', in M. R. Powicke and T. A. Sandquist (eds), *Essays in Medieval Society* (Toronto: University of Toronto Press, 1969), pp. 371–82.
30. Tuchman, *Distant Mirror*, p. 504.
31. M. Prestwich, *Armies and Warfare in the Middle Ages: The English Experience* (New Haven, CT: Yale University Press, 1996), p. 260.
32. Keen, 'Richard II's Ordinances', p. 46.
33. A. Curry, 'English Armies in the Fifteenth Century', in Curry and Hughes (eds), *Arms, Armies and Fortifications*, p. 47.
34. Jamieson, 'Recruitment of Northerners', p. 111.
35. Curry, 'English Armies'.
36. Ibid., pp. 61–5.
37. Ibid., p. 50.
38. B. Geremek, *The Margins of Society in late Medieval Paris,* trans. J. Birrell (Cambridge: Cambridge University Press, 1987), p. 65.
39. J. Bradbury, *The Medieval Siege* (Boydell Press: Woodbridge, 1992).
40. Geremek, *Margins of Society*, pp. 38, 129, 133–4.
41. Meron, *Henry's Wars*, pp. 146–9.
42. '*Énemies de toute la chose publique*', Archives nationales, *Livre bleu du Châtelet* (1405), quoted in Geremek, *Margins of Society*, p. 126, fn139.
43. M. Foucault, *The Order of Things: An Archaeology of the Human Sciences,* trans. Sheridan (London: Tavistock, 1970).
44. Contamine, *War in the Middle Ages*, p. 169.
45. Tuchman, *Distant Mirror*, pp. 587–8; Geremek, *Margins of Society*, pp. 126–31.
46. B. G. H. Ditcham, 'Mutton Guzzlers and Wine Bags: Foreign Soldiers and Native Reactions in Fifteenth-Century France', in C. Allmand (ed.), *Power, Culture and Religion in France, c.1350–1550* (Woodbridge: Boydell Press, 1989), pp. 1–13.
47. Contamine, *War in the Middle Ages*, pp. 247–8; Geremek, *Margins of Society*, pp. 127–8.
48. C. Allmand, (ed.), *Society at War: The Experience of France and England During the Hundred Years War* (Edinburgh: Oliver & Boyd, 1973), pp. 51–7.
49. M. Foucault, 'Politics and Reason', in *Politics, Philosophy and Culture: Interviews and Other Writings, 1977–84,* ed. L. D. Kritzman (London: Routledge, 1988), pp. 57–85; 'Governmentality', in G. Burchell *et al.* (eds), *The Foucault Effect: Studies in Governmentality* (London: Harvester Wheatsheaf, 1991), pp. 87–104.
50. Allmand, *Society at War*, p. 54.
51. Quoted in M. Vale, *War and Chivalry: Warfare and Aristocratic Culture in England, France and Burgundy at the End of the Middle Ages* (London: Duckworth, 1981), pp. 148–9.
52. Phillipe de Commynes, *Memoirs: The Reign of Louis XI, 1461–83,* (trans. and ed. M. Jones) (Harmondsworth: Penguin, 1972), p. 187.

PART FOUR: EARLY MODERN

11

Two Sources of Military Modernity: Burgundy and the Swiss

The late medieval duchy of Burgundy had achieved a unique relation to kingship through the particularistic negotiations which had constituted the French body politic, most notably in its exemption from the means by which private war was proscribed. The resultant indeterminate status of the Burgundian duchy under the French Crown enabled it to develop 'precociously' along the lines of state formation. The kingdom of France provided a domain in which the Duke of Burgundy could intervene without directly risking his own jurisdiction, an option closed to the 'universalistic' French Crown itself, while quasi-autonomy enabled relatively unconstrained administrative development within Burgundian lands. Burgundy thus offers a crucial counter-example to teleological projections of a historical rationality inherent in the structural conditions of the emergence of the modern state. Perry Anderson's structural Marxist historical sociology of the state does not accord Burgundy any analytical autonomy, but subordinates it to 'France',[1] while Giddens', *The Nation-State and Violence*[2] gives it little consideration despite the duchy's pioneering implementation of precisely the techniques which Giddens supposedly accords a central role to in the historical constitution of the modern state and states system. The Burgundian example is even marginalized in Tilly's macro-sociological overview of the relation between coercion, capital and the state, by his latent evolutionary model of competitive selection.[3] In Elias, late medieval Burgundy figures as the last 'rival' of the kings of the Ile-de-France and its nobility as an exemplar of the old mode of chivalric affect-control, i.e. as an anachronism in both aspects of the civilizing process.[4]

However, fifteenth-century ducal Burgundy was the most advanced regime in terms of the characteristics of the western European transition to political modernity. A highly developed fiscal state apparatus, shifting from tribute-taking to administrative revenue extraction, financed the development of gunpowder weapons technology and techniques of military organization to the most advanced degree in all of Europe. Politically, a stable alliance between the prince and the highly commercialized cities marginalized the nobility, which became a caste of state functionaries whose cultural capital was subjected to princely control through the reconstruction of knighthood in a royal order of chivalry and in a carefully managed 'court society', with structures of surveillance and sanction over individual behaviour.[5] Its neglect in historical sociology may be explained by its exception to sociological narratives of state formation, which abstract theoretically privileged factors from a field presented by historiography to construct the ideal-typical models that generate general sociological theory. However, neglect of Burgundy conceals significant continuities and developments that had far wider effects throughout Europe. In particular, Burgundian development of governmental techniques made the crucial transition from household to political government, while its military organization produced new capacities which were transmitted beyond its catastrophic demise as a territorial and dynastic entity, the form that provides the unit of analysis for historical macro-sociology.

The entire process of medieval development described so far can be seen in accelerated form in the emergence of a nascent state in the duchy of Burgundy from the end of the first phase of the Hundred Years War. Its rise cannot be reduced to geo-strategic factors or to economic determination, as the duchy was comprised of fragmentary and economically heterogenous lands, but can be explained in terms of political techniques and their effects. Similarly, its fall cannot be attributed to its elimination in a process of competitive evolution; it was destroyed in the reinstatement of decisive battle by an entirely different military subject, embodied in the mass Swiss pike phalanx.

The project of Burgundian policy

In an examination of the rise of the House of Burgundy, we can see how the integration and accelerated development of administrative and political practices and techniques in a policy of government produced a princely sovereignty, constituting the duchy as a virtual state extending over a heterogenous terrain of domination and social forms, including the governmentally problematic urban communes of the Low Countries. We can also identify the development of the principle of 'police' which was subsequently transmitted to the Habsburg regime and into Germany, where it developed into the governmental science of *polizeiwissenschaft*.[6]

Philip the Bold, first Valois Duke of Burgundy (1363–1404), assembled his dominions by conventional medieval strategies of marriage, purchase and diplomacy, rather than conquest. Though formally a vassal of France, the Burgundian duchy maintained persistent alliances with the English Crown and seems to have adopted the English model of political kingship that emerged out of extended household government. When the English kings embarked on their policy of conquest during the Hundred Years War, the dukes of Burgundy again adopted this model of territorial expansion.

Like those of the English, the Burgundian dukes' campaigns drew upon heterogeneous forces (John the Fearless' armies have been calculated as comprising 38 per cent Flemish, 33 per cent mercenaries and 29 per cent Burgundians[7]), and as with the English expeditions, the method of assemblage did not invoke permanent political relations, so these forces could also be used to suppress urban revolts and could be discharged back into the space of war. Again like the English kings, to defend his own strongholds, John the Fearless used garrisons of 'alien' mercenaries, personally dependent upon him, rather than quasi-independent members of the body politic. As offensive wars shifted to siege, so Burgundian field armies also developed 'trains' carrying siege equipment and the logistical support required to maintain forces in stasis, a vast mass of wagons and service followers, requiring pioneers to prepare the way for its passage through the land, widening roads and repairing bridges as they went. In 1414–15 Burgundian ordnance resources were reorganized on the model of the English privy Wardrobe to create new strategic capacities, with a central depot where *gens de comptes* continuously updated an inventory of the stock, monitoring its distribution and circulation in the garrisons and the trains of war. Duke Philip the Good doubled the size of his domains by investing his forces where resistance in the field was most weakened by the decline of horizontal vassalage and vertical feudal obligations, so he had only to lay siege to garrisoned towns.[8]

Extensive rule over the geographic, economic, political and cultural diversity of the Burgundian dominions, ranging from feudal Luxembourg to the urban communes of commercial Flanders, effectively constituted the regime of Burgundy as a transcendent political authority. In the diplomacy of take-over, prospective ducal rule presented itself as mediating local domination, enabling the dynasty's campaigns of conquest in Holland, for example, to recruit the communal levies of the towns against the resistant rural nobility.[9] The regime also promoted the Estates General in the Low Countries as a means for co-operative economic development, providing itself with a collective subject represented in the combined assembly to which it could apply pressure and appeal for taxes to finance wars that strengthened the duchy as a whole. The ducal regime outflanked the capacity for resistance generated by this mode of government by integrating administrative techniques into its policy, which aimed at political reduction by 'the elimination of all existing franchises', feudal, ecclesiastical and communal.[10] But rather than following a rationality of state, its measures could be described as constructing a rationality of *government*. Burgundian policy was concerned with creating a mode of subjectification; acknowledging protest, resistance and demands for reform, and in its positive response to them securing the active desire of its subject in the administration and princeship of the ducal house. The Burgundian regime thus appears strikingly modern, rather than archaic. This governmental modernity can be illustrated by its policies of fiscal reform and internal order, which produced a precocious 'military–fiscal state', and in its administrative enrolment of status hierarchy into the wider political project.

Burgundian fiscal reforms shifted the basis of taxation from the nobles' franchise to the tax-paying subjects, resituating the lord as intermediate agent of the ducal administration by requiring him to pay all the revenue collected to the duchy's treasury, from which he was then recompensed with a third of the share of the taxes duly collected. These reforms addressed the common complaints of the tax-paying lower orders, since the lord no longer had any interest in over-taxing them. They also advantaged the duchy, freeing money for temporary enterprises such as war by deliberately delaying recompense to the lords, who lost all fiscal independence, becoming functional mediums in a process that both produced and linked the interests of sovereign princeship and subject commoners against their customary role. The Burgundian ordnance system enabled the duchy to use its arsenal, along with the specialist troops maintained as garrisons, to quickly and precisely reduce the castle of any recalcitrant lord, in the manner of Henry II, before rebellion could spread, without the need to raise extra money or forces. This synthesis of the juridical and forceful converted the ducal right of rendability into princely power, laying the basis for the constitution of a body politic under the duchy.[11]

In this new context, the ducal right to grant patents of nobility was exploited to create a distinctly Burgundian nobility whose status and (standardized, rather than particular) privileges were directly dependent on the duke, while existent nobles were redifferentiated by ducal usurpation of the right to create new titles to which they could be elevated, so that both old and new nobilities depended for their differentiation on the duke's claim to princely status. Even as their 'traditional' opportunities were eroded by fiscal reform, the nobility were offered life-careers in administrative, political or diplomatic service to the duchy on a pension, prospects to which they were predisposed by the institution of a half-year's service in the duke's household.[12] Existing forms of relation were thus not obliterated, but transformed into means, providing sources of aspirations and expectations for government to operate through and upon, producing a policy of rule which projected its own object, princely status, onto the willing desire of its subjects. Social and systems integration in late medieval Burgundy was a unitary political accomplishment, an effect of policy, rather than an organic or mechanical function.

To reduce other local privileges and jurisdictions to its project, the Burgundian regime adopted an instrumental suspension of political judgement, ordering reforms that cut across existing privileges and abolishing existent institutions, referring itself to a superordinate administrative rationality, but reinstating the traditional order of things where it encountered resistance, thereby rendering the restoration of traditional privileges dependent on the duke's 'wise' governmental intercession in the administrative apparatus.[13] In such policies, Burgundian government sought to create subjective investments in its rationalizations, rather than to impose a 'reason of state' from above, thus instituting a principle precociously like Foucault's notion of 'governmentality',[14] simultaneously the *reason of government* and the *government of reason*, even as they produced a new object of princely sovereignty.

Cyropaedia: The military government of Charles the Bold

In the military domain, too, the Burgundian regime integrated discrete late medieval administrative technologies into policy. Under Charles the Bold, the capacity for this systemic integration to project its own object hypertrophied into grandiose projects for the recovery of the ancient kingdom of Lotharingia, extending from the Italian Mediterranean to the North Sea. We can contextualize his apparently overreaching ambition in the correspondence between emergent governmental practices and the Renaissance recovery of the texts of the ancient world from the dogmatic interpretations of medieval Scholasticism. Charles the Bold commissioned the first translation of Xenophon's *Cyropaedia*,[15] a text which sets out the principles of an art of government, with a rationality located not in the ends of the preservation of the state or the security of the prince, but in the means of achieving the willing obedience of the subjects of rule. The exemplary site and model object presented by Xenophon in his exposition of the principle of the art of government is not the household, which Foucault read as the model used in the development of the discourse of government in early modern Europe,[16] but the *army*, which had reappeared as a space for the exercise of administrative and political technologies.

The *Cyropaedia*[17] opens by observing the failure of Aristotelian political and pre-political forms (monarchy, oligarchy, democracy, tyranny, and patriarchy) to secure obedience against a recalcitrant human tendency to self-government, while the pastoral alternative (rule on the model of the shepherd over the flock) is disqualified by the species-differentiation it assumes. Neither domination nor domestication provides a satisfactory model for the government of men, but Xenophon's critique is redeemed by the example of Cyrus the Persian, whose regime governed through the very desire of men to govern themselves, stimulating this general tendency into a desire to obey him, so that he always governed through the willing obedience of his subjects. Xenophon enquires into the conditions necessary for this mode of rule, especially the pedagogical instruction of the ruler. Cyrus was instructed first in the laws of Persia, which have as their object the common good, but do not operate through prohibitions and sanctions, aiming, rather, to preclude permissiveness by constituting subjects who will try not to behave badly, and who will thus seek guidance in how they might behave well. The education of the ruler follows the same principles. His tutors neither proscribe nor prescribe, but first enquire into his own opinions, uncovering their rationality and operating upon it by posing him problems to think through. The young Cyrus' desire to think for himself thus provides the means of his education in reason.

The army is presented by Xenophon's educators as the archetype for the exercise of this practical rationality of government. It is the condition of all good rule, but also a model from which principles of government in general can be abstracted. Military order will proceed from the duality of government; guiding men in both how to command and how to obey. In the military domain, care of the soldiers figures as the common good, and so must be the object of command. Good generalship consists not in tactics, but primarily in achieving their condition; that is, the government of the army's economy, health, morale, the exercise of arms and, above all, its obedience. Economy consists not merely in provision, but also in calculated expenditure; health consists not in the healing arts of the physician, but in the prevention of sickness through a positive regimen of the body; exercise consists not in the leisure to practise, but in continuous employment; courage is inspired not by deceiving men, but in addressing their rational expectations; and obedience is achieved not by sanctions, but by making men want to obey. Willing obedience, the proper object of government, is distinguished from enforced obedience, and though the well-governed army makes domination possible through conquest and repression, its government through willing obedience also provides a rationality and an ethics, the principles for government in general. Xenophon thus lays out in detail the ways in which the army is to be governed according to these principles, so that obedience will constitute its order and military tactics will appear as an effect of its government, rather than as an *a priori* function to which the army must be made to conform. Conquest and strategy, and the rule of the peoples and lands of the dominion, similarly, flow from this rationality of government.

For Charles the Bold, the order of the army became a positive obsession. In 1470 he was reported to be engaged daily in writing military ordinances for an administrative structure that transformed the late medieval host into a new military object by applying the principles of Xenophon's *Cyropaedia*. Printed in gold-covered books, the ordinances were presented to the captains of the new Burgundian army before the assembled troops as they took their oaths to the duke. The series of ordinances produced between 1468 and 1476 were renowned throughout contemporary Europe, and exerted an unprecedented influence on early modern military organization, technique and discipline in the sixteenth century.[18]

The first of the series, from 1468, instituted an order for a particular campaign, setting out the arms to be supplied for each tactical category of 'lances' comprising the companies to be provided by indenting captains and specifying the logistical supplies (not only of ordnance, but also of equipment; tools, ropes, etc., after Xenophon's injunction for detailed 'economy'), which the marshal was to draw from the arsenal at Dijon. Their disciplinary provisions, however, were largely proscriptive in detail, after the English and French models.

The second set of ordinances, issued from Abbeville in 1471, provided for the permanent establishment of mercenary companies, organized into multi-tactical lances, again carefully prescribing the requisite equipment for each category of arms. They also map out a military hierarchy, displacing the customary order of military companionship by developing the fusion and delegation of administrative authority and responsibility under the prerogative jurisdiction of the prince that had developed in the English forces. However, these ordinances establish intermediate offices between the captains and the commander-in-chief, so that administrative delegation no longer depends on the unit of the company, but is tiered in levels which distribute it downwards throughout the permanent force, establishing a hierarchy of superordination, rather than the horizontal series produced by indenture. Each officer in the hierarchy is owed obedience by someone, down to the common soldiers. A simple pyramidal hierarchy would constitute ranked identifications with exclusive interests and divisive solidarities, but these ranks overlap, so that each captain, or *conducteur*, of a company is also responsible within his company for ten of the lances, as are his immediate subordinates, the *diseniers*, while each of these are also responsible for one of the two divisions of the *dix*, along with their immediate subordinates, the *chef de chambre* who commands the other *dix*. With these overlapping ranks, no single rank of officers has any interest in exploiting its subordinates, whose responsibilities they share; each level also contains members of the immediately superordinate rank, so that all levels must themselves perform the orders they issue. The result is a structure of government in Xenophon's sense, designed to inculcate in each officer a rational interest in the common good of the order of the army, providing not only a 'chain of command', but also establishing the condition of willing obedience through administrative organization, producing an order of subjects who both command and obey.

The 1473 ordinances modified the disciplinary code, replacing the proscriptive mode, by which the French and English hosts of the Hundred Years War were maintained against decay and flight by differentiation from their environment, with positive injunctions which had as their object the creation of a voluntarily obedient subject. For instance, where the English ordinances banned 'harlots' from the proximity of the host, the Burgundian ordinances provided for 30 women to be held in common by each company, investing desire in the provisions of military organization. The 1473 ordinances also provide detailed instructions for the regular exercise in arms of the ordinance companies, indicating a 'micro-physics' of the body[19] in precisely prescribed movements and co-ordinated manoeuvres for each tactical category.[20] The ordinances even specify how the soldiers are to be introduced to this discipline in small groups who can then instruct others, so that the soldiers themselves become the *virtuosi*, with no grand pedagogical disciplinarian, the order of exercise again constituting subjects who both command and obey. Rather than routinization, a continuous *predisposition* for disciplinary exercise is to be created by varying it randomly, so the soldiers will not know when they will be called on to perform their duty and will have to maintain themselves in a state of permanent readiness for the rehearsal of war. Displayed to visiting envoys and diplomats, these drills produced a powerful spectacle of orderly movement in voluntary obedience, so that the army appeared as a single, automatic body.[21]

The most advanced regime in Europe

By 1476, *compagnies d'ordonnance* comprised almost all of the Burgundian army in the field, while the urban levies were used to garrison the towns, minimizing internal resistance to the duchy's increasingly military pursuit of its ambitions. However, the carefully administered field armies were disastrously defeated three times in battle in less than a year by the massed pike phalanxes of the Swiss cantons, which had no cannon, no administrative structure and no logistical support system. In the final battle at Nancy (January 1477), the Burgundian army was utterly destroyed. The body of Charles the Bold was discovered among the corpses by women stripping the dead.[22]

The nascent state of Burgundy was abruptly ended by these purely military defeats, but its destruction cannot be attributed to the factors conventionally used to explain the elimination of states in early modernity. Its financial administration had not been substantially weakened, and when the lands of the duchy were divided (not among conquering rivals, but between the French monarchy's assumption of dominion over Burgundy with the end of the ducal dynasty and Habsburg acquisition of the Low Countries through marriage), both these regimes acquired a fully functional administrative system of government, in which state legitimation and civil obedience in the form of tax payment and revenue collection continued even after the final and militarily decisive defeat at Nancy. Strategically, the well-known Swiss alliance with the French regime post-dated Nancy and no other regime provided support to the cantons. In terms of military technology, the Swiss pike was not a new weapon, but had been deployed for a quarter of a century by the foot soldiers of the urban communes against mounted lances. In terms of formal structures of military power, the army of the *compagnies d'ordonnance* was composed as a machine designed to integrate its internally differentiated elements, quite unlike the hosts of feudal array or the barely integrated hosts of indenture of the Hundred Years War, but also unlike the mass it met in the Swiss phalanx. It was able to accomplish complicated manoeuvres, to respond flexibly in the field, to co-ordinate its divisions and operate in a tactical synthesis with other elements, including newly-developed field cannon. Its companies were not composed of 'toy soldiers', but of selected veterans from across western Europe, permanently maintained, with no moral divide between them and their commander: Charles the Bold addressed them directly, in their own languages, and made the welfare of the soldiers his personal concern.

The fall of Burgundy was consequent upon purely military factors, but it illustrates that a sudden shift in the mode of war itself can occur as an effect of contingency, indissolubly linked to the political constitution of force, and that effective military obedience, discipline, and tactics can be transformed radically by such shifts, rendering useless what previously appeared as the epitome of competence. The constellation of events that was to sweep Burgundy from the field and fundamentally alter the course of European history was also novel. The Swiss cantons' devastating tactics of mass assault were neither rooted in tradition nor the product of strategic genius or technological innovation, but constituted the only possible response by the cantons in the face of the military policy of the most advanced state in Europe.

Conquest, cities and cantons

Initially, Charles the Bold attempted to emulate the mode of warfare by which the French had driven the English from France at the end of the Hundred Years War. However, in besieging the chartered city of Neuss, the nascent Burgundian state was confronted by another order of organization of bodies, resources and subjects, with its own discipline, capable of resistance more sustainable than the English garrisons of territorial occupation in France. Chartered cities constituted self-governing jurisdictions which could mobilize all available resources within their walls in their self-defence,[23] protracting war beyond the capacity of field armies to maintain themselves in static siege. Failing to take Neuss, Charles sent his army into Lorraine 'to save it from starvation and to refresh itself' in plunder,[24] reverting to a policy of territorial extension by seizing garrisoned strongpoints by speed and surprise, with the army making forced marches, often by night, as the *écorcheurs* had done. The army's advance spread terror, invoking a rationale of capitulation by operating upon the differentiation of the garrison from the town (garrisons were executed unconditionally, but the town would be spared if it did not resist). In Lorraine, Burgundian forces only laid siege to the principal fortified city, Nancy, once the land had been terrorized into submission and the army restored to vigour.[25] The policies by which the duchy sought to form a greater Burgundy while evading engagement with resistant cities, however, drew it into an engagement more fatal even than the stasis of siege.

The communities of the Alpine forest cantons were an isolated enclave, ignored by the medieval lords of the Holy Roman Empire over centuries, during which the local nobility had expired. The poor, remote valley communities of subsistence farmers and the still more marginal mountain population had thus not been subjected to domination by castellar lordship. Their freedom consisted simply in the collective right to practise the customs and activities necessary for survival in the harsh Alpine environment. Like that of the chartered cities, it was a particular liberty, formalized in their thirteenth-century acquisition of a charter of purchase of their lands from the Habsburgs, placing them under the juridical protection of the Holy Roman Emperor.

However, their 'ancient' political constitution was also effected by changing relations with the external world. Pastoral transhumance had created market contacts through the towns at the valley entrances, but also placed a premium on grazing rights, thus strengthening the internal political organization of the communities as a means of dispute settlement and as collective representation in disputes over rights to pasture on the margins of the enclave. The traditionally self-defensive communal military mobilization of freemen, who all held the right and obligation to bear arms, was increasingly called upon in extensive assertion of the general right of pasture, requiring regular collective exercise, but precluding the conventional military distinction between defence and attack in favour of a rapid response in which all encounters tended to become an 'endgame', without space for negotiation and in which an economy of violence would be exercised only after a decisive outcome. The cantons' location between the two halves of the Holy Roman Empire also became strategically significant when the construction of a bridge over the gorge of Schoellenen opened the Gotthard Pass, transforming the medieval Alpine 'end of the world' into a major route of passage, taking two-thirds of the traffic between the burgeoning economies of Italy and the Low Countries. The new passage transformed the cantons in both external and internal relations. Under pressure of a Habsburg blockade intended to reduce them to subjection, the mountain cantons, Uri, Schwyz and Unterwalden, signed a defensive pact against outside aggression in 1291. As they successfully trapped and annihilated expeditions of knights sent against them in the valleys, their pact expanded into a political union which made further defensive alliances with the towns of Lucerne, Zurich, Glarus, Zug and Berne, forming a bloc of eight allies. The towns were small by the standards of the commercial cities of north-western Europe,[26] but just as the forest cantons asserted an aggressive right to extensive pasture on the marginal mountain slopes, so the cities did over trade-routes. In 1393, the *Sempacherbrief* united the eight allied cantons into a political union, represented in the Diet.[27]

The primarily defensive purpose of the union was reflected in the military organization of the communities, which were not centred on the cantonal assembly, but in the scattered valley settlements, which formed the basis for mobilization. Within each of the eight cantons of the Confederation all men aged 16–60 were full members of the political community and obliged to assist in communal defence against aggression, constituting a military–political identity. By the fifteenth century, however, as the defence of particular, customary liberty merged into expeditionary sallies into the margins, cantonal rolls specified the number of armed men each community was to provide for general mobilizations, with their own weapons, maintained subject to regular inspection by the local community leader, according to the number of households, with substitutes acceptable only for households of widows or the sick. Smaller expeditions selected volunteers, to be paid at a relatively high wage, from the young male population surplus to the transhumant economy, *knaben*, who had learnt the art of herdsmanship, but were still too young to marry. Often, unpaid volunteers also accompanied the expedition in anticipation of booty. Roving *knabenschaften* bands were also available for hire in private feuds, whether over minor wrongs which could be restituted by descending on the household of the wrongdoer to help themselves to food and drink, or for more serious blood feuds.[28] The volunteering system projected this surplus male age-band beyond the domestic discipline of the household and the local political discipline of their home valley, into an order in which a customary economy of violence operated in the permissible seizure and imperative killing of feud, an economy which carried over into the expedition.

For general mobilizations, each soldier brought food for several days, enabling the forces to rendezvous before an attack, but not to maintain a campaign, making speed imperative and foreclosing in practice any capacity for negotiation or ransom. The politics of the cantonal military alliance, under which all could be called upon to come to the support of any one, also required the duration of mobilization to be as short as possible. These logistical and political factors combined to produce a tendency to engagement almost immediately once the full forces were assembled. There was thus no great strategist or tactician behind the Swiss mode of warfare. The war council of captains appointed by cantonal or town council to lead their contingents could only decide tactics to maximize the advantages of terrain, through woods, along obscure trails and over hills, enabling them to lay ambushes and make surprise attacks. Historically, the mountain cantons had resisted noble domination by trapping mounted, armoured forces sent against them in the narrow valleys. Unlike knightly expeditions, Charles the Bold's campaign enabled him to choose the ground on which he met the Swiss, who were forced to come out of their own valleys to protect customary cantonal rights to marginal lands in the Vaud, which were under the Burgundian occupation. However, over the course of the Middle Ages, foot soldiers had been deployed in the open field of battle only as defensive walls or the 'hedgehogs' of the urban communes of the Low Countries, which had been able to hold their place, but not to attack, and even in 1475, the cantonal foot-soldiers had protected themselves behind a field fortress comprised of wagons against the Burgundian knights.[29] The Swiss tactic of all-out assault thus appears to have been an effect of increasing pressures on the system of cantonal alliance in general mobilization and a response to the new form of military power presented by the Burgundian forces.

Three battles and an end

Charles the Bold did not seek war with the Swiss, a 'bestial people' of little worth,[30] but was drawn into it when Burgundian territorial expansion by garrisoned strongpoints was threatened by Bernese attempts to maintain free trade in the Vaud, blocking the passage of Italian troops to reinforce the *compagnies d'ordonnance*. In alliance with the city of Fribourg, Berne raised its militia, took the garrisons in the Vaud, then assaulted and sacked the city of Neuchâtel, opening the Vaud to pillage by troops from other cantons. As well as the strategic need to maintain the passage of troops from Italy, Charles the Bold was drawn directly into war through his governmental policy of granting the nobility offices in the state apparatus in substitution for their particular franchise, which personally and inextricably implicated the duke in a petty conflict between his noble subject, the count of Romont and the Bernese. He declared that he would go in person to restore the rule of reason, with absolute faith in his military programme.[31]

The Swiss had been isolated by treaties which Charles had signed in the same year with both Louis XI of France and the Holy Roman Emperor. Furthermore, the cantons even appeared to be divided amongst themselves as the eastern members of the Confederation had declared that they were only bound to go to war against a threat to the territory of the Confederation itself, thus pressuring Berne to withdraw to Grandson. However, when the Burgundian army set up a well-fortified camp, with the largest artillery park that had been seen in Europe at the time, reduced the Grandson fortress, and slaughtered the Bernese garrison, the factor of blood-feud enabled Bernese appeals to prevail on the Confederation to mobilize in its support.

From his camp, Charles the Bold was able to choose open ground for battle to give maximum room to manoeuvre his *compagnies* and deploy his cannon, so that battle could replicate its practised simulation. The Confederation forces who were assembled in a square formation on the plain suffered heavy losses and two contingents that arrived late at the rendezvous had to descend from hiding in the hills on either flank to draw off the enemy attack. However, in the face of their surprise appearance, the *compagnies* withdrawal to enable the artillery to fire again was misinterpreted as a rout, panicking the Burgundian army into mass flight. Without any substantial mounted force, the Swiss were unable to pursue their enemies, but took the Burgundian camp intact, carting the assets of the grandest prince of Europe back to their valleys and towns. The booty included four hundred pieces of artillery and vaster riches than most of the Swiss had ever dreamt of. The wrangles over its distribution occupied the Diet into the fifteenth century.[32]

The unprecedented success of their victory led the Swiss to adopt a new tactical form corresponding to the political requirements of cantonal alliance. From this time, the tactical formation of the great squares of massed pike became the conventional military policy of the councils of war and the conventional form in which Swiss volunteers served for other enterprises. Force-marching to within a few kilometres of the enemy, local knowledge enabled the cantonal contingents to assemble into three great squares under cover of the terrain, each comprised of three ranks of pike on the outsides, providing a wall of steel against the charge of men-at-arms to protect the crossbowmen and the halberdiers, axemen and swordsmen who would engage at close quarters. The war council elected the commanders for the squares, but within them the local contingents were grouped together under the captains appointed by their own community (only unofficial expeditions elected their own captains), projecting their military–political identity into battle itself. Division into three major units enabled some flexibility, since the proportions of the squares could be varied and their order of engagement was not fixed by custom. In addition, advance skirmish groups (the *verloren laufen* or *enfants perdus* consisting of the marginal social elements most expendable to the communities), distracted the enemy on the open field. Appearing out of concealment, the main square would move at high speed to close with the enemy, its impetus as an impenetrable body carrying it through almost any composition of defences to release its close-quarter combatants within the body of the enemy forces. Even the front ranks of the squares wore only light armour, to facilitate their speed. Where surprise failed, the square could be maintained defensively for hours, while the enemy exhausted itself in futile onslaughts, enabling the Swiss to either wait for an opportunity to attack, or else to withdraw in formation from the field without catastrophic losses.[33] This tactical policy reduced all calculations to speed, mass and surprise, radically foreshortening time and space in battle. The novelty of the formation as a regular tactic is borne out by the absence of disciplinary codes or any set form for the communal exercises in arms before the Burgundian war.

The mass assault reinstated the decisiveness of battle after its occlusion by siege toward the end of the Hundred Years War, but its emergence out of political necessities also invoked an imperative elemental discipline in a new, mass subject of war. Once in the field, the soldiers maintained the order of the square for their very survival. The item of the Swiss disciplinary code drawn up after Grandson instructing any soldier to summarily kill anyone attempting to break ranks appears almost superfluous, since flight would only have resulted in certain death, either cut down by enemy horsemen or trampled underfoot by the impenetrable mass. Any choice between static defence and attack was foreclosed by the presence of cannon in the field, and the enemy guns became the first object of assault of the squares as they expanded their presence on the battlefields of Europe, concentrating the determination of life or death into one moment. The phenomenology of the reinstated order of battle also extended to those who faced the Swiss in the field, as the disciplinary code issued by the Diet for subsequent general mobilizations expressly forbade the seizure of prisoners, ordering all to be killed,[34] in order to preclude the politically destabilizing effects of trade in ransoms within the communities.

The political constitution of the Confederation also prevented territorial expansion by the cantons, but conflicted with internal social forces. The Diet disbanded its army immediately after Grandson and ordered Berne not to establish any more extensive garrisons, but unofficial raiding by *knabenschaften* into Burgundian territory perpetuated the conflict by preventing the reinstatement of Burgundian governmental policy, which was dependent upon the pacification of its domain.[35] While the Diet demobilized, Charles the Bold was able to draw upon the resources of his administrative apparatus to re-assemble his forces at a base only 50 miles from Berne, hiring new mercenaries and replacing his lost artillery. The new army, however, was unconditioned and could only be subject to proscription and operation upon the body, rather than the will. The ordinances of 1476 ordered the expulsion of prostitutes from the *compagnies* and instituted the death penalty against anyone who disobeyed its injunctions. Recovered fugitives from the field of Grandson now served as criminals, deserters, rather than as subjects of willing obedience. By June, Charles lay siege to the Bernese garrison at Morat with greater forces than before. Once again, cantonal disputes delayed mobilization, enabling him to choose the ground of battle, but not the time.[36] After awaiting the enemy for a week in full armour, the Burgundian army was disarrayed to receive its pay when the delayed Confederation contingents finally arrived. The main Swiss square attacked at such speed out of hiding in the woods that it reached the Burgundian field fortifications without advance warning, overrunning and seizing the camp while the Burgundians were still trying to re-arm. The other two squares swept round by herdsmens' paths through the hills to drive the enemy into the lake, methodically slaughtering about a third of the Burgundian army.[37]

Despite this further defeat, the political legitimacy of the Burgundian regime remained intact and its fiscal administration continued to function effectively. The main damage to the regime was caused by the pillage of deserting soldiers, who were summarily executed, since continuing fiscal revenue enabled recruitment of English and Italian mercenaries for another campaign to reconquer Lorraine from the duke of René.[38] Besieged at Nancy, René's appeal was rejected by the Diet, which refused a general mobilization, but granted authority to recruit volunteers at a stipulated monthly salary. Over 8,000 knaben marched out of the valleys, forming a tactically mixed force with the levies, allies and array of the duke of René, but, bent on loot before any military objective, they advanced relatively slowly, committing pogroms against Jewish communities along the way. The siege of Nancy had reduced the Burgundian forces, as well as the defenders, to starvation by the time the relief force reached the city in freezing weather. Under cover of a heavy snowstorm, the surprise Swiss assault overran their positions and guns. This time there was no escape. The duke of René's men-at-arms pursued the fleeing Burgundians and the locals finished them off. The Chronique de Metz records that, 'three days afterwards, the peasants were still killing the fugitives along the roads as far as Metz, so that for five or six leagues … one would find nothing but people killed and stripped by the roads'.[39] After two days searching, the corpse of Charles the Bold was identified. For Hans Delbrück, writing the history of war 'from the perspective of political history',

> [t]he Middle Ages in military history came to a close on the day of Murten [Morat] where in the person of the duke of Burgundy and his army, medieval methods of war were theoretically overcome – not by chance, not in a moment of weakness, not in a condition of decay, but on the contrary, at their highest imaginable degree of perfection and even especially supported by the new discovery of firearms … [40]

Capitulations

The Swiss defeat of Burgundy vastly inflated demand for the mercenary services of their collectively self-disciplined contingents. Mercenary entrepreneurship served the otherwise divergent external interests of both urban and mountain cantons, providing income from the exploitation of surplus population resources for the rural cantons, while enabling the towns to negotiate territorial guarantees and alliances, and it thus became politically imperative for the Confederation to regulate mercenary service to maintain the conditions that endowed those bodies with their military value. The need to provide for common defence, on which the Confederation had been founded, demanded that all official agreements allowed for the recall of forces in case of need, while Swiss discipline further required that mercenaries in external service continue to be subject to their own laws.

The disciplinary rules for the Confederation forces are given in a number of orders, based on the *Sempacherbrief*. A judge and executioner would accompany major expeditions to administer justice under the code; only in smaller forces would this would be left to the captains. Though they could not be subjected to the prerogative authority of the prince over his army, Swiss self-subjection, sworn to their own discipline under their captain, provided a pre-formed military instrument, with the additional assurance that the mercenary contingents would return home when discharged. The Diet also sought to monopolize mercenary contracting to ensure that it did not serve interests prejudicial to the cantons or set one against another in battle. In the wake of the Burgundian wars, it attempted to ban all non-negotiated recruitment. However, the Confederation was not a state and the Diet not a government, but merely a representative body ultimately comprised of the communities of mountains, valleys and towns, for whom the *knaben* were a marketable resource and mercenary contracting a means of expediting a problem of order. It was thus not in their interests to limit mercenary service to official contracts negotiated by the Diet, and applicants who were refused an official recruiting franchise were able to find ample co-operation to raise volunteers at community level.[41]

A web of unofficial recruiting agents rapidly developed, able to supply quite precise requirements for a military labour market that drew in non-Swiss seeking mercenary employment. Renowned captains acted as sub-contractors, personally selecting and recruiting companies, underwriting their pay, equipping them out of the communal arsenals and leading them in the field. They thus functioned much like the indenting captains of the Hundred Years War, but with the crucial difference that the men recruited retained their juridical identity, swearing their oath to the captain rather than to the employing prince. Captainship came to represent an authority in communities permeated by the recruitment network and economically invested in the provision of bodies for mercenary service. However, conditions of service were regularized after the traumatic defeat at Marignano in 1516, when the Diet signed a 'Perpetual Peace', effectively a military contract, with the French. This was consolidated in 1521 as the Treaty of Alliance that established the Capitulation system, giving the French king the right to raise levies through local leaders in the cantons if his domains were attacked directly, at a minimum of 6,000 and a maximum of 16,000 men. The Capitulation system provided a model for agreements with other external princes and corporations. Once a Capitulation was agreed, the captains appointed by the Diet traversed the communities, recruiting and selecting from cantonal rolls and exercising authority to enforce the standard Swiss disciplinary code in the field, though Swiss law demanded that offenders were sent home for hearing and punishment where no judge accompanied the expedition.[42]

Pay is often thought to have been the key to the employment of the Swiss through the mercenary system (*pas d'argent, pas de suisse*), but this mistakes the role of money in the mercenary economy. In fact, the Swiss often continued in their service even when unpaid for years, bound not by money, but by the discipline and law in which their military value and identity was invested, the law of a confederated community inextricably tied into a dromological circuit by a complex of historical and sociological factors, and it was there that money had its effect. Under the Treaty of Alliance, the French monarchy paid pensions to mayors, local officials and innkeepers, butchers, tanners and blacksmiths, whose shops provided recruiting points in the dromological network. Unofficial pensions were also secretly distributed to individuals and still more 'gratifications' paid for specific services. This was the true cost of mercenary procurement, not the chronically deferred wages to soldiers. For the French monarchy, this supply of self-disciplining bodies solved the problem of how to raise the large numbers of men demanded by warfare in the new space of territorial conquest of strongpoints which could only be taken by siege. The Swiss would hold the centre of a battle or guard the artillery to their deaths and would storm a breach in the teeth of defensive fire, but when they were not needed they could simply be discharged under their own law back into the Confederation.[42]

The very means by which the Diet managed the mercenary system on behalf of the Confederation's communities infused pecuniary interests into key political and sociological junctures, enabling the French monarchy to bypass the Diet's regulation, since a Capitulation set in motion more extensive interest-mechanisms, extending far beyond the Diet's capacity to regulate political authorities. The communities became enmeshed in a dependency on mercenary supply that constituted the captains as local authorities, while the Diet's attempt at regulation trapped it into producing increased dependence upon exterior powers through the very means by which it attempted to maintain the independence and internal cohesion of the Confederation. The liberty of the Swiss thus became a means, with peasant families literally breeding bodies as a resource for mercenary service, and the discipline in which Swiss liberty was invested became an iron rule holding the soldiers to long and often impoverished contractual service in foreign lands.

Synthesis: Fusing techniques and free bodies

Charles the Bold's *compagnies d'ordonnance* had produced the idea that a military order could be constructed, rather than merely recruited in pre-formed units under an indenting captain in whom the right of command was invested by virtue of his personal relationship with his company. The political technologies of Burgundian government had also produced a service nobility of subjects invested in their technical expertise and its provision as an official service. Two members of this service nobility, escaping the slaughter at Nancy, now applied Burgundian techniques of military formation to produce new bodies on the model of the Swiss discipline.[43] In their offices as military governors and commanders, the counts of Nassua and Romont organized the communes of the Low Countries in resistance to incorporation into the French royal domain after the expiry of the Burgundian ducal dynasty with the death of Charles the Bold. The Swiss model provided a new *form* in which the counts were able to deploy the Flemish communal militias flexibly and aggressively, rather than merely defensively, against mounted knights, in the mass assault of the manoeuvrable square rather than the collective self-defence of their traditional immobile 'hedgehog' form, which had been able to withstand mounted men-at-arms, but depended upon terrain to decisively defeat them. The counts used the techniques set out in Charles' military ordinances to reproduce the technology of the Swiss battle-machine, training their 'raw material' by collective exercise with pikes. At Guinegate in 1479, they were already able to field these forces effectively against an army of French *compagnies d'ordonnance* and levied *francs-archers*.

Habsburg acquisition of the Low Countries through marriage opened the possibility of more direct military entrepreneurship for the Counts. For such an enterprise, their repute (or military capital) no longer lay in the permissive discipline of the captains of the Hundred Years War, but was now vested in the technical and administrative expertise that could produce ordered bodies in battle condition. The successful inculcation of these techniques guaranteed the soldiers' safety upon the field of mass battle and maximized their prospects of booty from baggage trains and stormed towns, comprising a new content to the 'reputation' by which such entrepreneurs were able to recruit. The new techniques of formation required subjects already free from domination by a master or lord to submit themselves to the discipline of training and drill. The cities of Flanders provided the initial subjects to which the new techniques could be applied, but the urban militias were subject to an identity in the particular liberty of their town, so they could not be maintained as forces after the Battle of Guinegate relieved the threat to the Flemish cities. For the creation of permanent companies on the Swiss model, men were required who were subject to no other jurisdiction, but could be formed within the prerogative jurisdiction that constituted a purely military order and maintained it in distinction from its environment. The Habsburg domains included parts of upper Germany bordering on the Swiss Confederation, where the economically surplus youth population formed semi-nomadic bands, living off the traffic of the road when not employed in the feuds of the urban leagues and the nobility. As displaced subjects these 'liberties' of the road provided the human material condition for the exercise of the new techniques of formation. 'Given these underlying sociological facts, the state could work on them ... Maximilian von Habsburg could enrol these men, following the advice of the former faithful councillors of Charles the Bold like the counts of Romont and Nassau.'[44]

Unlike the Swiss, the identity of the *landsknechte* or *lansquenets* was invested only in their military function. Subjection to a specifically military jurisdiction, order and discipline enabled the new formations to be deployed against the estates as well as against rival princes; in 1485, the count of Nassau entered Ghent at the head of 5,000 'Germans' marching in disciplined order.[45] Burgundian techniques could be applied to inculcate Swiss battle-discipline in almost any body that was projected outside the particular jurisdictions of late medieval polity and community, thus transmitting the imperative collective discipline of the square across the battlefields of Europe. Similarly, the king of France experimented with a training camp for foot soldiers, after the Burgundian model, hiring Swiss contingents to demonstrate their methods to the army he assembled there. The exercises produced complex articulations of 'an entire mass ... so that they appeared to form a single body'.[46] The pike-squares were also adapted to accommodate handgunners and other weapons, and were tactically flexible, used to storm field fortifications and town defences breached by cannon.

However, the creation of these bodies did not produce the subjects of willing obedience which Charles the Bold had envisioned through the *Cyropaedia*. Unlike the Swiss, these bodies were subject only to the law of their own formation, and were thus politically unreliable, particularly since the opportunity of plunder no longer functioned as a political gift, but continued to condition their assembly. Their interests were not formed in the order of the army as an integrated machine, but in the fraternity and cohesion which imbued them with their tactical utility and military value. Most particularly, they could not be made to perform menial labour, especially digging field fortifications and entrenchments, and thus these bodies remained ultimately resistant to integration in the new assemblage of warfare emerging in the space constituted by networks of strongpoints, fortifications, supply depots and arsenals, with its flow of cannon, powder and vehicles, and its own form of knowledge in logistics and mode of perception in the survey.

Notes

1. P. Anderson, *Lineages of the Absolutist State* (London: New Left Books, 1974).
2. A. Giddens, *The Nation-State and Violence: Vol. 2 of A Contemporary Critique of Historical Materialism* (Cambridge: Polity Press, 1985).
3. C. Tilly, *Coercion, Capital and European States,* AD 990–1992 (Oxford: Blackwell, 1992).
4. N. Elias, *Civilizing Process: The History of Manners and State Formation and Civilisation*, trans. E. Jephcott (2 vols) (Oxford: Blackwell, 1994).
5. R. Vaughan, *Philip the Bold: The Formation of the Burgundian State* (Longman: London, 1962); *John the Fearless* (London: Longman, 1966); *Philip the Good: The Apogée of Burgundy* (London: Longman, 1970) and *Charles the Bold: The Last Valois Duke of Burgundy* (London: Longman, 1973).
6. G. Oestreich, *Neo-Stoicism and the early Modern State* (Cambridge University Press, 1982); H. Caygill, *Art of Judgement* (Oxford: Blackwell, 1989).
7. R. Vaughan, *Valois Burgundy* (London: Longman, 1975), p. 124.
8. Ibid., pp. 150–4.
9. Ibid., p. 131.
10. C. A. J. Armstrong, 'Had the Burgundian Government a Policy for the Nobility?', in J. S. Bromley and E. H. Kossman (eds), *Britain and the Netherlands,* Vol. 2 (Groningen: Walters, 1964) pp. 9–32.
11. Ibid., pp. 10–11.

12. Ibid., pp. 15–20.
13. Vaughan, *Charles the Bold*, pp. 183–8.
14. M. Foucault, 'Governmentality', in G. Burchell *et al.* (eds), *The Foucault Effect: Studies in Governmentality* (London: Harvester Wheatsheaf, 1991), pp. 87–104.
15. Vaughan, *Charles the Bold*, p. 163.
16. M. Foucault, 'Politics and Reason', in *Politics, Philosophy and Culture: Interviews and Other Writings, 1977–84,* ed. L. Kritzman (London: Routledge, 1988), pp. 57–85.
17. Xenophon *Cyropaedia*, trans. Mongan (London: James Cornish, n.d).
18. Vaughan, *Charles the Bold*, p. 205
19. Foucault, M. *Discipline and Punish: The Birth of the Prison* (London: Penguin, 1977).
20. '... charging in close formation ... to withdraw on command, and to rally ... the archers ... to march briskly forwards and to fire without breaking rank. The pikemen ... to advance in close formation ... [and] kneel, holding their pikes lowered to the level of a horse's back so that the archers can fire over them as if over a wall. [The archers] to place themselves back to back in double defence, or in a square or a circle ... the pikemen outside them ...', quoted in Vaughan, *Charles the Bold*, p. 210.
21. Ibid.
22. Ibid., p. 431.
23. Ibid., p. 357. Urban mobilization for resistance had high and uncertain costs, however, requiring the total conversion of the city into defensive resources. Strasbourg, in fear of the Burgundian advance, prepared itself by demolishing five monasteries and 620 houses beyond its walls to create a two-mile *glacis* which any attacker would have to cross under fire from the walls, levying 800 men to dig a moat, stocking itself with powder and artillery from Nurnberg and provisions of corn for ten years and salt and wine for three, but was not, in the end, besieged at all.
24. Phillipe de Commynes, *Memoirs: The Reign of Louis XI, 1461–83,* trans. Jones (Harmondsworth: Penguin, [1491] 1972), p. 241.
25. Vaughan, *Charles the Bold*, pp. 352–7.
26. K. Von Greyerz, 'Switzerland', in B. Scribner *et al.* (eds), *The Reformation in National Context* (Cambridge: Cambridge University Press, 1994), p. 31.
27. J. McCormack, *One Million Mercenaries: Swiss Soldiers in the Armies of the World* (London: Leo Cooper, 1993), pp 4–10.
28. Ibid., pp. 11–13.
29. H. Delbrück *The History of the Art of War within the Framework of Political History*, vol. III, trans. W. J. Renfroe (London: Greenwood Press, 1985) p. 654.
30. Vaughan, *Charles the Bold*, p. 387.
31. Ibid., p. 360–7.
32. Ibid., p. 377; Delbrück, *History of the Art of War*, vol. III, pp. 606–12; McCormack, *One Million Mercenaries*, pp. 27–9.
33. J. McCormack, *One Million Mercenaries*, pp. 15–20.
34. Ibid., p. 29.
35. Vaughan, *Charles the Bold*, p. 378.
36. Delbrück, *History of the Art of War*, vol. III, pp. 612–17.
37. McCormack, *One Million Mercenaries*, p. 29; Vaughan, *Charles the Bold*, pp. 390–4.

38. Vaughan, *Charles the Bold*, pp. 400–15.
39. Quoted in ibid., p. 430.
40. Delbrück, *History of the Art of War*, vol. III, p. 655.
41. Charles VIII of France's call for volunteers against the Diet's refusal drew 10,000 men out of the Confederation in 1494, with 20,000, one-fifth of the adult male population, responding to a second call in the following year, from which Charles was able to select the 8,000 he needed.
42. McCormack, *One Million Mercenaries*, pp. 62–4, 74–7.
43. Delbrück, *History of the Art of War*, vol. IV, pp. 5–7.
44. P. Contamine, *War in the Middle Ages* (Oxford: Blackwell, 1984), p. 137.
45. Delbrück, *History of the Art of War*, vol. IV, pp. 10–12.
46. Quoted in ibid., p. 12.

12

Republic and Monarchy: Two Texts on Government, Discipline and the Subject of Violence

Two early modern texts map out the problematics presented by the new space of war. In Claude de Seyssel's *The Monarchy of France*,[1] first published in 1519, the army appears as a structurally differentiated site in which new forms of subjectification could be accomplished, corresponding to a new mode of government by edict rather than government under given law and custom, since in the military domain, discipline provides an alternative pre-political order. In Nicolo Machiavelli's *Art of War*,[2] first published in 1521, the army and its discipline provide the conditions for the recovery of ancient liberty. Again, in this text, the pre-political appears not as the *socius* of patriarchal domination in the household or fraternal equality in property ownership, but as discipline under arms, with its site beyond the city, in the camp of the war-zone where men's interests are subject to common existential necessity. In both these texts we find particular problematics of the organization of force mapped out, with discipline and obedience as the key elements of a military order that is the model for new political orders.

Machiavelli

Art of War, military history and political theory

In terms of the history of military technique, *Art of War* appears already outdated and even regressive, but these histories assume a given instrumentalization of violence for the strategic deployment of a sovereign power, retrospectively attributing a historically determinant role to the development of gunpowder weapons.[3] The English translator's addition of the definite article to Machiavelli's text, published in Italian as *Arte della guerra*, relocates the text in a discourse in which it is read as a formal military manual after Vegetius' *De Re Militari*, one of Machiavelli's sources, as an attempt 'to conceive of the art of war as a science by attempting to systematize its principles'.[4] Divested of its discursive strategy, abstracted from its context and reduced to ahistorical categories, it is thus conventionally evaluated by criteria according to which it will always be found inadequate. Rather than reading the text in terms of essential military forms, situating Machiavelli's project historically and discursively enables us to see, in Skinner's terms, what the text actually *does*.[5] This approach requires us to consider its format and marginalia and to attend to the Renaissance Florentine context.

Art of War does not expound military techniques in the form of a manual addressed to military professionals, but its form of presentation as a Socratic 'conference' conducted between friends and equals in a Florentine garden establishes it as political discourse situated in the culture of Renaissance civilization. The expositor, Fabrizio Colonna, presents his credentials not only as a military practitioner, but also as a military governor,[6] and Machiavelli uses his character not merely to propound the value of ancient techniques as means of warfare, but to explicate them as political technology for the reconstitution of the republic and the citizen–subject. Neal Wood's introduction to the modern edition of an eighteenth-century English translation by Ellis Farnesworth argues that

> ... the ideal military community that is prescribed by Machiavelli in *The Art of War* becomes something like the well-ordered civic community which he advocates in *The Prince* and *The Discourses* ... Machiavelli's rational order serves as a model for his concept of civil society.[7]

In his preface, Machiavelli begins from the differentiation of the contemporary soldier 'as a creature different from all other men', but argues that this difference occludes a 'close, intimate relationship' between the military and civil condition.[8] In *Art of War*, the former provides the model and the means for the reconstitution of the latter. Contextualization can help us to grasp the significance of this project.

J. G. A. Pocock situates *Art of War* as a Florentine textual intervention in the crisis of the Renaissance discourse of the city-republic invoked by the collapse of major Italian city-states before the invading forces of the French monarchy.[9] His contextual restoration enables us to read it as a political programme concerned not only to facilitate the organization of forces of resistance, but also to reconstitute the order of the republic mobilized in that organization, so that its military techniques appear as political technology, as the means by which Machiavelli proposes to reform the republic and its subjects. However, while useful in situating *Art of War* as a political crisis intervention, Pocock's reading from context leads him to treat it only as a programmatic text, neglecting its problematization of the reformation of the republic and its citizen–soldier–subject in military order and discipline. Pocock is concerned with the ends to which Machiavelli applied these techniques (simultaneously the ends of defence in liberty and of the constitution of liberty itself) and thus focuses on the first book, which deals with the relation of organized force *to* the republic, without any deeper enquiry into the conditions established by its military construction or the problematics invoked by the project, which appear at the end of the text, when Fabrizio reflexively asks of his own discourse where men could be found who would obediently submit to such discipline.[10]

The city of grace and the virtuous subject: Toward political reformation

In the political discourse of the Italian Renaissance, Florence exemplified the 'fallen' republic, the city of men fallen from grace, a condition brought home to the Italian city-states by Charles VIII's invasion of 1494, which utilized the mobile artillery and siege train developed by the Bureau Brothers at the end of the Hundred Years War to reduce their urban fortifications and force their subjection to French royal hegemony. In Florence, the French invasion led to the collapse of oligarchic rule in a series of revolts in which Pocock identifies a convergence between the traditions of Judaeo-Christian apocalypticism and classical civic humanism.[11] In the serial time of apocalyptic and messianic religion, each moment is uniquely significant, a moment in which any community might 'be' an Israel or a Rome. The particularity of the early modern city as a source of law in itself reached its highest degree of development in Renaissance Italy, where the northern concept of lordship had never successfully taken hold. This particularity had isolated the community in the present moment, cutting it off from continuous dynastic time and providing conditions in which the projects of civic self-realization in political community and of spiritual realization in religious community converged in the refoundational recovery of the republic as simultaneously a community of justice and a community of grace.

Articulating the popular anti-oligarchic Florentine revolt, the apocalyptic preacher, Savonarola, interpreted the political crisis as such a moment of convergence. Relatively stable and enduring Venice conventionally provided the ideal constitutional model for Renaissance republican discourse. However, Savonarola argued that the fixed constitutional arrangements underpinning Venetian stability closed off the moment in which the constitution of the republic might also be the moment of grace, since it indefinitely deferred the apocalyptic-political moment by projecting a 'second nature' in which primary nature (the *prima forma* of the city, its *soul*) saw itself reflected, so that the security of established political arrangements took precedence over the reformation necessary for *virtù* and grace. Their very security thus prevented the Venetians from ever taking the momentous step of risking their city's stability. Pocock argues that Machiavelli took Savonarola seriously, but recognized that the step demanded by the apocalyptic priest left the prophet unarmed and the republic defenceless. Rather, Machiavelli proposed a programme for the recovery of the republic that would work through the second nature which Savonarola saw as an obstacle, eschewing an essentialist concept of the soul in favour of a subject which could be constructed by using political technologies to impose form and design on the disordered space and time of contingent conditions (*fortuna*). Machiavelli's concept of *virtù* brings these technical effects together with the aim of 'modifying men's natures from what custom has made them after custom itself has ceased to be operative'.[12]

The self-realization of the city and its subject required a civic reformation; 'Machiavelli was in search of social means whereby men's natures could be transformed to the point where they became capable of citizenship'.[13] Such means of subjectification were to be found in the order, exercise and discipline of military organization according to the ancients and more recently exemplified in some respects by the Swiss. In this project, the figures of both the original legislator and the prophet of grace are substituted by techniques of mobilization which project the city into the realm of necessity, the field of war, under the military order and discipline that had produced the preconditions of the ancient Roman republic, as recounted in the first four books of Livy's *History*. Political *virtù* (if not soteriological grace) thus consists in the condition of mobilization, military formation and discipline, so that these become political technologies producing a citizen-soldier, who

> ... is more than an instrument in the public hand or in the hand of the prophet, since his *virtù* is his own and he fights out of knowledge of what it is he fights for ... By basing the popular republic on the *virtù* of the armed citizen, Machiavelli had transformed the problem of popular participation from one of knowledge to one of will.[14]

Military–political technology

In order to reform the citizenry, to recover *virtù* from contingent *fortuna* (*Art of War*) or from corruption (*Discourses*), Machiavelli does not project these operations upon the city in its given order, but proposes to march the citizens out beyond the walls (to drive them out if necessary) into the space of war where they will by necessity have to subject themselves to military discipline, order and formation if they are to survive. Though Vegetius provides his main source, Machiavelli ascribes the corruption of the republic to the appearance of men who made warfare their sole occupation, rupturing the identity of the military and civic order of the city. Rather than adopting a Vegetian ontology, he seeks to recover the principles of Roman military order, *virtù*, asceticism, order, discipline, fraternity, unity and the public good.[15]

This problem of the disposition of professional commanders applies also to the soldiery, and Machiavelli addresses the problem of the return to domestic or civic life of those raised up into military order by referring it to the criteria of selection, under which a commander should mobilize 'only such men as will cheerfully serve him in war when it is necessary, and be as glad to return home after it is over'.[16] Since inexperienced men will fear war, those who would volunteer themselves to serve under contemporary conditions will be robbers and vagabonds who make war their profession, but the authority of the prince can provide a 'middle course' whereby men are 'motivated by the obedience they think due to their governors to expose themselves to a little hardship rather than incur their displeasure'.[17] Such a predisposition is best inculcated by strict laws and ordinances to enforce the practice of exercises in peacetime, a spectacular simulation which sustains the republic as a militarily disciplined body *in potentia* without maintaining an army permanently in the field, but also reproduces the condition of agonic citizenship, extending to the physical exercise of the individual body by the addition of weights to the practice equipment, so that the exercise of arms in real conditions would seem relatively easy.[18] The operational divisions that Fabrizio recommends are derived, like the form of arms and the primacy of foot soldiers, from a synthesis of ancient Roman and contemporary Swiss sources, to fit together 'like staves of a barrel'. The subjective disposition to order produced by drilling in battalions is similarly a microcosm of the order of the army as a whole, so that the interchangeable units can be deployed independently or in co-ordination without disturbing it.

Against the reduction of the city-states by siege, Machiavelli invokes the Swiss reinstatement of battle as the primary mode of warfare. The third book of *Art of War* comprises an account of an imaginary battle in which the order of drill is set in constant motion, with the forces deployed not merely as a dense mass, but in precisely specified and calibrated spaces, to enable changes of formation. The numbering of battalions and the functions of ranks are essential to their flexible manoeuvrability, and the troops must conduct themselves in silence in order to enable communications to be heard. There is order everywhere throughout the battle, except in the face of the cannon, which fire to signal the start of the battle and must be stormed at speed before they have the chance to fire again. In the charge against them, order is abandoned to dissolve the mass body they would target, producing a phenomenological encounter of each soldier with his own death staring from the mouth of the cannon. This encounter with the modern technology of warfare thus recovers the ancient *agon* of the individual citizen–warrior, but only in its singular moment, since the aftermath of the battle-charge does not release the men from their discipline to plunder at will, but is subject to military administration. Independent military economy is precluded by establishing the custom that the spoils of war pass directly into the public treasury for administrative distribution, making the soldiers 'more intent on victory than on plunder'.[19] Like Vegetius, Machiavelli also recommends that the soliders' pay and share of spoils be deposited with the standards for the duration of the campaign, thus investing the soldiers' individual material interests in the administrative order.

The fourth book deals with stratagems and intelligences, discussing weather and topography, spies and reconnaissance, surprise, evasion, dissimulation, concealment, traps and false intelligence. Intelligence figures not merely as the means of gaining advantage over an enemy, but also of manipulating the morale of the soldiers, and in both respects these operational stratagems are subject to principles of government. The fifth book is concerned with the march. The environment must always be considered hostile and commanders must have good intelligence of the land by maps and by reconnaissance. March is ordered in precise dimensions and proportions (as for the order of drill and battle) and such disposition is again a technique of subject formation as well as of spatial order. It is not sufficient that the army be drawn up according to the correct specifications; the soldiers must also be accustomed to form and march in this order, to expect attack, to exist on bread they prepare themselves, to drink only water, to carry loads, and to clear their own path and construct their own camps. Machiavelli devotes the sixth book to the camp, again specifying its dimensions after ancient sources. As for the Romans, the order of the camp constitutes a moving city, and directions to separate

245

combatants from non-combatants suggest there could be equal numbers of camp-followers to soldiers. The camp provides an exemplar for 'popular' government, i.e. the order and rule of subjects undifferentiated by status privileges. In this simulacrum of the city, Machiavelli expounds the conditions of discipline most fully, revealing the problematics of the entire project.

The circumscription of the camp constitutes a prerogative order of command over the disposition of bodies, its perimeter demarcating those who have gone absent without leave, and again this order is not merely spatial but also moral, since the preoccupation of the bodies within it is subject to regulations prohibiting games of vice and prescribing functional activity. Its spatial order and regulation also ensure the health of the physical bodies within it. The regime of the camp is thus a regime of the body both in a collective and an individual sense, operating upon and through the body formed by its military order to produce self-disciplined subjects. Strict rationing of provisions imposes a common order of frugality, without privileges, and the dimensions of the camp's roadways and spaces provide for mutual surveillance. The result is a body of subjects of self-constraint. The armed camp provides a test case for governmental technologies because 'neither fear of laws nor reverence to man are sufficient to bridle an armed multitude'.[20] Fabrizio points out that the ancients used religion as a means of social control, but cannot offer a contemporary equivalent, since the universality of the Christian community of mercy corrupts military discipline. Sovereign prohibitions would also undermine the intended effect of political subjectification, but military peer judgement constitutes a means of *government* which preserves the liberty of subjects in disciplinary order, providing a model for the administration of popular justice in the city itself.

Problematics of military-political reformation

At the end of the text Fabrizio acknowledges that the programme of disciplinary formation he has outlined is conditional upon its own effect. It is possible to raise an army 'out of the earth', but this requires subjects of a disposition willing to submit themselves to discipline and training, i.e. predisposed to order and obedience, which is precisely the quality that the programme is designed to produce. Fabrizio's reflexively critical questions relate not to fighting, for which the condition of battle in itself would suffice, but to the condition of exercise, deployment, moral regulation, obedience, and subjectification. Ancient discipline provides the technology to inure bodies and fortify minds, and the co-operation of a prince provides the necessary authority, but the intended effect could only be achieved in their operation upon 'raw, honest men who are their own subjects', precisely the condition which the project is intended to recover.

Mercenaries would not subject themselves to the discipline and rigours necessary to form an army that could recover the liberty of the ancients, but nor would the citizens of existing Italian cities. Even exercises require self-subjection to the simulated anxieties of the field, but a militia is not immanent in the order of the city itself. In describing military order in terms of masses, ranks, ratios and proportions, in conjunction with terms of military administration and regulation, Machiavelli brings together the technologies of architecture and military command, tying the prince (a necessary but instrumental factor in the army's formation) to the form of the city. The republic's military reformation, however, takes place in a field camp outside the city, in the space of insecurity and necessity, where a military order is formed in the operation of techniques upon the 'raw' body rather than reproduced as a copy of an original order given in the city-republic or in the sovereign prince.

Machiavelli cannot simply adopt the Swiss identity of citizen-soldiers in the field under the law of the political community because the Florentines are a people fallen from ancient liberty, which persists only in the mountain enclaves on the margins of civilization, providing the Swiss with a tradition that can be admired, but not reproduced immediately. In any case, the Swiss could not be subjected to new techniques of discipline to produce new effects because their constitution is fixed in its particularity *outside* of historical time.[21] Rather than the law of the community, the order of the militia camp envisioned by Fabrizio has to be like that of other armies, excepting the Swiss, i.e. a jurisdiction beyond the law of the republic, a space in which laws are established for the formation and maintenance of the army itself, dictated by function and necessity, rather than by reference to political justice or will. The problem of obedience thus reappears at the very centre of the discourse of the army.

Fabrizio's reflexive turn projects its problematization of obedience back through his preceding exposition, but Machiavelli has provided a range of practices drawn from ancient Roman sources which can be deployed as techniques to inculcate a *positive*, wilful, rational obedience. Together, all these techniques, technologies and their conditions (discipline, architecture, exercise, dromology, extra-juridical law, stratagems, etc.) can be subsumed under one term, government, which has the object of obedience, the primary condition of the militia army and the project which it is to realize. Government thus emerges from *Art of War* as the art of arts, the art of deployment of technologies of subjectification in general, with obedience as its end, enabling all other operations. And military government provides the model for all government, since, 'there is no case whatsoever in which the most exact and implicit obedience is as necessary as in the government of an army'.[22]

De Seyssel

Monarchy, governmentality, military

In his lecture on 'Governmentality', Foucault notes the appearance in early modern Europe of 'a series of treatises that are no longer exactly "advice to the prince" and not yet the treatises of political science, but are instead presented as works on the "art of government"'.[23] These deal with a problematic of 'government in general', a discourse which can be differentiated from the juridical theory of sovereignty. Where the former seeks to distinguish the power of the prince from all other kinds of power, the art of government seeks to establish a continuity – upwards to the prince, who must first learn to govern himself, downwards so that individuals know how to govern themselves. While the target of sovereign power is the territory and its inhabitants, government operates upon the relations between men and things (resources, ways of life, events). The end of the sovereign exercise of power lies in the 'common good', understood as obedience to the laws (divine, juridical, sovereign) and hence has law as its instrument and its legitimation, but the ends of government are found in the relations it has as its object, and its means are thus tactical, particular, heterogenous.

The movement Foucault describes as historically embedded in the early modern emancipation of the discourse of the art of government from juridical theories of sovereignty and pre-political patriarchal domination can be traced in one text, Claude de Seyssel's *The Monarchy of France*, first published in 1519. This text sets out, quite explicitly, to establish the *principles* of government, a task facilitated by the form of the text and the transitional juncture of its authorship. De Seyssel had served Louis XII as a counsellor of state and wrote *The Monarchy* in three months between his retirement from office following the death of the king and the commencement of an ecclesiastical career. The speed of its composition and its transitional authorship traverses the domains it lays out in ways that more scholarly or authorized forms could not, in an entirely new kind of text on government which is neither pedagogical instruction nor memoir, enabling him to develop and map out its principles. In the fifteenth century, those recording the practical wisdom to be gained from the study of the past, either derived the lessons they propounded from ancient historical authority available to scholars (but safely distinct from contemporary powers), or else used the form of the memoir (for which the rules of discourse were very different), to derive cautious and incidental generalizations from an account of events authorized by personal involvement. The treatise form provides de Seyssel with a space for generalization conventionally open only to scholars working at a distance from power and patronage, but within it he abstracts general principles from his experience as royal counsellor, which endows the text with a validity beyond the reach of scholarly commentary. In contrast to de Commynes' *Memoirs*, for example, where detail provides the occasion for generalization only in digress from a narrative to which it is subordinate, detail in de Seyssel's text is subordinate to the presentation of principles of government, appearing only, 'by political reason, approved authority and authentic historical example' to validate and verify his abstractions.

An archaeology of *police*

The importance of this text lies not in the place we can allocate it to in traditions or great movements of thought,[24] but in the movement within it (perhaps an effect of the speed and transition of its authorship). In his concept of *police*,[25] de Seyssel incorporates the Burgundian development of discrete late medieval political technologies into policy, as a means whereby the rational interests of subjects and the legitimation of the regime can be brought into correspondence, effecting voluntary obedience. In its abstractions from such practice, the text provides a bridge between late medieval practices of government and the *polizeiwissenschaft* of Enlightened absolutism,[26] a bridge that is articulated, like his text, by the army. Within the structure of the text itself, we can see how the concept of *police* shifts from a means for the preservation of given relations between the estates, the prince and the polity as a whole, to their augmentation and finally to the production of obedience in orders that are not given, i.e. in the domain of conquest.

The Monarchy's five parts map out different domains for the operation of government; the monarchy itself and the estates (corresponding to the mystical body of medieval political theology); the person of the king and his counsel and offices of state; military power; foreign relations; and war and conquered states. The object of the text is to establish the 'principle' of 'government in general', rather than the transcendent authority of the discourse of sovereignty. As in Foucault's overview, government is differentiated from both domination through force and subjection through law, but operates through reason constituted in the particular relations between men and things in particular situations, with *police* as a means of operating upon those relations to produce its effects. However, though the same general principles apply throughout (to secure and govern through rational obedience), different objects, different rationalities, different ends and different means apply in each of the domains mapped out by the divisions of the text. Means adapt to operate upon the rationalities particular to each domain. In the government of the estates and of the offices of state, *police* is still essentially conservative, constituting at once a means, an object and a limit for kingship; only in the domain of military power (which in the structure of the book articulates the other four domains) does it actually produce order.

The government of the laws and the estates

The Monarchy opens with a conventional Aristotelian disputation of the best of the three forms of government, presenting the French monarchy, with its fundamental historical laws, as exemplary. The text is conventionally interpreted as a conservative and orthodox legal and political work in which princely authority is 'bridled' by religion, justice and *police*, mediations of power unavailable to democratic and oligarchic regimes, where the interplay of divided civil authority with military forces disintegrates the polity, so that government is replaced by the rule of force. However, military force already appears distinct from the polity, an extra domain that is not addressed by conventional Aristotelian constitutional analysis. The nobles' right to bear arms does not constitute military force, but is simply the means by which the noble estate is maintained in office or income from the king and is thereby enabled to fulfil its function in the social order by maintaining others. The French *gens d'armerie*, created to rid the realm of socially displaced bands discharged from the armies of the Hundred Years War, de Seyssel argues, 'was instituted for the defence of the realm and to have a sufficient number trained in arms and also for the maintenance of gentlemen'; it is disbanded when not needed, 'so that they can live part of the time in their own houses and save a part of their wages'.[27]

The order of the estates is inherent in their interdependent functions. Relations between them are self-regulating and only to be facilitated by government, so that in this domain, 'it is only necessary to maintain each estate in its liberties, privileges and praiseworthy customs, and so to superintend all of them that one cannot lord it over

250

the others excessively nor all three join against the head and monarch'.[28] Since the functional division of the estates is entirely transparent, this structural order operates through reason rather than law. 'In this way the estates think only to live in good order [*police*], in concord with one another and especially in obedience to the king.' Just as the division of functions constitutes a limit for the effective action of each estate which is also the limit of law, so for the prince reason in the exercise of authority is also the limit of legality, given in the fundamental laws and the three bridles. Governmental rationality is thus not merely an attribute of the prince, but also of the estates, though their preservation and augmentation still requires 'remedies to correct them and thus render it as perfect and perpetual as the wisdom and the fragility or imperfection of earthly things allow'.[29]

The government of kingship and counsel

'*La police*' provides the means for this preservation and augmentation, which must begin with the person of the king himself, but since the affairs of the realm are too complex and extensive for any one man or group to understand and manage, counsel provides a mode of *knowledge* or *intelligence* for government in this domain. While the order of knowledge pertaining to the first domain of government was that of hierarchical *transparency*, in this second domain it is ordered in a concentric concentration of *secrecy* around a centre so that knowledge and government of the minutiae of life is not delegated to remote functionaries. Rather, it is brought under increasingly detailed and regular surveillance towards the innermost circle of counsel, which operates as a political lens, monitoring and ordering secret reports on offices and nominees, its scope extending from actions of state to the personal morality of the prince, household and court expenditure, and monetary regulation.

In this domain, *police* is concerned with *circulation*, the moving, effective, economic aspects of the relations between things, rather than with *distribution* within a static order. It is concerned with the money of the kingdom, the effects of trade upon the nobility, the moral and financial effects of tax collection upon the popular estates, and even with facilitating and regulating social mobility.[30]

The government of the army: Producing military power

The last three sections of the book, dealing with military power, foreign relations and conquest, appear very different to the first and second. The third part, lying at the heart of a work which has the identity of the kingdom at one pole and conquest at its other, articulates the whole. The army figures in this central section as a domain of government beyond both the estates and the embryonic offices of the state. Power is not productively generated in the distribution of the estates or the circulation of the riches of the realm, but only in this third domain, dealing with the government of 'military power'. In relation to the estates and even to counsel, *police* operates conservatively, to maintain what is existent in good order (even counsel is the condensed wisdom of centuries of practice). It is only in relation to the army that *police* acts upon relations newly and continuously constituted.

The military domain is comprised territorially by fortifications, materially by their provision and socially by the army. The memory of the *écorcheurs* of the previous century was deeply imprinted upon the sixteenth-century discourse of government and the problematic for government in this field does not consist in the armed nobility, but in the soldiery. Though foreign mercenaries cannot be reduced by reason to discipline and sanctions, as an alternative source of forces, de Seyssel writes not of the estates, but of 'the people'. He proposes a levy of men by ballot or quota, to be assigned captains from the same locality whose authority would be more personal and extensive, and concerned with the men both as a unit and individually, in a micro-government of the regiment, though (as for Machiavelli) the order of the army would consist in its reduction to discipline, rather than in a given order. In contrast to Machiavelli's *Art of War*, however, *The Monarchy* focuses directly upon the preconditions that problematized Fabrizio's exposition of its exercise.

The first condition of discipline is obedience, but rather than reading this off from command, de Seyssel considers both sides of the dyadic form of disciplinary sociation, command and obedience. Command consists in the technical qualifications of the commander and their summary execution of a military justice determined not by abstract principles or tactical contingency, but by its function as a means of establishing discipline. Severe administration of justice brings the soldiers to reason, establishing within each and every one the conditions for government to operate upon. Additionally, the commander must cultivate a personal relationship with his soldiers. Treating them according to merit has a negative object in this economy of reason, 'to deprive the soldiers of all occasion to disobey him and engage in mutiny',[31] but by sharing their hardships and treating them courteously (in short, by evidencing his love for them), the commander will make them *want* to obey him.

A second condition of discipline consists in the moral order of the army, and this requires operation upon the soul and the body rather than upon reason, establishing conditions of discipline that are completely internal to the soldier and independent of their relation to their commander. This condition has to do with 'the way the soldiers live amongst themselves'.[32] It operates through the soul since soldiers are

> most of the time in danger of their lives. For this reason they should especially put and keep themselves in a state of grace, a thing that is little cared for in France, particularly among the infantry, who ordinarily are so ill conditioned in everything.[33]

But the body of the soldier also provides an object for government to operate upon in the camp. A regime of military asceticism serves three functions; toughening the body and accustoming it to the possible shortage of rations in the field, enabling the army to dispense with the tactical liability of a baggage train, and regulating the desires of soldiers so that they can live upon their pay and are not tempted to loot. Pay, the 'material' condition of discipline upon which modern commentators usually focus in their readings of early modern texts on military government, is thus secondary to the establishment of moral military order, since a properly ordered army will be constrained to abandon their posts and seek the means of life by violence only if it does not have enough to live upon. Regular and sufficient pay is thus not a primary condition of discipline, but only a secondary factor, conditional for its effect upon moral government. (This view was not peculiar to de Seyssel; even for Machiavelli's prince, pay 'is not enough to make them want to die for you'.[34])

The government of conquest

In war, all considerations are subordinated to imperative *speed* and all the aspects of kingship otherwise so carefully governed according to the first parts of the text become merely means to accelerate conquest. However, if war requires *foreshortening* government, the retention of conquered lordships requires its *extended* duration.[35] The presence of the army may secure the goodwill of conquered subjects by defending and enforcing justice, *police* and finance – the task of a government of occupation – but in the space of conquest the army itself becomes an estate, so that 'matters concerning the armed force in general', are here very different. Its internal order here is considered as given; the problematic of military power in the domain of conquest is rather to maintain the army in static inactivity within an environment that is not ordered by ancient institutions or intrinsic functions.

The main problem for government of conquest does not come from the people of the conquered lands, but lies in the means of security, because the economies which constitute the government of the army in its own discipline have negative effects in the duration of conquest. Customary military economy undermines government of duration, as those with booty will only want to return home with it, while those without will be forced to abandon a foreign land in which they cannot maintain themselves on their pay. Even the honour of soldiers works against military occupation by garrisons, since there is no honour in such duty and they will ultimately seek an excuse for withdrawal. However, the principle of government, operating through economies (rather than force) to achieve its objects, suggests the problem can be reconfigured in the terms peculiar to this new domain, invoking the colonial model; 'means must be sought to make most of them or their leaders love the land and desire to stay there by giving them a stake that they cannot sell, or marrying them off in the country'. Trustworthy inhabitants may also be civilized by the conqueror taking them into his pay, 'teaching them his people's way of living and waging war'.[36]

Besides military colonies, government of the army in the duration of conquest is to be achieved by maintaining garrisons as a totally alien military presence in rigorous isolation from their social, material and moral environment, in strongholds provisioned to withstand a year of siege and supplied by a bureaucratic order subject to continual surveillance. The fortress is thus not a part of the same field of government as the rest of the conquered land, which is invested by military colonists and inhabitants raised into the forces. Commanders must maintain the space of fortification in a continuous simulation of the state of siege.

> Such commanders must not on any condition have any charge or mix in matters of justice and *police* in the town, or do anything but provide for and keep their strongholds. It is essential that neither they nor their men ever go far from their places ... and that they have no important dealings with the inhabitants of either town or country, nor admit them to the stronghold except on business necessary for the stronghold.[37]

The stronghold is thus to be maintained as a purely military set of relations, supplied by contracts not between equal parties, but between individual contractors and the military establishment in its fortification, which exists in a different space and time of government to that of the land and its inhabitants. The strongholds and their garrisons are not a force of domination, but a distinct governmental regime in itself. The garrisons thus do not function to dominate the domain of conquest; they do not even patrol it, but are closed off even by the minimalization of contractual relations of supply. Rather, they maintain the time of war in insulated pockets, enclaves of military power frozen in internal discipline, a thing apart, existing in its own space and hence able to maintain its own time of unrelenting vigilance.

Domination is effected by other, political, means, replicating the government of the domain of the army to produce the conditions of obedience where an ancient constitution and intrinsic order do not operate. As in the army, the substance of the laws is secondary to the instrumentalization of justice as a means of government. The conqueror's law is not to be imposed, judges are to be chosen from men of the conquered country and only administered by the governor, 'some great and good person' who must cultivate personal relationships with the conquered subjects. Offices of the land should be given to local leaders, so that their distribution operates as a means of government, to construct a rational allegiance to the regime of conquest. Only in the very final chapter of *The Monarchy*, where he deals with the government of irreducible factions, does de Seyssel advocate political rather than administrative measures. The prince should, 'seek by all means available to extinguish party strife and bring about an accord in devotion to him if that seems possible'.[38] Finally, and only where this proves impossible, is there repression.

Notes

1. C. de Seyssel, *The Monarchy of France,* ed. D. R. Kelley, trans. J. H. Hexter (New Haven, CO: Yale University Press, 1981).
2. N. Machiavelli, *The Art of War,* ed. N. Wood, trans. E. Farneworth (New York, NY: Da Capo Press, 1965).
3. F. Gilbert, 'Machiavelli: The Renaissance of the Art of War', in P. Paret (ed.), *Makers of Modern Strategy: From Machiavelli to Nuclear Strategy* (Princeton, NJ: Princeton University Press, 1986); G. Parker, *The Military Revolution: Military Innovation and the Rise of the West, 1500–1800* (Cambridge: Cambridge University Press, 1988).
4. N. Wood, 'Introduction' to Machiavelli, *Art of War,* p. xxxix.
5. Q. Skinner, 'Meaning and Understanding in the History of Ideas', in J. Tully (ed.), *Meaning and Context: Quentin Skinner and his Critics* (Cambridge: Polity Press, 1988), pp. 97–118.
6. Machiavelli, *Art of War,* p. 23.
7. Wood, 'Introduction', in ibid., pp. lxxiv–lxxv.
8. Machiavelli, *Art of War,* pp. 3–5.
9. J. G. A. Pocock, *The Machiavellian Moment: Florentine Political Thought and the Atlantic Republican Tradition* (Princeton, NJ: Princeton University Press, 1975).

10. Machiavelli, *Art of War*, p. 208.
11. This convergence corresponds to the synthesis of the pastoral and political traditions of governmental discourse which Foucault identifies as characteristic of 'daemonic' modernity in his thesis on governmentality.
12. Pocock, *Machiavellian Moment*, p. 184.
13. Ibid., p. 193.
14. Ibid., pp. 203, 212.
15. Machiavelli, *Art of War*, pp. 12, 17.
16. Ibid., p. 21.
17. Ibid., p. 29.
18. Ibid., pp. 57–8.
19. Ibid., p. 141.
20. Ibid., p. 165.
21. Ibid., p. 209.
22. Ibid., p. 163.
23. Foucault, M. 'Governmentality', in G. Burchell *et al.* (eds), *The Foucault Effect: Studies in Governmentality* (London: Harvester Wheatsheaf, 1991), p. 87.
24. *The Monarchy* is usually read in the context of constitutional political thought, focusing on de Seyssel's sketch of the constraints operant upon kingship, which positions it at a point of articulation between conservative formulations of the body politic and the Huguenots' radicalization of the idea of constitutional constraints to produce a theory of revolutionary resistance. Q. Skinner, *The Foundations of Modern Political Thought* (Cambridge: Cambridge University Press, 1978); D. Kelley, *The Beginning of Ideology: Consciousness and Society in the French Reformation* (Cambridge: Cambridge University Press, 1981). However, I am not concerned so much with *The Monarchy* as a constitutional or ideological text, but with the principles and rationalities along which it operates.
25. Hexter's translation elides de Seyssel's distinction between *politie, policie* and *police*, but this edition usefully provides an index of the usage of these terms in the French against the translation, thus enabling the distinction to be recovered.
26. See H. Caygill, *Art of Judgement* (Oxford: Blackwell, 1989).
27. De Seyssel, *The Monarchy*, pp. 59–60.
28. Ibid., p. 95.
29. Ibid., pp. 65–7.
30. Ibid., pp. 100–6.
31. Ibid., pp. 123–4.
32. This text thus confounds the idea that the intervention of rule in the everyday lives of subjects first took place through the fiscal activities of the state. Its also situates the convergence between pastoral and political modes of government that Foucault posits as a phenomenon of modernity in an original military context.
33. De Seyssel, *The Monarchy*, pp. 59–60.
34. N. Machiavelli, *The Prince,* trans. G. Bull (Harmondsworth: Penguin, 1961), pp. 77–8.
35. De Seyssel, *The Monarchy*, p. 149.
36. Ibid., p. 152.
37. Ibid., pp. 154–6.
38. Ibid., pp. 159–60.

13

The Early Modern Army and Historical Sociology

We can already see the discursive formation of the early modern army mapped out between the extra-political technologies of de Seyssel and the pre-political problematics of Machiavelli. We can treat them both as a military–political discourse in which obedience appears as the problematic condition of discipline over subjects abstracted from the given order, enabling us to see them as complementary attempts to define new political technologies through the domain of the army, rather than in terms of an ideological opposition between monarchism and republicanism. Their focus on the condition of obedience also provides us with a set of considerations very different to those of the forms, structure and resources of the state which have conventionally oriented historical sociology. Drawing its terms of analysis from modernity, this posits the army as a political instrument *a priori*, definitively linked to the state. However, the most important military developments in the early modern period can be located in the organization of forces in civil wars, where state formation was contested and emergent, rather than established.

Military power and state formation

For both Tilly and Mann, the early modern development of military power is structured by the historical context of eliminatory competition between various forms of political organization, in which states proved most efficient in terms of the historically determinant criteria of the accumulation of capital and the accumulation of means of coercion and administration.[1] Changes in the organization and distribution of violence appear as a function of the emergence and organization of the modern state-form, epiphenomena of an inexorable process of progressive centralization and rationalization which has its teleological outcome in the modern state's territorial monopoly of legitimate violence and political administration.

Giddens provides a more sociologically specific account, though positing the state *a priori* as the norm of political organization, and military power as a function of social systems, so that his account of the development of military modernity is defined against the preceding military function of feudal lordship.[2] Giddens argues that medieval royal authority could not develop into state formation because, in the absence of accumulated material and administrative resources, it needed to utilize the lords to fulfil the ruler-function of societal defence, fostering centrifugal forces that tended to assert their own autonomous authority. Giddens identifies weapons technology and the development of 'administrative power' in the armed forces as the main types of change which transformed this constitution of 'military power' in directions that led to the modern monopoly of the means of violence by the state.[3]

His treatment of weapons technology as an independent variable in historical change, however, assumes that one form of weaponry determines the tactical dimension at any given time; first, the mounted armour of knights, second, the bows and pike of the commoners of the late Middle Ages and early modernity, and third, gunpowder weapons, which demanded investment and logistical resources, stimulating the development of state administration and tending toward the monopolization of the means of violence and elimination of rivals by states which could regularize the supply and co-ordination of financial and manpower resources. Ultimately, this exercise is tautological, since identifying weapons-systems with social forces simply refers technological determinism back to what it sets out to explain.

Furthermore, although Giddens argues that 'the emergence of standing armies is of greater sociological interest than is ordinarily recognised', the civil–military dichotomy which emerged in this period is assumed as an *a priori* distinction between violence and the social which finds its teleological expression in the emergence of the modern state's function of mediation between the organization of violence and society. However, restoring contemporary problematics to early modern military developments reveals an uncertain process of struggle around the normative dichotomization of violence in its abstraction from society and the reduction of the subject of violence to instrumentality as an object of discipline and surveillance.

The problem of obedience in early modernity was general, rather than specifically military, and civil wars were evidence of its endemic ubiquity. The army was not a separate and distinct form; rather, command, authority and expertise were reconstituted in the struggle to make it so. Similarly, the army's relation to the monarchical state, the permanence of its organization and even the superiority of particular forms of weaponry, were neither self-evident nor sociologically given, but were the outcome of contestive struggles. Gunpowder weapons-systems initially offered little tactical advantage and were resisted, most notably in the collective refusal of quasi-autonomous military formations to dig field fortifications, a refusal grounded not in their relation to the state, but in their self-differentiating autonomy from the domestic discipline of household and workshop. Reducing to discipline the 'vagabond elements' raised up into *lansquenet* bands by military entrepreneurs was not simply given in a right of command, effected by regular pay, or determined by weapons technology. Above all, it was not mechanically given in the organization of violence in the form of a standing army, which for early modern political theorists presented a great danger to the state. Historical sociology, its sights firmly fixed upon 'explaining' the emergence of a modernity already preconceived in normative terms of the monopoly of violence in the state and social and systems integration, resolutely neglects the early modern struggles over precisely these conditions of disciplinary subjection of the forces of violence.

Like Tilly and Mann, Giddens draws uncritically from the highly complex historiographical debate over the 'military revolution', mistaking the contestable constructions of historiography for a positive knowledge of the past which only requires a framework of grand-theoretical abstraction to provide an 'explanation'.

The 'military revolution', history and the condition of discipline

In the original formulation of the 'military revolution' thesis, Michael Roberts[4] identified a far-reaching historical catalyst in an apparently minor innovation of battle order instituted by the military commanders of the forces of the United Provinces in their struggle against Habsburg domination, switching from the phalanxial formation of Swiss-style squares to a 'proto-linear' file formation that enabled gunfire to be utilized as a decisive battlefield weapon by producing the capacity for volleys to be delivered by infantry soldiers who could rapidly reform into close defensive order. Their success led to an unprecedented emulatory escalation of military organization and weaponry from 1560–1660, driving military enterprise to a scale that could only be competitively sustained by intensive development of the administrative and extractive resources of states. Though the claims of its original formulation appear over-reaching (Roberts traced the emergence of the contemporary nuclear weapons-system, and its strategy, from this single innovation), we can locate in it the origin of the analysis of military strength in terms of 'firepower' that still dominates some analyses of military power in the present era of globalization.[5] Subsequent historical studies have expanded the range of explanatory factors, but have done so in technological terms which detract from Roberts' focus on discipline, so that the concept of 'military revolution' has been reformulated as an explanation of European state formation by reference to the development of gunpowder weapons and defensive systems. Geoffrey Parker's influential and critical adaption of the idea of military revolution shifted the role of catalyst from discipline to technology, specifically the design and diffusion of a new form of defensive fortification in the sixteenth century; this was itself a response to the technological development of mobile siege guns. Gunpowder-weapons development and the *trace italienne* thus provide Parker with the two factors precipitating the same long-term historical process traced by Roberts.[6]

These technologically deterministic versions provide historical sociology with support for accounts of the emergence of the modern state as the outcome of a world-historical process of rationalization, since only the modern state-form could develop the resources necessary for effective military competition.[7] However, Roberts' argument was implicitly based upon the prior condition of discipline, which had enabled commanders to subject their men to the drill necessary to learn new formations. Max Weber had formulated a very similar thesis more sociologically. For Weber, 'the discipline of the army gives birth to all discipline',[8] but his definition already elides the problematic confronting early modern commanders such as Maurice of Nassau.

> The content of discipline is nothing but the consistently rationalized, methodically prepared and exact execution of the received order, in which all personal criticism is unconditionally suspended and the actor is unswervingly and exclusively set for carrying out the command. In addition, this conduct under orders is uniform. The effects of this uniformity derive from its quality as social action within a mass structure. Those who obey are not necessarily a simultaneously obedient or an especially large mass, nor are they necessarily united in a specific locality. What is decisive for discipline is that the obedience of a plurality of men is rationally uniform.[9]

However, for Machiavelli and de Seyssel, *mass structure*, which for Weber is the condition of the peculiar quality of discipline, was the *effect* of discipline. Mass obedience was for them the precondition of discipline, and thus of mass structure. As Machiavelli's Fabrizio laments, this general precondition was absent even in the Swiss, who could not be subjected to drill to learn *new* tactics. The problem was not so much how to secure loyalty as how to construct the rationality upon which voluntary obedience depended.

Against such contemporary perceptions, historical sociology reduces even military discipline to the narrative of state-system formation in accounts which argue that modern military forms first developed in the United Provinces because it had the allocative and administrative resources necessary to pay its soldiers regularly. However, regular pay does not in itself constitute the condition for discipline, either theoretically or historically. Firstly, pay would not secure the obedience unto death implied in Weber's definition and in the practical conditions of military service. Secondly, to substitute for a theory of obedience, pay would have to operate consistently across historical examples, but the model armies of discipline of early modernity (those of the United Provinces under Maurice of Nassau and of the New Model Army in the English Civil War), were frequently in chronic arrears.[10] Plunder provided an alternative form of subsistence for armies, but its significance was more than material; the right to plunder was a value in itself in the military economy. Plunder and pay were not interchangeable because they did not function as contractual equivalents, but as distinct symbolic values in a moral economy. Thirdly, for contemporary military–political theorists (such as Machiavelli), the condition of the paid soldier appeared to be at odds with the condition of discipline, while for others (such as de Seyssel), pay functioned to maintain the army in its differentiation from the social environment, but only to produce a domain in which techniques of government could operate upon bodies free from the given, domestic order of the estates.

Another prospective condition for the achievement of obedience lies in Giddens' account of 'the formation of a body of experts holding exclusive knowledge of certain essential administrative techniques, and the simultaneous creation of a "de-skilled" population of ordinary soldiery',[11] but this apparently straightforward sociological premise comprises a complex knot of assumptions within an *a priori* definition of 'the army' that depends upon what the statement purports to explain. Most obviously, 'administrative techniques' can only be 'essential' when the body of the army becomes dependent upon them, which requires its continuous differentiation and isolation from its environment, a major problematic of military order both in the field and in the duration of peace. Furthermore, the formation of a body of experts invested in administrative knowledge presupposes an object of administration, which is again what Giddens is supposedly explaining. It also assumes the service of this body of experts, i.e. their subordination to the administrative regime comprised by the operations of their knowledge. For this, Giddens refers to the concept of 'military professionalism' as a form of expertise characterizing modern military formations.

Murray Feld grounded this conceptualization by identifying the origins of military professionalism in Maurice of Nassau's reforms. Feld's essay is only one version, but nevertheless represents a consensus viewpoint underpinning the entire research programme of 'military sociology', which continues to have as its object the study of the modern 'professional army'.[12] However, arguing that the authority of command consists in expert instrumental knowledge brings us no closer to the early modern problematic of obedience, which was what military expertise had to produce. Like Giddens, Feld resolved this problematic by defining armies *a priori* as functional social systems, but this simply means that the order that is realized in expert knowledge in the military professionalization thesis is pre-existent, that is, given in the object of knowledge which the thesis is supposed to explain. The final dimension of Giddens' formulation, a 'population' of soldiery (which can be known, classified, ordered), similarly depends upon the administrative techniques that are monopolized by an elite. In comparing early modern flow-charts of arms drill with industrial Taylorism, Giddens (despite his own critique of Foucault) infers the constitution of this 'docile body' from its disciplinary exercise.

Military technique in the sixteenth century

The attribution of modern military transformation to the reforms instituted by Maurice of Nassau as commander of the forces of the Dutch Revolt has also been challenged on empirical grounds. David Eltis[13] has recently claimed the 'military revolution' for the earlier sixteenth century, pointing out that Roberts' indicators (drill, training, a hierarchy of ranks and specialist expertise) provided the means by which Swiss tactics were translated onto mercenary forces. The institution of drill and the emergence of 'professional' specialist military knowedge were not causally dependent upon either gunpowder weapons or the resources of 'the state', but more directly linked to changing conditions of knowledge and subjectivity.

Swiss tactics and organization, Eltis reminds us, transformed the pike phalanx from a defensive formation into an offensive force.[14] Early sixteenth-century battles revealed the Swiss square's vulnerability to concentrated firepower, while foot-soldiers equipped with firearms required the pike's protection against cavalry, resulting in what military historians call a 'combined-arms tactical synthesis', a single formation combining pike-and-shot that could move at the speed necessary for offence, offer close protection against cavalry, and allow for the deployment of firearms from within the square. Construction of this composite body required mathematical expertise for abstract calculations on the basis of a standard unit of body-space for each weapons-bearer. The complex articulations necessary for movement and for deployment of the two weapons-forms also required standardization of bodily exercises, commands, speeds of execution, etc. Individual bodies had to be reduced to numerical quantities of equivalence, while for their effective articulation each separate and individual movement had to mimic a uniform model.

Eltis' extensive reading of the sixteenth-century proliferation of tactical manuals, exercise charts and mathematical tables shows that military expertise required literacy and numeracy prior to Maurice of Nassau's reforms.[15] Contemporary military discourse also debated whether technical expertise was in itself sufficient, arguing that a commander had to be 'experimented' in the practical operationalization of technical procedures, suggesting that contingent innovation was a necessary element of command on the field of battle. Eltis further argues that battlefield command was not exercised by the captains and colonels, the recruiting agents and entrepreneurial proprietors of regiments, but by the subaltern figure of the sergeant-major, who on the field of battle actually commanded their obedience as well as the soldiers', through sergeants who knew the precise composition and equipment of their platoons.[16] A division of labour thus emerged between subaltern tactical command and the administrative functions of the commissioned officers.

The condition of discipline given in the solidarity of battle, where, 'scattered or disordered individuals had little chance against a fast-moving, tightly packed formation',[17] did not render the army a strategically instrumental force, but constituted an identity which still found a space of liberty in the wider space of war, requiring continuous simulation of the fear of battle to maintain it in order. In different ways, the orders of battle and of the camp were both circumscribed by the termination of the body. The gallows of prerogative military justice marked the threshold of the military condition just as did the mangled corpses of the fallen on the field of battle, but the regulations of the camp were proscriptive, in contrast to the imperatives of battle. Camp regulations could not in themselves provide the condition of voluntary obedience, but effected a collective body with a capacity for resistance.

Within the perimeter that marked it off from the hostile environment, the camp constituted a simulated city, a republic, in which the particularity of military identity and liberty endowed its subjects with capacities of resistance. Willing obedience was limited to the necessary functions of battle, where discipline operated only upon the condition of a phenomenology of arms. Though the camp was externally structured by similar necessities in a hostile environment, the condition of obedience still had to be established in the will of the soldier.

However, the city was not the only model available to early modern military–political thought. In the new modes of knowledge of the Renaissance, the army also appeared as a body, an object of knowledge rather than the subject of violence. Like the New World that the cartographers were mapping from 1540 onwards, the body was mapped in two stages,[18] a process as evident in technical-military knowledge as in natural philosophy. The military body was mapped in its dispersal, as the layout and divisions of the camp, the composition of the square, the order of the march,[19] just as the new cartography charted the features and contours of the land and anatomical illustrators drew the human body with its features distinctly marked and labelled. Just as cartography was transformed from the art of making itineraries to that of charts, and the depiction of the body in natural philosophy changed from the description of Galenic systems traversing the body to an anatomy informed by dissection, so military technique also took on these new modes of knowledge and representation. The new empirical knowledge could not be inferred from epistemological principles, but only acquired by 'experimentation', venturing into the 'dark interior', the inner space of lands, corpses, or fields of war, to colonize it by naming, marking and representing it as a mode of instrumentalization.

Notes

1. C. Tilly, *Coercion, Capital and European States, AD 990–1992* (Oxford: Blackwell, 1992), passim; M. Mann, *The Sources of Social Power*, vol. 1 (Cambridge: Cambridge University Press, 1986) p. 450.
2. A. Giddens, *The Nation-State and Violence: Volume 2 of a Contemporary Critique of Historical Materialism* (Cambridge: Polity Press, 1985).
3. Ibid., pp. 105–7.
4. M. Roberts, 'The Military Revolution, 1560–1660', in M. Roberts, *Essays in Swedish History* (London: Weidenfeld & Nicolson, 1967), pp. 195–225, G. Parker, *The Military Revolution: Military Innovation and the Rise of the West, 1500–1800* (Cambridge: Cambridge University Press, 1972).
5. D. Held, A. McGrew, D. Goldblatt and J. Perraton, *Global Transformations: Politics, Economics and Culture* (Cambridge: Polity Press, 1999), pp. 87–148.

6. Jeremy Black's critique of Parker is still more technologically deterministic, and argues that the changes involved cannot be assimilated by conceptualization, but only organized into chronological periods. J. Black, *European Warfare, 1660–1815* (London: UCL Press, 1994).
7. Tilly, *Coercion, Capital*; J. Brewer, *The Sinews of Power* (London: Unwin Hyman, 1989); M. Mann, *States, War and Capitalism: Studies in Political Sociology* (Oxford: Blackwell, 1988).
8. M. Weber, 'Discipline', in H. H. Gerth and C. W. Mills (eds), *From Max Weber: Essays in Sociology* (London: Routledge & Kegan Paul, 1948), p. 261.
9. M. Weber, *Economy and Society*, eds. G. Roth and C. Wittich (Berkeley: University of Califorina Press, 1968), p. 1149.
10. B. Nickle, 'The Military Reforms of Maurice of Orange' (unpublished PhD, thesis, University of Michigan, 1984).
11. Giddens, *Nation-State and Violence*, p. 113.
12. M. D. Feld, 'Military Professionalism and the Mass Army', *Armed Forces and Society*, 1, 2 (1975), pp. 191–214; see also, for example M. Janowitz, *Military Conflict: Essays in the Institutional Analysis of War and Peace* (Beverley Hills, CA: Sage, 1975); M. Blumenson, 'The Development of the Modern Military', *Armed Forces and Society*, 6, 4 (1980), pp. 670–82.
13. D. Eltis, *The Military Revolution in Sixteenth-Century Europe* (London: I. B.Tauris, 1995).
14. Ibid., p. 23.
15. Ibid., p. 61.
16. Ibid., pp. 55–6.
17. Ibid., p. 60.
18. J. Sawday, *The Body Emblazoned: Dissection and the Human Body in Renaissance Culture* (London: Routledge, 1995).
19. See, for example, D. Digges, *Stratioticos: An Arithmetical Militare Treatise* (Amsterdam: Theatrum Orbis Terrarum, 1968).

14

Military Reformations

The city as the condition of political and pastoral reformation

The early modern European city was characterized by its particularity. Its liberties under its own laws and institutions provided the condition for both the Renaissance reconstruction of civic relations of the citizen and the city, and pastoral reformation of the relationship of the subject and the soul. Machiavelli sought to operationalize one side of this convergence while implicitly recognizing the other strand, represented by Savonarola, not in the city as it was given, but in the virtual city of the camp. The Calvinist Reformation, too, operated upon a virtual condition, the city besieged.

The American scholar R. W. Kingdon has shown how the pastoral Reformation converged in a uniquely fertile affinity with civic political humanism in the cities of the Swiss Confederation,[1] where secular city government sought to establish itself independently of both hierocratic and aristocratic jurisdictions. John Calvin and his followers in Geneva were drawn even more strongly into this convergence than were more moderate reformers, since their emphasis on radical refoundation was less able to maintain a distinction between ecclesiastical authority and secular rule. Calvin thus found himself impelled to develop an ethics for city government, which was to be transformed in its extension to very different conditions in the French Reformation.

Ideological historiography and the ethical economy of Calvinism

Mid-twentieth-century historiography reflected Cold War preoccupations in its conceptualization of early modern 'international Calvinism' in terms of a generic conspiratorial model of revolutionary movements, with the implication that such 'extremist' forces tended to institute civil

266

war because they were were immanently totalitarian, inherently unable to engage in rational political compromise, and ultimately causal agents of wide-scale 'unlimited' violence.[2] In contrast, more recent work has emphasized the defensive reflex of Calvinism, at least in its extension to France, focusing on the contingent conditions of its formation, rather than imputing to it a strategic programme.[3]

The importance of Calvinism for the early modern transformation of subjectivity was established by Max Weber in his essays on asceticism and 'the Protestant Ethic'.[4] However, subsequent sociological attempts to extend this thesis to the subject of violence and the formation of the modern state have either followed Cold War-era historiography, crediting the Protestant ethic with creating 'a set of organizational and political strategies through which disciplined, militant minorities could capture power',[5] or else reduce Weber's analysis of the ethical imperative to the more simplistic formulation of an ethic of conviction or even simply to 'faith'.[6] The instrumentalism and reductivism of these revisions are at odds with Weber's sociological reasoning from methodical comparison of Protestant sectarian practices, and substitute a relatively crude psychology in which belief directly affects subjectivity for his Nietzschean framework of an ethical and soteriological *economy* in which subjectivity is something produced rather than simply acted upon by belief. In Weber's analysis, the reformed Protestant faced the question of salvation alone, but for the Calvinist to seek soteriological certainty would have been an act of unfaithfulness, an indication of damnation; for Calvin, only those who are certain in themselves are predestined to election to grace.[7] Weber argues that this injunction was unsustainable as a guide to the conduct of inner life in the world. Calvin's followers thus had to develop objective criteria of certitude by transposing the much older Christian concept of the vocation (which had come to refer specifically to the dedication of life to the search for grace in subjection to the austere monastic regulation of life-conduct) on to the everyday life-situation in which believers found themselves.

> On the one hand it is held to be an absolute duty to consider oneself chosen, and to combat all doubts as temptations of the devil ... On the other hand, in order to attain that self-confidence, intense worldly activity is recommended as the most suitable means.[8]

Calvinism reintroduced this project into the world as a discipline which could be practised by every believer in answer to the dilemma of salvation-anxiety,

... not in everyday life as it is given, but in methodical and rationalized routine-activities of workaday life in the service of the Lord. Rationally raised into a vocation, everyday conduct becomes the *locus* for proving one's state of grace.[9]

Observance of rules did not supply the Calvinist with the instrumental means to achieve grace, but merely provided a framework within which the individual could practise the ascetic discipline of self-subjectification as a way of governing the soteriologically insecure self. The routine of the vocation need not have been, as Weber suggests above, in the service of the Lord, but only needed not to have been against it; the content of the work itself was irrelevant since the criterion of unconditional faith was vested in the work of self-subjectification, not in any external sign. This required total and voluntary subordination of desires and impulses to the purely technical aspects of one's providentially given vocation, an 'inner-worldly asceticism' which could be facilitated by the instrumental rationalization of tasks, reducing them to functional techniques of performance. Worldly ends were thus subordinated to the performance of tasks as the means to displaced ends, since the end of ascetically undertaken vocational activity did not lie in the worldly effect of that performance, but only in the individual's continuous self-subordination to its technical demands.

However, such rationalization and 'selfless' dedication itself produced success in the world, and as the Puritans came to see in these worldly effects the evidence of their correct way of life, so worldly success in a rationalized vocation came to appear as an indicator of moral propriety, the criteria for dispelling the demon of doubt, even if it could not be assumed as an indicator of grace in itself. This second-order effect of predestinarian doctrine appeared in the translation of Calvinism on to the French Reformation; comparing the condition of Calvin's original formulation and Beza's revisionist interpretation enables us to move beyond simple contextualism to see how both were mediated by particular forms of political organization and the constitution of violence.

Calvin's Geneva: The city besieged

The ethic of providentially conditioned action informed the ecclesiastical ordinances that Calvin drew up for the pastoral government of Geneva, but their institution must be set in context. The city had already undergone political reformation in its struggle to assert the civic authority vested in its charter of liberties over the administration of charity, against the episcopal jurisdiction of the bishop and the resistance of the mendicant orders. Anticipating siege against its actions, the city council had rationalized civic organization and welfare provision along military lines and called upon Calvin to reorganize the ecclesiastical government of the city. The principles he had established in his *Institutes of Christian Religion* were thus extended over a militarily mobilized urban political order through ordinances shaped by, and frequently referring specifically to, institutions and functions of urban siege organization, which provided an operational model for Calvinist reform. For instance, the *procureurs* of the rationalized urban welfare administration held jurisdiction over many of the issues that concerned the elders of Calvin's consistory, and the cases before them were screened by *dizaniers* who were in charge of the military divisions of the city. Similarly the same system used to provide supervisors of the city's fortifications was utilized to select the deacons of Calvin's ecclesiastical constitution.[10] Civic mobilization of the city for siege thus provided the model for the organization of ecclesiastical government, and for the vigilance of the conscience of individual believers in anxious uncertainty of salvation.

The capacity of the reformed city actually to enforce moral laws is often located in Calvin's original institution of the consistory. Civic reforms had already sought to enforce moral regulation by applying the traditional urban sanction of banishment to prostitutes and adulterers, in common with many German cities. Welfare administration, integral to the medieval urban constitution, and the culture of charity, constituting the city as a Christian community, were both thrown into crisis by the mass influx of destitute bodies produced by the deployment of hired armies in prosecution of war upon the body politic, which ate up the countryside, displaced populations and blocked supplies, thereby invoking a dual crisis of urban welfare and security. Emergency responses often vested singular authority for both aspects in the same offices and institutions, operating through the divisions of the late medieval city into discrete quarters not only for trade and production, but also for the administration of justice, for militia mobilization, and for the redistribution of resources for siege. This same spatial organization provided Calvin with the model for the ecclesiastical government of a city under 'moral siege'.

On his return in 1541, Calvin persuaded the council to establish a consistory, constitutionally modelled on the standing committees dealing with fortifications and grain supply, its membership representing the city's military districts. Like those committees, the consistory was formally subordinate to the council, but had absolute authority within its own functional division of the urban jurisdiction. Pastoral power was simply grafted on to this model with the provision that the consistory had to consult the pastorate, who shared in the selection of deacons and elders.[11] As with the military and logistical committees, the consistory was not intended to govern *over* the populace, but to inculcate self-government and self-discipline within it. The principles of consistorial administration of moral regulation thus corresponded to the condition of siege, attempting to produce collective self-mobilization while conserving human and material resources. Just as the government of siege sought to reduce the population to co-operative discipline, rather than to expel malefactors, the consistory used interrogative methods to induce *voluntary* submission to the moral order without invoking excommunication. Consistorial sanctions were intended to produce their effect through shame in public exposure, rather than through deduction from or of the body. For the regime of siege, every body was a resource, and every loss a possible source of defeat; for the consistorial regime, every soul held the possibility of salvation, and each lost soul could cast everyone's salvation into doubt, every fall into sin invoking the possibility of damnation. For the more recalcitrant, the small executive council administered summary justice in punishments exposed to the public gaze, rather than banishment.[12]

Consistory elders were also known as *surveillants* or monitors.[13] In *Discipline and Punish*, Foucault uses the concept of surveillance to conceptualize techniques of subjection which operate through spatial division:

> ... an architecture that would operate to transform individuals: to act on those it shelters, to provide a hold on their conduct, to carry the effects of power right to them, to make it possible to know them, to alter them.[14]

By using the military divisions of the city as a spatial order for moral regulation and by operating a crisis economy like that of the state of siege, the Calvinist consistory turned the city into a disciplinary space, an alternative 'ideal model' for the disciplinary technique of surveillance, alongside Foucault's exemplar of the military camp.

In its reception into historical sociology, the Foucaultian concept of surveillance is often at once reduced to bureaucracy and supervision and elevated into an instrumental resource for 'power over'. It is reconceptualized as the 'control of information and the superintendence of the activities of some groups by others', or, 'the supervisory and information gathering capacities of organizations of

270

modern society'.[15] However, these formulations lose the crucial point of Foucault's analysis, that techniques of surveillance constitute objects and subjects of power. The Calvinist consistory shows this Foucaultian aspect in the way that the elders were charged by Calvin's ecclesiastical ordinances 'to keep an eye on everybody',[16] to keep themselves informed and to maintain continuous concern, not through compiling and scrutinizing bureaucratic records, but through a moral structure of community constituted by mutual surveillance, effecting 'hierarchized reciprocal observation'.[17] Calvinist surveillance thus operated at the level of everyday life, just as the regulation of the camp subjected all aspects of life to its imperative rationality. In Calvinist Geneva, the consistorial regime of moral surveillance combined with civic emergency discipline to produce an 'identity of believer and citizen' which was manifest in the combination of the civic oath and the confession of the faith.[18]

However, these techniques were predicated upon the particularity of the early modern city in its urban liberties. Calvinism took the particular form that it assumed in Geneva, on the model of the city under siege, because of Geneva's extreme insecurity stemming from its location on the borders of Catholic France, but outside the Swiss Confederation. The doctrine and its effects as a mode of subjectification were transformed by their extension over a body politic, rather than a city-republic, in the Calvinization of the French Reformation, where they operated upon a *displaced* subject, rather than that emplaced and even confined within the besieged city.

The Reformation in France

Historians have posited pre-Reformation France in conservative, Durkheimian terms as a mechanically integrated society,[19] but in the terms of the discourse of government in the sixteenth century, the functional interdependence of the estates appears already subject to the active *police* of their relations by the Crown in *its* function, which de Seyssel extended to the *police* of religion. This regal function of *police* provides us with the key to seeing how authoritative political practices interacted with the Reformation in France, without requiring the reifying categories of Durkheimian analysis.

Since the function of active kingship was to maintain the self-regulation of the estates, and since religion formed part of the domain of *police* by active royal offices, so Francis I first authorized the prosecution of heresy through the Crown's criminal courts, rather than through the ecclesiastical courts. However, while the centralization of reports by royal itinerant justices produced the appearance of increasing levels of heretical activity, further inflating demand for effective royal prosecution, the criminal prosecution of heresy removed the grounds for jurisprudential judgement (since theological truth could not be assessed by secular criteria), even as the perceptions of heresy and pressure on the crown increased to crisis proportions.[20] As frustrations with legal prosecution slid into persecution, the loosely focused movement of reformation coalesced around Calvinism, which enabled clandestine religious practice by requiring only a lay pastor, with guidance readily forthcoming from Geneva, where Calvin himself relied upon the refugee French community for support in the city's politics. With growing uniformity of Reformed practice and doctrine, Calvinist churches formed in distinct urban quarters and under the protection of nobles with jurisdiction over their own rural domains. In 1559 a national synod met to draw up a Confession of the faith and a Discipline, founding the Reformed Church of France.

Subjectively, too, Calvinism provided techniques conducive to the condition of the Reformed faith in France. Its transference of the organizational rationality of the besieged city on to a subject defensively enclosed against the world while maintaining self-subjection to vocational performance in a providentially given worldly order, facilitated the resolution of a persecuted religious minority. Calvin's writings not only used military imagery to represent the defence of conscience against assailing doubt; his commentaries and sermons were also infused with an exilic sense of loss of belonging as the ideal condition for spiritual rebirth in evangelical conversion,[21] which in Catholic France mapped quite literally on to alienation from the social environment and inner reorientation of the self through conscience.

The work of allegory: Battles without war

Natalie Zemon Davis' anthropological approach shows that the sectarian violence of popular persecution was neither instrumentally rational nor simply a socially encoded discharge of affect, but was both meaningful and imperative. Davis describes how the persecuting crowd enacted the role of both king and magistrate, inflicting humiliations, mutilations and tortures.[22] After the Edict of Toleration, in which the regent sought to restore the authority of the Crown and its monopoly of legitimate violence by proscribing popular religious persecution, Protestant crowds took on the same role, not merely defending themselves, but actively 'prosecuting' the implications of the Edict by punishing their religious opponents for their disregard of its injunction to allow the free profession of faith, which Protestants believed included the right publicly to demonstrate against the magical presumptions of Catholic rite.

Sectarian violence had its own economy. Conflict between religiously fractured urban quarters was conducted in the public space of representation, in the street, in cemeteries, in churches, and derecognized the private sanctuary of the home. Its theatrical forms – disinterment and reburial of bodies, profanation of the sacral, murder as enactment of animal slaughter – all 'work' as allegory, as symbolic representations in which 'truth' can be *shown*. Protestant dissenters crumbled the holy wafer in front of Catholic worshippers to demonstrate the illusory nature of magical investment; Catholics stuffed the mouths of slaughtered Protestants with pages torn from their own Bible to show that their words could not save them; Protestants strangled priests with their own rosaries. The Huguenots claimed to 'make war' only on objects, but while the work of allegory translated this for Catholics into violence perpetrated upon the body politic, on the bonds of the social body, and even upon the body of Christ, for the Huguenots it translated allegorically into physical attacks on the clergy and those participating in the performance of Catholic rite. Catholic violence was similarly produced by the work of allegory as violence against de-humanized bodies, against Huguenots as pollution and a source of contagion.[23]

Davis argues that symbolic representation enabled the perpetrators to overcome innate constraints against interpersonal violence by providing a mechanism to repress affect or to disguise their own agency from themselves, but if we acknowledge truth-value as relativized by the conflict of faiths, and allegory as the work of its production (rather than as dissimulation), we can then begin to see how the violence of the conflict was constituted as an imperative. Allegory functioned in the disputation of faith because truth no longer represented itself, but needed to be shown. Faithfulness lay in the performance of truth, in 'witness' to truth being done, a productive and active 'confession' of faith that readily became a profession of violence. Men and women could make truth manifest in the public theatre of allegory, and truth could be shown most absolutely in the physical subjection of the untruthful to allegorically meaningful violence.

From right of resistance to vocational force

However, the theatre of violence only became the theatre of war when other imperatives also came into play. Quentin Skinner[24] has established that the Huguenot political theorists' development of a right of resistance was derived from secular political concepts and reason, rather than from religious justification or theology. However, he fails to show how this right became the *duty* that produced the violence of the Wars of Religion, but infers this imperative from his imputation that Huguenot political thought developed to justify a seizure of sovereign power. Skinner shows how Huguenot political theory drew upon medieval concepts of the body politic to reason that the legitimate authority of the king was only given in popular accession and was thus subject to constitutional constraints. Within the polity, certain magistrates had the right of resistance (including the use of force where events moved beyond the law) to ensure the legitimate constitution of royal authority against tyrannous usurpation. However, since the magistrates to whom the popular consent to establish and maintain legitimate royal authority was delegated included the elected officers of cities,[25] organized and fortified for self-defence, Huguenot self-legitimation did not need to develop any justification of seizure of sovereign power. The cities themselves constituted a sufficient force of resistance. The constitutional model of the *Standestaat*, which Poggi characterizes as a nexus of political negotiation between the monarchy, the nobility and autonomous urban formations,[26] appears to offer a more plausible object of Huguenot strategy.

Skinner is forced to explain the transition from magisterial right to dutiful resistance in Huguenot political theory by second-order inference of a strategy to seize sovereign power because his opposition to sociological reductionism neglects the way that right was articulated by Calvinist conscience. In Genevan doctrine, the concept of the vocation had no decisive political significance, since the city was already an independent civic formation, but in France it translated onto a magistracy that offered the only prospect of legitimate defence of the faith against a persecuting society. However, even legitimate defensive interests are not sufficient to explain how the imperative to violence in the Wars of Religion sometimes overrode political expediency.

Huguenot claims to legitimation used medieval constitutional thought to infer the authority of kingship from popular consent, reconstituting magistracy as the political representation of that proper constitution of authority. Furthermore, in defence of the faith guaranteed by the Edict of Toleration, this constitutional function of magisterial resistance became an imperative vocation. Common subjects themselves had no vocation to proffer resistance, but the Calvinist rule of conscience decreed that all believers must maintain themselves in a state of certainty of election to grace, and since doubt itself was the object of avoidance, where scripture provided no answer to the question of whether a political command could be obeyed in conscience, Béza referred believers to natural law.[27] The Huguenot minority were thus imperatively predisposed to question all commands, and Huguenot magistracy was vocationally charged to use its legitimate capacity actively to resist even indirect threats to the conscience of believers. In default of failure to obtain resolution in law, magistracy was legitimately and vocationally charged to respond with force, thus invoking war irrespective of political expediency. Such an ethical imperative may not have determined action in all cases, but nevertheless constituted its subjective condition.

The nobility and military knowledge

When the theatre of violence became the theatre of war, technical rationality substituted for allegory. The cultural historian, Johann Dewald, describes how the military function of the nobility had been transformed in the late Middle Ages into captainship, opening onto alternative sources of social status differentiation that invested identity in the concept of a career in service to the body politic.[28] In Burgundy, the most advanced late medieval polity, governmental reforms created interests and identifications in the princely state by derecognizing traditional and customary noble privileges, while creating new opportunities in administrative service. De Seyssel's *Monarchy* mapped out a similar model for France, where the sixteenth-century nobility had become invested in service to a monarchy conceived in constitutional terms.

Military administration of the organization and deployment of violence required both theoretical knowledge of technical principles of warfare recovered from ancient sources and practical experience of their application. Even as noble subjectivity was 'civilized' through investment in the mannerisms of courtly conduct,[29] their specialist monopoly of military administration constructed another economy in which affect was substituted by *raison de la guerre*, the instrumentally calculative employment of technical principles in warfare, a rationality that had its own imperatives, operating in abstraction from social sources of ethics. Controlled capacity to violence thus became a resource to be carefully cultivated in this corollary of courtly civilization, rather than a representation of a contrary 'de-civilizing process'.[30] Blaise de Montluc's *Commentaires* of 1592 provide us with a picture of the techniques of self that constituted this subject of military civilization. De Montluc's nobility and his position in the court hierarchy were invested not only in his accomplishment of ritual forms and the self-discipline of violent affect, but also in his military reputation, and thus depended upon a personal, rather than an official, capacity of command as an experienced practitioner of *raison de la guerre*.

Though he refers to the rationalized use of terror as an instrument in war, it is only when commanding a city under siege that de Montluc refers to the necessary 'sin' inherent in military leadership. While commanding the besieged city of Siéna in the winter of 1554–55, he calculated the resources available to the defenders and citizens against the probable time they would have to hold out, and expelled over 4,000 'useless mouths', of whom 3,000 died slowly over the next eight days, driven back against the city walls by the besieging forces. De Montluc rationalized this action in a way that subordinates the self and its soteriologically mediated affect (the fear of sin), to the rule of necessity:

> These are the effects of war. We must of necessity sometimes be cruel to frustrate the designs of the enemy. God had need to be merciful to men of our trade, who commit so many sins and are the causers of so many miseries and mischiefs.[31]

His subordination of affect to the practice of *raison de la guerre* also extends to hatred. Though the Huguenots are his personal enemies, he argues that his slaughter of captured townsfolk is purely instrumental,

> ... so as to strike terror into the country, that they dare not make head against our army ... And as severity (call it cruelty if you please) is requisite in the sense of a resolute opposition, so on the other side mercy is very commendable and fit if you see that they in good time surrender to your discretion.[32]

Social and self-subjection to the rationality of war have substituted technical criteria for even the ethical capacity to exercise mercy, just as it has substituted for the expression of affective violence. The investments of the self have shifted radically from the code of chivalry, and ethics are now determined by abstract principles of instrumental calculation, rather than by custom or law. The governing principle of 'necessity' is constructed in this rational calculus on the basis of criteria abstracted from technical, practical manuals. Even the concept of honour now corresponds to the rigorous application of these principles. The construction of a rationality of war and its investment with social identity and moral value thus produces a violence which is not insensible to humanist considerations, but masters and redeploys the affect that they produce, so that 'passion' is reconfigured as the pursuit of a technical vocation. War and the career of warfare 'detached men from their settings',[33] propelling them in search of experiential knowledge not merely into other geographical spaces, but into other social spaces, other conditions of perception, and into moral uncertainty. These were the conditions into which the Reformation was thrust as it mapped on to noble factional politics in France.

For the Huguenot magistracy, the practice of war was a vocation, and as the proper mode of its performance, *raison de la guerre* overrode other ethical and political considerations. Beza's *Right of Magistrates* clearly set out the vocational imperative to violence in the magistracy's constitutional function, which Sproxton has further traced in the career and writings of the Huguenot noble, D'Aubigné. Such texts show how the inexpedient, apparently irrational violence of the Wars of Religion was produced in the vocational articulation of political right with conscience, which substituted for political reason an ethical imperative to adopt the technical rationality of war. This enables us to see how politics *produces* violence rather than strategically deploying it as a resource, but without ascribing it to a simple dichotomization between the ethics of conviction and responsibility.[34]

The dismemberment of the body politic

Noble competitive rivalry in the service of the monarchy had become mediated by courtly constraints, but Calvinist vocationalization of the noble estate's function of magistracy transposed religious division onto political functions, so that with the paralysis of regal authority vested in judicial administration, the feud between the princely houses of Guise and Condé was carried into the public domain, invoking *raison de la guerre* in the cause of legitimacy. Between 1557 and 1562 the French Reformation was politicized on two fronts. Geneva provided the model for control of city government where Calvinists seized power through town councils and established consistories alongside secular authority, while the conversion of noble patrons established rural enclaves under their protection.[35] In response, Catholic reaction organized around the Guise noble alliance and mobilized common confraternities dedicated against heresy.

After public disputation intended to produce ecclesiastical reconciliation simply entrenched doctrinal division, the royal function of *police* attempted to depoliticize religious fracture by asserting a transcendent political authority in the Edict of Toleration of 1561, but

277

the *parlement* refused to ratify it on constitutional grounds, arguing that the Crown in its private capacity would implicitly be offering refuge to heretics in contravention of the law, and that the edict's recognition of religious division was against the interests of the monarchy as a whole, since this consisted in religious as well as political unity. This constitutional resistance opened the space through which war entered. With *parlement*'s suspension of the process of law, the noble magistrates assumed their legitimate executive function, invoking the rationality of war in defence of public interests, in place of political reason. After soldiers of the Catholic Guise faction massacred Reformed worshippers at Vassy, the Huguenots congregated under arms.

Huguenot discipline

The Calvinist national synod elected Prince Condé Protector-General of the Reformed Church to uphold the Edict of Toleration.[36] His call for troops was administered by Beza through ecclesiatical organization, despatching mustering orders to the local synods to mobilize volunteers, enabling Condé to assemble forces quickly at Orléans, where military articles and an oath were drawn up for their formation and government as an army.

The Huguenot armies of the 1560s were primarily comprised of merchants and artisans from the urban strongholds of Calvinism, who subjected themselves to military displacement as a confirmative act of faith in their own election, but considered themselves levied in defence of the public interests of the monarchy, expressed in the Edict of Toleration and under the constitutionally legitimate authority invested by default in the Protector-General. The articles drawn up for the Huguenot army wove together military and ecclesiastical discipline to produce a military vocation.[37] Public prayer, chaplaincy and consistorial 'advice' were instituted within the Huguenot armies, reproducing the moral governmentality of the beleaguered city in a form that was not dependent on particular, chartered liberties. The articles delineated the army against its social environment by providing a code for moral and physical regulation, 'two excellent nerves in order to hold vices in check and the soldier to his duties',[38] but the soldier's obedience to these orders was vested in the cultivation of individual conscience and collective surveillance. This articulation of consistorial surveillance and self-government in conscience with military discipline to produce a military-political vocation effectively subordinated civic and religious identities to apolitical and amoral imperatives of war. The new mode of discipline enabled armies to be deployed in duties that conventional, mercenary forces refused, such as entrenchment.[39] The Huguenots used the term *police* to describe this novel disciplinary conjunction, in which an internally constituted rationality could be brought into correspondence with externally given objective ends (in this case, the imperatives of war), producing willing obedience unto death. In the vehicle of the army, Calvinist techniques of self-subjection were liberated from dependence upon a given (urban) order, while the rationality of war was liberated from the legitimate function of the nobility. The army now comprised not only a new body in the political landscape, but was also invested with a self-governing conscience.

The army and the city

However, the discontinuities of politicized 'civil' war precluded the maintenance of a permanent, unitary force, especially as it became apparent that Huguenot security could be guaranteed most effectively in the form of the city. Though a few towns were taken by external force, more were brought under Huguenot control through internal coups, producing a strategic field in which the cities did not function passively to maintain an army in the field for seizure of sovereign power, or to support nobile factional politics, but themselves constituted a military power. Study of the campaigns shows that the city proved a stronger military form than the armies in the field, and this imbalance, rather than fiscal inadequacies, produced the discontinuous and fragmentary mode of warfare of the Wars of Religion. Both Huguenot and royal armies provided for themselves in the field, but the stasis incurred by laying siege to well-fortified, internally mobilized urban strongholds wasted them more decisively than battle. Successive peace treaties confirmed the security of strongholds, while the field armies became indisciplined and their command increasingly autonomous. After the massacre of the Huguenot nobility, gathered to celebrate a royal marriage in Paris, on St Bartholomew's Eve, 1572, the movement took refuge in the townships, effectively repudiating the politics of faction and rejecting noble strategies. During La Rochelle's successful resistance to siege by an army that was reduced by half through catastrophic casualty rates, disease and desertion, the town council expelled its noble commander, Gaspard de Coligny, because of his willingness to negotiate, and consistently refused to discuss peace terms without guarantees for the security of other Huguenot strongholds.[40]

The Huguenots' cities thus marginalized their own noble faction. When their urban strongholds were secured in the Peace of La Rochelle, the king was free to pursue a depoliticized suppression of the Guise-dominated Catholic League. Henry IV (who acceded to the throne in a politically expedient conversion to Catholicism) reconstructed the court as a source of authority and a means of surveillance over the nobility, but the reconstruction of the devastated kingdom was undertaken by a minor Huguenot noble, Maximilien de Béthune, duc de Sully, who had served the king as a gunner and engineer in the campaigns against the League.[41] Through a number of crucial administrative offices, Sully established the administrative and spatial structure that became the basis for seventeenth-century French absolutism.

Reforming France as a domain of conquest

Sully's reconstruction programme operationalized de Seyssel's plan for government of 'the domain of conquest'. As *grand voyer* (royal surveyor), charged with repairing the Roman roads and medieval bridges ruined in the Wars of Religion, Sully utilized the services of artillery and siege engineers to construct a military-logistical infrastructure of roads and canals, centred on Paris, that also enabled control of commercial traffic and its revenues. The maintenance of fortifications had previously been a joint responsibility of the royal treasury and local authorities, but as *surintendant* of fortifications from 1600, Sully instituted a new administration, personally appointing to garrisons *ingénieurs du roi* who would annually inspect the frontier provinces, drawing up contracts for necessary work according to standards issued from his central office, which local authorities then put out to tender. Their surveys produced scaled maps, thus enabling the surveillance of the militarized domain to be reproduced as a form of archival knowledge. The *ingénieurs* also reduced non-royal fortifications, and rather than repairing city walls, built citadels in which garrisons could be maintained in isolation from the urban environment. The reconstruction thus precluded noble rebellion, urban armed resistance and the autonomy of armies in an integrated, unitary policy. As *grand maitre d'artillerie*, Sully also instituted standard written examinations for officers, uniform drill for gunners and precise specifications for guns and all other equipment, subjecting the entire stock of the royal arsenals to regular survey, centralizing records to produce the knowledge and organization necessary for the calculable strategic deployment of firepower batteries.

Sully was well aware of the political nature of this work, explicit in his letters patent from the king in 1605, which establish the royal project to monopolize all ordnance, but his reforms also mark a new condition of military discourse. Under his administrative regime, his technical works (*Traité de la Guerre*, *Maréchal de Camp* and *Instruction de Milice et de Police*) would have circulated as manuals among the offices which they addressed, rather than as general military–political discourse. In the new order, the technical function of military office had absorbed the political aspects of the organization of violence, and one of those functions was now to ensure its monopolization.

Through these policies, the reconstructed kingdom was governed by Henry IV as de Seyssel's domain of conquest, where the prince is not bound by precedent, custom or ancient law, producing the sovereignty of Jean Bodin's *Six Bookes of the Commonweale* of 1583. Bodin asserts that the sovereign power to 'give laws to subjects', 'contains' all others,[42] but reading beyond his own claims for his text, we can identify in it another irreducible, definitive characteristic of sovereignty: the power of the sword. This second characteristic is irreducible to the first because the capacity to make war requires prerogative extra-legal techniques which cannot be grounded in the law of the sovereign.

Sovereignty in the power of the sword

However, though the power to make war is contained by the condition of sovereignty, the capacity to do so, requiring the maintenance of armed forces even in peace, is preconditional to sovereignty and cannot be assimilated under the power to make law, which cannot maintain orderly forces since soldiers 'by nature' do not obey laws (whether natural or regal). Though Bodin's normative constitution implicitly excludes armed forces from the commonweal of lawful sovereignty, the full text provides not only juridical principles, but also practical techniques, its less-read chapters engaging with the government of military power that is preconditional to sovereignty.[43]

Lawful sovereignty both produces and is produced by this extra-legal dimension, since disarming subjects to extend legality and civility among them places those who must bear arms beyond the law, demanding special powers to govern them; this undermines Bodin's claim that the power to make law contains all others. The power of the sword is only exceptionally applicable to subjects, at the limits of civility and law, but pertains 'always' to rule over the army,[44] since it is a condition of military discipline, which substitutes for the rule of law over soldiers. As for Machiavelli, discipline provides a means whereby popular subjects may be reformed:

> The subject then being instructed in military discipline, is not infected with lust, licentiousness, impiety and sloth, but being wicked and impious, they immure to themselves all kinds of virtue if they learn the precepts of the Roman military discipline and art of commanding.[45]

However, training in arms and order under discipline effectively places these bodies beyond the law, because soldiers are by definition and by nature thieves and robbers: 'It was thus impossible to train all the subjects of a Commonweale in arms and to maintain them in the obedience of laws and magistrates.'[46] Those subject to discipline are those not subjectable to law and the military domain of the army and men of war is to be kept distinct from that of law and men of justice.

Situated in garrisoned citadels on the frontiers, the army is to provide a means for the emergency repression of political rivals, the function which Giddens ascribes to the armies of absolutism,[47] but the power of the sword and its military domain of extra-legal regulation also has a more regular function.

> There is yet another a reason of great moment, to show that it is necessary to entertain martial discipline, and to make war, for that there is no city so holy nor so well governed that hath not in it many thieves, murderers, idle persons, vagabonds, mutins, adulterers, and diceplayers which lead a wicked life and corrupt the simplicity of good subjects, neither can laws, magistrates, nor any punishment keep them in awe ... There is no better means to purge the Commonweale of this infectious filth than to send them to the war.[48]

Discipline consists in pay (which functions to remove the need for soldiers to rob and steal), in orders of 'excellent description' (i.e. comprehensive regulation of life in the army) and in daily training in arms, after the model of the Romans, making the camp 'a school of virtues', in which these subjects of essentially irreducible vices under law (and thus already beyond it), can be reduced to the order and virtue of discipline by maintaining them beyond law. Bodin leaves the chapter with the proposal that these bodies of discipline could be supported on lands on the frontiers they are sent to garrison. The problems of order of a field army within the kingdom are thus quite literally extruded into another domain, quite distinct from the republic governed by law, a proposal which seems to reverse the order of the commonweal, since this policy may take up to a third of the revenues of the kingdom, but at once provides forces for external defence and internal repression, guarantees rational social pacification, civility and social order, and establishes a necessary ruler-function of defence of the pacified commonweal.[49] With this policy, sovereignty operates as a power of exclusion that is also a condition of territorial sovereignty as the rule of law. However, all this takes place outside the order of legitimate sovereignty. The militarization of marginal elements is not a function of political repression, since these military subjects are not the subjects of law and politics, but the subjects of the sword, of sovereignty in its violence.

Notes

1. R. M. Kingdon, *Church and Society in Reformation Europe* (London: Variorum Reprints, 1985).
2. See, for example, H. G. Koenigsberger, 'The Organization of Revolutionary Parties in France and the Netherlands in the Sixteenth Century', *Journal of Modern History,* XXVII, 4 (1955), pp. 335–51.
3. M. Greengrass, *The French Reformation* (Oxford: Blackwell, 1987), and 'France', in B. Scribner *et al.* (eds), *The Reformation in National Context* (Cambridge: Cambridge University Press, 1994); M. Nicholls, 'France', in A. Pettergree, (ed.), *The Early Reformation in Europe* (Cambridge: Cambridge University Press, 1992).
4. M. Weber, *The Protestant Ethic and the Spirit of Capitalism,* trans. and ed. T. Parsons (London: Unwin, 1930).
5. P. S. Gorski, 'The Protestant Ethic Revisisted: Disciplinary Revolution and State Formation in Holland and Prussia', *American Journal of Sociology*, 99, 2 (1993), pp. 265–316.
6. J. A. Aho, 'The Protestant Ethic and the Spirit of Violence', *Journal of Political and Military Sociology*, 7 (1979), pp. 103–19.
7. Weber, *The Protestant Ethic*, p. 110.
8. Ibid., pp. 111–12.
9. M. Weber, *From Max Weber: Essays in Sociology,* eds H. H. Gerth and C. W. Mills (London: Routledge & Kegan Paul, 1948), p. 291.
10. Kingdon, *Church and Society*, VI, pp. 57, 63.
11. Ibid., VIII, p. 7.
12. Ibid., VIII, pp. 10–11; H. von Greyerz, 'Switzerland', in Scribner *et al.* (eds), *Reformation in National Context*, p. 38.
13. N. Z. Davis, *Society and Culture in Early Modern France* (London: Duckworth, 1975), p. 11.
14. M. Foucault, *Discipline and Punish: the Birth of the Prison,* trans. A. Sheridan (London: Penguin, 1977), p. 172.
15. A. Giddens, *The Nation-State and Violence* (Cambridge: Polity Press, 1985), p. 2; C. Dandeker, *Surveillance, Power and Modernity: Bureaucracy and*

Discipline from 1700–the present day (Cambridge: Polity Press, 1990), p. 2.

16. John Calvin, quoted in M. P. Holt, *The French Wars of Religion, 1562–1629* (Cambridge: Cambridge University Press, 1995), p. 25.
17. Foucault, *Discipline and Punish*, pp. 170–7.
18. M. Walzer, *The Revolution of the Saints: A Study in the Origins of Radical Politics* (London: Weidenfeld & Nicholson, 1965), pp. 55–6.
19. Holt, *French Wars of Religion*.
20. Ibid.; Greengrass, 'France', Scribner *et al.* (eds), *Reformation in Rational Context*, pp. 47–66.
21. J. Sproxton, *Violence and Religion: Attitudes Towards Militancy in the French Civil Wars and the English Revolution* (London: Routledge, 1995).
22. Davis, *Society and Culture*, pp. 162–4.
23. Ibid.
24. Q. Skinner, *The Foundations of Modern Political Thought* (2 vols) (Cambridge: Cambridge University Press, 1978).
25. Ibid., p. 330.
26. G. Poggi, *The Development of the Modern State* (London: Hutchinson, 1978).
27. T. Beza, *The Right of Magistrates*, trans. J. H. Franklin, in J. H. Franklin, (ed.), *Constitutionalism and Resistance in the Sixteenth Century: Three Treatises by Hotman, Beza and Mornay* (New York, NY: Pegasus, 1969), p. 102.
28. J. Dewald, *Aristocratic Experience and the Origins of Modern Culture: France, 1570–1715* (Berkeley, CA: University of California Press, 1993).
29. N. Elias, *The Court Society*, trans. C. Jephcott (Oxford: Blackwell, 1983).
30. J. Fletcher, *Violence and Civilization: An Introduction to the Work of Norbert Elias* (Cambridge: Polity Press, 1997).
31. B. de Montluc, *Commentaires: The Hapsburg–Valois Wars and the French Wars of Religion*, trans C. Cotton, ed. I. Roy (London: Longman, 1971), p. 166.
32. Ibid., p. 222.
33. Dewald, *Aristocratic Experience*.
34. M. Weber, 'The Profession and Vocation of Politics', in P. Lassman and R. Speirs (eds) *Political Writings* (Cambridge: Cambridge University Press, 1994).
35. H. Heller, *Iron and Blood: Civil Wars in Sixteenth-Century France* (Montreal: McGill-Queen's University Press, 1991).
36. Kingdon, *Church and Society*, XI, p. 222.
37. Walzer, *Revolution of Saints*.
38. Quoted in ibid., p. 86.
39. J. B. Wood, *The King's Army: Warfare, Soldiers and Society during the French Wars of Religion, 1562–1576* (Cambridge: Cambridge University Press, 1996), p. 112.
40. Ibid.
41. D. Buisseret, *Sully and the Growth of Centralized Government in France, 1598–1610* (London: Eyre & Spottiswoode, 1968).
42. J. Bodin, *The Six Bookes of a Commonweale*, trans. R. Knolles, ed. K. D. McRae (Cambridge, MA: Harvard University Press, 1962), p. 162.
43. The relationship of the army to law is dealt with by Bodin in the section on the power of the sword in Book III, Chapter V, while Book V, Chapter V, considers the military power necessary to make war.
44. Ibid., p. 331.
45. Ibid., pp. 603–4.

46. Ibid., pp. 610–11.
47. Giddens, *Nation-State and Violence*.
48. Bodin, *Six Bookes*, pp. 602–3.
49. Ibid., p. 614.

15

Military and Civil Society

The revolt of liberties

As I have discussed above, the 'military revolution' of early modernity is usually traced to the reforms of Maurice of Nassau as commander of the forces of the United Provinces of the ex-Burgundian Netherlands in their struggle against Spanish Habsburg domination. After the defeat of Charles the Bold and successful resistance to French domination, the lands of the Low Countries had passed by marriage into the Habsburg dominions, and by patrimonial division to Philip II of Spain. The northern provinces' struggle against Habsburg authority was not grounded in universalistic ideals, but in the particularities of provincial political identities invested in the patchwork of liberties and charters that Burgundian governmental policy had worked upon and had fostered rather than oppressed. The rebellion was primarily 'conservative' in its defence of particularities against absolutist reduction to universal conditions of subjection, and only 'modern' by necessity, in terms of the contingently emergent structures, institutions, political processes and modes of subjectification produced in the struggle.[1]

Uniting to expel the forces of domination in defence of their particular and traditional liberties, the provinces' civic self-assertion mapped on to the religious schism of early modern Europe. As with Louis XII's Revocation of the Edict of Nantes and repression of Huguenot enclaves, Phillip II's macro-policies operated in tandem with the strategies and techniques of the Counter-Reformation, but resistance only assumed coherent form when the Spanish soldiery was permitted to loot and plunder the religiously reformed cities in retaliation for armed piracy by the self-styled 'sea-beggars', urban-based seafarers operating under the informal command of military–aristocratic adventurers. The towns and the impoverished nobility then found themselves pitched into a conflict perceived as a struggle for survival, against the greatest monarchical dynasty of Europe.[2]

286

The English policy

In the early stages of the conflict, the United Provinces sought a protective alliance with Protestant Elizabethan England, but Elizabeth I's commission to the Earl of Leicester to govern the Netherlands as her protectorate, produced a renegade authority in which his attempt to garner his reputation overrrode strategic considerations. Apparently operating as an autonomous command seeking favour in royal patronage, his military governorship effectively derecognized provincial authority, exercising prerogative, seizing towns, and negotiating independently with the enemy.

Leicester's expedition was part of a long series of English military–political experimentation that combined the projection of armed force with the *police* of the margins of society in England. There are no English military–political treatises equivalent to those of Machiavelli, de Seyssel or Lipsius, since dromological order sufficed for this purpose. After the anarchy of the Wars of the Roses, the Tudor regime had been established in Henry VII's programme of administrative reforms, constituting a 'national economic space' for the radical shift in *moral* economy effected by the Reformation's 'de-sanctification' of the poor.[3] In the new order, the offices, governmental principles and operations of the state corresponded to an economized commonwealth, with both closed against an object of exclusion embodied in the figure of the vagrant, who was subject to neither political nor domestic discipline. Experimental military expeditions provided a vehicle for policy by incorporating these vagrant bodies into the special, extra-political jurisdiction of logistical dependence, dromological control and prerogative adjudication that had developed during the Hundred Years War. This policy is clearly evidenced in the records of the Privy Council and the proliferation of anti-vagrancy legislation and decrees of the Tudor regime.

Such expeditions integrated military experimentation (the source of practical knowledge for Renaissance military discourse) with domestic *police*. They imbued Elizabeth's Irish campaigns with an instrumental brutality, but in the context of the Low Countries appeared as military incompetence. In addition to the displacement of strategic objectives by Leicester's clientary command, his forces were inherently unstable and indisciplined, amounting to an inept instrument which tended to decay almost immediately. His communications with England consist of almost continuous demands for more men and invective against those he was sent. English intervention simply added to the chaos of the resistance by *ad hoc* emergency commands conducting separate campaigns with provisional, often mutinous forces. Only Habsburg redeployment for an invasion of England provided a respite, enabling the United Provinces to adapt the medieval office of Stadholder (already subordinated by earlier Burgundian reforms to the representative assemblies of the States General) to the role of military command under Maurice of Nassau, whose reorganization of the defence forces is conventionally seen as the origin of military modernity.

Neo-Stoicism and the military reformation

Gerhard Oestreich has established how these reforms were informed by the neo-Stoic philosophy of Justus Lipsius, Maurice's tutor and correspondent.[4] Against the vulgar sociologism that identifies an 'international Calvinism' as the singular vehicle for new modes of government and discipline, Oestreich shows how neo-Stoicism provided a more generic source of early modern political and military reformation. Calvin's ecclesiastical reformation had drawn on the Stoic tradition, but Lipsius' *Six Bookes of Politickes*[5] applied Stoic philosophy to the secular project of reformation of citizen and state in abstraction from political particularities by using the army rather than the city as its exemplary organizational model. Lipsius decries the use of mercenaries, but in contrast to Machiavelli, divorces the military from the political subject by recommending that permanent core units be maintained in garrisons in lieu of active operations. For military selection, Vegetius' criteria provide a necessary, but not sufficient condition of virtuous force, which also requires discipline and obedience. Lipsius' analytical exposition of discipline in the Fifth Book breaks this binary problematic of early modern military power into four elements: exercise, order, example and self-constraint, providing a new ethos which will effect moral reformation of the soldiery from within, rather than through the external functions of operational imperatives and draconian military law. To supplement the rod of iron, Lipsius proposed prizes for good conduct, which would constitute rational interests correponding to the object of discipline, rather than the contradictory interests generated by military government through the customary economy of plunder. However, even though the rod is now supplemented by inner strength, the new techniques require a special field of internal operations, a subjectivity beyond traditional orders.

In relation to the *Six Bookes of Politickes*, Oestreich ultimately dismisses Lipsius' earlier work, *De Constantia* of 1584[6] as, 'merely a preliminary treatise on morals and society'.[7] However, this earlier work can be related to the problematization of obedience which provides the key to the condition of discipline. Reducing Lipsius' project for disciplinary self-constraint to a utilitarian system of sanctions and rewards constituting subjective rationality in externally given material interests does not provide for the self-government necessary for discipline to continue to operate in the absence of such provisions, in the deprivations of the field. It does not make obedience a virtue for the subject itself, but only inculcates instrumentality. However, *De Constantia* can be seen as a manual for subjectification in the conditions of physical and moral uncertainty characterized by the state of war extending across early modern Europe.

Lipsius presents the struggle to master the self under these conditions in the form of a Socratic dialogue in a garden. Despairing of the warfare and insecurity besetting his country, the supplicant of philosophical advice asks how he can flee when neither town nor countryside can offer safety, and is told to 'not forsake thy country, but thy affections. Our minds must be so confirmed and conformed that we be at rest in troubles and have peace even in the midst of war.'[8] *De Constantia* thus promises to provide a model for the self-maintenance of reason in the absence of security, a mode of self-government of affect in the ethically and socially indeterminate environment of war. Lipsius represents the troubled interiority of the subject as a reflection of the warfare without and uses military operations as an allegorical model for the necessary operations of self-government. Where there appears chaos and indeterminacy of ends, he implies, there is yet a practical order in instrumentality itself. His technique orders the 'forces' of Constancy and Inconstancy under 'captains', classifying them into distinct categories each designated by the banner under which they are assembled, enabling the subject to counter each of the forces of despair with appropriate virtues, on the model of deployments in battle, so that the interiority of the subject becomes a theatre of war in which a tactically co-ordinated campaign of virtualization is conducted.

Military problematics and policy in the Dutch Revolt

Just as Lipsius' object in *De Constantia* is to overcome affect and restore the subject to a reason that no longer lies in the security of a given identity or the given order of things, so Maurice of Nassau's main objective in his military reforms was not to assemble a force of citizens whose order would be given in particularities, but to form the available mercenary companies into a force governed internally by a reason that brought its own interests into conformity with the tasks confronting it, irrespective of previous investments. In the defence of the United Provinces, this meant integrating the hired soldiery with a military system comprised of fortified towns, citadels, ordnance, canals and above all temporary field fortifications, especially earthworks. Contrary to Parker's thesis that the military necessity of expensive fortifications provided the catalyst for state formation around a military–fiscal nexus,[9] early modern urban fortification often consisted of packed earth, more resilient to the impact of ordnance than expensive brickwork or masonry, but requiring continuous maintenance.[10] Maurice's own estimate of his success was that he could get his soldiers to dig, a boast that had both a practical and a symbolic dimension, requiring their self-subjection to manual labour, below the customary calling of the soldier and beyond the military economy vested in the right to plunder that was conventionally used to govern forces of violence. This could not be achieved by pay alone, but required the reformation of the military subject modelled on the Roman legion that had engaged in the military engineering campaigns in the time of Frontinus, rather than of Vegetius. Maurice subjected support services, engineers and logistical provision (including even the sutlers) to martial law, integrating these elements into a military order with a clear definition of the duties of personnel and offices[11] that also drew on the Burgundian organizational model.

The forces of the United Provinces faced a Habsburg army considered the best in Europe at the time. The order of the *tercios* was constituted by their alienation, their projection in logistical dependence along the 'Spanish Road' of barracks and depots calibrated to their march across western Europe into a land in which they were strangers, producing both dependence and internal solidarity.[12] Long-term, distant campaigning was made possible by pay, which in turn was dependent on an imperial economy drawing silver from the New World and converting it into the means of domination of seafaring western Europe to secure the circuit; but pay only constituted a means of military government in combination with permissive plunder and a draconian code administered by a military service aristocracy. The *tercios'* strategic deployment in the Low Countries presented two quite different problematics for their government. Governing forces in the field through permission to plunder established a military economy and rational interests at odds with the need to secure territorial control by garrisoning fortified strongholds, where soldiers could mutiny in demand of pay, while the possibility of a permanent functional division of forces for field and garrison was precluded by the long-term tendency for the latter to 'decay' by assimilating into local communities. The military value of the *tercios* – their experience and solidarity, and their governability by pay and plunder – thus problematized their strategic instrumentality in the Low Countries.

In the protracted struggle, the United Provinces' reliance on mercenary forces presented the Nassaus' command with the same problematics, but their reforms enrolled them in a general policy of military government. This integrated approach was not effected by the simple quantitative accumulation of resources or by the centralization of authority. The United Provinces lacked the regular economic supply of the Habsburg empire and were frequently unable to procure the men or resources to follow up victories or prosecute long sieges. Their commanders' military strategy was subject to severe constraints, rather than enabled, by their mercantile political economy, in which the role of capital was to increase itself through circulation, primarily in international trade, not to secure political sovereignty by subsidizing military expenditure. The States General was often divided over the distribution of defence costs between the various provinces, and its politically decentralized form precluded the emergence of a military–fiscal state in which revenue and defence could be brought into rational correspondence. Standardized pay was an effect of these political constraints, enabling costs to be reduced to calculable sums, so that forces could be discharged or hired in response to financial negotiations within the States General. Maurice's political paymasters also took over the military economy of expropriation through 'contributions' levied on the communities of occupied territories against the threat of pillage, enabling disciplined armed occupation to be financed from those who received its immediate services,[13] but removing the autonomy of the army and one of the principal means by which the forces of violence were conventionally governed. Removal of direct military expropriation reconstituted the function of pay, which no longer operated as a means simply to secure the services of the companies, but reduced them to dependence. The effect cannot be explained solely in terms of exchange, since it operated in a moral economy. Soldiers on active service for the United Provinces only received their pay in part, and often irregularly, with arrears that could take years 'to account'.[14] Maurice's soldiers did not dig because they were paid twice as much for it; rather, they were promised a double rate for such work because they would do it, the double pay constituting a recognition of the abject self-abasement of the soldier who had been reduced to dependence on public wages.

In active operations, regular rotation of companies between garrison and field enabled surveillance by muster and inspection, controlling fraud, preventing decay, maintaining conditions, and providing continuous knowledge of the forces available to command.

Administration of the need to maintain permanent core forces in garrisons for urban defence became a means of positive control, since the companies retained were transformed from voluntary associations of solidarity in arms under negotiated authority, into interchangeable units subject to permanent administration and piecemeal adjustment of their numbers, with reductions often accompanied by an increase in wages for those remaining.[15] The prospect of retention also provided an incentive to seasonally engaged captains and companies, further investing their interests in the security of the United Provinces, in contrast to standard temporary military employment, which fostered an interest in the state of war.[16]

The forces of the United Provinces were often deployed in close proximity among the non-military members of the society they were employed to defend, but the social distance between soldier and the citizen was maintained by a disciplinary code as draconian as any other of its time. The self-subjection of the soldier did not release him from the peculiar prerogative jurisdiction constituting the army as a domain apart, but was, rather, dependent upon it. Nickle suggests that Maurice's military code of 1590 was modelled on articles that Leicester had earlier drawn up for the government of the expedited English bands under his authority.

Leicester's Articles in turn draw upon the techniques and forms developed in the Hundred Years War, but also address themselves to a new object, established in the preamble, to provide a discipline and an administration of justice as a means of government for an 'estate' that has no given order. The articles are almost entirely proscriptive, concerned to constitute and maintain the vehicle of English expeditionary policy. The first five substantive articles provide for compulsory religious worship, but their moral regulation consists in prohibiting blasphemy, games, drunkenness and vagrant women in the army. Of 55 articles, only four deal with external relations; the rest with internal order, and only eleven by positive injunction. The major innovation over the ordinances of the Hundred Years War is the 'devil's Article', which provides for an almost absolute prerogative jurisdiction in the commander's discretion to summarily punish 'all other offences and acts that may tend to disorder not comprised in these articles ... as if it had been specially expressed and set down'. Death in various forms is the most frequently cited sanction.[17]

Of Maurice's 82 'Articles of War, or Ordinances Concerning Military Discipline', only seven are concerned with external relations, and only 23 specify non-capital punishments (of those, two demand amputations). The articles also suggest that pay did not procure obedience, with one proscribing demands for pay before the enemy, another the solicitation of pay owing and a third positively adjuring the soldier to 'content himself with a reasonable partial pay until the money arrives', all on pain of death.[18] Internal order and military economy are regulated in greater detail than in Leicester's code, with the army's quarters particularly clearly delineated, perhaps in response to the chronic decay of the English forces. These regulations, then, are intended to provide the conditions for the government of the forces of violence by constituting its subject as dependent upon the state, closing-off other social relations and means of subsistence, while expressly denying it any scope to represent its interests politically and curtailing all customary internal economy. Its domain is inscribed in the integrity of the body, not of the legal person, and its sanctions are exacted at the limits of its domain, so that the thresholds across which the soldier or the army would become something else (a vagrant, a free company, or simply indisciplined) become terminals of the life of the body.

Vagrancy and government

Just as the French Wars of Religion can be seen in terms of a struggle over the constitution of violence, so a similar struggle can be seen underlying English 'internal' conflicts of the seventeenth century. English royal household military organization had developed through the adoption of *chevauchée* as a means of prosecuting public warfare against the body politic, producing techniques that found ready correspondence with the new problems of public order under the Tudor regime, as a policy of expediting excluded social elements. From the time of Henry VIII's 1545 expedition to France, wars were accompanied by the enforcement of vagrancy legislation.[19] The convergence of military and domestic policy can be traced through the office of provost which had originated in the proxy prerogative jurisdiction over indentured and levied forces. Appointments to this office proliferated in the sixteenth century as English monarchs imitated the disciplinary machinery of other European royal regimes, especially France, where the political alliance of the Crown and the cities was articulated in the official jurisdiction of the provincial *prévot* over discharged military forces, vagabonds and highway traffic in both peace and war.[20] It would be anachronistic to differentiate military provosts, concerned with the execution of military order under the articles of war, including the apprehension of deserters, from the emergency appointments of 'civilian' provosts responsible for dealing with the disorder perceived on the return of discharged soldiers to England. Both held the same office, with jurisdiction over men reduced from legal personhood to military embodiment, and both operated the policy of expeditory impressment of apprehended vagrants for military service abroad.

The numbers of returning soldiers were not insignificant[21] and even though not all soldiers had been impressed, they appeared as the return of a violence that had supposedly been discharged through the terminals of the polity into the space of war and the domain of royal prerogative. The symbolic violence of their reappearance in a society invested in legal and economic mediations of domination and violence combined with their grievances (they were often discharged unpaid, and many deserted when military service failed to provide wages and provisions) to produce a condition closely associated with flight from the moralized economic criteria of labour, subjecting both vagrants without visible means of support and soldiers without passports to regulate their passage home to the provosts' administration of martial law.

The subject of violence and the subject of the constitution

Repeal of the Statute of Winchester formally rationalized the effective divorce of warfare from the Tudor political constitution, in which scutage had effectively long been substituted for personal liability to military service. However, this repeal further liberated the identity of the subject in the political order from any constitutional subjection to prerogative military authority, and divorced the jurisdiction of the Crown in war (and the power of the sword) from the legitimate constitution of the polity. This triple divorce is illustrated in the events leading to the Petition of Right, which established the political positions for the Civil War. Rather than reducing this constitutional struggle to an ideological expression of class interests, the terms in which it was articulated indicate the moral dimensions of contemporary concerns motivating its actors. The alarm of the parliamentarized gentry at the appearance of prerogative jurisdiction over the forces of war in England was not expressed in economic terms. Their fiscal concerns appear as second order, ideological rationalizations of a fear of the *moral* disorder invoked by the declaration of 'martial law' and its implied assembly of vagrant bodies dependent on the Crown. The gentry were not so much fearful of the prospect of 'royal military power' in control of such a force, as concerned that such forces could not and would not be controlled.

Charles Stuart agreed to provide troops to Louis XIII in 1626 for the reduction of La Rochelle, the last Huguenot stronghold withstanding the Revocation of the Edict of Nantes, as part of a dynastic strategy of marriage. By royal prerogative, martial law was declared to govern the army raised for the campaign, and the right of *prise* exercised to provision and billet the soldiers in private households while they awaited embarkation. Whatever the realities of their order, the force was suspected of comprising elements irreducible to discipline, prompting complaints of their conduct; regardless of remuneration, billeting on private householders was deemed an infraction of the pre-political domestic order of settled society by another pre-political form, that of the sovereign's household; and irrespective of royal intentions, it was feared that the concentration of a force of potential disorder in itself provided the king with a political lever to gain parliamentary assent. Parliament's Petition of Right of 1628–29 declared illegal the extension of martial law to subjects of the commonwealth and the billeting of troops on private households in the realm, as well as the collection of taxes without parliamentary approval. It aimed to remove the prerogative means by which the Crown could raise and govern mass forces of violence in England, requiring the king to revoke the commissions for martial law as 'contrary to the laws and franchises of the kingdom'. The king was forced to sign to gain consent for taxation, but did not call another Parliament until 1642.

Faced with rebellion in the north of England in 1638, the Lieutenant of the Northern Army was advised to pardon a soldier he had condemned for mutiny, on the grounds that martial law was illegal except in proximity to the enemy. He warned that such restrictions removed the principal means by which armed forces could be kept in order and subjected to discipline, potentially creating the conditions for a general crisis of authority,[22] but the issue remained constitutionally unresolved when some companies raised to suppress a Scottish rebellion in 1639 and 1640 mutinied, plundered and even murdered their officers, before the royal army was routed at Newburn.[23] The issues of the English Civil War were heavily ideologized, but the issue of prerogative authority over forces of war runs through almost all interpretations, from the economic relations of the rising bourgeoisie and the political relations of the gentry to the state, to the juridical discourse that referred resistance to an originary popular sovereignty repressed by 'the Norman yoke'.[24]

The New Model Army: A new constitution of violence

The early years of the Civil War were chaotic. The forces on both sides were comprised of multiple armies under *ad hoc* commands. Local interests and tactical considerations distorted the definition of a field for strategy and obstructed co-ordination. Recent historiography has revealed a multiplicity of forces in the field, where command was not immediately given in direct alignments of interests, but had to be constructed organizationally in practices that had their own effect, invoking a struggle over the constitution of violence within those forces themselves.

Throughout the course of the war, only the cavalry was mostly composed of volunteers. Impressment was introduced by both sides as early as 1643, but recruitment through county authorities produced a multiplication of small forces, while existing armies were depleted by desertion to new formations offering fresh equipment and the prospect of commissions. As strategic significance became increasingly uncertain in the fragmentary theatres of highly mobile warfare, the proliferation of minor fortifications further localized the conflict. Battles in this early phase were relatively small and therefore indecisive. In 1644, three Parliamentary armies defeated the king at Marston Moor, but were unable to follow up the victory, so that by the autumn the war was unravelling again into unco-ordinated military rivalries.

Against the tendency of localization to empower especially those who held both political and military authority, obstructing strategic co-ordination, the creation of the Parliamentary New Model Army was underpinned by the Self-Denying Ordinance, debarring MPs from military command. Undercutting the titled gentry's traditional dual function, it deprived many Parliamentary forces of commanders, enabling them to be incorporated into the New Model.[25] However, the numbers fell far short of the project, and half the New Model's foot soldiery were involuntarily impressed under an Act of 1645. A long list of exemptions reveal that it was aimed at the poor. The desertion rate was high; half the 1646 quota had been enlisted by March of that year, but half of those deserted within a few weeks. Parliament had to rely upon the county authorities both to apprehend deserters and to provide it with levies, with the result that 'most counties press the scum of all their inhabitants, the king's soldiers, men taken out of prison, tinkers, vagrants that have no dwelling'.[26]

The New Model's transformation into the self-disciplined, revolutionary army of popular reknown was not the result of the uniform conditioning of Weber's thesis on discipline, or even of the ideological identification of Walzer's 'military Protestant ethic', or even of a civilizing social transmission of elite modes of affect-control.[27] Though focusing on different means, all these neglect the condition of subjectification necessary for the transformation of this resistant body into an army of self-denying, proselytizing ascetics that proclaimed itself to be the instrument of God before Parliament and refused to disband when ordered. This condition was effected by two conjoint techniques; marking-off the body of the army by excluding it and circumscribing it in violence, while inculcating a subjectivity of self-conduct within it. Analysis in these terms employs the Foucaultian concept of governmentality as 'the conduct of conduct',[28] but shows that subjectification can only operate upon a subject circumscribed against conditions of acute insecurity beyond a disciplinary domain.

The articles to which soldiers and officers swore on enlistment (their 'engagement', an entry into another domain, unlike contract and more like marriage, reconstituting identity) were rigorously enforced within the New Model.[29] They appear closely related to those drawn up for the reformed forces of the United Provinces, presenting themselves for the *conduct* of the New Model Army, suggesting that the intention was not so much to facilitate sovereign command as to inculcate self-constraint. Their lower ratio of capital and even corporal punishments appeals to reason, rather than vesting the internal order of the army solely in its circumscription against a society into which it might decay in desertion or indiscipline. They provide for close regulation of the camp, but many also refer to contacts with external society, ensuring that merchants were always paid, guaranteeing the reliability of provisions to secure a flow into the New Model of experienced men who deserted from less well-provisioned Parliamentary and even royal armies.[30] They also transform the negative proscriptions of previous codes into positive injunctions for the performance of specific duties and operations of the army, sanctioned mostly by punishments inflicted upon the body and executed by the provost-marshal in public before the ranks and officers.[31] Puritanism made the division of the body and the soul the concern of each believer, a division extending to the political dimension, so that mastery of the body took on a political significance.[32] The body's punitive public marking (cropping ears, boring tongues and branding) shamed the soldier through the body, just as laying waste the land had provided a means to impose indirect pressure upon the medieval body politic, and thus did not require external material economic interests to operate upon.

New Model training was imbued from the beginning with an instrumental asceticism toward the body. In 1642, Essex had instructed his officers only to train their recruits 'to use their arms readily and expertly, and not to busy them in practising the ceremonious forms of discipline'.[33] Rather than providing a spectacular display, New Model drill exercised an intensive micro-political technology of the body that utilized every part to produce a practical effect. For instance, training men to hold spare musket balls in their mouth reduced reloading time, enabling the New Model to reduce the ten files of Maurice's innovative formations to six, with three ranks firing at a time. The significance here was not an 'invention' of what was probably old soldiers' common practice, but its appropriation to a disciplinary regime in specific instructions.

The early modern model of the body as a vehicle of instrumental reason and economy was both practically and epistemologically associated with developments in cartography and anatomy, and the qualities produced by such new techniques appeared to the empirical mode of knowledge as inherent qualities of its objects in military as in other sciences. The New Model achieved tactical advantages by utilizing the micro-topography of landscape, employing surveyors to make cartographic charts that superseded the old form of itineraries. Though its speed of march was facilitated by open roads, it sought to engage the enemy in close terrain, where it excelled in 'hedge-fighting'.[34] Much of the fighting of the Civil War was conducted in skirmishes, not in set-piece battles. Rather than uniform mass discipline in docile bodies, tactical initiative, improvisation and individual self-control, with solidarity at the level of small units of men, were needed in situations where the course of the battle and the deployments of the rest of the force were unknown.

Another important innovation was the introduction of a *regimental* jurisdiction, with its own courts and orders. New Model soldiers were engaged to serve in a particular regiment, where military justice and the regulation of everyday life was subject to discretionary administration in the colonel's Standing Orders (written down but not necessarily distributed) authorized under the 'devil's Article'. Rather than rationally efficient military instruments, the regiments comprised sites of struggle between magical faith on the part of the officers and carnivalesque irreverence in the ranks, in which the regiments became the vehicle for the moral reformation of the army. The 'masterless men' comprising the foot soldiers of the early New Model scorned religion as they did all discipline of domestic society, flouting the Sabbath, blaspheming, denying divinity, and enacting parodies of religious worship,[35] while for the providentialism of their commanders, correct conduct was more significant as an indication of faith than as a direct means of military effectiveness, since victory in the field was dependent on the grace of God. However, participation in prayer was mandated by the articles, and ascetic techniques such as fasting in disciplinary preparation for battle could be instituted through a combination of the colonel's discretionary authority and the soldiers' dependence on military administration in their exclusion from society. In a universally mobilized land, there was literally nowhere to desert to, and local authorities fearful of predation apprehended deserters and returned them to the army. Commanders personally appointed military chaplains for their regiments, but sought to reform the soldiery through inculcation of the rule of conscience, rather than in conformity to any particular doctrine, condoning lay preaching and disputation.[36]

It seemed that the New Model succeeded against worldly deprivations, the political mistrust of Parliament, the contradictory strategies of the Scots allies, the treachery of the royal party, and the hostility of local communities and authorities, to win a succession of victories that finally reduced its enemy. By 1647, providentialism appeared as a manifest truth, and offered the soldiery a vocation in their instrumental exclusion from a corrupt world, which was transformed into a divinely sanctioned role. The reformed army now constituted a vanguard of the rule of conscience, its exclusion from society reconfigured as virtuous self-enclosure, in which the common soldiery spurned popular entertainments in favour of prayer, proselytizing and doctrinal disputation. The instrumentality of the New Model had also been transformed in this process, and since military as well as moral discipline appeared to manifest divine providence, so the identity of the army became invested in its role as the unitary instrument of a higher purpose, against any necessary enemy.

The constitution of the army contested

When the prospect of disbandment at the end of the Civil War presented the New Model Army with an almost ontological threat, it responded by exercising the seventeenth-century equivalent of the *secessio plebis*, marching on London and encamping in military order. We can identify in this *secessio* the return of what Pocock calls the 'Machiavellian moment',[37] outside the cycle of time and opening on to an entirely new foundation. The New Model had reformed the subject of violence into a military condition that united the salvation of the soul and of the polity, bringing into correspondence the project of establishing a community of grace and the constitution (or recovery) of a community of justice.

There is no space here to undertake a lengthy analysis of the documents issued by the Army and its supporters, or of the debates between the regiments' elected representatives, the Army command, and delegates from Parliament.[38] However, where these are usually read in terms of ideology, they also present three distinct positions within the overall question of the identity of the Army, comprising a key moment in the struggle over the constitution of violence in early

European modernity. Parliament's order to disband, and the Army's response, ruptured the tacit military-political constitution and opened the question of whether pre-constitutional legitimacy lay with the political or the military power, of whether the power of the sword is constitutive of the political or vice versa. Thus, the fundamental problem of the constitution of violence, and thus of society, is implicit in the otherwise obscure question of 'what the unity of the Army consists in', which was addressed in the opening discussions of the first debates at Putney in October and November 1647. Positions adopted over this primary question grounded the secondary ideological arguments about political forms.

In this preliminary debate, the commanders argue that the Army is the instrument of Parliament, the radicals that it is the instrument of God and justice. However, a third position is opened by Cromwell, for whom the Army is indeed more than a political instrument, but by invoking the sovereignty of conscience, he shows that the radicals' claim for the Army to act as the instrument of God, even when grounded in the providential manifestation of its victories, would place it in danger of the sin of presumption. He thus projects the entire struggle against the forces of doubt and despair which the radicals claim for the Army back into the subject of violence itself, arguing that the Army cannot be defined in terms of its function, which is given only in divine providence, but that the virtue of its identity lies in its instrumentality, which is effected in its self-subjection to the vocation given in the articles to which the soldiers have sworn their oath, constituting a 'prior engagement' over all worldly projects. The subject of violence is first of all a subject of conscience, and thus the subject of vocational obedience. Deferring the debate to conscience, to the self-conduct of subjectivity, enables Cromwell to accommodate both the radical believers, who must submit themselves to obedience under the articles as the condition of their claim, and the advocates of the sovereignty of Parliament, who must be constrained in their utilization of the army by its vocational constitution, given in the articles.

This retrojection of the question of politics and violence enables the continual reassertion of political order under the moral precondition of a prior exclusion of violence, which becomes the conditional responsibility of subjectivity. It immediately enabled Cromwell to reduce the regiments, redeploying them in division and using his command to enforce the order of the articles, seizing radical leaders for court martial in night raids on the camps at Burford in 1649. Following the principles of military government, executions were minimized and men permitted to exercise the right of conscience either to leave the Army or submit to command and go to serve in Ireland, where all other considerations were displaced by the severest application of vocational, instrumental reason of war in ruthless suppression of the Catholic Irish.

No military settlement

With the Restoration, Parliament wanted to disband the army altogether, but on the pretext of their role in suppressing minor sectarian disturbances in London, some regiments were retained during peacetime in forts and houses of the royal household at the expense of the Crown. By projecting the organization of violence into the personal domain of royal prerogative, this solution resolved fears of financial costs to the commonwealth, but simply reinstated the constitutional problems of the condition of the government and discipline of forces of violence which had led to the Petition of Right and precipitated the Civil War. From 1666, Parliament controlled the finance and in effect the declaration of war through the Supply system, procedures requiring the Crown to submit military estimates and accounts to a parliamentary enquiry before it would vote a sum earmarked for specific goods and services, a procedure formalized in the Subsidy Act of 1667.[39] But since military discipline remained dependent on articles issued on the personal prerogative authority of the monarch in the royal household, when Parliament sanctioned war by voting finance for the Crown to maintain an army in the field, it opened the question of whether royal prerogative for military government by martial law extended to the whole realm, and, conversely, whether the army in the field was subject to the jurisdiction of common law. Beneath this political contestation of jurisdictions, it is possible to discern the far more fundamental question of the relation between violence and society. Ideologically, this was conducted through a debate over the respective virtues of a militia and a standing army,[40] but the increasing dichotomization of the orders of violence and society and their repression into subjectivity tended to project the more fundamental question into fantastic forms, in contrast to the practical reason of previous military-political discourse.

A series of constitutional skirmishes ensued between James II and Parliament over the unsettled military constitution of the Restoration in jurisdictional forms. Parliament could only refuse the means for the king to exercise prerogative to maintain and govern an army, but could not control his exercise of that authority, which the king sought to maximize by appointing to senior military offices Huguenots and Catholics who were dependent upon his personal protection in an alien and hostile political environment. The Test Act of 1672 made property and Protestantism (i.e. a stake in the regime) necessary qualifications for military office at Parliament's expense,[41] but James responded by enlarging the army through recruitment in Ireland, officering it with Catholics at his own cost, and in 1688 encamped this force on Hounslow Heath, overlooking London. Parliament responded by inviting the king's sister, Mary, to assume the throne, backed by her husband, William of Orange, who landed in command of experienced and disciplined forces while James' army deserted. The Mutiny Act of 1688 was an emergency measure to legitimate the new monarch's command over armed forces within the realm. It did not provide a disciplinary code, but sanctioned and delineated the jurisdiction of the Crown to draw up the Articles, enabling the government of the army for a strictly limited duration.

The military constitution of civil society

The preamble's reiteration of the formula of the Petition of Right reaffirmed the constitutional subordination of the Crown to parliamentary sovereignty and the principle that no army was to be maintained within the kingdom without its explicit approval. The Mutiny Act never provided for a permanent army, but was renewed annually, with modifications, until the early nineteenth century, when extensive parliamentary reports on military organization provided the basis for a thorough reconstitution of British land forces. Thus, during the time in which the English army was vastly enlarged and deployed on a global scale, there was no constitutional guarantee of its permanent establishment and (with the exception of the personal Household Guards of the monarch) its regiments in England were maintained in a state of continuous transition as privatized franchises of colonels commissioned by the Crown, in an executive jurisdiction beyond the protection of common law. However, focusing on the constitutional formalities of this arrangement would neglect the wider sociological effect of the Act's accumulatively detailed regulation of relations between civil and military jurisdictions, regulation which effected much more than juridical differentiation.

Because of the peculiarities of moral economy and conditions of life in an army now affirmed as a distinct jurisdiction in law, successive Mutiny Acts sought to ensure that the law of contract applied to contacts between the army and civilians, interactions problematized by the army's impermanence, which required it to be dispersed in England in almost permanent transit upon the road. The constitutional settlement precluded any institution of systematic state provision, other than the supply of arms, ammunition and military equipment from the Board of Ordnance, but, though an abstraction in Parliamentary debates, the army was in practice embodied in soldiers who had to be quartered, transported and fed, physical needs which had to be met *ad hoc*, by soldiers and officers making individual account with their landlords for billet and quarter. The soldier's fortune is not an estate and military and domestic economy were very different, so that soldier and officer alike were popularly seen as incapable of holding civil property. Additionally, the relative anonymity of itinerant soldiers, subject to the authority of a distant regimental colonel rather than a local master, opened a space of uncertainty and mistrust in contractual dealings, which became a persistent issue of political and popular contestation. Hence, the Acts made rigid and increasingly detailed specification of the rates, provisions, and accounting and payment procedures for billet, quarter and wagon transport.

The jurisdictional, rather than administrative, regulation of this fundamental military–civil interface persisted well into the nineteenth century, with increasingly complex specifications and a cumulative burden of clauses expanding the Mutiny Act into a vast and cumbrous code. This mode of regulation resulted from the Supply procedure's displacement of logistical maintenance of the army on to royal budgetary management and royal commission of colonels to raise regiments as private franchises. In this case, the sociological assumption that surveillance creates a rationale of efficiency in organizational development[42] seems to derive from the normative utilitarian rationality applied by the great parliamentary enquiries and reforms of the early nineteenth century, rather than from the historical process, in which political imperatives took precedence.

The other group of regulations by which the Mutiny Acts constituted and policed the division of society into civilian and military subjects concerned the adjustment and repletion of the strength of the army. Historical sociology has been curiously inattentive to the early modern dichotomization which constituted and maintained *civil* society by siphoning-off elements irreducible to private, domestic discipline and economy. In England, justices were ordinarily empowered to consign convicts to the army, and recruitment clauses were periodically added to the Mutiny Act, empowering them to 'take up' men without visible means of livelihood. As Christopher Hill has pointed out, the subjection of those 'who could not give an account of themselves' to extra-legal economy and discipline also functioned to consolidate domestic relations of domination.[43] Even John Locke, whose political theory advocated that those who could not find liberty in the constraints of domestic society should take flight to the New World, proposed in his 1697 Report to the Board of Trade that conscription into disciplinary colonial institutions on the model of expeditory military organization could rid England of its burdensome beggars and indigent poor.[44]

Impressment did conflict with customary conceptions of liberty in the 'moral economy of the crowd',[45] and mobs sometimes liberated men enlisted by justices under the Recruitment Acts from the gaols where they were held pending embarkation abroad. However, the jurisdictional differentiation of military and civil society did not correspond to ideological, political or even moral dichotomies. Even after 1714, when the army was first used as a means of internal control, soldiers were as frequently a part of the crowd that enacted the moral economy of popular politics as they were opposed to or targeted by it. By contrast, in France and other states with permanent, and thus garrisoned, military institutions, spatial divisions also demarcated moral and ideological identities, and barracks provided an ideal model for regimes of disciplinary surveillance.[46] In England, constitutional and political considerations combined to preclude this. In addition to the impermanence of the army under the Mutiny Act, Parliament was fearful of massing together under arms those 'without a stake in the commonwealth', as Ireton had referred at Putney to the propertyless in order to disqualify them from political participation.[47] The division of the military from political power was secured by dispersing the army through through the transient spaces of society – inns, roads, and ports – in small groups subject to dromological control of their speed of transit in jurisdictional differentiation from their social environment and regulated by tight definition of their contractual relations with civil society, rather than through continuous surveillance. In overseas regimental postings, even in peacetime, the rate of decay from death, disease, injury and desertion varied unpredictably from high to catastrophic.

The Recruitment and Mutiny Acts policed the transition between legal personhood under protection of the law and reduction to embodiment in military subjection by requiring all new recruits to appear before justices, who verified either their assent to voluntary enlistment or their vagrant disqualification from the protection of law. Though recruiting officers and justices with quotas to fill notoriously distorted these conditions of enlistment, a large proportion of the ranks, if not the majority claimed by some, were nevertheless filled by volunteers. The army offered an escape from some of the common plights of civil and domestic economy, discipline and law, such as pauperism, indenture in apprenticeship or service, debt, criminalization, familial burdens, and even unwanted marriage. Army recruiters contrasted domestic bondage and civil discipline to a fantastic, carnivalesque domain of liberty in fraternity and the freedom of the road.

The operation of the Mutiny Acts thus constituted civil and military societies as differentiated, if interpermeable, social spaces, each with its own rationality and economy, and distinct subjectivity and moral order. Eighteenth-century Acts followed the conventional policy established under Elizabeth Tudor, using the opportunity of war to rid the kingdom of marginal elements: vagrants, the indigent poor and convicted criminals. But popular resistance reveals this translation of the civil–military division onto a moralized formation of society as a process *of* marginalization rather than one which has its subjects already marked out for it, effectively creating a military class subject to policy but outside the protection of common law, a structural repository of both violence and social exclusion as the threshold of a civil society.

The Mutiny and Recruitment Acts demarcated this threshold as the peculiar jurisdiction of prerogative authority and its reduction of legal personhood to embodiment, mapping this onto moralized social categories and domestic policy. Although the Articles of War produced under this constitutional permission contained no universal category like that of contract in civil law, it achieved universality within its own jurisdiction in another way, by the 'devil's Article', which could find offence in any action that was not expressly sanctioned. The threshold was only the first step into a secular damnation that was often for life, short as it might be. The courts martial of military law made no pretensions of operating under a code that was anything less than demonic in its constraints and punishments upon the body, proceeding from the assumed moral condemnation of those already subject to it by their condition of exclusion from civil society and constitutional identification with violence.

Notes

1. P. Zagorin, *Rebels and Rulers, 1500–1660, Vol. II: Provincial Rebellion, Revolutionary Civil Wars, 1560–1660* (Cambridge: Cambridge University Press, 1982).
2. S. Schama, *The Embarrassment of Riches: An Interpretation of Dutch Culture in the Golden Age* (London: Collins, 1987).
3. P. Corrigan and D. Sayer, *The Great Arch: English State Formation as Cultural Revolution* (Oxford: Blackwell, 1985); A. L. Beier, *Masterless Men: The Vagrancy Problem in England, 1560–1660* (London: Methuen, 1985), pp. 4–7.
4. G. Oestreich, *Neo-Stoicism and the Early Modern State* (Cambridge: Cambridge University Press, 1982).

5. Justus Lipsius, *Sixe Bookes of Politickes or Civil Doctrine*, trans. W. Iones (Amsterdam: Theatrum Orbis Terrarum, 1970).
6. Justus Lipsius, *Tvvo Bookes of Constancie*, trans. J. Stradling, ed. R. Kirk (New Brunswick, NJ: Rutgers University Press, 1939).
7. Oestreich, *Neo-Stoicism*, p. 32.
8. Lipsius, *Tvvo Books*, p. 72.
9. G. Parker, *The Military Revolution: Military Innovation and the Rise of the West, 1500–1800* (Cambridge University Press, 1988).
10. J. A. Lynn, 'The *trace italienne* and the Growth of Armies: The French Case', in C. J. Rogers (ed.), *Military Revolution Debate: Readings on the Transformation of Early Modern Europe* (Oxford: Westview Press, 1995).
11. B. Nickle, 'The Military Reforms of Maurice of Orange' (unpublished PhD thesis, University of Michigan, 1984), pp. 112–30.
12. F. Tallet, *War and Society in Early Modern Europe, 1495–1715* (London: Routledge, 1992); G. Parker, *The Army of Flanders and the Spanish Road, 1567–1659* (Cambridge: Cambridge University Press, 1972).
13. Nickle, 'Military Reforms', p. 80.
14. Ibid., p. 91.
15. Ibid., pp. 177, 190.
16. Ibid., p. 182.
17. Reprinted as Appendix 12 in C. G. Cruickshank, *Elizabeth's Army* (Oxford: Oxford University Press, 1966), pp. 296–303.
18. Reprinted as Appendix C in Nickle, 'Military Reforms'.
19. Beier, *Masterless Men*, pp. 93–5.
20. L. Boynton, 'The Tudor Provost-Marshal', *English Historical Review*, 77 (1962), pp. 437–55.
21. Beier cites the instance of 1,500 men returning from Ireland in 1575, whose passage recalled the route of the medieval bands. Cruickshank estimates that 20,000 men were despatched on expedition to France alone in the 1590s, of whom half returned.
22. C. M. Clode, *The Administration of Justice under Military and Martial Law* (London: John Murray, 1872), p. 24.
23. C. H. Firth, *Cromwell's Army: A History of the English Soldier during the Civil Wars, the Commonwealth and the Protectorate* (London: Greenhill Books, 1921), pp. 12–14.
24. C. Hill, *Puritanism and Revolution* (London: Secker & Warburg, 1958), pp. 50–122.
25. I. J. Gentles, *The New Model Army in England, Ireland and Scotland, 1645–1653* (Oxford: Blackwell, 1992).
26. Venn, quoted in ibid., p. 33.
27. M. Weber, *From Max Weber: Essays in Sociology*, eds H. H. Gerth and C. W. Mills (London: Routledge Kegan Paul, 1948), pp. 253–61; M. Walzer, *The Revolution of the Saints: A Study in the Origins of Radical Politics* (London: Weidenfeld & Nicolson, 1965).
28. A. Barry, T. Osborne and N. Rose (eds), *Foucault and Political Reason* (London: UCL Press, 1996), 'Introduction', pp. 1–17.
29. Reprinted as Appendix L in Firth, *Cromwell's Army*, pp. 400–12.
30. Firth, *Cromwell's Army*, pp. 35–6; Gentles, *The New Model Army*, pp. 30–52.
31. Firth, *Cromwell's Army*, p. 289.
32. J. Sawday, *The Body Emblazoned: Dissection and the Human Body in Renaissance Culture* (London: Routledge, 1995).

33. Essex, quoted in Firth, *Cromwell's Army*, p. 93.
34. Ibid., pp. 98–9.
35. Gentles, *The New Model Army*, pp. 99 and 89; C. Hill, *The World Turned Upside Down: Radical Ideas in the English Revolution* (London: Penguin, 1972).
36. Gentles, *The New Model Army*, pp. 100–1, C. Hill, *God's Englishman: Oliver Cromwell and the English Revolution* (London: Weidenfeld & Nicholson, 1970).
37. J. G. A. Pocock, *The Machiavellian Moment: Florentine Political Thought and the Atlantic Republican Tradition* (Princeton, NJ: Princeton University Press, 1975).
38. A. S. P. Woodhouse, (ed.), *Puritanism and Liberty, Being the Army Debates (1647–9) from the Clarke Manuscripts* (London: J. M. Dent, 1938).
39. Clode, *Administration of Justice*, pp. 58–9.
40. Pocock, *Machiavellian Moment*; L. G. Schwoerer, *'No Standing Armies!': The Antiarmy Ideology in Seventeenth-Century England* (Baltimore, MD: Johns Hopkins University Press, 1974).
41. Clode, *Administration of Justice*, p. 68.
42. A. Giddens, *The Nation-State and Violence* (Cambridge: Polity Press, 1985); C. Dandeker, *Surveillance, Power and Modernity: Bureaucracy and Discipline from 1700 to the present day* (Cambridge: Polity Press, 1990).
43. C. Hill, *Liberty Against the Law: Some Seventeenth-Century Controversies* (London: Penguin, 1996), pp. 162–76.
44. J. Childs, *The British Army of William III, 1698–1702* (Manchester: Manchester University Press, 1987), p. 109.
45. E. P. Thompson, *Customs in Common* (London: Penguin, 1991).
46. Y-M. Bercé, *History of Peasant Revolts: The Social Origins of Rebellion in Early Modern France,* trans. A. Whitmore (Ithaca, NY: Cornell University Press, 1990); M. Foucault, *Discipline and Punish,* trans. A. Sheridan (London: Penguin, 1977).
47. Woodhouse, *Puritanism and Liberty*.

16

Reflections

This study has followed a research proposal outlined by Michel Foucault first in 1976, in an interview for the journal *Hérodote*[1] and then again in 1983:

> ... I would like to study ... the problem of war and the institution of war in what one could call the military dimension of society. There again one would have to cross into the problem of law, the rights of people and international law, etc ... as well as the question of military justice: what makes a Nation entitled to ask someone to die for it.[2]

Between these formulations, Foucault's work in other fields had developed in method and approach, transforming his conceptualization of the object of this unrealized research proposal around the theme of military power. That shift illustrates one of the methodological premises of the present study: that our objects of enquiry, like the objects of strategy, are not given in *a priori* definitions, but emerge out of practices and the mapping of their effects. The second proposal also points toward the inextricable entwinement of sovereignty and military power. In between the two proposals lies Foucault's programmatic rejection of the essentialism of the sovereign conception of power, his work on discipline, the subsequent focus on the government of self and others, and his later work on political theory, which reintroduced the problem of sovereignty in a way that was transformed as a result of the intermediate studies. The problem of military power is thus addressed indirectly, as an ongoing but never substantiated project, throughout the trajectory of his work.

The second formulation of the problem is set within the wider question posed by the interview's title, 'What Our Present Is'. The 'present' for this study, the condition of military power in modernity, consists in the taken-for-granted categories of the disciplines of international relations theory and macro-sociology respectively: sovereignty and the state. In his study of the genealogy of sovereignty,[3]

Jens Bartelson points out that international relations theory and historical macro-sociology both play the same game in relation to these respective fundamental objects, both taking for granted precisely what is problematic about their object of enquiry. Sociology first emerged as an attempt to reveal the objective realities behind the juridical concepts of political theory, prominent among which was the concept of sovereignty. Both Marx and Weber referred the sovereign power of the state to an ultimate and original source in the means of violence, an axiom that has assumed a privileged place in subsequent macro-sociological theory. But the more that military power comes to the fore as an explanatory concept, the more it escapes explanation itself. The problematization of 'what our present is' consists then in questioning the instrumentality of violence, or military power, a question for which the concept of sovereignty, as an *a priori*, given right of command, provides no resolution.

The present study is similar in approach to Bartelson's 'genealogy of sovereignty' in eschewing assumptions of the essence of its object (which could only be supplied by *a priori* definition), asking not what military power is, but rather, 'how it has been spoken of and known throughout a period of time'. This question also invokes enquiry into the process by which the privileged concept (whether military power or sovereignty) became such an indefinable essence and yet such a necessary factor in explanation. Macro-sociology posits a solution to the indefinability of the normative concept of sovereignty by analytically substituting it with the state, and then explains the power of the state in terms of military power. However, if military power is explained by a right of command, we simply return to the problem of sovereignty, while if it is traced to relations of domination within military forces, we embark upon an infinite regression, since this domination in turn would require resources which could only be secured through force, which would then need to be explained, and so on. The paradox can only be evaded in theory by positing the instrumental forces of domination as separate from the social, as an on-tologically distinct domain in which social theory can be liberated from the onus of explaining domination, but this again invokes precisely what needs to be explained – a dichotomy between organized violence and society.

Weber's 'types of legitimate domination' do not help us here either, since they ultimately refer command to the ruler's capacity to reward the original forces of domination, presupposing either an original pre-social domination (analytically problematized in Hobbes' account of the state of nature), or the model of a contract in which the subject speculatively invests obedience in exchange for a prospective share in material or other-worldly reward. For such investment to secure obedience unto death, and so function as a source for the instrumental deployment of forces of violence in which the body and life itself is risked, the leader must be able to defer even earthly reward indefinitely. More than life itself has to be invested, demanding some form of government of the self, which is not necessarily a source of 'power over'. The *a priori* possession of 'charisma' which Weber posits as a source of authority through promissory dispensation of other-worldly reward, is merely one form of such governmental power, and, as I have suggested, can generally be understood as itself an effect of strategic operations upon the terrain produced by political practices.

The problem of military power is thus in a general sense identical with the problem of sovereign power as Foucault formulated it for a critical theory of modernity,[4] and can similarly be shown as a political construction. The present study began by refusing any given or essential source as a theoretical *locus* of origin of such a right or power, and rather than focusing on the emergence of 'the state', focuses on the problematics concealed within the modern state's monopoly of violence. As Elias reminds us, this monopoly is significant not only in terms of the constitution of the state, but also for the subject of civilization and the constitution of society.

Bartelson also points out that international relations and macro-sociological theory invert one another's assumptions. Both systemic and realist models of international relations theory retain the perspective of the sovereign from which it emerged in the diplomacy of early modern, absolutist Europe, grounded in a contrast between territorial and external order. Macro-sociology reverses this order of theorizing by problematizing the sovereign state and demanding an empirical account of its historical and territorial formation and transformation. However, it tends to construct that account in terms of 'generative structural features of a sphere of social action that it posits as existing prior to the state'.[5] Where systems macro-sociology infers those structural conditions from 'essential' functions of social reproduction, conflict theory locates an equivalent of the 'anarchy' of realist international relations theory in the tension of social relations, with the monopoly of violence emerging contingently, but by an inexorable logic of the emergence of 'order out of disorder, presence out of absence', in the same way that realist international relations theory conceives of the emergence of a contingent international order out of its absence in relations between sovereign states. 'The logical ancestor of the state', Bartelson points out, is implicit in the on-tologically necessary assumption of some integral agent of conflict, whether it be 'small groups of power-hungry men' (Tilly) or 'warrior families' (Elias). In systemic theories, sovereignty is immanent in structure; in realist and conflict theories, it is intrinsic in their conception of the agent.[6] Sovereignty is always present in such theories, in the guise of one side or other of the structure/agency antinomy, whether displaced onto essentially functional systems (producing an account in which the function of protection becomes domination), or onto the subject of a 'realist' state of conflict (producing an account in which original violent domination becomes a legitimized social function).

The implicit theoretical assumption that force is essentially instrumental in producing a structure of social domination presupposes the social structure and the agent of domination that it is supposed to explain, and reduces violence *a priori* to instrumentality as a source of sovereign 'power over'. Furthermore, social structure is posited as inherently spatialized and agency as intrinsically territorializing, so violence appears instrumental for territorial and structural social domination, producing 'a materialist drama of mutual reinforcement between territory and power, between the spatialization of politics and the politicization of space',[7] in which the outcome of state formation as military control over territory is already given in the abstract theoretical framework of analysis. As Bartelson points out, 'there seems to be no space for nomads in macrosociology, neither literally not metaphorically'.[8]

The problematization of military power cannot be pursued through an *a priori* method which would trace the different organizational forms and social context of something defined in a way which posits it as a given object, for example, in terms of its function or of intrinsic qualities of agents. The premise that violence is always social and yet constitutive of the social, if taken seriously, implies that violence cannot be defined in terms of its difference from society, since their interrelation is not a dialectic in which the two can be opposed antithetically. However, the formulation of a model of society distinct from violence projects it onto disorder, onto the excluded, and onto the category of the 'other' or the 'nomad' (just as the theory of sovereignty projects it on to an 'outside'), which serves as a repository of 'violence', legitimating 'force' and moralizing its exclusive social order.

This study has in part been guided by historical textual mappings of the social field which perform precisely this function. These texts often appear to be primarily concerned with sovereign order in its historically variable forms, but we can also read them as programmatic surveys of the social field which engage practically with the problematic of the constitution of violence. In this sense, they offer us an insight into how that constitution is not simply an effect of generative sociological laws, but is political in the sense that it relates to and is susceptible to strategic action. Such texts also offer us a way to trace the changing meaning of concepts, to restore them to their historicity, which is necessary if we are to use them to understand the political as a field for strategy.

Without engaging with the history of ideas, particularly the changing meaning of concepts, and the way that these structure the field of the possible and provide objects for strategy, we have to resort to a universal model of agency, of invariant subjectivity, uniformly rational, possessed of a given perception of the world, with foreknowledge of the field of objective possibilities, deriving its ends from long-term historical tendencies. History, the grand-narrative logical structure, thereby becomes identical with the acting subject of history, an identity which is constantly revealed in the 'presentist' teleology of outcomes. There is thus no distinction between the sovereign theorist, the sovereign actor, and the sovereignty of the narrative itself.

This identity is mirrored in the methods of historical sociology. Giddens almost exclusively, and Anderson and Mann primarily, rely on secondary sources, with negligible methodological reflection, verifying data by cross-indexing. Such historical sociology proceeds as though history is a field of facts, without reflexive regard for the shifting field of the discourse of historiography, which has its own theoretical battles, terrain and strategies, to which macro-sociology remains blind. In these campaigns, the deployment of historical evidence becomes an instrument, just as the deployment of data provides the ammunition for partisan debates in sociology. Lifting data out of these contexts as unalloyed fact is a far more problematic venture than this standard verification procedure allows, as sociologists are all too well aware in relation to data collected by their contemporaries.

Elias engages in more reflective consideration of the relations between history and sociology, though he sometimes refers to historiography in terms that reduce it to a positivist model of accumulation of knowledge of the past, which could be relieved of its interpretive function by sociological theory.[9] His studies use a more sophisticated methodology than Giddens, Mann and Tilly, engaging with primary sources and acknowledging strategies in the production of cultural texts, as in his analysis of the strategic construction of values and dispositions of mannered civility among a nobility at court, where the strategic construction of etiquette intentionally operated upon a subjectivity structured by relations of dependence to habituate that dependence, but he infers the object of such strategy from its outcome (absolutist kingship through the reduction of a warrior nobility to dependence-habituating status competition). The strategic options open to action and discourse are thus inferred from their location in long-term macro-structural processes, i.e. 'the civilizing process', Elias' own version of social evolutionism, rather than in the exigencies of contemporary situations and their discursive constructions. His reflection on the historical role of cultural documents does not extend to the modern secondary sources used as supporting evidence of the formation of a court society from the late fifteenth century onwards. The contingency of actors' contemporary situations is therefore neglected in favour of (or obliterated by) the theoretical macro-structure of historical development into which their actions and texts are inserted. Strategy is then projected back upon action and discourse as though this situation in long-term trends provides an explanation of social and political action.

In order to trace the practical rationality governing historical acts we need a 'thicker' understanding of the political field in terms of the changing meaning of its conceptual markers and its construction as a field for social action. Without this we will simply be imputing rationality to and inferring political objects from historical action either in the form of ahistorical concepts (such as 'sovereignty' as the goal for 'rulers'), or of abstract systemic models of the social context of functionally defined action. These two alternatives are basically the same as those which Skinner castigates political theory for imposing upon its field of study by reading texts either as expressions of a given social structure (objectively known to the observer with the benefit of historical hindsight, and therefore not necessarily apparent to the original authors) or else as approximations of a transcendent meaning immanent in concepts themselves. However, if we are to begin to read such texts as a source of historical sociology beyond their mobilization, deployment and redefinition of normative concepts in historical context, then we need to attend to the conditions of their production in two senses. One of the premises of this study is that history is not a field of facts; this means that we need to apply to historical sources the same reflexivity we would apply to data in the contemporary world. Just as dealing reflexively with cross-cultural data requires us to engage with a 'thick description' of their meaningful cultural context, so we need to restore the historicity to historical data. We also need to acknowledge that authors engage in strategies.

Quentin Skinner's operational premise that we should analyze the rationality of statements in terms of the author's own world, rather than seeing the texts as simply a reflection of our 'objective' definition of that world (contextualism) or evaluating them as an approximation to transcendent truths (textualism),[10] opens them to us as active constructions of the world, in the same way that anthropologists have come to understand the accounts of their informants. However, neither acknowledgement of the objective sociological conditions of enunciation of statements, nor meaningful cultural context, are enough. We need also to situate the social position of authorship, not so much in terms of interests that can be inferred from an objective analysis of their structural location (as though the author were 'bearer' of a class consciousness or culture), but in terms of discursive possibilities and the ethics of performance governing that authorship. The status of statements as 'sanctioned' knowledge is also given in the relation of their authorship and discourse to technical political practices. Such analysis of locations and ethics can help to untangle the knot of situating texts in social structures and wider discourse.

For instance, in the eleventh century, the role of clerics in political practices was a condition of John of Salisbury's mapping of the social relations constituting a body politic, of his reformulation of particular problems of the contemporary constitution of violence, and of his redefinition of the object of kingship. Similarly, the 'political game' of the Roman senatorial aristocracy conditions Cicero's reformulation of the late republic. The condition of monopoly patronage and functional career specialization also foregrounds Frontinus' military discourse. The role of jurists in the political practices of the king's peace and their administrative extension in territorial and social reconstruction provides the conditions for Bodin's formulation of sovereignty. However, Salisbury's body politic, Cicero's political vehicle, Frontinus' command, and Bodin's sovereignty, do not describe forms *a priori*, but trace the constitutive effect of heterogenous practices, descriptions in which their formal objects are given definition. Thus, rather than tracing the emergence of a particular form, the state, we can follow Bourdieu's argument that the state arises and is reproduced in the activities of functional specialist elites.[11] The state (or the power of command) is understood here not as an object which can be normatively defined in terms of functions for a given social system, or even as a strategic project which has this normative ideal as its object (as Skinner supposes when inferring the object of Huguenot political theory), but as an effect of heterogenous practices and as an object appearing out of their mapping. Theoretical texts begin from such practices, mapping out their effects and formulating practical problematics for those practices, thereby informing and delineating a field and objects for strategy, since only on this basis is situated strategic rational calculation possible. Indeed, such programmes constitute that rationality by outlining the range of practices, effects and objects, so that 'rationality' appears as given, as universal rather than contingent.

Such textual readings provide us with the equivalent of what Bartelson calls 'manuals' as distinct from 'traditionary' texts, which reinterpret concepts over time, providing 'blueprints for reality' that manuals translate into practical projects.[12] The texts in this study can be read in both senses, the traditional reading being privileged when the texts are read conventionally as normative political theory. However, as my critique of Skinner's imputation of strategy to Huguenot political thought shows, the methodologically necessary analytical exclusion of contextualist approaches inclines Skinner to disregard sociological approaches that would enable a broader understanding of authorial strategies without reducing them to the determinations of social structure. As well as their rationality, we also need to attend to the form of statements in terms of their condition of knowledge, and it can be argued that Foucault's methods are of wider utility here. Skinner's work is restricted to the analysis of political thought, that is, primarily to reading transformations and the rationality of strategies within the textual production of normative ideology, and is not designed to deal with the practical rationalities of action in a field constituted by heterogenous practices. While his methodological premises open up texts for us to read as practical treatises, Skinner himself is unable to do so because of the rigid division of labour imposed by the way he establishes his methodological framework. Ultimately he has to refer to a contextual understanding of political action which neglects insights that could be gained from reading texts in 'political theory' as practical political discourse.

In contrast, Foucault's concept of discourse was developed in studies of the formation of statements which provided a guide for practical action, in his studies of the discourse of madness and of medicine. The conventional reception of Foucault's work posits a rupture between his early method of archaeology and the later genealogy, and a final abandonment of both approaches in favour of more conventional historiography. Dean, however, points out that Foucault's archaeological concerns with the condition of knowledge and 'regimes of truth' were not abandoned, but provided a background for his later researches, where the method of genealogy articulates them with enquiry into 'regimes of practices'.[13]

The later studies focused primarily on practices of 'political subjectification' which produced the capacities and predispositions that constituted self-governing subjects. Such practices enable rational strategic action conditioned by, but acting back upon, discourse. There is thus no master-strategist of power, whether posited in the historical innovator or in determinant social structure.[14] Dean's discussion of the 'minimal rationality' of strategy enables us to see how it is a primarily practical, rather than normative reason, constituted by the formulation of a field of possibilities and the definition of particular problems arising as an effect of the deployment of multiform practices. Strategic (sovereign) capacity and its autonomous subject are not given in a pre-possession of power, but are themselves constituted in this constellation as the object of strategic action, contra Giddens and Weber, for whom sovereign agency is identical with the possession of means of governmental technologies as resources.

> A part of the resources available to strategy are these programmes, the planful attempts to render the real amenable to government and administration, to render it governable and administrable. Strategy also presupposes assemblages of techniques, inventions, material and intellectual means of government, which might generically be called technologies of power and government. Yet strategy is never identical to either the explicit political rationality of the programme or the governmental technologies, techniques and practices on which this rationality depends ... Programmes and technologies of power have to do with the formation of the real in a governable, programmable, form, while strategy consists in turning that real into an instrument for certain ends.[15]

In applying this method in substantive studies, we can see that these 'ends', the object of strategy, are not given in interests which could be inferred from 'objective' macro-structural relations or long-term historical processes, but appear in the construction of the 'real' in programmes which map out the effect of political practices. There is thus no 'sovereign', neither actor nor determinant structure, though such an object may appear in the mapping of the relations produced by multiple practices.

Utilization of Foucault's work in historical sociology has tended to substitute derivative historiographical frameworks for further explorative methodical enquiry, following a general tendency to reify substantive analyses as 'theory'. At best, this reifies the processes of political subjectification traced by Foucault into historically periodized structures of subjectivity; at worst, even subjectivity is displaced from the picture, and the analysis is treated as a totalizing schema, for example, in the terms 'disciplinary' or 'surveillance society'. Foucault's comments in interviews often lend themselves to this treatment, particularly pronounced in generalizations of 'orders of discourse' which tend to overlook strategies and reduce the status of programmatic texts to an expression of periodized discursive formations, ironically foreclosing the relation between such programmes and strategic political action addressed by Foucault's later work. Such deterministic periodization is inadequate for understanding political rationalities. Where discursive formations are further identified with particular ensembles of practices, resources, or institutional forms, the approach collapses back into schemas of determinant macro-structural totalities.

For instance, Dean's historically periodizing distinction between discourses of government which refer themselves to the laws of God and those that are explicitly secular and artificial[16] is misleading in terms of a shifting politico-cultural field. The order of God was not always the same throughout the period in which governmental discourse deferred to it, and the relationship between the order of God as creation, his officers on earth, and the forms of political domination was not fixed, but underwent an identifiable series of transformations. This is not to say that religious legitimation was ideologically contingent or could analytically be subordinated to the interests of groups using it to justify their actions. Rather, its significance lies primarily in the ethics of practice governing authorship and action, which translated into the conditions of strategy and political rationality. Such ethics were problems that actors engaged with, not determinant structures or ideological opportunities. As such, we can trace their genealogy through other values, such as liberty or honour, which also effected ethical economies as conditions of action. The conduct and economy of violence is also a matter of government of the self and conscience.

Today, our fixation on technology and technical solutions, our very technicality itself, raises the danger that we may forget this insight in a self-certitude for which the object of action always appears immediate. Today's legitimation of violence refers itself only to normative claims, which in themselves are reduced to purely technical conditions of value or truth within their own sphere of specialist rationality, and we neglect the politics of the practical operations which are normatively dictated in this process. However, such bases for judgement may be nearing their limit, and thus already begin to appear illegitimate both in their claims and in their effects. This study comes at a time when the constitution of violence may be undergoing deep and fundamental changes, as the monopoly of legitimate violence in the territorial sovereign state shifts at both local and global poles.

Social theory today is faced with a new field emerging from practices no longer framed primarily by the functionally integral nation-state as the unitary subject of violence, a field in which strategies and economies of violence no longer have the state as their object. In such a new constellation, we need to study military rationality and its technical practices as operating upon and playing a major role in effecting political terrain no longer definitively comprised of states as singular strategic actors. Sovereignty may be shifting to other *loci*, or may no longer provide the principal object of strategy. Violence in itself is not dependent on an object, is not instrumental *a priori*, but if the object of strategy is mistaken and hence becomes unrealizable, then intentional and disciplined violence, operating a purely technical rationality to achieve that object, may lack economy. The study of military practice and rationality *before* the constitution of the state and of the states-system as strategic terrain may thus provide us with a guide to begin to grasp the constitution of violence *beyond* the state, a task which is today crucial as a critical complement to the normative discourse of legitimacy, since normative concepts alone cannot constitute an order, but can invoke endless violence.

Notes

1. M. Foucault, *Power/Knowledge: Selected Interviews and Other Writings,* ed. C. Gordon (Hemel Hempstead: Harvester Wheatsheaf, 1980), pp. 63–77.
2. M. Foucault, 'What Our Present Is', in M. Foucault, *Foucault Live: Collected Interviews, 1961–1984,* ed. S. Lotringer (New York, NY: Semiotext(e), 1989), p. 415.
3. J. Bartelson, *A Genealogy of Sovereignty* (Cambridge: Cambridge University Press, 1995).
4. M. Foucault, 'Two Lectures', in *Power/Knowledge,* pp. 78–108.
5. Bartelson, *Genealogy of Sovereignty,* p. 35.
6. Ibid., p. 39.
7. Ibid., p. 41.
8. A radically alternative 'nomadology' of the 'war-machine' is explored in G. Deleuze and F. Guattari, *A Thousand Plateaus: Capitalism and Schizophrenia,* Vol. 2, trans. B. Massumi (London: Athlone Press, 1987).
9. N. Elias, *The Court Society,* trans. C. Jephcott (Oxford: Blackwell, 1983).
10. Q. Skinner, 'Meaning and Understanding in the History of Ideas', in J. Tully, (ed.), *Meaning and Context: Quentin Skinner and His Critics* (Cambridge: Polity Press, 1988), pp. 3–53.
11. P. Bourdieu, *Practical Reason: On the Theory of Action* (Cambridge: Polity Press, 1998).
12. Bartelson, *Genealogy of Sovereignty,* p. 9.
13. M. Dean, *Critical and Effective Histories: Foucault's Methods and Historical Sociology* (London: Routledge, 1994), p. 35.
14. Where attempts to mediate the structure/agency dichotomy in social theory displace this sovereign historical determination into a dialectical relation between the two, as in Giddens' structuration theory, Foucault simply dissolves the problem altogether. Indeed the problem itself could be seen as an effect of the way that social theory continues to map the field of social relations in terms of a particular model of domination, as sovereign power.
15. Dean, *Critical and Effective Histories,* pp. 158–9.
16. Ibid., p. 183.

Select Bibliography

Allmand, C. T. (ed.), *Society at War: The Experience of England and France during the Hundred Years War* (Edinburgh: Oliver & Boyd, 1973).

Anderson, P. *Passages From Antiquity to Feudalism* (London: New Left Books, 1974).

Anderson, P. *Lineages of the Absolutist State* (London: New Left Books, 1974).

Austin, N. J. E. and Rankov, N. B. *Exploratio: Military and Political Intelligence in the Roman World from the Second Punic War to the Battle of Adrianople* (London: Routledge, 1995).

Ayton, A. and Price, J. L. (eds), *The Medieval Military Revolution: State, Society and Military Change in Medieval and Early Modern Europe* (London: I. B. Tauris, 1995).

Bachrach, B. S. *Merovingian Military Organization, 481–751* (Minneapolis, MN: University of Minnesota Press, 1972).

Barnwell, P. S. *Kings, Courtiers and Imperium: The Barbarian West, 565–725* (London: Duckworth, 1997).

Bartelson, J. *A Genealogy of Sovereignty* (Cambridge: Cambridge University Press, 1995).

Bartlett, R. *The Making of Europe: Conquest, Colonization and Cultural Change 950–1350* (London: Penguin, 1993).

Beier, A. L. *Masterless Men: The Vagrancy Problem in England, 1560–1640* (London: Methuen, 1985).

Bodin, J. *The Six Bookes of a Commonweale,* trans. R. Knolles, ed. K. D. McRae (Cambridge, MA: Harvard University Press, [1583] 1962).

Boétie, de la E. *The Politics of Obedience: The Discourse of Voluntary Servitude,* trans. H. Kurz (Montreal: Black Rose Books, 1975).

Bourdieu, P. *In Other Words: Essays Towards a Reflexive Sociology,* trans. M. Adamson (Cambridge: Polity Press, 1990).

Bourdieu, P. *Practical Reason: On the Theory of Action* (Cambridge: Polity Press, 1998).

Bradbury, J. *The Medieval Siege* (Woodbridge: Boydell Press, 1992).

Brown, P. *Power and Persuasion in Late Antiquity: Towards a Christian Empire* (Madison, WI: University of Wisconsin Press, 1992).

Brunt, P. A. *Social Conflicts in the Roman Republic* (London: Chatto & Windus, 1971).

Brunt, P. A. *Italian Manpower, 225 BC–14 AD* (Oxford: Oxford University Press, 1971).

Brunt, P. A. and Moore, J. M. (trans. and eds), *Res Gestae Divi Augusti: The Achievements of the Divine Augustus* (Oxford: Oxford University Press 1967).

Buisseret, D. *Sully and the Growth of Centralized Government in France 1598–1610* (London: Eyre & Spottiswoode, 1968).

Caesar, Julius *The Civil War,* trans. J. F. Gardner (London: Penguin, 1967).

Campbell, J. B. *The Emperor and the Roman Army: 31 BC–AD 235* (Oxford: Clarendon Press, 1984).

Childs, J. *The British Army of William III, 1698–1702* (Manchester: Manchester University Press, 1987).

Cicero, Marcus Tullius *De Re Publica,* trans. C. W. Keyes (London: Heinemann, 1928).

Contamine, P. *War in the Middle Ages,* trans. M. Jones (Oxford: Blackwell, 1984).

Corrigan, P. and Sayer, D. *The Great Arch: English State Formation as Cultural Revolution* (Oxford: Blackwell, 1985).

Cruickshank, C. G. *Elizabeth's Army* (Oxford: Oxford University Press, 1966).

Curry, A. and Hughes, M. (eds) *Arms, Armies and Fortifications in the Hundred Years War* (Woodbridge: Boydell Press, 1994).

Dean, M. *Critical and Effective Histories: Foucault's Methods and Historical Sociology* (London: Routledge, 1994).

Delbrück, H. *The History of the Art of War within the Framework of Political History* (5 vols), trans. W. J. Renfroe (London: Greenwood Press, 1985).

Deleuze, G. and Guattari, F. *Anti-Oedipus: Capitalism and Schizophrenia, vol.1,* trans. R. Hurley *et al.* (London: Athlone Press, 1983).

Deleuze, G. and Guattari, F. *A Thousand Plateaus: Capitalism and Schizophrenia, vol.2,* trans. B. Massumi (London: Athlone Press, 1984).

Dewald, J. *Aristocratic Experience and the Origins of Modern Culture: France 1570–1715* (Berkeley, CA: University of California Press, 1993).

Duby, G. *The Chivalrous Society,* trans. C. Postan (London: Edward Arnold, 1977).

Duby, G. *The Three Orders: Feudal Society Imagined,* trans. A. Goldhammer (London: University of Chicago Press, 1980).

Duby, G. *The Legend of Bouvines: War, Religion and Culture in the Middle Ages,* trans. C. Tihanyi (Cambridge: Polity Press, 1990).

Elias, N. *The Court Society,* trans. E. Jephcott (Oxford: Blackwell, 1983).

Elias, N. *The Civilizing Process: The History of Manners and State Formation and Civilization,* trans. E. Jephcott (2 vols) (Oxford: Blackwell, 1994).

Eltis, D. *The Military Revolution in Sixteenth-Century Europe* (London: I. B. Tauris, 1995).

Firth, C. H. *Cromwell's Army: A History of the English Soldier during the Civil Wars, the Commonwealth and the Protectorate* (London: Greenhill Books, 1921).

Foucault, M. *Discipline and Punish: The Birth of the Prison,* trans. A. Sheridan (London: Penguin, 1977).

Foucault, M. *The History of Sexuality, vol. 1: An Introduction,* trans. R. Hurley (London: Penguin, 1979).

Foucault, M. *Power/Knowledge: Selected Interviews and Other Writings,* ed. C. Gordon (Hemel Hempstead: Harvester Wheatsheaf, 1980).

Foucault, M. *The Care of the Self: The History of Sexuality, vol. 3,* trans. R. Hurley (London: Penguin, 1986).

Foucault, M. *Politics, Philosophy and Culture: Interviews and Other Writings 1977–84,* ed. L. D. Kritzman (London: Routledge, 1988).

Foucault, M. *Foucault Live: Collected Interviews, 1961–1984,* ed. S. Lotringer (New York: Semiotext(e), 1989).

Franklin, J. H. (ed.), *Constitutionalism and Resistance in the Sixteenth Century: Three Treatises by Hotman, Beza and Mornay* (New York, NY: Pegasus, 1969).

Froissart, J. *Chronicles,* trans. and ed. G. Brereton (London: Penguin, [1389] 1978).

Frontinus, Sextus Julius *Strategemata,* trans. C. E. Bennett (London: Heinemann, 1925).

Geary, P. *Before France and Germany: The Creation and Transformation of the Merovingian World* (New York, NY: Oxford University Press, 1988).

Gentles, I. J. *The New Model Army in England, Ireland and Scotland, 1645–1653* (Oxford: Blackwell, 1992).

Geremek, B. *The Margins of Society in Late Medieval Paris,* trans. J. Birrell (Cambridge: Cambridge University Press, 1987).

Giddens, A. *The Nation-State and Violence: Volume Two of a Contemporary Critique of Historical Materialism* (Cambridge:

Polity Press, 1985).

Greengrass, M. *The French Reformation* (Oxford: Blackwell, 1987).

Hewitt, H. J. *The Organisation of War under Edward III, 1338–62* (Manchester: Manchester University Press, 1966).

Hill, C. *Liberty Against the Law: Some Seventeenth-Century Controversies* (London: Penguin, 1996).

Hogg, O. F. G. *The Royal Arsenal: Its Background, Origin and Subsequent History* (vol. 1) (London: Oxford University Press, 1963).

Holt, M. P. *The French Wars of Religion, 1562–1629* (Cambridge: Cambridge University Press, 1995).

John of Salisbury, *Policraticus*, trans. and ed. C. Nederman (Cambridge: Cambridge University Press, 1990).

Jones, A. H. M. *The Later Roman Empire, 284–602: A Social, Economic and Administrative Survey* (2 vols) (Oxford: Blackwell, 1964).

Jones, A. H. M. (ed.), *A History of Rome Through the Fifth Century, Vol. II: The Empire* (New York, NY: Harper & Row, 1978).

Kaeuper, R. *War, Justice and Public Order: England and France in the Later Middle Ages* (Oxford: Clarendon Press, 1988).

Kantorowicz, E. *The King's Two Bodies: A Study in Medieval Political Theology* (Princeton, NJ: Princeton University Press, 1957).

Keen, M. H. *Laws of War in the Later Middle Ages* (London: Routledge, Kegan & Paul, 1965).

Keppie, L. *The Making of the Roman Army from Republic to Empire* (London: Batsford, 1984).

Kingdon, R. M. *Church and Society in Reformation Europe* (London: Variorum Reprints, 1985).

Lefebvre, H. *The Production of Space*, trans. D. Nicholson-Smith (Oxford: Blackwell, 1991).

Le Goff, J. *Medieval Civilization, 400–1500*, trans. J. Barrow (Oxford: Blackwell, 1988).

Le Goff, J. (ed.), *The Medieval World*, trans. L. G. Cochrane (London: Collins & Brown, 1990).

Lipsius, Justus, *Tvvo Bookes of Constancie*, trans. J. Stradling, ed. R. Kirk (New Brunswick, NJ: Rutgers University Press, [1584] 1939).

Lipsius, Justus, *Sixe Bookes of Politickes or Civil Doctrine*, trans. W. Iones (Amsterdam: Theatrum Orbis Terrarum, [1589] 1970).

Little, L. K. and Rosenwein, B. H. *Debating the Middle Ages: Issues and Readings* (Oxford: Blackwell, 1998).

Livy, Titus *The History of Rome, Books I–V, The Early History of Rome*, trans. A. de Sélincourt (Harmondsworth: Penguin, 1971).

Luttwak, E. *The Grand Strategy of the Roman Empire from the First*

Century AD *to the Third* (Baltimore, MD: Johns Hopkins University Press, 1976).

Machiavelli, N. *Art of War,* trans. E. Farneworth and ed. N. Wood (New York, NY: Da Capo Press, [1521] 1965).

McCormack, J. *One Million Mercenaries: Swiss Soldiers in the Armies of the World* (London: Leo Cooper, 1993).

Mann, M. *The Sources of Social Power, Vol. I: A History of Power from the Beginning to* AD *1760* (Cambridge: Cambridge University Press, 1986).

Mann, M. *States, War and Capitalism: Studies in Political Sociology* (Oxford: Blackwell, 1988).

Montluc, B. de, *Commentaires: The Habsburg–Valois Wars and the French Wars of Religion,* ed. C. Roy, trans. I. Cotton (London: Longman, [1592] 1971).

Morillo, S. *Warfare Under the Anglo-Norman Kings, 1066–1135* (Woodbridge: Boydell Press, 1994).

Nickle, B. 'The Military Reforms of Maurice of Orange' (unpublished PhD thesis, University of Michigan, 1984).

Oestreich, G. *Neo-Stoicism and the Early Modern State* (Cambridge: Cambridge University Press, 1982).

Parker, G. *The Army of Flanders and the Spanish Road, 1567–1659* (Cambridge: Cambridge University Press, 1972).

Parker, G. *The Military Revolution: Military Innovation and the Rise of the West, 1500–1800* (Cambridge: Cambridge University Press, 1988).

Pisan, C. de *The Book of the Body Politic* trans. and ed. K. Langdon Forhan (Cambridge University Press, [1406] 1994).

Pocock, J. G. A. *The Machiavellian Moment: Florentine Political Thought and the Atlantic Republican Tradition* (Princeton, NJ: Princeton University Press, 1975).

Poggi, G. *The Development of the Modern State* (London: Hutchinson, 1978).

Poly, J-P. and Bournazel, E. *The Feudal Transformation, 900–1200,* trans. C. Higgitt (New York, NY: Holmes and Meier, 1991).

Pounds, N. J. G. *The Medieval Castle in England and Wales: A Social and Political History* (Cambridge: Cambridge University Press, 1990).

Powicke, M. *Military Obligation in Medieval England: A Study in Liberty and Duty* (Oxford: Clarendon Press, 1962).

Prestwich, M. *The Three Edwards: War and State in England 1272–1377* (London: Methuen, 1980).

Prestwich, M. *Armies and Warfare in the Middle Ages: The English Experience* (New Haven, CT: Yale University Press, 1996).

Rich, J. and Shipley, G. (eds), *War and Society in the Roman World* (London: Routledge, 1993).

Roberts, M. 'The Military Revolution' in M. Roberts, *Essays in Swedish History* (London: Weidenfeld & Nicholson, 1967).

Rogers, C. J. (ed.) *The Military Revolution Debate: Readings on the Military Transformation of Early Modern Europe* (Oxford: Westview Press, 1995).

Scribner, B. *et al.* (eds) *The Reformation in National Context* (Cambridge: Cambridge University Press, 1994).

Seward, D. *The Monks of War: The Military Religious Orders* (London: Penguin, 1995).

Seyssel, C. de *The Monarchy of France,* ed. D. R. Kelley, trans. J. H. Hexter (New Haven, CT: Yale University Press, [1519] 1981).

Simmel, G. *The Sociology of Georg Simmel,* trans. and ed. K. H. Wolff (New York, NY: Free Press, 1950).

Skinner, Q. *The Foundations of Modern Political Thought* (2 vols) (Cambridge: Cambridge University Press, 1978).

Southern, R. W. *The Making of the Middle Ages* (London: Arrow Books, 1959).

Southern, R. W. *Western Society and the Church in the Middle Ages* (Harmondsworth: Pelican, 1970).

Sproxton, J. *Violence and Religion: Attitudes Towards Militancy in the French Civil Wars and the English Revolution* (London: Routledge, 1995).

Strickland, M. (ed.), *Anglo-Norman Warfare* (Woodbridge: Boydell Press, 1992).

Strickland, M. *War and Chivalry: The Conduct and Perception of War in England and Normandy, 1066–1217* (Cambridge: Cambridge University Press 1996).

Stein, P. *Roman Law in European History* (Cambridge: Cambridge University Press, 1999).

Suger, Abbé *Deeds of Louis the Fat,* eds and trans. R. Cusimano and J. Moorehead (Washington, DC: Catholic University of America Press, 1992).

Tallett, F. *War and Society in Early Modern Europe, 1495–1715* (London: Routledge, 1992).

Thompson, E. P. *Customs in Common* (London: Penguin, 1991).

Tilly, C. *Coercion, Capital and European States,* AD *990–1992* (Oxford: Blackwell, 1992).

Tuchman, B. *A Distant Mirror: The Calamitous Fourteenth Century* (Harmondsworth: Penguin, 1979).

Tully, J. (ed.), *Meaning and Context: Quentin Skinner and his Critics* (Cambridge: Polity Press, 1988).

Van Gelderen, M. *The Political Thought of the Dutch Revolt, 1555–1590* (Cambridge: Cambridge University Press 1992).

Vaughan, R. *Charles the Bold: The Last Valois Duke of Burgundy* (London: Longman, 1973).

Vaughan, R. *Valois Burgundy* (London: Longman, 1975).

Vegetius, Renatus Flavius. *De Re Militari (Epitome of Military Science)*, trans. and ed. N. P. Milner (Liverpool: Liverpool University Press, 1993).

Veyne, P. *Bread and Circuses: Historical Sociology and Political Pluralism*, trans. B. Pearce (London: Allen Lane, 1990).

Virilio, P. *Speed and Politics: An Essay on Dromology*, trans. M. Polizotti (New York, NY: Semiotext(e), 1986).

Wallace-Hadrill, J. M. *The Long-Haired Kings and Other Studies in Frankish History* (London: Methuen, 1962).

Walzer, M. *The Revolution of the Saints: A Study in the Origins of Radical Politics* (London: Weidenfeld & Nicolson, 1965).

Weber, M. *The Protestant Ethic and the Spirit of Capitalism*, trans. and ed. T. Parsons (London: Unwin, 1930).

Weber, M. *From Max Weber: Essays in Sociology*, ed. and trans. H. H. Gerth and C. W. Mills (London: Routledge & Kegan Paul, 1948).

Weber, M. *Economy and Society: An Outline of Interpretive Sociology*, ed. G. Roth and C. Wittich (Berkeley, CA: University of California Press, 1978).

Weber, M. *The Agrarian Sociology of Ancient Civilizations*, trans. R. I. Frank (London: New Left Books, 1976).

Wood, J. B. *The King's Army: Warfare, Soldiers, and Society during the Wars of Religion in France, 1562–1576* (Cambridge: Cambridge University Press, 1996).

Woodhouse, A. S. P. (ed.), *Puritanism and Liberty, Being the Army Debates (1647–9) from the Clarke Manuscripts* (London: J. M. Dent, 1938).

Xenophon, *Cyropaedia*, trans. J. Morgan (London: James Cornish, n.d.).

Index